"The Transportation sector of the Natural Gas business has never been covered so comprehensively in one place. This is the book that natural gas has needed for a long time. Sylvia has distilled decades of experience into an informative and readable book. This book has much to offer everyone in the business, regardless of their level of experience."

Rusty Braziel, RBN Energy

"This is the reference book every QA person needs to be an effective natural-gas pipeline tester. I have *Trading Natural Gas* by Fletcher Sturm for my marketing clients and now I have *Contents Under Pressure* by Sylvia Munson for my pipeline and transportation clients."

Opral Wisham, IT Quality Assurance Consultant

"This will become required reading for all Latitude employees."

Leigh Spangler, President, Latitude Software

"This book is two books in one. It covers the basics of the gas industry for someone who wants to understand the business, and it covers in-depth workings of the industry for someone who has a good working knowledge of their area and wants to know more. I have 20+ years in the Natural Gas business, and I learned new things from this book."

Jeff O'Block, Chorus Solutions

For more on ***Contents Under Pressure*** and for continuing up-to-date industry information visit

ContentsUnderPressureBook.com

The Complete Handbook of Natural Gas Transportation

Contents Under Pressure

The Complete Handbook of Natural Gas Transportation

Contents Under Pressure

First Edition, September 2015

Sylvia F Munson

Farris Ventures
Houston Atlanta Jacksonville

Contents Under Pressure
The Complete Handbook of Natural Gas Transportation

The information contained in this book captures a point in time in the Natural Gas Industry. It is not intended to capture the nuances of every pipeline contract or every operational constraint. It is, however, intended to give the reader enough information that they can ask the right questions in order to fully understand the business. The book is not intended to advise on how a pipeline business should be run but, rather, to give clarity on the diverse ways that a pipeline may be run so that industry participants can realize the breadth of business practice

Photos – KoEd Photography, Houston, Texas

Bulk purchases available via ContentsUnderPressureBook.com

Published in Houston, TX by Farris Ventures.

Printed in the United States of America by Ingram Printing

Acknowledgements:

There are so many people who helped to make this book possible that I am afraid to mention names at the risk of leaving one out. If I leave you out, I apologize and please autograph my copy of the book for me.

First – my kids and my sisters, Amanda Farris, Allison Munson, Susan Farris, Delores Stover, Farris Few – for believing in me, pushing me, and giving me time and space to get this done.

Also First – Averyl Re, my editor, for patiently rewording my passive sentencing structures, for learning so much about the gas industry, and for reading this book again and again and again.

Next – the huge group of people in the gas industry who have encouraged me, questioned me, doubted me, and pushed and prodded- you have helped me grow in this knowledge and encouraged me in so many ways. Particular sound-outs to Dale Davis, Jeff O'Block, Keith Bishop, Mike Schisler, Kim Van Pelt, Mark Gracey, Dawn Brown, Opral Wisham, and all of the people who continued to ask me about the book.

Thank you Don Busby, Stephen Schwarz, and Trip Ray for getting me through the initial legal minefield.

Thank you Cindy Albert for getting me the access to facilities for the photos.

Thank you Koed Photography for making yourselves so available to capture the photos.

Thank you Reg Harman for excellent layout design.

Thank you Randall Neighbour for your enthusiasm and patient hand-holding through the publishing process.

Contents

Contributing Authors

Leigh Spangler is president of Dallas-based Latitude Technologies Inc., which provides technology services, including EDI services and Internet-based nomination systems, to LDCs, energy marketers, pipelines, and natural gas storage facilities nationwide. As a member of the NAESB board of directors, the NAESB Wholesale Gas Quadrant (WGQ) executive committee, and co-chair of the WGQ Electronic Delivery Mechanism subcommittee, he participates in both the business and the technology aspects of industry standardization.

Greg Lander is presently a partner in the energy consulting firm, Skipping Stone LLC. In the 1980s, he co-founded the gas marketing firm Citizens Energy, which he ran for six years. Following that, he formed TransCapacity, a natural gas transaction software and information services firm. During his six years with that firm, he helped found GISB, now NAESB, and was instrumental in drafting for passage hundreds of GISB/NAESB standards. He has served as a Board Member with NAESB since the late 1990s. In 1999, Skipping Stone acquired TransCapacity, where he currently runs the natural gas logistics and information services practices.

Joe Casey, Project Manager, Standards and Regulatory Compliance, Spectra Energy Corporation. Casey has been project manager of Standards and Regulatory Compliance in the Regulatory Affairs department of Spectra Energy Corporation since 2014, and is a member of the executive board of the Wholesale Gas Quadrant of the North American Energy Standards Board. He began his career more than 30 years ago as a pipeliner, moving up the ranks as his assignments took him to locations in Texas, Louisiana, and Pennsylvania. Casey has been involved in commercial operations and business system development, developing an expertise in Nominations, Segmentation, Volume Management, Scheduling, and Capacity Release.

Mike Schisler is the owner of Composite Data Systems, a supplier of NAESB standards compliant gas logistics and B2B software. Schisler's background includes interstate pipeline system and web portal management and commercial software development for the pipeline shipper community. He graduated from Texas A&M with a BS in Geology.

Steve McCord is an energy professional with more than 28 years of experience working with a major natural gas pipeline in Houston, Texas.

Mike Stender retired from the El Paso Corporation after 26 years of service. For the past 15 years, he has worked extensively with EDI while leading the Technical Subcommittee of NAESB. Stender holds a BS from University of Nebraska and an MBA from University of Iowa. Today, he consults for companies when he has time from his wife, family, horses, and corgis.

Micki Hoffee has been involved with EDI for nearly two decades, from the perspective of an end user to data mapping to business and technical support. She has been an active member of the NAESB Wholesale Gas Quadrant (WGQ) information requirements and technical subcommittees for the last 12 years. Hoffee is a Senior Business Systems Analyst with Northern Natural Gas where she oversees daily EDI operations as well as coordinates the implementation of related business and technical aspects of industry changes.

Jim Buccigross is an experienced attorney specializing in energy, including standards, contracts, regulatory compliance, e-commerce, and related electronic transactions. He is vice president of Energy Industry Practice for Group 8760, LLC. He is the current chairman of the North American Standards Energy Board (NAESB) Executive Committee. Buccigross received a Bachelor of Science Degree from Framingham State College, an MBA Degree cum laude from Babson College, and a Juris Doctor Degree cum laude from Suffolk University Law School. He is admitted to the bar in Massachusetts, the District of Columbia, and various federal districts.

Kathryn Burch worked for Spectra Energy Corp in a variety of departments, starting as an analyst in Gas Control, then customer services, measurement, marketing, the LINK Group, and finally in Regulatory Affairs. She served as Spectra Energy's representative on the Executive Committee for the North American Energy Standards Board, and was influential in the development of key business standards for the interstate gas pipeline industry.

Jeff O'Block has worked as a software engineer in the energy industry for more than 25 years. O'Block was the original architect and developer for Panhandle Eastern, Trunkline, and Texas Eastern's customer systems. He was also the original developer of GMS and GTMS, and Altra and Sungard's natural gas accounting and management systems. He is currently president of Chorus Solutions, a custom software development company for the energy industry

Michael E. Novak, Asst. General Manager, National Fuel Gas Distribution Corporation. Novak oversees federal regulatory affairs within the National Fuel Gas Distribution Corporation ("National Fuel") Rates & Regulatory Affairs Department. His career at National Fuel includes positions in Gas Control, Gas Supply Administration, and Transportation Services. He is a long-time member of American Gas Association's (AGA) federal regulatory committee and serves on the North American Energy Standards Board (NAESB) Executive Committee and board of directors. At the state level, he participates in a variety of working groups, committees, and task forces addressing retail customer choice matters, EDI, and reliability issues. Novak holds a Bachelor of Science Degree in Civil Engineering and an MBA from the State University of New York at Buffalo.

*The views and opinions expressed in this article are those of the author and do not necessarily reflect the official policy or position of National Fuel Gas Distribution Corporation.

Introduction

I. Why this Book

In my career, I have had the opportunity to teach many people – mainly IT people – about the natural gas business. It amazes me how many people work in various business groups in our industry and do what they are told by someone without truly understanding the nature of the business they are supporting. Others have worked in their specific areas of the business for several years, but do not have an understanding of the processes of the business as a whole. Understanding the business allows everyone to ask the right questions and to interpret the gaps in information in a much more successful manner.

In the last 19 years of my career, since the Federal Energy Regulatory Commission (FERC) first adopted the standards of the North American Energy Standards Board (NAESB) (aka Gas Industry Standards Board (GISB)) as operational standards for the interstate gas industry, I have had the opportunity to teach many people about the standards. I have found that, in many cases, an understanding of the North American natural gas business must be taught first, so that the NAESB standards make sense.

This book comes from the heart. I love to teach. I love the natural gas industry. I find it a very interesting industry to be a part of because it incorporates so many different types of people and processes. There's the chemistry side of things - natural gas is methane or CH4, plus a host of secondary components. There's the engineering side with pipelines and flow-control valves. There's the geology side with exploration and drilling. There's the financial side with trading and risk and hedging. My list could go on and on. But really, the gas industry consists of a lot of real people who are trying to make sure that they keep your house warm in the winter and your gas grill working well in the summer. Good people doing a great job.

I based this book on the North American gas business - primarily the business in the United States. It focuses on the transactions and interactions required to transport gas from its point of origin to the burner on your heater or grill. Getting the gas from the well to your burner may require many transactions, many different business parties, and must comply with many regulations in the lifecycle of that gas flow.

One of the fun aspects of the natural gas business is that it is always changing. Technology changes in exploration, production, and transportation create new opportunities, cause market shifts, and cause companies to create new services to utilize those shifts. Additionally, the computer-technology changes that are constantly added to the market place create opportunities to see the business in a different way. On top of that, the Federal rules governing the business change, and the NAESB rules to implement the business change. This keeps the industry constantly shifting. It makes being a part of this industry fun. Change is good and a great opportunity to learn.

II. Who is the Audience?

Who is this book for? This book is for anyone who wants to understand the transportation of natural gas. It is for business people who work in a specific area of the gas business and want to understand what their counterparts do. It is for support staff, such as legal and IT people, who want to understand the business that is being conducted in the areas they support. It is for experts in the industry who may want to round out their knowledge. It is for anyone.

III. About Me

I have been working in the natural gas industry for more than 30 years. My background is in chemistry and computer science. My primary role these past 30 years has been as a consultant helping companies implement technology solutions for natural gas while meeting the requirements of regulatory compliance. I have had the privilege of working in production, gathering, midstream, intrastate, interstate, and local distribution companies, but have not worked for an end-user/consumer (yet) even though I, myself, am a consumer of natural gas. During this time, I have worked in IT, Regulatory Affairs, Marketing, Sales and, my favorite, Training. I have had the opportunity to contribute writing to several energy publications and to be interviewed by several energy-trade publications during this time.

I have also participated in NAESB since its inception, serving as the chair of multiple subcommittees, teaching standards classes, serving on the Board of Directors and Executive Committee, and writing standards; I have also been employed by NAESB for a time.

The most important things to know about me are that I love to learn, I love the gas industry, and I am proud to be a part of the work that I have done. But what you really want to know is that I love my two daughters and two grandchildren. I prefer dogs over cats, chocolate over vanilla, and I love my God and country.

IV. Origin of Materials

The information in this book comes from many years of working in this industry in all of its different segments. This book will give you a thorough understanding of the gas transportation business. The primary sources of reference will be FERC regulations and the NAESB standards and implementation guides. You will need the NAESB standards and implementation guides as additional information if you are implementing a business process that needs to be compliant with regulations.

The NAESB standards, along with the Code of Federal Regulations related to Natural Gas Transportation, comprise the governing rules for conducting business in natural gas transportation. These standards set the boundaries within which the industry works. The standards are primarily focused on the pipelines that transport gas, but they impact all industry participants because, to get the gas from point A to point B, it must go through a pipeline. To transport gas through a pipeline requires the owner of the gas and a contract. It may also involve purchases, sales, agents, etc.

Additionally, that pipeline may be a gathering system, a state-level pipeline, an intrastate, an interstate, a 311 pipeline, a Hinshaw pipeline, a local distribution company, or a utility. Generally, to get gas from point A to point B, at least two of these types of pipelines must be involved. In many cases, a single transportation plan may involve all of the pipeline types listed above. There are always exceptions. Always. For this book, we will refer to interstate pipelines as interstates and all other pipelines as non-interstates.

In addition to my own experience and knowledge, I have asked experts in the industry to contribute their stories, relevant to certain sections of the book. These experts come from many different types of companies within the gas industry and have graciously contributed their experiences to make the book's information relevant to the reader.

Caveat: This book references the NAESB standards. However,

1. It is not intended to replace the NAESB standards nor to interpret them.
2. There are many implementations of the standards that will not be addressed in this book.

The NAESB standards provide specific rules that must be incorporated into an overall business process, but do not define the business process that must be accomplished. The standards establish a set of boundaries within which to operate, but they do not always dictate a specific solution. Therefore, there will be many implementations of the standards that appear to be very different but are within the boundaries of the standards. This is a very important concept to understand. A clear reading of the NAESB standards is essential before attempting to use them. This book is intended to aid the reader/implementer in understanding the variances and opportunities in the business process, within the standards, and in understanding how all of the pieces of the business process work together within the industry.

Appendix B includes a description of the NAESB organization and process, as well as an understanding of important components of the Wholesale Gas Quadrant (WGQ) standards implementation guides.

Foundation Information

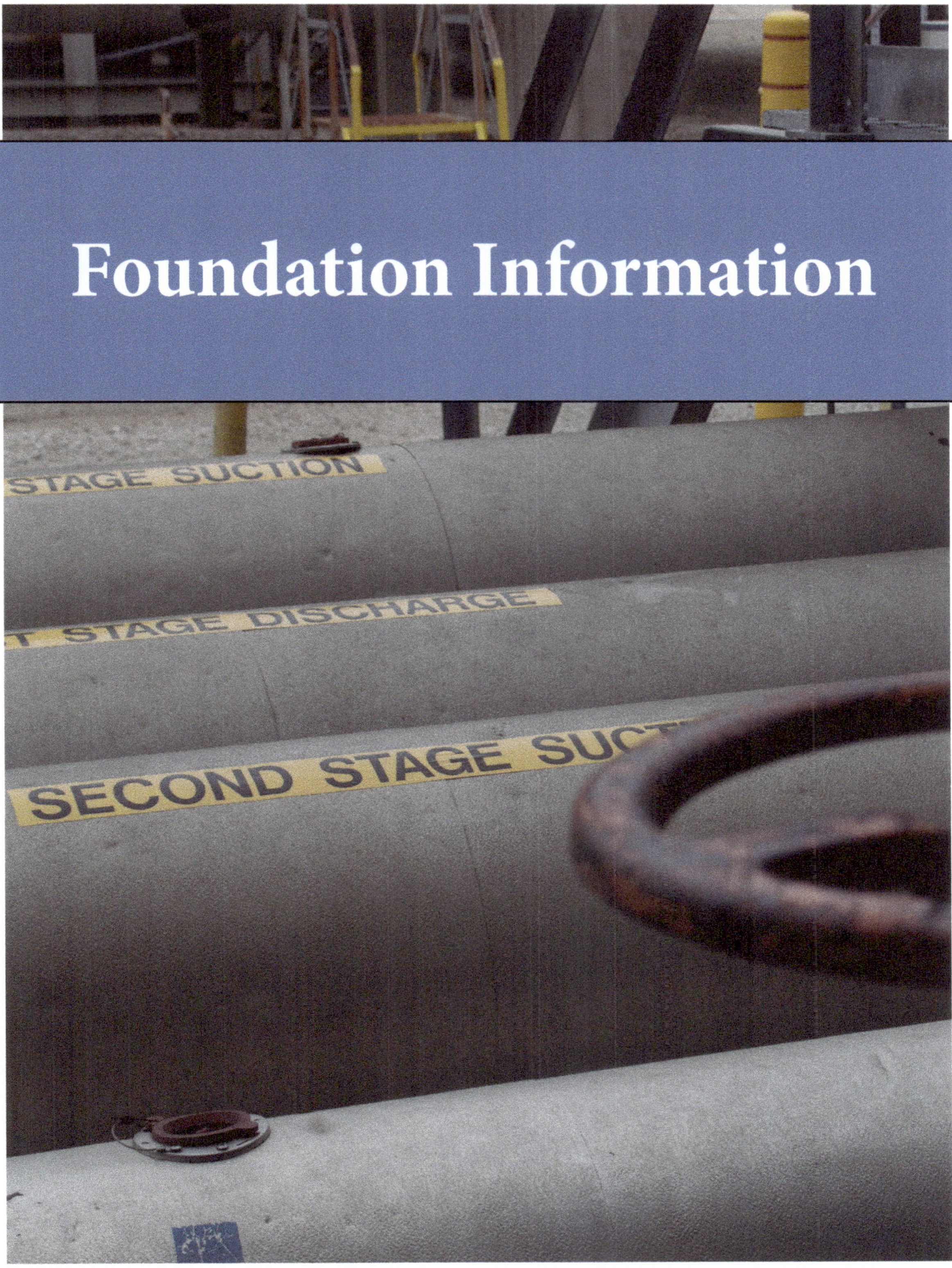

Before diving into the overall business and processes, it is good to have a basic understanding of what natural gas is, where it comes from, and how natural gas transportation fits into the overall natural gas industry. There are many participants in natural gas such as exploration, drilling, production, processing, distribution, and utility management. The transportation sector is a key component because it moves the gas from the source to the destination, but there are other relationships worth understanding. In addition, natural gas and transportation are highly regulated. It is good to introduce those parties at the federal, state, and local level.

1. High-level picture of the Natural Gas Industry

What is natural gas?

Let's start at the beginning – natural gas consists of methane – CH4. It's as simple as that? NO! When gas comes out of the ground, it may have many other components in it, but the goal is to have as pure methane as possible when transporting and burning natural gas. What's it really made of?

Natural gas is by nature a random grouping of chemicals. Natural gas coming out of the ground may have heavier carbon gases with it as high as octane. The content of the gas will vary by where the gas is coming from. The heavier the hydrocarbon in the gas, the less of that gas there will be. Additionally, it may contain water, sulfur, and other impurities. Gas that contains sulfur is described as sour. All of these extra components may affect the heating value of the gas. Gas with too many additional components will be sent through a processing plant to remove them. The gas going into the plant is considered "wet" gas, and the pure-methane gas that comes out of the plant is referred to as "dry" gas.

The heating value of the gas is measured in British Thermal Units (BTUs). Volume of gas is measured in thousand-cubic-feet (MCF), million-cubic-feet (MMCF), or billion-cubic-feet (BCF) units. Gas that has been converted to a quantity of heating value is referred to in Dekatherms (DTH). U.S. transportation contracts most commonly use the DTH measurement of gas.

Name	Number of Carbon Atoms	Molecular Formula	Structure	Word Root
Methane	1	CH4	CH4	Meth
Ethane	2	C2H6	CH3-CH3	Eth
Propane	3	C3H8	CH3-CH2-CH3	Prop
Butane	4	C4H10	CH3-(CH2)2-CH3	But
Iso-Butane	4	C4H10	CH1-(CH3)3	But
Pentane	5	C5H12	CH3-(CH2)3)-CH3	Pent
Iso-Pentane	5	C5H12	CH2-CH-(CH3)3	Pent
Hexane	6	C6H14	CH3-(CH2)4-CH3	Hex
Heptane	7	C7H16	CH3-(CH2)5-CH3	Hept
Octane	8	C8H18	CH3-(CH2)6-CH3	Oct
Nonane	9	C9H20	CH3-(CH2)7-CH3	Non
Decane	10	C10H22	CH3-(CH2)8)-CH3	Dec

Table 1.1
Molecular Formulas

The larger the molecule, the more energy is released when the molecule is burned. Burning is simply combining the hydrocarbon with oxygen. The reaction for methane is as follows:

CH4 + 202 = C02 + 2H20

So, one methane molecule combines with two oxygen molecules to form one carbon dioxide molecule and two water molecules. This is why natural gas is called "clean", as the by-products of combustion are water and plant loving CO2.

Molecules C6 and greater are often liquids. The state of each molecule is determined by its saturation as well as the temperature and pressure of the gas. Note the bigger the molecule, the more high dollar value it has. The term "plant processing" is used to define the process of separating out these molecules from the "natural gas."

The natural gas industry

The natural gas industry spans a wide range of activities and responsibilities. From the geologist who explores potential gas reserves to the utility-company employee turning the gas on at a house, there are many different roles to get the gas from the ground to the consumer.

The exploration and production area of natural gas is where the gas is discovered; the wells are drilled; and the gas is brought up from the ground, cleaned through plant processing, and made ready for transportation. Producers, well operators, gatherers, midstream transporters, and plant operators manage these processes. This area of the business is also referred to as gas gathering.

Figure 1.1
Gas industry participants in relative order of the flow of gas

The transportation side of the industry takes the gas from the wellhead or other point of readiness in the production system to the burner tip or last point of delivery on the transportation system. The pipelines, transporters, and storage operators who conduct business in the interstate and non-interstate marketplace manage this part of the business. Non-interstate transportation may occur on intrastate pipelines, midstream systems, or local distribution companies that transport gas for others.

The distribution side of the industry takes the gas from the transportation pipeline, a local distribution company (LDC), and brings it, through smaller pipelines, into the businesses and homes where the gas is consumed. That LDC may be the utility that delivers gas to both industrial users and to consumers, or that LDC may deliver to one or more utility companies that are the distribution center for industries and consumers. In many states, the LDC has become an open-access transporter that offers transportation services for others just like an interstate pipeline. In most states, the LDC also purchases and sells gas for delivery to ultimate consumers. Utility companies are still, generally, purchasers of gas for their customers and the ultimate sales entity to those customers for the gas.

In between all of the entities bringing the gas from the wellhead to the burner tip, there may be marketers and traders who buy the gas, aggregate and disaggregate bundles of gas, and sell it to downstream parties. There are many books that cover the trading aspect of the natural gas business.

For this book, the focus will be on transportation of gas. That transportation could be on the upstream, mainline, or downstream side of the transportation stream. The mainline pipeline is the pipeline where the current activity takes place. The upstream pipeline is the pipeline connected to the mainline pipeline where the flow of gas enters the mainline. The downstream pipeline is the pipeline connected to the mainline where the flow of gas exits the mainline. There will be touchpoints into the two other areas of the business to tie the pieces together.

The gas-transportation business is carried out by natural gas pipelines. Pipelines generally fit into two classifications: interstate and intrastate. Interstate pipelines travel through more than one state and are regulated by the FERC. Intrastates operate inside of one state and are regulated by that state's regulatory entity. Intrastates may be gathering pipelines that bring the gas from the point of production and move it onto higher-pressure pipelines, or they may be distribution pipelines that take the gas from other high-pressure pipelines and move it onto local distribution company lines or utility lines for delivery to the consumer.

When you link all of these industry participants together, and look at the flow of gas, then a single unit of gas could travel from the wellhead, through a gathering system, be processed by a processing plant, be delivered to an intrastate pipeline, then transported through an interstate pipeline, delivered to an LDC, delivered to a utility company, and then to the ultimate consumer. In any of these situations, there may be multiple participants; for instance, the gas delivered from a gathering system may go into an intrastate pipeline and then be delivered into a second intrastate pipeline before being delivered into additional pipelines for downstream delivery. In another scenario, the gas may go from gathering to an intrastate to delivery to an industrial end-user without ever having flowed through an interstate pipeline, an LDC, or a utility. As you can see, there are many combinations of flows through the various participants that may occur. Additionally, at any of the points where the ownership of the gas changes, there may be one or more marketers buying and selling the same unit of gas several times before it continues to flow in the pipeline system.

2. The Names in Regulation

There are several different entities involved in the regulation of natural gas and natural gas transportation. The FERC[1] sits at the top of that list. It is the federal-level governing body for energy. Each state that has natural gas transportation also has a state-level regulatory body that governs the drilling, production, gathering, transportation, and delivery of gas in that state. Some states assess taxes on the delivery of gas in that state. At the next level, there may be county, local, and city regulations that apply. Any company buying, selling, or transporting gas in a state will be subject to the local regulatory bodies that govern that area. Additionally, if the gas is transported into or out of that state, the service will also be subject to the FERC regulations that apply.

Along with these federal, state, and local entities is the NAESB[2]. NAESB is a membership-sponsored, industry-driven, standards-setting organization. An understanding of natural gas transportation in North America would be incomplete without consideration of NAESB.

Refer to Appendix A for more on each of these entities.

The Business Process

3. The process and timeline

It is time to introduce the transportation business-process flow. This is a very high-level and general business-process flow that shows how the pieces and the terms that will be discussed in the book will fit together in the much bigger end-to-end picture. The flow includes the steps in the business process from contract initiation through accounting. It also includes the timeline for each of these steps. Some of the steps are on a broad, as-needed timeline while others have very tight and regulated timeline components.

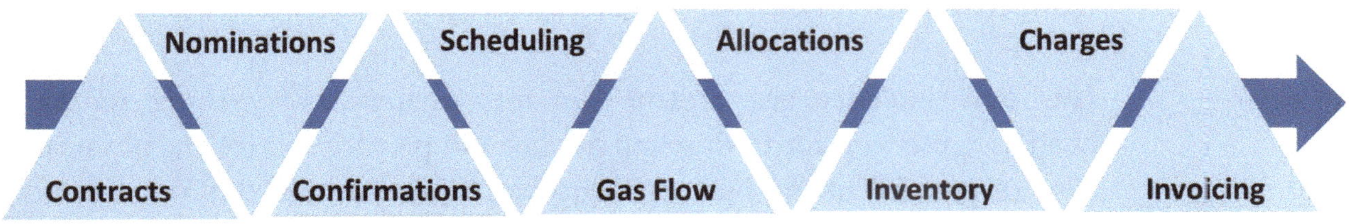

Figure 3.0
Each of the business process groupings in the order of flow for end to end processing

The business-process flow initiates with creation of a contract prior to any gas transactions. The flow continues through the transaction lifecycle to complete in the invoice process.

The Contracts section includes the core data of pipeline setup, tariffs, locations, and rates. Capacity Release and Service Types are included. Contracts are the foundation of the relationship between the shipper or shipper's agent and the pipeline.

Nominations initiate the flow of gas on the pipeline. They contain the request for the transportation service to begin. They define the receipt location and delivery location for the request. The receipt location is where the gas is delivered from the upstream pipeline and received onto the transporting pipeline. The delivery location is where the gas is delivered from the transporting pipeline and received onto the downstream pipeline.

Nominations include regular transportation, requirements for make-up gas, and the concept of business cycles.

Confirmations

Confirmations occur between interconnected pipelines to ensure that the gas will be delivered onto the pipeline and will be taken off of the pipeline in concert with the nomination that the shipper has provided. The confirming parties use the information provided in the nomination to match the transactions that cross the interconnect.

Scheduling

Scheduling is where the pipeline operator compares the gas available to flow versus the gas requested to flow, and schedules the requests to flow based on pipeline constraints. In Scheduling, segmentation and flow-day redirects are also discussed.

Gas flow

Gas flow includes gas control and measurement. Everything in the business process prior to this step has been in preparation for the physical flow of gas. All of the business processes subsequent to this step are in response to the physical flow of gas.

Allocations

In Allocations, the pipeline operator looks at the gas that actually flowed versus the gas that was scheduled and allocates the actual flow to the requested flow. There are multiple allocation methods that may be utilized between the pipeline tariff rules and the preferences provided by the operator regarding how the gas should be distributed among the shippers.

Inventory

Inventory accounts include imbalances, imbalance trading, inventory in storage, and other accounts on the pipeline. Inventories give the pipeline an indication of the balance of flow on and off the pipeline. It give shippers a report of imbalances as well as the utilization of its contract capacities.

Charges

With Charges, the pipeline applies the quantities of gas to the contractual rates and charge types to determine the charges that are to be assessed to the shipper. Cash-out charges may be included to resolve imbalances.

Invoicing

The Invoicing process assembles the charges into a comprehensive shipper bill. Invoicing contains the generation of the invoice as well as the generation of the back-up statements to support the invoice, the assignment of General Ledger account codes and interfaces to accounting.

When does all of this occur?

Contracting takes place ahead of any scheduled gas flow. It may take time to negotiate a transportation pipeline contract when it includes the determination of available capacity and the evaluation of the shipper's credit. At the same time, if the shipper is a known shipper on the pipeline with an established credit base and the contract is for capacity release, a known capacity, the contracting process can take place in as little as one hour. (See more on the capacity-release process for more information.)

Figure 3.1
Contracting may occur months, days or hours before the nomination deadline.

Nominations are governed by the nomination deadlines. There are multiple nomination deadlines, referred to as cycles. Some of these occur before gas flows, and some occur during the day of gas flow. Nomination cycles that occur after the timely nomination deadline are referred to as intraday-noms.

Figure 3.2
Nominations may occur months, days, hours, or minutes before the nomination deadline.

Confirmations and **Scheduling** occur during a window of the associated nomination cycle. This means that the confirmations and scheduling process will occur multiple times on the day before the gas begins to flow and will occur multiple times during the day of gas flow. The process must be complete before the gas begins to flow and the results provided to both the shipper and the operator.

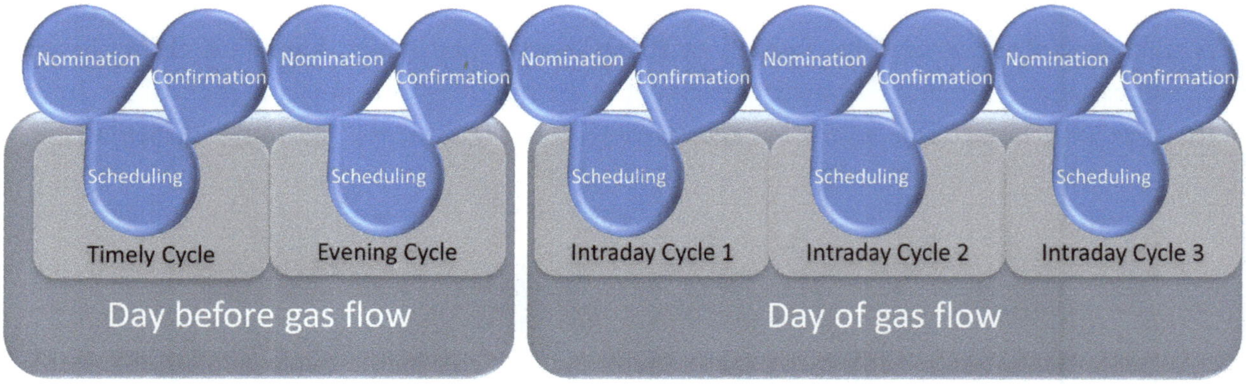

Figure 3.3
The nominations, confirmations, and scheduling process occurs during each of the nomination cycles.

Gas Flow takes place on the day of the requested gas service. This is when the gas is flowing into and out of the pipeline and is being measured by measurement meters and monitored by gas control. When a nomination has been submitted for an intra-day cycle, then the flow of gas may be for a partial day of flow.

Allocations may be calculated by the pipeline immediately after gas flow, on a daily basis, or on a monthly basis at the end of the month. Allocations are then provided back to the shipper and the point operator.

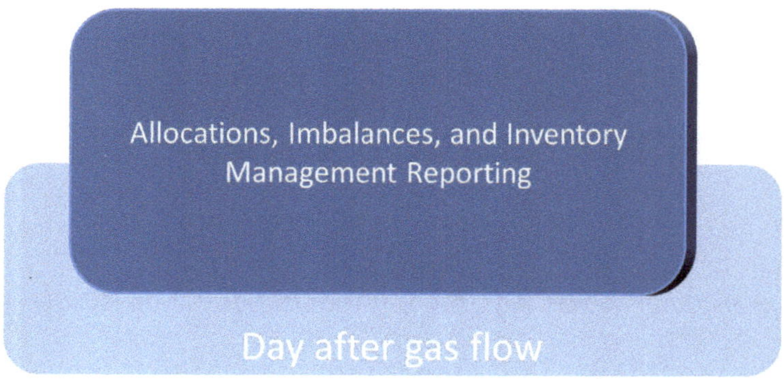

Figure 3.4
Allocations, imbalances and inventory management occur after gas flow.

Inventories are calculated concurrent with Allocations, and are the difference between the best available quantity[3] at a receipt location and the best available quantity at a delivery location. With the determination of imbalances, inventory accounts are updated and the imbalances may be paid back, cashed out, or traded.

Charges are assessed on the finalized allocated volumes and interfaced to the accounting process for accounts receivable and payable tracking.

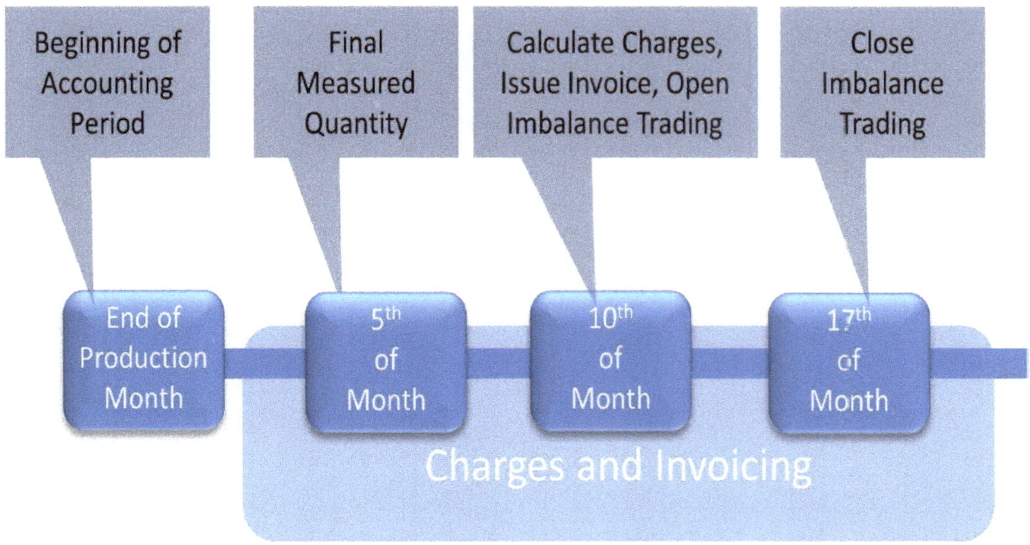

Figure 3.5
A calendar of the deadlines for charges and invoicing.

Invoices are issued according to a regulatory timeline after charge calculations are complete and verified and contain bundles of charges by shipper and shipper contract. Invoices include the back-up documentation that supports them.

Contracts

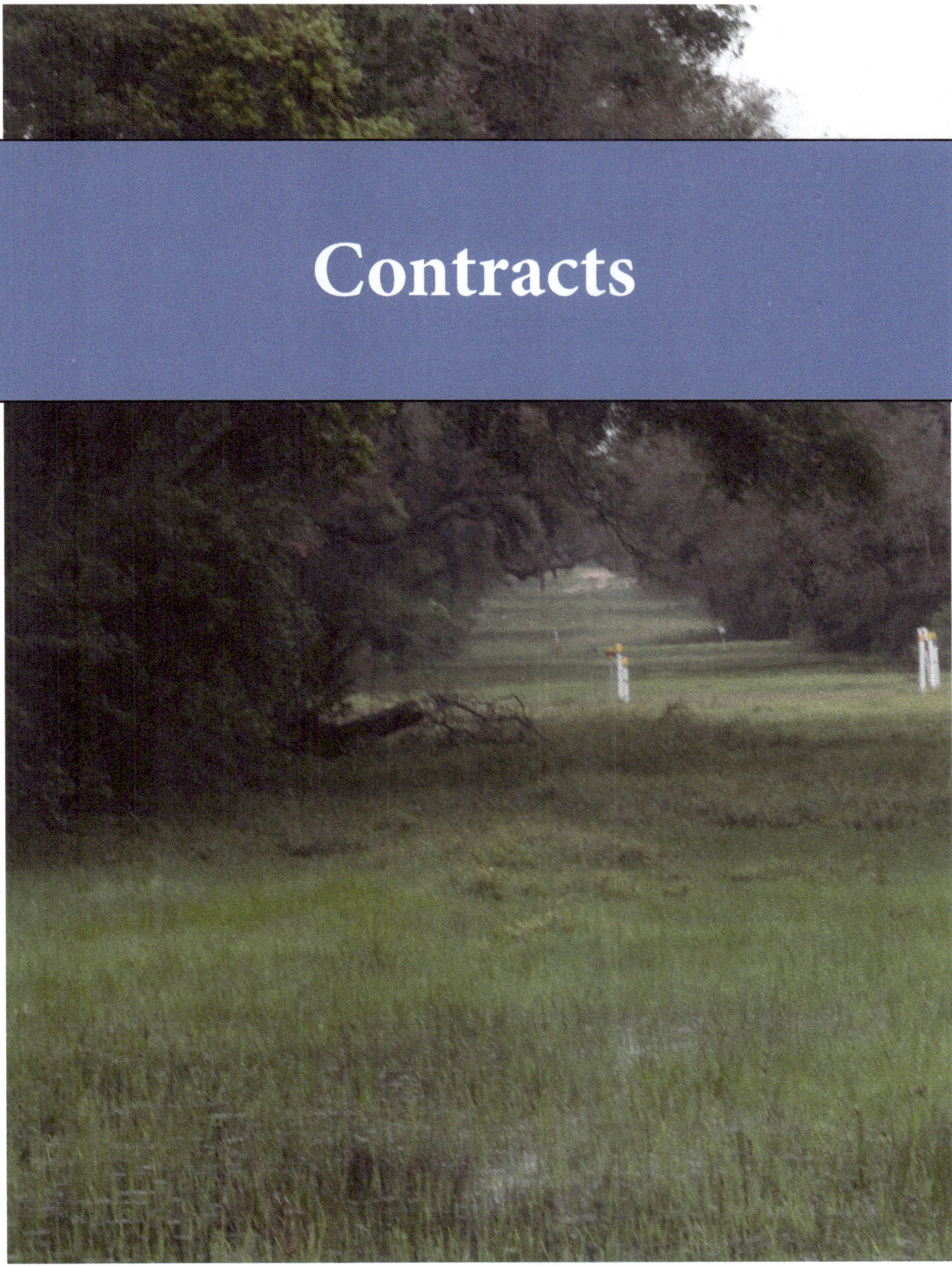

Contracts are the foundation of all natural-gas transportation transactions. The definition of a contract includes identification of the pipeline, the pipeline tariff, the terms of service, the contracted parties, locations and quantities for the service area, rates and charges to be assessed, credit terms, and management as well as the possibilities from the capacity release program.

The service contract outlines the agreement between the pipeline and the service requester for a service on the pipeline. The service requester may be a shipper, agent, or operator requesting a service. The contract defines the terms of the relationship within the confines of the pipeline's published Tariff or Statement of Operating Conditions (SOC). The contract will identify the time period of the service, the type of service (one offered by the pipeline), any exceptions to the pipeline's pro-forma agreement, the rate(s) for the service, and the location(s) to be used.

To transact business in natural gas, there is a group of core data that a company must gather and maintain. This information does not cause the gas to be bought, sold, or transported, but is the ancillary information that must be gathered and collected to validate the business transaction and to give all of the parties involved the assurance that they are achieving the expected business result. This information gives the pipeline the foundation data to build the contract. With this information in place, everyone involved in the gas transaction will know the product that they will receive and how much they will pay for that product.

Information in the core-data group includes the pipeline, pipeline tariff information, contract terms, type of service, parties to the contract, pipeline locations, quantities, and rates.

4. Pipelines

Pipelines is a large general topic in the North American transportation industry. The term is generally used to encompass the physical transportation pipeline, storage facilities, gathering facilities, and distribution companies. Often these facilities include gas-processing plants, meaning that the pipeline may be transporting wet or dry gas.

In North American natural gas, NAESB has defined all of these entities as the Transportation Service Provider (TSP)[4], an all-encompassing term used to describe the pipeline services companies listed above.

In some circles, companies engaged in primarily gathering or midstream services do not consider themselves a "pipeline." Likewise, companies that position themselves as a local distribution company or utility do not consider themselves pipelines. However, for the purposes of this discussion, any company, whether it is gathering, midstream, or a local distribution company, is considered a TSP if it provides services to transport gas for other parties.

A facility generally refers to the functional area on the pipeline. A pipeline may have one or more storage facilities; it may have one or more gas-plant facilities; and, of course, the transportation pipeline itself may be defined as a facility. Some TSPs group all of these entities together into one pipeline facility. Other TSPs separate each of the facilities into distinct entities.

5. Pipeline Tariff

The tariff or statement of operating conditions is the governing document for a pipeline. It explains all of the service offerings of the pipeline, the rules for those service offerings, the rates and charges, and the business rules that the pipeline will use to govern transactions.

An interstate pipeline files its tariff with the FERC. Additional filings are made to the FERC as rates change, as rules change, or when a new service is offered. The FERC has specific instructions for the pipeline that determine the content of the tariff and identify the sections the tariff must contain. These sections include pro-forma agreements, a description of each of the service offerings on the pipeline, identified as Rate Schedules, the rates for each of these offerings, pipeline maps, and General Terms and Conditions.

For a non-interstate pipeline, there may be a tariff to define operations, or there may be a statement of operating conditions (SOC). Some state regulatory entities require that every contract that is filed for a pipeline becomes part of the tariff. For these pipelines, the SOC may be very small because the operating details are defined in each of its contracts.

When a pipeline seeks to modify a tariff, it will submit, via a filing, the pages that it proposes to change. The filing may concern a change to a single page, or it may concern the addition of new pages, such as a new type of service being offered. For a new service offering, the filing may contain the new pages that describe the service offering, an updated table of contents, updated rate sheets, and updated sections of the General Terms and Conditions to incorporate language for the new service. Rarely will a pipeline file a completely new tariff.

Once a filing is made with the FERC, customers and affected parties are given an opportunity to comment on the filing and to express their favor or disfavor with the proposed changes. After customer comments and any necessary changes, the FERC will issue an order that the tariff changes are accepted and will give an implementation date for the changes. Often, the FERC grants the pipeline the ability to implement the changes on a date that has already passed, corresponding to the date in the original filing request.

6. Terms

The pipeline's pro-forma agreement provides terms of the service, and the service requester may ask for modifications or exceptions to those terms. If the pipeline is an interstate pipeline, then any exceptions to the standard agreement must be filed with the FERC. The terms of service may include basic information, such as the start and end of the gas day, the nomination cycle deadlines, terms of force majeure, etc.

The service contract is for a specific range of dates - the beginning date and ending date. The contract may be for a limited number of days in one month, a subset of months spanning several years, or may cover several complete years. Firm contracts may have an "Evergreen" clause, meaning that the contract self-renews each year unless the shipper informs the pipeline that it does not want to renew the contract.

The service contract will refer to the pipeline's General Terms and Conditions for generic contract terms that are not specified in the contract language.

The tariff also contains the business-processing rules for that pipeline in the General Terms and Conditions section on an interstate pipeline. This section identifies the transportation rules and expectations for a shipper entering into a service agreement on the pipeline. The general terms and conditions will identify items such as the gas day, nomination deadlines, nomination model type, imbalance-resolution procedures, procedures for handling of any remaining imbalances/amounts due at the end of a contract, procedures for force majeure, etc. It is critical that a shipper review this section of the pipeline tariff before entering into a service agreement with a pipeline because it identifies the shipper responsibilities and the pipeline's business-processing rules.

Type of Service

Most pipelines offer more than one type of service. In addition to traditional transportation, they may offer storage, gas processing, pooling, parking and loaning, balancing services, imbalance trading, and/or operational balancing agreements. This list comprises the services that are commonly offered on interstate pipelines. Services such as pooling and imbalance trading are required to be offered by interstate pipelines. Any given pipeline may offer fewer services or more specialty services than those listed.

Any of the services may be offered as either a firm or an interruptible service. Shippers holding firm service have capacity reserved on the pipeline for a specified period of time while those shippers holding interruptible service use pipeline services on an as-needed basis, where capacity is available, without reserving capacity full-time.

On an interstate pipeline, these services may be used by the contract holder or by an agent for the contract holder. If the contract holder chooses to use an agent, then the agent will also need a contract with the pipeline. The agent becomes a contract holder just like the original contract holder. For interstate transportation, federal regulations require the contract holder, not the agent, to hold title to the gas. This is often referred to as the "shipper must have title rule." Another way that the interstate contract holder can get the best use out of its transportation contract is by using an asset manager or Retail Choice Program. The asset manager has the right to transport its gas and its customer's gas under the same contract without violating the "shipper must have title rule." This sounds like a simple process when described here, but there are very important rules that must be adhered to in order to use the rights of an asset manager[5] or Retail Choice Program[6].

On an intrastate pipeline, the state in which the transportation occurs determines whether or not the shipper must have title to the gas it contracts to transport. There are still many service opportunities for agents to participate in the intrastate market.

Transportation

Transportation service describes the movement on a gas pipeline from a receipt location to a delivery location. The transportation may be short-haul or long-haul. It may also be firm or interruptible.

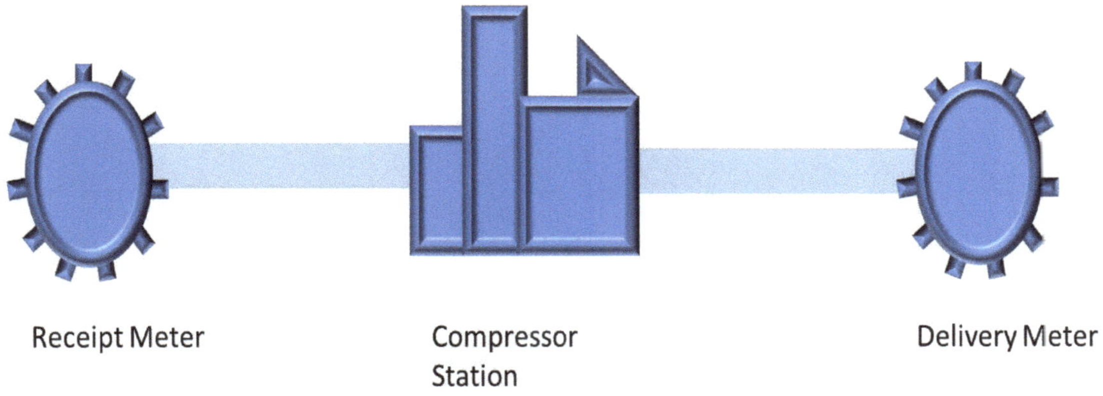

Figure 6.1
Gas received onto a pipeline may go through one or more compressor stations before being delivered

When a pipeline receives gas at a receipt location, the gas may require compression to bring it into the pipeline because the upstream source of gas is at a lower pressure than the pressure on the transportation pipeline. Along the path of the gas being transported, there may be additional compression required to keep the pressure of the pipeline at an appropriate level to push the gas down the pipe. The energy used to compress the flow of gas on the pipeline is referred to as "fuel." The gas received for transportation at a receipt location is reduced by the fuel amount to determine the quantity to be delivered at the delivery location. At the delivery location, the gas will flow into a similarly pressurized pipeline or a pipeline of lesser pressure. In this case, the gas requires no additional compression to take it from a high-pressure pipeline into a low-pressure pipeline.

Pipelines generally offer transportation service as firm or interruptible. Firm service reserves a designated space on the pipeline for transportation. This reserved service guarantees that the shipper will have space above all other non-firm shippers on the pipeline. Pipelines assess to the firm service contract a reservation charge or demand charge for the quantity of DTH specified in the contract. The pipeline assesses this reservation charge on a daily or monthly basis regardless of the use that the contract holder has on the pipeline.

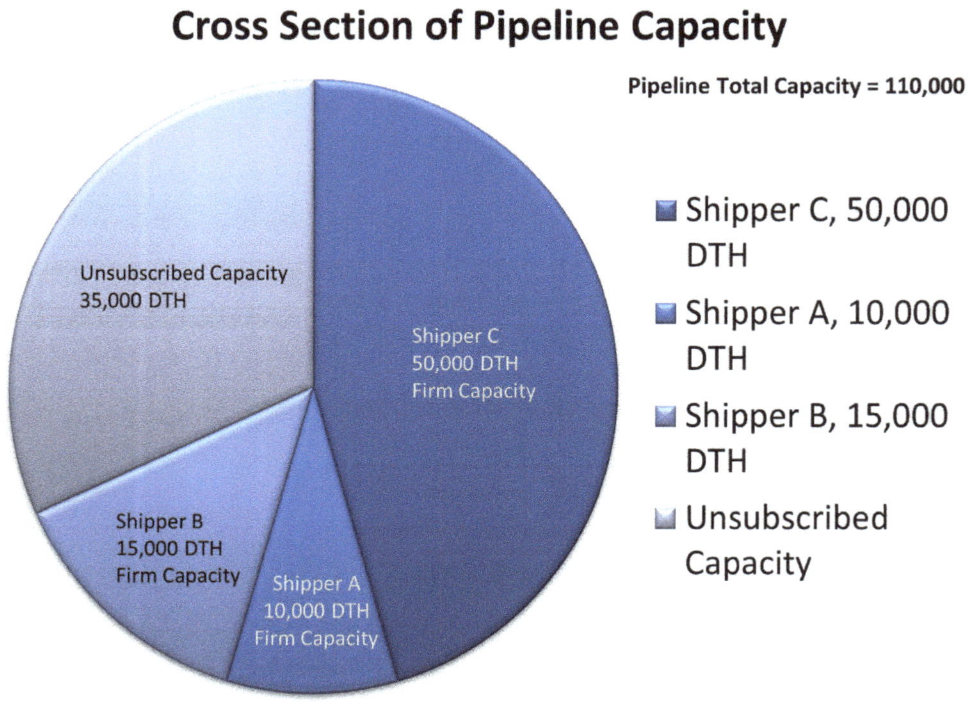

Figure 6.2
An example of pipeline capacity divided among several shippers with a quantity remaining unsubscribed

If a contract holder has a firm contract for 10,000 DTH per day, and the contract holder uses only 5,000 DTH per day for a month, then the contract holder will pay the reservation charge for the entire 10,000 DTH even though it only used 5,000 DTH. The value in a firm-service contract is that it guarantees the contract holder/shipper space on the pipeline as long as the pipeline has the operational ability to deliver any gas. Additionally, the firm contract is assessed a commodity or usage charge. This charge is based on the quantity of gas that is delivered on the contract. In the above example, the contract holder would pay a commodity charge for the 5,000 DTH of usage.

With an interruptible-service contract, the shipper avoids the monthly demand charge but pays a higher commodity charge for transportation. This service is more of an "on-demand" service that permits transportation only if pipeline capacity is available. With interruptible service, the shipper may nominate zero on one day and 1,000 DTH on the next day and will be charged, at the end of the month, for the 1,000 DTH. Interruptible service introduces risk for the shipper because this type of contract does not guarantee space on the pipeline. All firm-service contracts will move ahead of an interruptible-service contract. If a pipeline has a high level of operationally available capacity, then using an interruptible service for transportation provides little risk. This means that the pipeline has excess space on the pipeline that is not used on a daily basis.

Pooling

A pipeline may offer pooling to allow a shipper to aggregate its supply transactions into one larger unit of gas and then disaggregate that gas to its markets. With a pooling service, a shipper may nominate many transactions to be delivered into the pool, to create a total available pool quantity. The shipper may sell this quantity of gas at the pool or the shipper may purchase additional quantities of gas at the pool. Once the shipper has acquired all of the quantities it needs at the pool, it will submit one or more nominations to take the gas from the pool and deliver the gas to its downstream markets[7].

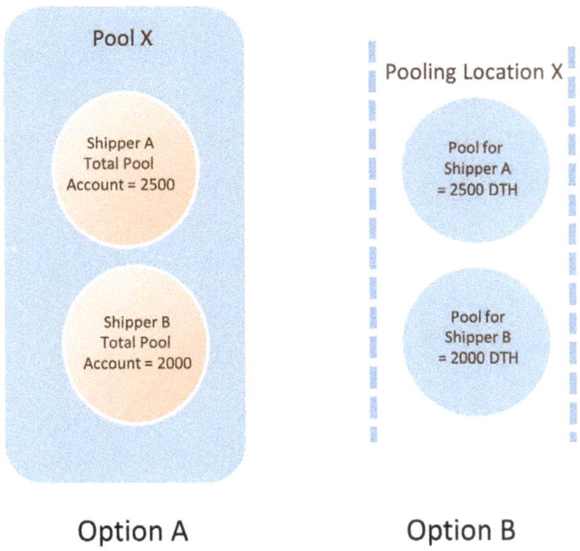

Figure 6.3
A pooling scenario where (A) each shipper is given a contract within a single pool on the transportation pipeline, or (B) is given a separate pool in a single location on the transportation pipeline

Interstate pipelines must offer pooling as a service and must offer one or more pools available reasonably proximate to receipt locations so that producers and other shippers can bring their supply gas to a pool to sell.

Some pipelines create their pools by shipper, such that each shipper on the pipeline has a distinct pool. Other pipelines create one or more pools and give each shipper a separate account on a pool.

These differences in pooling services accommodate the unique business offerings of the pipeline. For the shipper, the effect is the same. Selling gas from one shipper to another requires a pool-to-pool transfer transaction whether that transaction takes the gas from one pool (location) to another pool (location) or that transaction transfers the ownership from one party to another at the same location. Additionally, a pipeline may create multiple separate pools in different operational areas of the pipeline. For instance, the pipeline may have one pool where all of the receipt locations in the southern section of the pipeline come together into one pool and another pool where all of the receipt locations in the eastern section of the pipeline come together into one pool. This gives the pipeline the ability to accommodate operational considerations while still offering pooling services.

Pools may be associated with a physical location on a pipeline, with a geographic area on a pipeline, or may be unassociated with any geographic location. A pipeline determines its placement of pools by the operational priorities of that pipeline.

Storage

In pipeline storage service, a shipper may contract for the pipeline to hold its gas on the pipeline for a period of time. A pipeline storage facility may come from an underground salt dome, an underground gas facility that has been exhausted, an aboveground storage facility that the pipeline has built, or other operational sources.

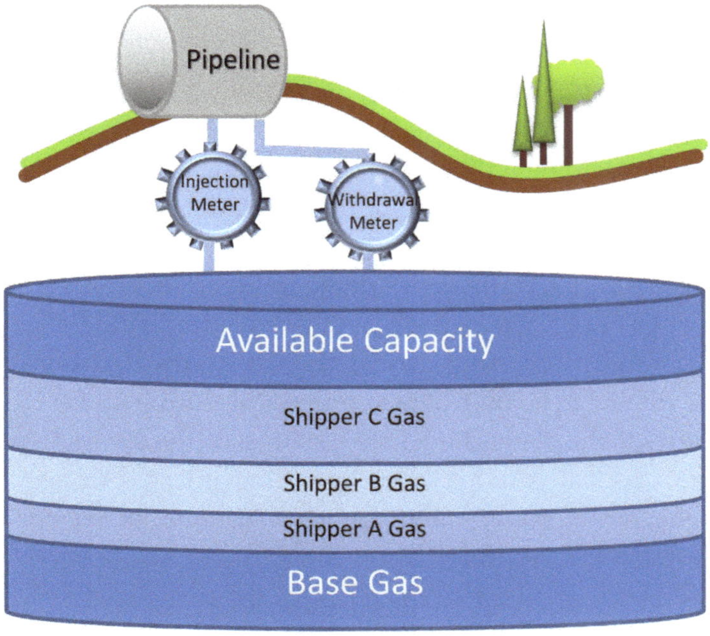

Figure 6.5
Multiple shippers with inventories of gas in a single storage facility

The shipper contracts for a right to inject gas into the storage facility, store gas for a period of time, and then withdraw the gas from the facility. The pipeline storage-service contract will state how much gas can be injected on a daily basis, how much gas can be withdrawn on a daily basis, and the total quantity that the shipper may have in storage at any given time. This service gives the shipper the ability to purchase gas throughout the non-peak season of the year, store it near the market or supply area for the gas, and then deliver the gas to market during the peak season of the year. The shipper will usually pay separate fees per DTH, as well as in-kind fuel, to inject the gas, to store the gas on a monthly basis, and to withdraw the gas.

Many storage contracts have an injection season and a withdrawal season in which pipelines expect the gas to be injected during non-peak periods and withdrawn during peak periods. During the injection season, a pipeline may require that a minimum amount of the target storage quantity be injected by a certain date so that the shipper cannot try to push all of the gas into storage at a peak injection period. The corollary exists that the same pipeline may require that a certain percentage of the gas be withdrawn by a certain date so that all of the gas is not withdrawn during a peak withdrawal period. These rules on how much may be injected or withdrawn to meet contract terms as the injection and withdrawal seasons progress is often referred to as storage ratcheting. Pipelines vary on how they implement ratcheting rules across the industry and on individual pipelines.

Type of Natural Gas Storage Facilities by Leigh Spangler

Billions of cubic feet of natural gas is stored underground all over the world. But not all storage facilities are the same. Subterranean geology varies radically, making some places ideal for underground storage, while others are not. This varying terra firma also creates differing types of storage, each with different features and drawbacks.

The most common type of natural gas storage is reservoir storage. Reservoir storage projects store natural gas in empty, depleted natural gas storage fields; that is, natural gas is re-injected into naturally occurring geological formations that once held natural gas. Reservoir storage facilities can be quite large, sometimes storing 40 BCF or more of natural gas. However, because of the sometimes fragile nature of the geology, reservoir storage is most often used as "seasonal" storage, with gas being injected during the summer and withdrawn during the winter. Reservoir storage can be found across the U.S., but is most common in the Midwest and Northeast.

Reef storage is similar to reservoir storage in that it uses naturally occurring geological formations to hold natural gas. The difference is that reef storage uses the reefs formed by ancient oceans, now underground, as the storage geology. Reef storage is mostly found around the Great Lakes.

Salt storage facilities utilize underground domes of salt as the storage geology. To create a salt storage facility, some of the domal salt is removed by injecting and then removing high pressure water that dissolves the salt, leaving behind a vertical "cavern." Because they are man-made, salt caverns storage facilities tend to be smaller than reservoirs, but more durable, able to support "high deliverability" or multiple storage cycles a year. Salt dome geology is most commonly found along the Gulf Coast.

Parking and Loaning (PAL)

PAL service is the abbreviation for "parking and loaning" service or "parking and lending" service on a pipeline. PAL service varies from storage service because it utilizes the physical capacity of the transportation pipeline instead of a separate storage facility on the pipeline. Because of this, there is usually less capacity for PAL service on a pipeline than there is storage capacity, and pipelines usually consider PAL service to be short-term and interruptible. The parking service takes place when a shipper has received gas onto the pipeline that it wishes for the pipeline to store for a period of time rather than simultaneously delivering the gas off of the pipeline. In this transaction, the shipper "parks" the gas onto the pipeline's physical capacity and pays a parking fee for the transaction to park the gas and a daily fee for the quantity of gas that is remaining in the parked balance each day, based on the quantity of gas. The shipper removes the parked gas from the pipeline through an un-parking transaction much like a transaction when the shipper withdraws gas from storage.

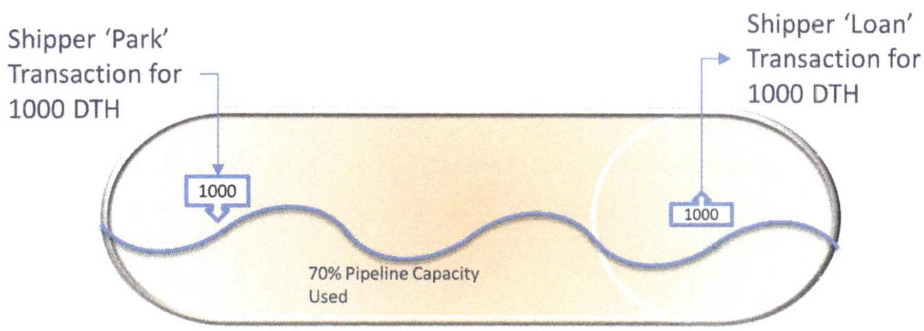

Figure 6.6
An example of gas being parked or loaned on a pipeline

The loaning service takes place when a shipper needs to deliver more gas off of the pipeline than it has received and wishes to borrow gas from the pipeline for a period of time to fulfill the delivery requirement. In this transaction, the pipeline "loans" the gas to the shipper on a previously agreed-to contract, for a loaning fee and a daily fee, based on the quantity of gas. To resolve the loaning service, the shipper must enter in a payback transaction to the loaning account to zero out the account.

Pipelines consider PAL services low-priority interruptible services. If any operational change occurs, the pipeline may demand that gas is un-parked or paid back immediately to resolve the operational issue. Just like in storage service, PAL service charges a fee for parking, un-parking, and daily parking of the gas. Some pipelines execute one contract for parking service and a separate contract for the loaning service; other pipelines execute one contract that encompasses both parking and loaning services. Pipelines are not required to offer a PAL service.

Balancing

A shipper balancing agreement between the shipper and the pipeline defines which services will be rolled into the overall shipper balance and how those balances and imbalances will be resolved.

Shipper balancing may occur for the shipper across all of its service contracts, or the balance may be maintained on each contract. If a pipeline has multiple rate zones or segments, then the pipeline may maintain shipper balances for each of those zones/ segments or the pipeline may group all shipper balances to the Operational Impact Area on the pipeline. The Operational Impact Area may span multiple zones and segments. The different mechanisms for maintaining shipper balances and resolving imbalances are discussed in more detail later in this book.

Some pipelines use their storage contracts as a balancing service. This method allows a shipper to designate that, if there is excess gas received onto the pipeline, the gas is automatically injected into its storage account, and, if there is insufficient gas received, the gas is automatically withdrawn from its storage account. This keeps the shipper in balance at all times with the pipeline and allows the shipper to make up any anomalies in flow by injecting and withdrawing from storage.

Operational Balancing Agreements (OBAs)

The pipeline will maintain balances with operators at interconnects through the use of an Operational Balancing Agreement (OBA). An OBA may cover one point between two operators or may cover multiple points between two operators. The OBA is used to keep the shipper's flow of gas "whole" and to pass the variations in flow and measurement to the operator level for the operators to resolve.

An interconnect is a location where one pipeline is connected to another pipeline. One of the pipelines, either the upstream or downstream pipeline is generally the operator of that location. In some instances, a third-party operator may be contracted to manage the location. The OBA contract is between the operator of the location and the connecting pipeline.

When an OBA exists at a location, the scheduled quantities for the shippers through that location are considered as guaranteed quantities. Any differences between the scheduled flow and the actual flow is absorbed into the OBA and resolved between the operator and the pipeline.

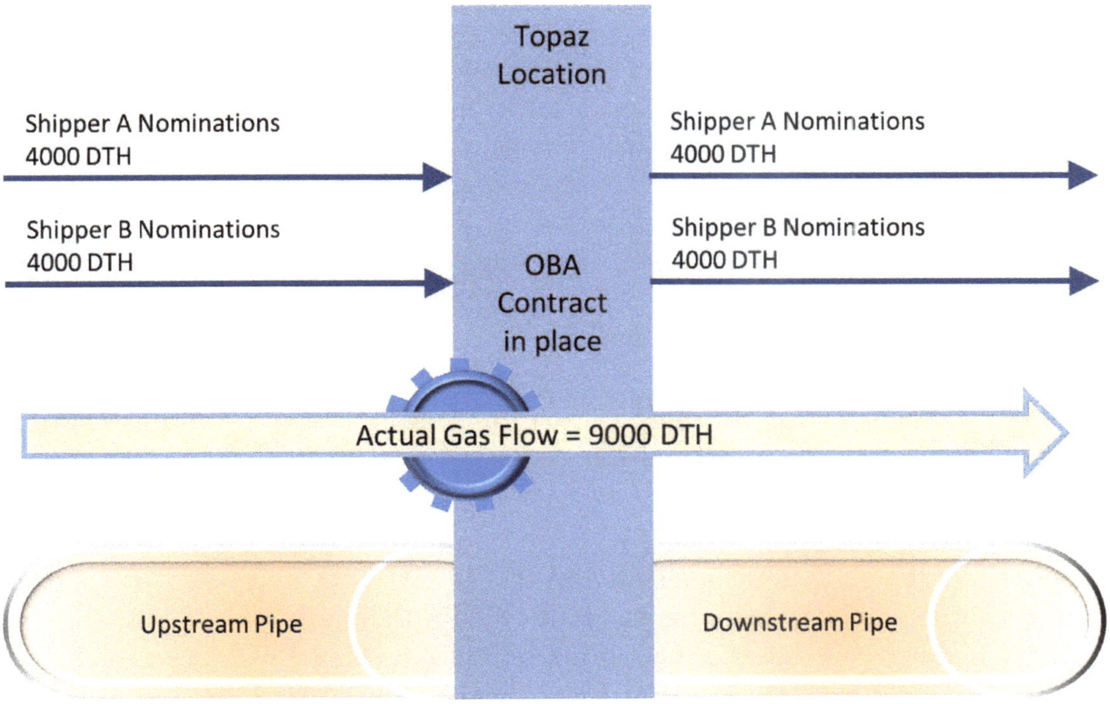

When 9000 DTH flows through the Topaz Location where only 8000 DTH was scheduled, the upstream pipeline has delivered more gas and the downstream pipeline has received more gas. This excess gas of 1000 DTH is placed into the OBA contract account as a quantity due the upstream pipeline.

Figure 6.7
An example of gas that is overdelivered on a pipeline and the excess quantity is allocated to an OBA.

Why Storage Operators Have OBAs by Leigh Spangler

An Operational Balancing Agreement (OBA) is a contractual arrangement between two interconnected asset operators (such as a pipeline operator and a storage operator) in which the asset operators agree to carry the daily imbalance between the quantity of gas scheduled to flow and the quantity of gas that actually flows through the interconnect. Since moving natural gas is not an exact science, these two quantities always differ, and that difference is added to the daily OBA Balance. By agreeing to manage this OBA Balance between themselves, the asset operators can keep their shippers "whole", i.e. the shipper's allocated quantity always equals its scheduled quantity.

Note that without an OBA, the shippers carry this daily imbalance. For pipelines, this is no big deal, but for storage operators this can cause problems, especially when a shipper nears the "bottom" of its storage inventory.

Suppose, for example that a shipper has 1000 DTH left in its storage inventory and wants to withdraw it all. The shipper submits a 1000 DTH withdrawal nomination to the storage operator. If the storage operator has an OBA in place with the withdrawal pipeline, the storage operator can allocate exactly 1000 DTH to the shipper's withdrawal, happily zeroing out the inventory.

But if there is no OBA in place, the shipper most certainly would be allocated an amount other than the planned 1000 DTH (say, 997 DTH). The three-DTH difference would remain in the shipper's inventory. The shipper would then try to nominate the withdrawal of the remaining three DTHs, only to be allocated, say 10 DTH, and end up with a negative-seven DTH inventory position! So a seven DTH injection nomination would be needed to bring the balance to zero. And so on.

To avoid this endless allocation, nearly every storage facility has negotiated OBAs with its interconnected pipelines, freeing storage operators and shippers from an endless race to resolve the imbalance.

Processing

On pipelines that are transporting unprocessed or "wet" gas, the transportation service may include a processing service. Processing services are used to extract the non-methane components out of the gas to make it suitable for long-distance transportation. More on gas processing is covered in the chapter on Gas Quality.

7. Parties

There are many different parties engaged in the transportation of natural gas. At the highest level, we have the legal entities that own the business parties conducting business. These entities may own one or more of the businesses involved in the transactions, and one business may be owned by more than one entity. Recognizing this, then, the parties that conduct the business are the ones that will be addressed here.[8]

The parties involved in gas transportation are:

- The **pipeline (aka transportation service provider)**, which may also be processing, gathering, storing, or distributing the gas.
- The **service requester** for the transportation service, which may be the shipper, the shipper's agent, the shipper's asset manager, or retail choice program.
- The **shipper** owns the transportation contract for service on the pipeline or at the service facility.
- The **agent** may, through a contractual relationship with the pipeline and the shipper, conduct business on behalf of the shipper.
- The **asset manager**, in a special relationship between a shipper and an agent, has enhanced rights that do not exist within the traditional shipper/agent relationship[9].
- The **upstream shipper** delivers the gas on the upstream pipeline to the current pipeline's receipt location. The pipeline will seek this party to identify when it confirms the requested gas flow with the operator of the receipt location. More information on this party and the activities described can be found in the chapter on Confirmations.
- The **downstream shipper** receives the gas on the pipeline downstream of the current pipeline's delivery location. The pipeline will seek to identify this party when it confirms the requested gas flow with the operator of the delivery location. More information on this party and the activities described can be found in the chapter on Confirmations.
- The **point operator** or operator of a location is, generally, either the pipeline delivering gas at the location or the pipeline receiving gas at a location. The operator may be a third party that one or both pipelines have contracted to measure and to allocate the gas at the location.

- The **confirming party** confirms the requested flow of gas at a location; it is either the point operator or the pipeline. In the Confirmations chapter, the role of the confirming party with the operator and pipeline is discussed.

- The **accounting party** is the party who will be receiving the invoices and accompanying reports for this contract. The accounting party may be the shipper, the agent, or another party designated in the contract.

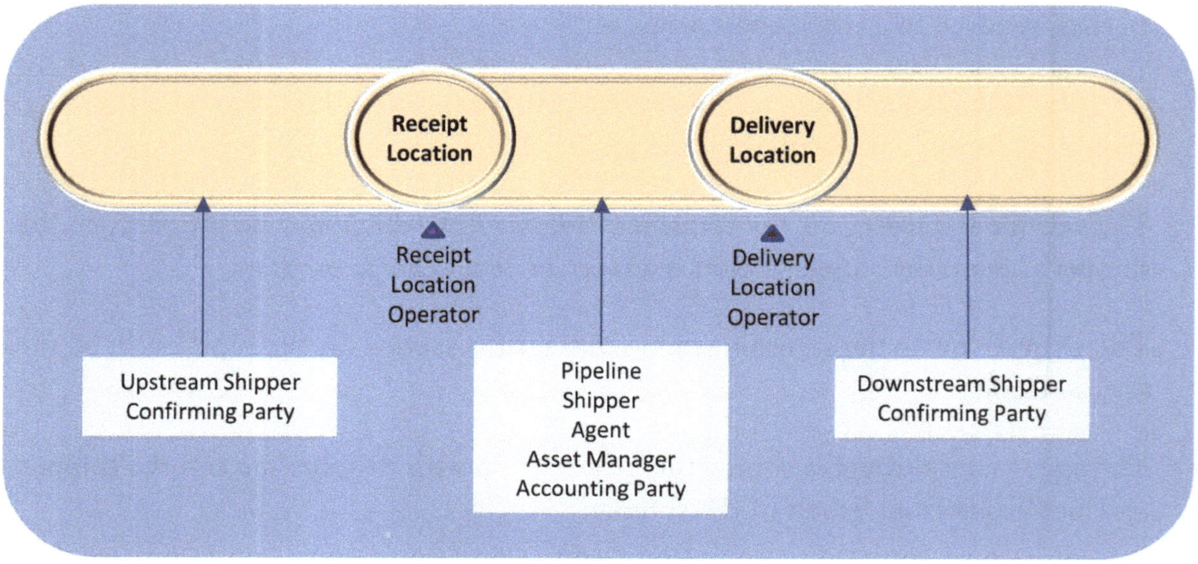

Figure 7.1
The parties involved in the transportation transaction on the upstream side of the meter, on the mainline pipeline and on the downstream side of the meter

8. Locations

The terms points, **locations**, and meters are used interchangeably on pipelines. It is important to recognize that there is a distinction between them. Location is the standard term used to identify where gas is received and delivered on a pipeline. Many business entities use the term **points** for the same purpose as the location. This book will use the terms interchangeably. A location may be a physical location, such as a meter station, or it may be a logical location, such as an accounting point for exchange of gas ownership on the pipeline. Some locations may have gas-measurement facilities at the physical locations while other locations may determine gas measurement by aggregating measurement from several other locations.

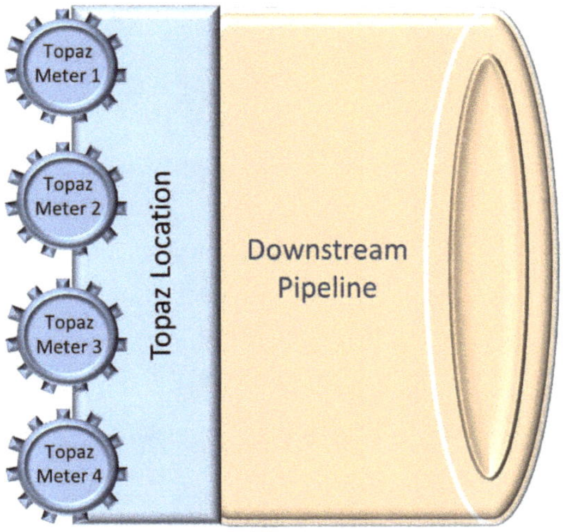

Figure 8.1
Multiple meters that comprise a single measurement location on the pipeline

Gas measured at a physical location may be comprised of one or more physical **meters**. Meters are the physical device that measures the gas at a location. Meters will be discussed in more detail in the Gas Flow section of this book.

Locations are one of the terms that are specified in the service contract. These terms may include:

- receipt and delivery locations for transportation,
- locations for pooling service,
- parking / loaning locations for park and loan service, or
- injection and withdrawal locations for storage.

When the service is for transportation, the receipt and delivery locations may be specified as one list of available receipt locations and one list of available delivery locations such that any combination of receipt and delivery locations is valid for use on the contract; or the locations may be specified as discrete paths where a receipt location is listed with a specific delivery for each of the approved path combinations.[10]

Example 1	Contract MDQ = 15,000 DTH	
	Locations:	Receipt A
		Receipt B
		Receipt C
		Delivery P
		Delivery Q
		Delivery R
		Delivery S
		Delivery T

Example 8.1
A contract with specific receipt and delivery locations assigned.

In the above example, the MDQ is specified at the contract level and a list of locations without quantity restrictions is provided.

Example 2	*Contract MDQ = 15,000 DTH*	
	Receipt A MDQ = 5,000 DTH	Delivery P MDQ = 4,000 DTH
	Receipt B MDQ = 5,000 DTH	Delivery Q MDQ = 3,000 DTH
	Receipt C MDQ = 5,000 DTH	Delivery R MDQ = 3,000 DT
		Delivery S MDQ = 2,000 DTH
		Delivery T MDQ = 3,000 DTH

Example 8.2
A contract with specific receipt and delivery locations and location level MDQs.
In this example the MDQ is specified at the contract level and a list of locations is rovided with a specific quantity restriction for each of the locations. In this example, the total of the MDQs for each of the locations is the same as that for the contract. A pipeline could also specify location level MDQs that exceed the MDQ of the contract so that the shipper has multiple receipt and delivery options for moving the gas.

Example 3

Contract MDQ = 15,000 DTH

Locations:	Receipt A	Delivery P
	Receipt B	Delivery Q
	Receipt C	Delivery R
		Delivery S
		Delivery T

Paths:				
	Path Receipt A	to	Delivery P	= 4,000 DTH
	Path Receipt A	to	Delivery T	= 1,000 DTH
	Path Receipt B	to	Delivery Q	= 3,000 DTH
	Path Receipt B	to	Delivery T	= 2,000 DTH

Example 8.3
A contract with specific receipt and delivery locations with no MDQ specified and paths with MDQ limits. Not all possible paths are listed, therefore, paths not listed do not have path level MDQ restrictions. In this example, the MDQ is specified at the contract level, and a list of locations is provided. This means that any of the locations can be used and combined to achieve the contract level MDQ, but the maximum quantity at the specified paths must be respected. A valid nomination would be from Receipt C to Delivery S for 15,000 DTH. This nomination would not encounter any of the path restrictions specified in the contract.

Example 4

Contract MDQ = 15,000 DTH

Locations:	Receipt A MDQ = 5,000 DTH	Delivery P MDQ = 4,000 DTH
	Receipt B MDQ = 5,000 DTH	Delivery Q MDQ = 3,000 DTH
	Receipt C MDQ = 5,000 DTH	Delivery R MDQ = 3,000 DTH
		Delivery S MDQ = 2,000 DTH
		Delivery T MDQ = 3,000 DTH

Paths:				
	Path Receipt A	to	Delivery P	= 4,000 DTH
	Path Receipt A	to	Delivery T	= 1,000 DTH
	Path Receipt B	to	Delivery Q	= 3,000 DTH
	Path Receipt B	to	Delivery T	= 2,000 DTH

Example 8.4
A contract with specific receipt and delivery locations containing location level MDQs as well as paths with MDQ limits. The MDQ limits of the paths must comply with the MDQ limits of the locations. Paths not listed do not have path level MDQ restrictions but must still comply with the location level MDQ. In this example, the MDQ is specified at the contract level, and a list of locations with MDQs is provided. This means that any of the locations can be used up to their MDQ and combined to achieve the contract level MDQ, but the maximum quantity at the specified paths must be respected. A valid nomination in this example would be from Receipt C to Delivery S for 2,000 DTH, utilizing the MDQ restriction for Delivery S. An additional nomination from Receipt C to Delivery P for 4,000 DTH would also be a valid nomination. The specified path does not limit the paths to those listed. It only limits the MDQs to those listed.

Example 5

Contract MDQ = 15,000 DTH

Locations: No Locations are listed on this contract.

Paths:				
	Path Receipt A	to	Delivery P	= 4,000 DTH
	Path Receipt A	to	Delivery T	= 4,000 DTH
	Path Receipt B	to	Delivery Q	= 4,000 DTH
	Path Receipt B	to	Delivery T	= 3,000 DTH

Example 8.5
A contract with no locations specified and no location level MDQs; however, paths are specified with associated MDQs. In this case, the only valid nominations for this contract are those nominations using the listed paths within the listed MDQs. In this example, there are only 4 paths available to the shipper. There are no options to rearrange the locations or the quantities. If the shipper wishes to utilize the maximum contract quantity on a day, then the 4 nominations for quantities as specified in the contract would be required.

The locations listed on a firm-service contract are considered primary locations. On many pipelines, all other locations on the pipeline system are available on the firm contract, but on a secondary basis. Other pipelines may specify any available secondary locations on the contract. The priority accorded to secondary points varies by pipeline. On some pipelines, priority is given to primary points, then secondary points, then interruptible; on other pipelines, the priority given to the secondary points is equal to interruptible. The terms in the General Terms and Conditions of the pipeline tariff will give the shipper the expectations on scheduling priorities.

Interruptible (IT) services may have specified points on the agreement but they will not have the primary/secondary priority designation.

9. Quantities

The service contract will contain a specified Maximum Daily Quantity (MDQ). This quantity is for the entire contract, and there may be additional path-specific or point-specific MDQs associated with the locations. It is this contract-level MDQ quantity that is used to assess the reservation/demand charge on a firm agreement. When a shipper wishes to exceed this quantity, then the excess use is charged at an overrun rate and scheduled as equal to interruptible service. Some pipelines do not associate an MDQ with interruptible service contracts. The assumption is that interruptible is available as long as space is available. Other pipelines assign an MDQ to interruptible service as a way to set a credit limit on service.

Some service contracts, such as storage contracts, will contain multiple maximum quantities and contain minimum quantities during specific peak-performance periods. The maximum quantities may be a maximum daily injection quantity, a maximum daily withdrawal quantity, and a maximum daily storage quantity, which refers to the total quantity in storage on any given day. The minimum quantities will identify a minimum injection quantity during a period of the contract and a minimum withdrawal quantity during another period of the contract.

There are variations to the quantities specified across many different pipelines. Some pipelines specify a maximum daily receipt quantity but no maximum daily delivery. The delivery quantity, in this case, is inferred by reducing the receipt quantity by the fuel amount. Some pipelines specify both the receipt and delivery maximums while others may specify only the delivery and infer the receipt.

The MDQ will always be maintained at the contract level, but also may be maintained at the location level, the path level, or both location level and path level on any given contract. The contract MDQ identifies the total maximum quantity that can be used across all locations and paths on a given day. A location-level MDQ[11] identifies the maximum quantity that can be used at that single location on a given day. A path-level MDQ identifies the maximum quantity that can be used on a location pair on a given day. All of these MDQs can exist on one contract at the same time. In processing, the path MDQ, if it exists, is examined first because it is at the lowest level[12]. If the quantity does not exceed the MDQ of the path, processing continues. The location MDQ of the receipt and delivery location is examined second. If the quantity does not cause the receipt location MDQ to be exceeded when examined with any other transactions for this contract at this receipt location, then processing continues. Next, if the quantity does not cause the delivery location MDQ to be exceeded when examined with any other transactions for this contract at this delivery location, then processing continues. The contract-level MDQ is examined last. The contract-level MDQ must be evaluated with all other transactions for this contract. If the contract-level MDQ is not exceeded, then processing may continue.

Another important consideration in MDQs is that the MDQ associated with a single location may be equal to or lesser than the MDQ associated with the contract. The sum of the MDQs at the location level may exceed the total MDQ for the contract. This is because the shipper has a choice on where to receive or deliver its gas on a given day within the terms of the contract.

An example of this situation in a contract is described below:

Contract KL1234	**Contract MDQ = 50,000 DTH**	
Receipt Location	**Receipt Location MDQ**	
A42	50,000	
B16	20,000	
C36	30,000	
Delivery Location	**Delivery Location MDQ**	
M18	40,000	
N22	40,000	
P88	40,000	
Path Receipt	**Path Delivery**	**Path MDQ**
A42	M18	30,000
A42	N22	30,000
A42	P88	30,000

Table 9.1
Example of contract, location and path level MDQs

In the example above, the total flow on a given day for contract KL1234 is the contract-level MDQ stated as 50,000 DTH. The first receipt location, A42, could be the only receipt location used on a single day because it also has a contract MDQ of 50,000 DTH. Or, for example, the shipper could choose to receive 20,000 DTH from A42, 20,000 DTH from B16, and 10,000 DTH from C36. Any combination that adds up to 50,000 DTH on the receipt side would be valid. If the shipper chose to receive the entire 50,000 DTH from A42, then the pathing restrictions would come into consideration.

The maximum quantity that A42 can deliver to M18, N22, or P88 is 30,000 each. If the entire 50,000 DTH was received at A42, then the delivery locations would need to be split into at least two different paths because of the 30,000-DTH limit on the path. On the delivery location MDQs, each delivery location has a MDQ of 40,000 DTH. The total delivery of 50,000 DTH cannot go to any single delivery location. If part of the quantity is coming from Receipt A42, then the maximum delivery from that location is restricted to 30,000 DTH for each delivery location because of the pathing restriction.

Receipt Location	Delivery Location	Quantity
A42	M18	30,000
B16	N22	20,000
Total Contract		**50,000**

Receipt Location	Delivery Location	Quantity
A42	M18	10,000
A42	N22	10,000
A42	P88	30,000
Total Contract		**50,000**

Receipt Location	Delivery Location	Quantity
B16	N22	20,000
C36	P88	30,000
Total Contract		**50,000**

Table 9.2
Example of valid paths based on the example contract, location, and path MDQ restrictions

Receipt Location	Delivery Location	Quantity	Reason
A42	M18	40,000	Exceeds path limit
B16	N22	10,000	
Total Contract		**50,000**	

Receipt Location	Delivery Location	Quantity	Reason
B16	M18	30,000	Exceeds receipt location MDQ
A42	N22	10,000	
A42	P88	10,000	
Total Contract		**50,000**	

Receipt Location	Delivery Location	Quantity	Reason
B16	P88	20,000	
C36	P88	30,000	Total delivered to P88 exceeds delivery location MDQ
Total Contract		**50,000**	

Table 9.3
Example of invalid paths based on the example contract, location, and path MDQ restrictions

10. Rates and Charges

Pipelines may be divided into zones, segments, or both. Often a zone is used to identify the boundaries of a specific rate area for transportation on the pipeline. If a pipeline does not divide the system into rate zones and, instead, uses a single rate for a service, this is often referred to as a flat rate or postage-stamp rate[13].

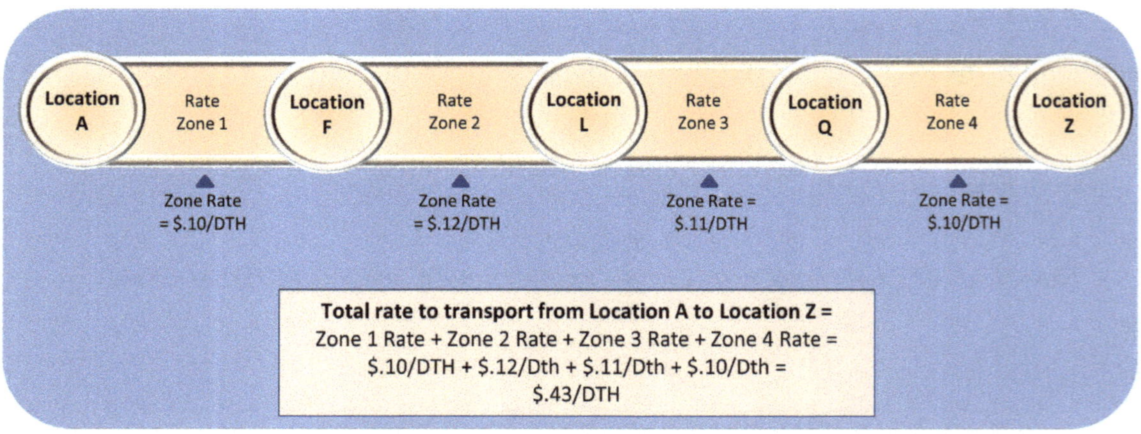

Figure 10.1
An example of multiple zones with individual rates

The pipeline tariff or SOC lists the standard rates for each service that the pipeline offers. These rates may be stated as minimum and maximum rates showing a range that may be negotiated for contracting or may be stated as a single fixed rate. There may be rates within a service that have rate ranges while other rates within that same service have fixed values.

Pipeline Tariff			
Firm Transportation			
CHARGE		Minimum Rate	Maximum Rate
Commodity			
	Zone 1	$0.01/DTH	$0.10/DTH
	Zone 2	$0.01	$0.15
	Zone 3	$0.01	$0.20
	Zone 4	$0.10	$0.50
Demand		$0.50	$0.80
Surcharge			
	Location F Deliveries		$0.03
	Zone 4 Receipts		$0.01

Example 10.1
A tariff excerpt for firm transportation with zone-based minimum and maximum rates for the commodity charge, a single rate demand charge, and surcharges that will apply in select situations

The service contract will contain either a reference to the tariff rate that is to be charged for the service, or it may contain contract-specific rates that are negotiated for the contract within the minimum and maximum rate range that is specified in the tariff. The rates may be specified at the contract level, at a contract/zone, at a contract/receipt location/delivery location (path), or at a contract/point. Many pipelines list the contractual points or paths on the contract as the primary points and make available all other locations on the pipeline as secondary points. On a firm contract, this means that the shipper will pay the demand charges for the primary points with a priority scheduling basis but may use other points without the same scheduling priority.

Contract Rates		
Within Tariff Terms		
Commodity		
	Zone 1	$0.10
	Zone 2	$0.12
	Zone 3	$0.11
	Zone 4	$0.10
Demand		$0.70
Surcharges	Location F Delivery	$0.03
	Zone 4 Receipt	$0.01

Example 10.2
Contract negotiated rates that are within the terms of the sample tariff shown in Example 10.1.

There are many rate options and permutations available when pricing service on a pipeline contract. The rates stated in a contract may take on many forms, including:

- index-based with a formula,
- index-based as the price difference between two indices and then a formula applied,
- a volume- or quantity-based rate within the minimum and maximum terms of the tariff,
- a percentage of maximum tariff rate,
- a discounted amount from the prevailing maximum tariff rate,
- a tiered rate where one rate is applied to the first block of volumes of flow, a second rate is applied to the second set of volumes of flow, and a third rate is applied to the third set of volumes of flow - this may be an increasing price where, as the volume increases, the price increases, or it may be a decreasing price where, as the volume increases, the price decreases,
- stepped rates where one rate is applied to the entire block of gas when the volume of gas falls within a certain range of volumes. In a stepped rate, the shipper will pay one rate if the total quantity is between zero and range-1, a second rate if the total quantity is between range-1 and range-2. In this case, the single rate is applied to the entire volume of gas rather than to a portion of the volume of gas as in the tiered rate,
- a combination of one or more of the options listed above.

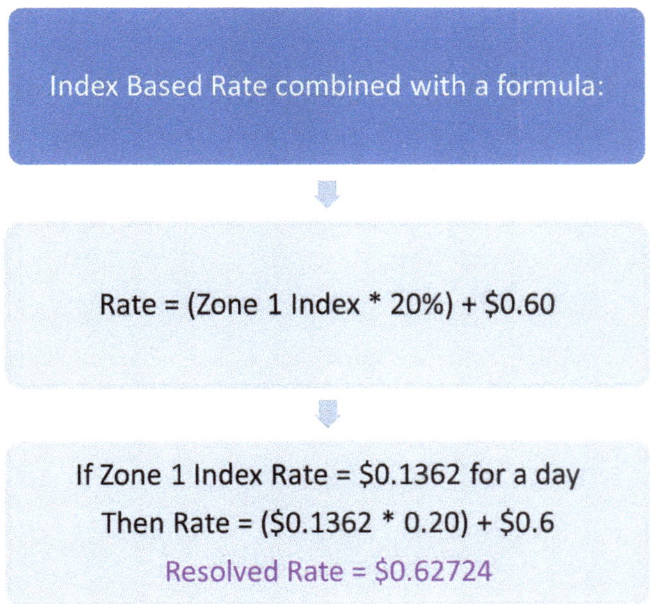

Example 10.3
An example of an index-based rate with a formula and how the rate is resolved

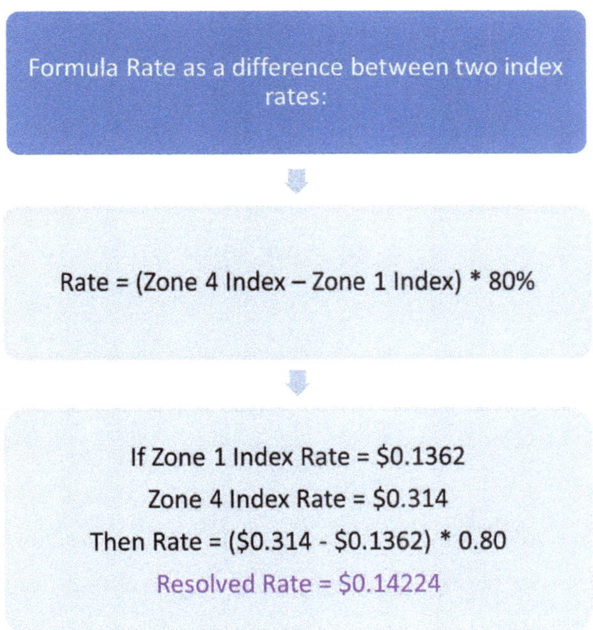

Example 10.4
An example of an index-based rate as the price difference between two indices, a formula, and the resolved rate

Pipeline Tariff			
Firm Transportation Service		**Minimum Rate**	**Maximum Rate**
Commodity	Zone 2	$0.01	$0.15
Contract Rate			
Commodity	Zone 2	$0.12	

Example 10.5
An example of a contracted quantity based rate within the terms of the tariff

Pipeline Tariff			
Firm Transportation			
Commodity		Minimum Rate	Maximum Rate
	Zone 2	$0.01	$0.15
Contract Rate			
Commodity	Zone 2	80% of prevailing Max Tariff Rate	
		Current Rate = $0.15 * .8 = $0.12	

Example 10.6
An example of a contracted rate that is a percentage of the maximum tariff rate

Pipeline Tariff			
Firm Transportation			
Commodity		Minimum Rate	Maximum Rate
	Zone 2	$0.01	$0.15
Contract Rate			
Commodity	Zone 2	Max Tariff Rate less $0.03	
		Current Rate = $0.15 - $0.03 = $0.12	

Example 10.7
An example of a contracted rate that is a discount from the current maximum tariff rate

Tiered Rates		
Tariff Commodity Rates		
Zone 3	0-5,000 DTH	$0.14
	5,001-10,000 DTH	$0.11
	10,001-30,000 DTH	$0.09
	30,001 + DTH	$0.08
Allocated Quantity = 35,000 DTH		
	Charge =	5,000 DTH * $0.14 + 5,000 DTH * $0.11 +20,000 DTH * $0.09 + 5,000 DTH * $0.08
	Total Charge =	$3,450

Example 10.8
An example of tariff level tiered rates and how the rate is resolved to a single price

Stepped Rates		
Tariff Commodity Rates		
Zone 3	0-5,000 DTH	$0.14
	5,001-10,000 DTH	$0.11
	10,001-30,000 DTH	$0.09
	30,001 + DTH	$0.08
Allocated Quantity = 35,000 DTH		
	Charge =	35,000 * $0.08
	Total Charge =	$2,800

Example 10.9
An example of tariff level stepped rates and how the rate is resolved to a single price.

Combination Rates		
	Cashout Rates	
Zone 2	**Rate Basis = Average of Zones 1, 2 & 3 First of Month Index Rate**	
	Zone 1 First of Month Index Rate	$3.146
	Zone 2 First of Month Index Rate	$3.25
	Zone 3 First of Month Index Rate	$3.3146
	Resolved Rate Basis = Average (Zone 1, Zone 2, Zone 3)	$3.2369
For Imbalance Due Pipeline :		
	If Imbalance Quantity </= 5% then Rate = Rate Basis	Resolved Rate = $3.2369
	If Imbalance Quantity > 5% and </+ 10% then Rate = Rate Basis + 20%	Resolved Rate = $3.8843
	If Imbalance Quantity > 10% and </= 30% then Rate = Rate Basis + 40%	Resolved Rate = $4.5317
	If Imbalance Quantity > 30% then Rate = Rate Basis + 50%	Resolved Rate = $4.8554
For Imbalance Due Shipper:		
	If Imbalance Quantity </= 10% then Rate = Rate Basis	Resolved Rate = $3.2369
	If Imbalance Quantity > 10% then Rate = Rate Basis - 30%	Resolved Rate = $2.2658

Example 10.10
Various examples of rates that combine the methods previously described.

Additionally, there are often multiple charges applied to a service contract. Generally, a contract is charged a demand or reservation fee if it is a firm-service contract. All contracts are charged a commodity fee, which relates to the volumetric use on that contract. Interstate pipelines charge an ACA charge, which is assessed for their share of the annual cost of operating the FERC. There may be additional surcharges and fees, depending on the section or segment of the pipeline for the specific transportation, to offset construction costs or other fees associated with operation of that portion of the pipeline.

A pipeline that has a single transportation rate for the entire pipeline may charge a rate for the gas received onto the pipeline at each receipt location or may charge for the gas leaving the pipeline at each delivery location. A receipt-based charge is very effective on a pipeline with many receipt locations that all funnel into a mainline pipe and deliver to a single delivery area or location. A delivery-based charge is effective on a pipeline that receives all of its gas in a single receipt area or location and then delivers gas to a broad range of delivery points. Additionally, a pipeline that uses other types of rates such as a single rate, zone-based, etc., may have additional charges assessed to receipts or deliveries at certain locations on the pipeline. There are several scenarios that can be used as an example of a receipt or delivery location supplemental charge, such as where gas is received at a **hub** location or where gas is delivered to a location that was built by the pipeline for access to a certain market, and the pipeline is using the supplemental charge to recover its construction costs.

Some pipelines state their rates as mileage-based rates. For this scenario, a pipeline has calculated the distance between each pair of nominatable points on the pipeline system and will assess a per-mile charge for the distance between each of those points. One of the terms used in mileage-based pipelines may be the "milepost." This is a mileage assigned to a location on the pipeline that is in relation to the upstream-most location on the pipeline so that the difference between two mileposts calculates the distance traveled for a path of gas. There are only a few pipelines in North America that assess their charges on a per-mile basis. Most are either a single rate or a zone-based rate.

Mileage Based Rates	
Example 1 - Simple Rate	
	Rate = Number of Miles * $0.0003/Mile
Example 2 – Zone Based Mileage Rate	
	Zone 1 Rate = Number of Miles * $0.0001 Zone 2 Rate = Number of Miles * $0.00016
Example 3 – Stepped Mileage Rate	
	For Mileage = 0-500, Rate = Number of Miles * $0.0005
	For Mileage = 501-1000, Rate = Number of Miles * $0.00036
	For Mileage = > 10001, Rate = Number of Miles * $0.00028

Example 10.11
Examples of different types of mileage based rates

Most pipelines do not charge for pooling services. There are, however, pipelines that do. They may charge for receipt/injection into the pool, delivery/withdrawal out of the pool, or both.

FERC-regulated pipelines are required to offer Title Transfer Tracking services at one or more pools on the pipeline. Pipelines are allowed to charge a fee for this service. On some pipelines, the fee assessed is a single charge for each transaction while, on other pipelines, the charge is a per-Dekatherm or volumetric-based charge. Many pipelines do not charge a fee for this service. This service is described in more detail in the Nominations section of this book.

A similar service to pooling services is hub services. A hub service is where a pipeline has a physical location that interconnects with many pipelines, forming a hub where gas may be transferred at that location, to one of several downstream or upstream pipeline options. There are fees associated with hub services, and those fees and the calculations for them may become complex. The details of those fees and their associated calculations are identified in the tariff or SOC for those facilities.

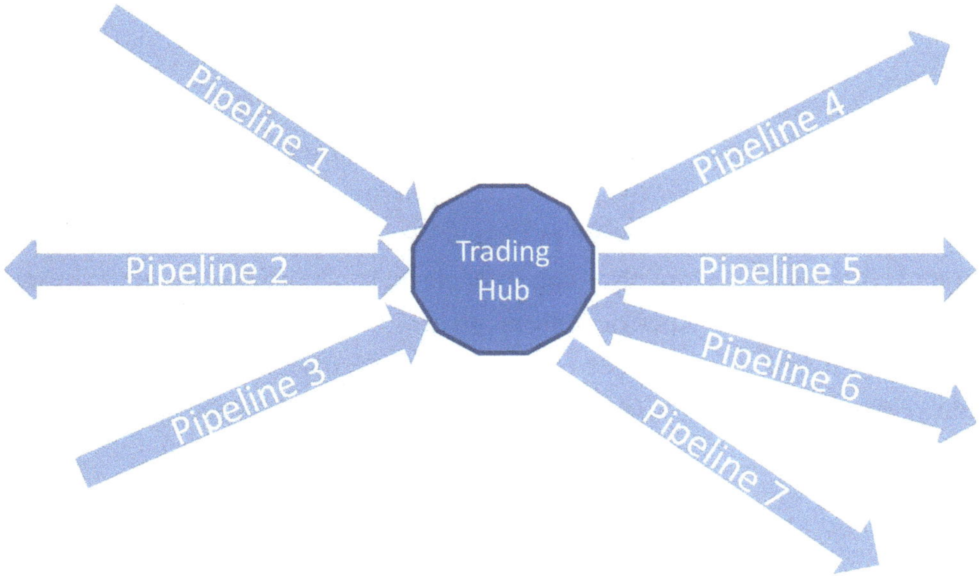

Figure 10.2
A trading hub where multiple pipelines may deliver and/or receive gas through a single location. Note that some of the pipelines both receive and deliver at the hub while other pipelines only receive or deliver.

Most pipelines charge fuel as an in-kind percentage of the gas being transported. For example, when a shipper receives 1,000 DTH of gas onto the pipeline, and the pipeline has a 5-percent fuel charge, then the shipper delivers 950 DTH of gas off of the pipeline. The pipeline's retainage of fuel is used to cover the fuel used to operate the pipeline and pipeline-compressor stations and to account for pipeline loss and unaccounted-for. Some pipelines offer the shipper the option of paying a charge for fuel rather than providing the gas in-kind. The pipeline must then purchase the fuel needed to operate the pipeline with the fees collected[14].

Fuel may be assessed on the entire path of gas, or it may be applied, on a cumulative basis, to each zone or segment that the path of gas is considered to have passed through. In this case, the pipeline may post the total fuel rate but apply the reductions on a zone-by-zone basis.

In addition to the charges assessed by the pipeline, the pipeline may be required to collect state and local taxes. This situation most often occurs when the pipeline is delivering to the ultimate consumer of the gas or is receiving from the production wellhead. There is no tax assessed for interstate transportation where the interstate transport is not the ultimate receipt location or delivery location for the gas.

11. Capacity Release

Capacity release was the first transaction process that the FERC required pipelines to conduct electronically. In capacity release, a shipper holding firm service on a pipeline decides that it does not want to utilize all or a portion of that service for a period of time. The shipper has the right to offer the capacity for release, make it available for bid to the highest bidder, and release that capacity right to the replacement shipper. When the capacity is released, the pipeline enters into a new contract for the terms of the release or amends an existing contract to include the terms of the release. The releasing shipper then receives a credit on its original contract for the amount that is paid by the replacement shipper.

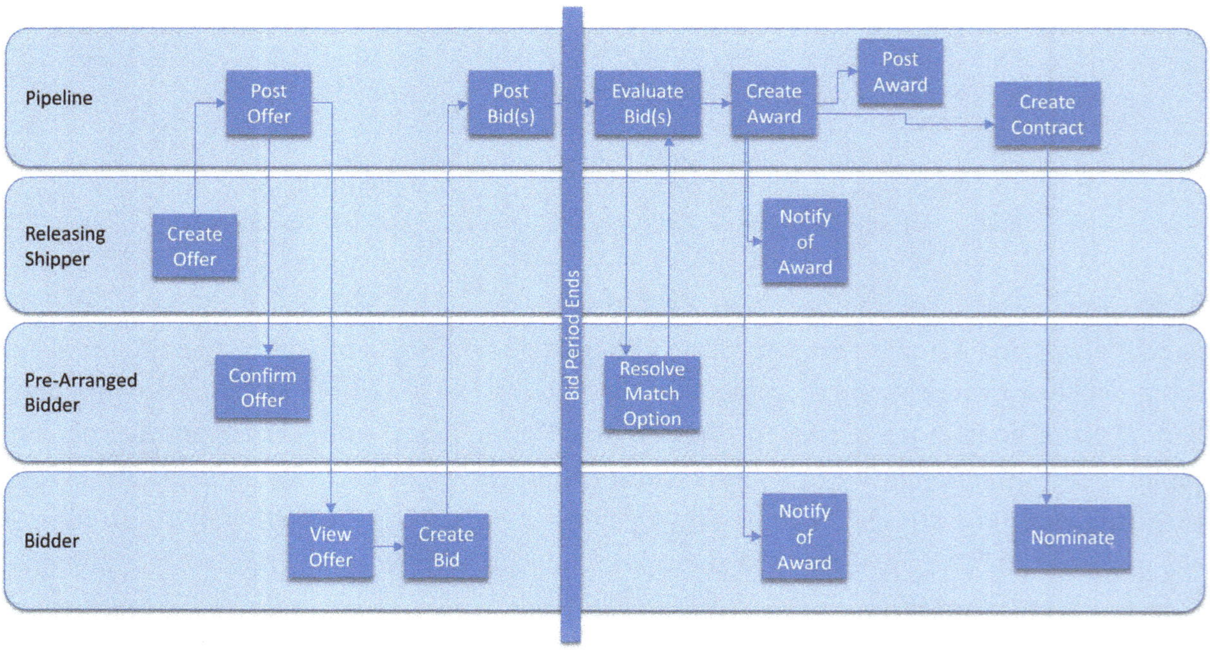

Figure 11.1
The business flow for the capacity release process

Because the new contract and the credits to the existing contract involve contracts between a shipper and the pipeline, the pipeline is the host of the capacity-release process, must conduct the offer, bid, and award process, and must oversee the resulting contractual terms. The capacity-release process is not a revenue-generating mechanism for the pipeline. It does, however, provide a tool so that more of the pipeline's capacity can be effectively used, increases the value of holding firm capacity to the firm-capacity holder, and provides a view of the liquidity of the market on that pipeline.

Post Offer/Bid/Award

To initiate the capacity-release process, a shipper holding a firm service agreement must post that capacity as available capacity. This posting occurs utilizing the Capacity Release Offer dataset[15]. The offer specifies the terms of the release - the date range, quantities, and rates being offered are the primary terms. There is a long list of secondary terms that the releasing shipper must select from when making the offer. One of the options when releasing capacity is that the releasing shipper may contact and arrange for an replacement shipper prior to making the capacity offer public. This replacement shipper is referred to as the pre-arranged bidder and must meet all credit requirements of the pipeline. If the offer of capacity release is for one month or less, then the offer is not required to go out for public bid but may be awarded as an executed contract immediately with the pre-arranged bidder as the replacement shipper. When the releasing shipper submits this pre-arranged bid, and the bid is confirmed, the pipeline is required to issue the new contract, available for nominations, within one hour of being posted.

The capacity release process is required to support index-based transportation rates. A pipeline must post an index representative of gas flow on that pipeline that may be used in capacity release transactions. Shippers may use this index as a basis of pricing for the released capacity offer, or they may provide another index for the pricing. A common practice is for the index-based pricing to be based on the difference between an index reflecting the gas price at receipt on the pipeline and an index reflecting the gas price at delivery off the pipeline. This difference is often referred to as the basis price.[16] This basis price is part of the calculation that may be used in determining the value of the transportation in a capacity release contract.

When the offer is entered as complete by the releasing shipper and validated by the pipeline, the offer is posted on the pipeline's web site. The terms of the offer determine the length of time that the offer must be made available for bid as minimum terms. The releasing shipper may request a longer bid period from the pipeline. The terms that determine the bid period are discussed later in this chapter under "Timeline."

If the capacity release offer is deemed biddable, then the offer is posted for bid[17]. Potential shippers who are shopping for firm capacity will view the offer and place bids against it. These bids must meet the minimum terms that the releasing shipper specified for the offer but can be for any terms between the minimum and maximum terms that were specified. For instance, a releasing shipper may state that the offer is for a three-month period for a maximum of 10,000 DTH per day, but the releasing shipper may also specify that it will accept a lesser term (period of time) and a lesser quantity. This creates an opportunity for a bidder to create a bid, using this example, for a period of two months for 5,000 DTH per day. The releasing shipper may have also specified minimum terms for period of time and quantity. As long as the bidder's terms are within those minimum terms, then the bid is a valid bid. Once a bid has been completed by the bidder, submitted to the pipeline and validated, then the bid is posted on the pipeline's website as a valid bid against this offer. This gives other potential bidders the opportunity to create a bid that complements or competes with the existing bid. The terms of the bid that must be captured and posted are described in the standards[18].

At the end of the designated bid period, the pipeline closes the bidding process on the offer and evaluates the bids to determine if one or more of the bids will be awarded the capacity. The original offer specified a bid-evaluation method that the pipeline is to use to determine which bid, or bids, will win the award. The standard bid evaluation methods are: 1) highest rate, 2) net revenue and 3) present value[19] [20].

Highest rate is a simple method where, without consideration of the volume or time period that is bid, the bid with the highest rate is awarded the capacity. Net revenue is calculated by Term x Quantity x Rate. In this scenario, a bid with a lesser term, but for a higher rate may be chosen over a bid for the full term at a lesser rate. Present value looks at the sum of all payments during the life of the acquired contract, "discounted to the present point in time, based on an accepted discount percentage rate.[21]"

Additionally, there are two formulas that may be applied, the first being for a stream of uniform payments and the second for a stream of non-uniform payments. NAESB standards provide comprehensive examples of these calculations[22].

There is a requirement that the bids are awarded until all of the capacity is utilized. Using the example above, if a second bidder placed a bid for one month for the full 10,000 of capacity and that month did not overlap the two months of the first bidder, then both bids would be awarded the capacity. The bid-evaluation method chosen by the releasing shipper determines which bid is awarded first, second, etc., and that same bid-evaluation method may mean that some capacity remains un-utilized by available bids.

Another aspect of the bidding process is that the bidder may specify that it will accept a lesser quantity, and the bidder may specify a minimum quantity that it will accept. In this scenario, if most of the capacity has been awarded and the next available bidder in line does not accept a lesser quantity, and the available capacity is less than it will accept, then the award could skip to the next bidder that has specified that it will accept a lesser quantity and the lesser quantity fits within the remaining capacity available. Additionally, the bidder may specify that it will accept a lesser term, and the bidder may specify a minimum term that it will accept. Again, if most of the capacity has been awarded and the next available bidder in line does not accept a lesser term and the available capacity is for less than the term it will accept, then the award could skip to the next bidder that has specified that it will accept a lesser term and the lesser terms fit within the remaining capacity available.

When the pipeline creates the awards, the awards are posted under the Award section of the Capacity Release heading on the website. The terms of the award that must be captured and posted are described in detail in the standards[23]. The pipeline then creates contracts for the newly awarded capacity. The pipeline may choose to create a new contract for each awarded capacity that an replacement shipper receives, or it may utilize a master agreement and amend that agreement with each package of awarded capacity that the replacement shipper receives. This is a business practice that is determined by the pipeline. In either case, when the capacity is awarded and the agreement is executed, specific terms of the capacity-release contract must be posted on the pipeline's informational postings website in the Transactional Reporting section under the capacity-release contracts sub-section. The specific terms that must be posted for this transactional-reporting posting are detailed in the related standards[24].

Charges

The charges that are assessed to an replacement-capacity contract are specified in the terms of the offer, agreed to in the terms of the bid, and specified in the award. All of the charges to which the replacement shipper will be subject must be specified either as a single rate that is inclusive of all charges or as a list of multiple charges.

When the replacement shipper is awarded a new contract, uses that contract, receives an invoice, and pays that invoice, then the reservation charges collected by the pipeline are credited to the releasing shipper's contract. This process is required because, if an replacement shipper does not utilize the capacity and/or does not pay the bill, then the original releasing shipper is still the party liable for the charges that are to be paid on the contract for the capacity that has been reserved in its name. The exception to this rule is when the release is issued as a permanent release. A permanent release is for the specified quantity for the remainder of the term of the contract. With a permanent release, the pipeline releases the releasing shipper from the financial contractual liability, and transfers the liability to the replacement shipper for the term of the contract.

Recall/Reput

Recalls and reputs are negotiated as part of the offer and bid process[25].

The ability to recall and reput capacity is unique to the capacity-release process. When a shipper has acquired capacity from a releasing shipper, that capacity would be expected to be available for exclusive use by the replacement shipper for the entire term of the capacity release. This is true if the releasing shipper has indicated, as one of the terms of the offer, that the capacity is not recallable. If the capacity is recallable by the releasing shipper, this means that, at any time during the term of the release, the releasing shipper may ask for the capacity to be returned to utilize the transportation space for a period of a partial day, several days, or the remainder of the term of the release. The recall of capacity may be a complete recall for the entire capacity-release quantity, or it can be a partial recall for only a portion of the released capacity.

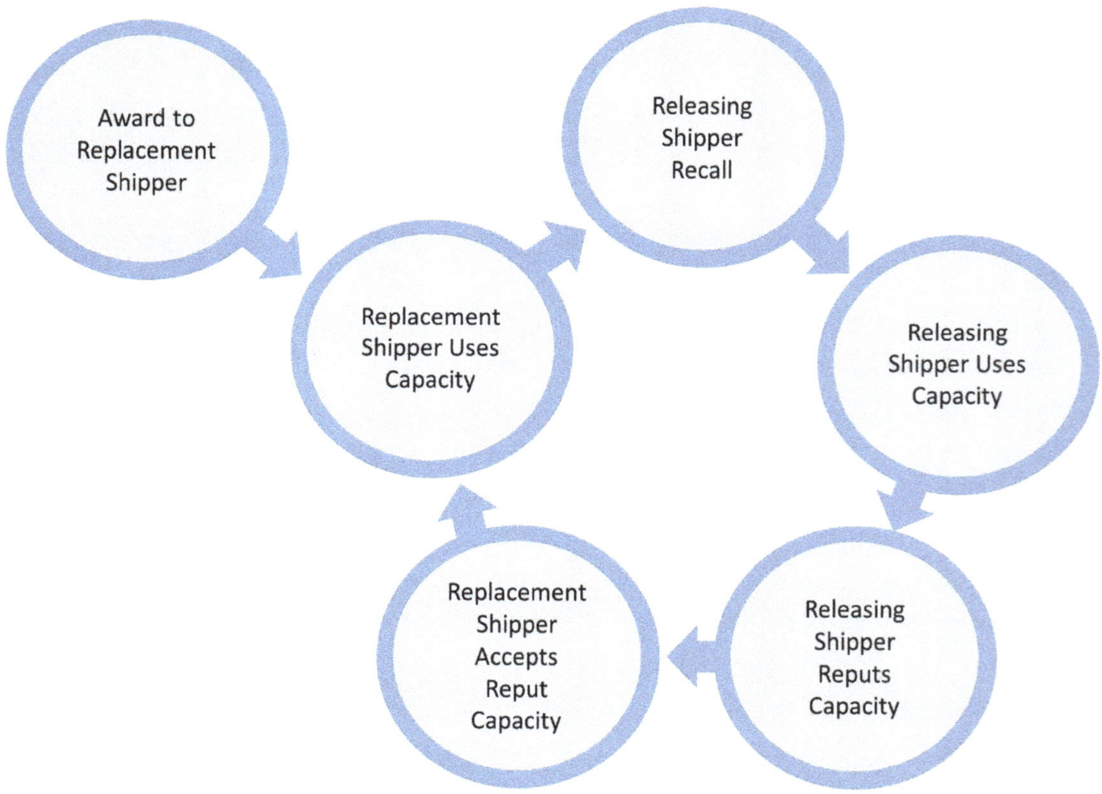

Figure 11.2
The cycle of recalling and reputting capacity

At the end of the recall period, the releasing shipper will reput the capacity to the original replacement shipper or to a new shipper, according to the terms that were negotiated as part of the offer process. This reputting of capacity means that the recalled capacity is returned to the replacement shipper on the original contract and with the original terms of the release in place. If the recalled capacity is not reputtable to the replacement shipper, then the releasing shipper will issue a new offer of capacity when the recall period has expired.

Recallable released capacity may be recalled and reput multiple times during the period of the release. If the capacity is recallable and reputtable to the original replacement shipper, the releasing shipper has no limit to the number of times it may exercise this right as long as the recall is only issued once per day.

When a releasing shipper posts capacity as an offer, it will select whether it wants the option to recall the capacity. If the shipper selects the option to recall the capacity, it is notifying the potential replacement shipper that it is keeping the right to recall the capacity on an as-needed basis. When the releasing shipper indicates the recall rights, it must also indicate the reput terms. The reput terms indicate to the replacement shipper whether the releasing shipper intends to return the released capacity to the replacement shipper after the recall has ended. The reput terms may be that the replacement shipper must accept the capacity at the end of the recall, or that the replacement shipper may choose whether to accept the reput at the end of the recall period. In addition to the reput terms, if the releasing shipper has indicated that the capacity is recallable, it must also indicate at least one of the nomination cycles that may be used to execute a recall. The releasing shipper could indicate that all cycles are available for a recall, or it could indicate that only one cycle would be used for a recall. In either case, at least one cycle must be selected by the releasing shipper when that shipper has indicated that the capacity is recallable.

When a releasing shipper exercises the recall right, certain standards determine the timing of the recall. The releasing shipper must give notice to the replacement shipper with enough time for the replacement shipper to take corrective action. This corrective action means that the replacement shipper must have time to change its nominations for gas under the replacement contract and to redirect that gas to another contract or to other locations, or to cancel the flow of that gas for the recall period. This notice is the responsibility of the releasing shipper. The releasing shipper must notify both the pipeline and the replacement shipper of the recall[26]. The pipeline is also responsible to notify the replacement shipper of the recall within one hour of receipt of the recall notice, if the recall period is within the designated business hours, and by 8 a.m. if the recall is outside of the designated business hours[27].

A number of additional NAESB standards provide instructions on how to conduct the recall/reput process, on how to format the email notification, and on the timing of reputs[28]. These standards should be evaluated together for a complete understanding of the rules of the recall/reput process.

Non-Biddable

The FERC sets the terms for determining whether a release is biddable or non-biddable. In layman's terms, a release is non-biddable if a) the offer is submitted with a pre-arranged bidder and the deal is for one month or less; or b) the offer is submitted with a pre-arranged bidder for one year or more at maximum tariff rate. A pre-arranged bidder is a party that has already been identified who wishes to acquire the capacity, and that party has agreed to the offer terms for this deal. Before the new contract can be awarded, the pre-arranged bidder may be required to confirm the terms of the deal with the pipeline.

Biddable

A biddable deal is one where the pipeline is required to post the releasing shipper's offer of capacity for a period of time on the pipeline's website so that bidders can bid on the offer. The biddable deal may have a pre-arranged bidder or may have no pre-arranged bidder. If there is a pre-arranged bidder, that bidder may have chosen an option to match any bids received through the pipeline posting. The length of time of the posting of a biddable offer is dependent on the terms of the offer.

The Timeline

The timeline for capacity release is a very important part of the capacity-release process. The determination of which offer/bid/award timeline applies to a release is governed by the type of release. The timeline is initiated when a valid capacity-release offer is received. The offer is considered valid when all of the terms of the offer are validated, the credit of the releasing shipper is verified, and there are no special terms to the offer that would cause it to be handled outside of the standard-release timeline[29].

Non-Biddable Releases	Biddable Releases one year or less	Biddable Releases greater than one year
Offer posted one hour before nomination deadline	Offer posted at 9 a.m. or earlier on a business day	Offer posted at 9 a.m. or earlier on a business day
N/A	Bid period ends at 10 a.m. on same day	Bid period ends at 10 a.m. after 3 open days
N/A	If no match, Award issued at by 11 a.m. If match, Award issued by 11:30 a.m.	If no match, Award issued at by 11 a.m. If match, Award issued by 11:30 a.m.
N/A	Award posted at Noon	Award posted at Noon
Contract issued within one hour of posting	Contract issued at 1 p.m.	Contract issued at 1 p.m.
Nomination available on next open cycle	Nomination available on next open cycle	Nomination available on next open cycle

Figure 11.3
The post, bid, and award timeline for different types of offers

There are variables in the offer that determine which of the capacity-release timelines are followed[30]. The first variable in the timeline is on whether the offer is biddable or non-biddable. The second variable is on the length of time of the offered capacity.

For non-biddable, regardless of whether they are for short-term or longer releases, the timeline is the same. Per Standard 5.3.2[31], the offer submitted and posted for the timely cycle must be posted by 12:00 noon, and the contract must be issued within one hour to provide the capability for nominations to be entered at the next timely nomination cycle. Similar timelines exist for offers submitted during the other cycles[32]. For an offer submitted and posted for the evening cycle, the offer must be posted by 5:00 p.m. Again, the pipeline is given one hour to issue the contract and to post the award. For an offer submitted for the Intraday-1 cycle, the offer must be posted by 9:00 a.m., and the pipeline is given one hour to issue the contract and to post the award. For an offer submitted for the Intraday-2 cycle, the offer must be posted by 1:30 p.m., and the pipeline is given one hour to issue the contract and to post the award. For an offer submitted for the Intraday-3 cycle, the offer must be posted by 6:00 p.m., and the pipeline is given one hour to issue the contract and to post the award. In all cycles, the goal is for the contract to be available in time for the next nomination cycle for the effective date of the contract.

Biddable releases follow one of two timelines regardless of whether there is a pre-arranged bidder or not: one timeline for offers of capacity that are one year or less, and the second timeline for offers that are more than one year. NAESB WGQ Standard 5.3.2[33] explains the details of both of these timelines. The timeline for offers of one year or less requires that, when an offer is posted by 9:00 a.m. on a business day, then bidding is open for one hour, until 10:00 a.m., and the award is issued by no later than 12:00 noon. The two deadlines inside of this timeline depend on whether the pre-arranged bidder has a match option or not. If the pre-arranged bidder has a match option, the match is communicated by 11:00 a.m., a match response is required by 11:30 a.m., and the award is issued and posted by 12 noon. If no match option exists, then the award is issued by 11:00 a.m. This timing gives the replacement shipper the opportunity to nominate in the evening cycle for gas to flow on the next business day.

The timeline for offers of more than one year requires a longer bid period. When the offer is posted by 9:00 a.m. on a business day, then there are three days given for the bid period. The bid period ends at the same time as the release for less than one year, at 10:00 a.m. on the day before the gas is to flow, and the same match response and award times apply as those described above for the offer that is for less than one year. The primary difference between the two timelines is that the longer-term release requires a bid period of three days, and the shorter-term release requires a bid period of one hour.

Capacity Release by Greg Lander

Prior to the introduction into the gas market of the capacity-release process, if a firm shipper did not have a use for its firm capacity, the capacity under its contract reverted to the pipeline. The pipeline could sell that capacity on an interruptible transportation (IT) basis to another shipper, and, when that shipper paid the pipeline for the IT service, the pipeline kept the money. In essence, the pipeline would be paid twice for the same capacity. Shippers did not like this. Before capacity release was introduced as a mandatory business process on interstate pipelines, its precursor was a form of gray-market temporary partial contract assignment. Under the temporary partial-assignment process, "favored" counterparties would be assigned "slices" of firm contracts. Generally, the assignors were Local Distribution Companies (LDCs), and the assignees were favored end-users and marketers (often marketers with an arrangement or affiliation with the LDC). Under this temporary partial-assignment regime, there was no transparency as to pricing, term, or other provisions of the assignment.

Several parties, including the FERC, became concerned that the temporary assignment of interstate pipeline capacity was or could be discriminatory. Ultimately FERC determined that it had jurisdiction over the terms of service on interstate pipelines, including the terms that might govern transfer of those service rights. What followed was a process involving the industry players; first, through an informal working-group process, and then through the nascent and formalized Gas Industry Standards Board (GISB – now NAESB) process.

In those processes, one of the first things that occurred was the creation of a common definition of a capacity right. By being defined and standardized, a capacity right that could then be "traded" by means of the capacity-release process. A capacity right became defined as the right to put a quantity of gas into a pipeline at one or more locations (receipt points) and simultaneously take that quantity out (less fuel, if any) at another location for a period of time for a rate per unit (DTH). This right to transport from receipt to delivery for term at price forms the underpinning of the capacity right that is now traded by means of capacity release. The same was done with storage. The difference between the two services, both of which move gas, is the following: Transportation is the movement of gas from point to point (across space) at time. Storage in turn is the movement of gas at point across time.

Once the concept of capacity rights was agreed upon, the industry consensus process was used to evolve the trading of that right into an automated process; and, in so doing, the rules for capacity-release were established.

In the end, the FERC had what it had sought to establish: a process whereby a defined right could be posted, all terms of the right and its use would be displayed and transparent, and in the end the FERC could be assured that the capacity would be made available to the party with the highest valued use able to "bid" on and either to get the capacity or to determine the price to be paid for that capacity by the replacement shipper.

Capacity Re-Releases

Firm contract capacity that has been released to a replacement shipper may be released again (re-released) by that replacement shipper to another party. There is no limit to the number of times at a block of capacity may be re-released. There are, however, restrictions on how the re-released capacity must be bounded in the re-release process.

Re-released capacity is limited to the terms of the replacement contract and does not have the full capabilities of the originating contract. For example, configure a firm contract with a capacity of 10,000 DTH per day, for four receipt locations and four delivery locations, each with a primary MDQ of 2,500 DTH per day. Now, release that contract for 5,000 DTH per day to two receipt locations and two delivery locations. The replacement shipper now wants to re-release that capacity. The re-released capacity is limited to the two receipt locations and two delivery locations for 5,000 DTH per day, total. The shipper acquiring the re-released capacity has no rights to the four original receipts or deliveries. Now, configure that same first release as recallable. The second release must also be recallable with the same or lesser rights than the original release. The re-releasing shipper cannot make the re-released contract not-recallable when the original contract has those terms already. In the converse, if the original release is not recallable, then the re-release could be made recallable by the original releasing shipper because the recallable terms are considered to be lesser rights than the original release.

Segmentation in Contracting

Segmentation has two components - a contractual component and a transactional component. The transactional component will be discussed in the Nominations and Scheduling chapters of this book. Segmentation is a FERC Order-637 requirement.

The nomination portion, in FERC, is referred to as "flexible point rights"[34], and pipelines are instructed to "... make the process of segmentation as easy as possible ... by permitting segmentation to take place quickly and efficiently through the nomination process"[35]. The contracting portion of the requirement "refers to the ability of firm-capacity holders to subdivide their capacity into segments and to use the segments for different capacity transactions."[36]

Why does segmentation matter? At the contract level, segmentation provides an opportunity for the firm-contract holder to fully utilize its transportation capacity by dividing that capacity into multiple segments and utilizing the demand component of that capacity more than once or releasing a portion of that capacity while retaining full capacity on another segment. This allows the contract holder to recognize revenue from portions of a contract that are being un-utilized. At the nomination level, segmentation works in the same way, allowing the contract holder to use the same contract capacity for multiple nominations but, in the case of the nomination, the contract is not modified and contract capacity is not released to another shipper.

Segmentation by Joe Casey

Segmentation, as the term is used in the natural gas industry, can be thought of as a "chopping up" (segmenting) of a shipper's firm capacity so that additional transactions can be scheduled or so that a shipper's capacity can be financially optimized.

In 1992, FERC issued Order 636 in which it established the principle of segmentation and the related principle of flexible point rights. Flexible point rights allow a shipper to use non-firm points to receive or deliver gas, which is a necessary aid to segmentation.[1]

Although FERC established segmentation as a principle in 1992, it did not incorporate the principle into its regulations at that time and as a result adoption and application of the principle was inconsistent across the industry.[2]

In 2000 FERC sought to rectify this by including segmentation and flexible point rights as a mandate in Order 637. Allowing shippers to segment their capacity is now required of interstate natural gas pipelines but FERC did not specify how this was to be implemented in Order 637, so some slight variations in segmentation practices exist between the pipes.

Fig. 1 - Typical contract path

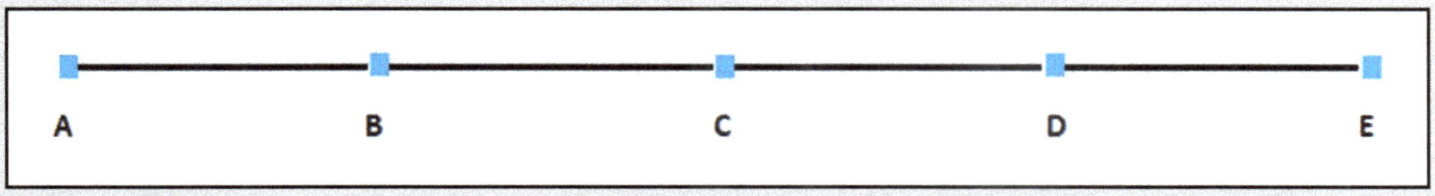

This figure shows what the path of a typical contract might look like on a pipeline using the path-threaded nomination model. In this example, the shipper has a contract path that originates at Point A and terminates at Point E. Assume that the contractual direction of flow is from left to right.

Fig. 2 - Segmentation through nominations

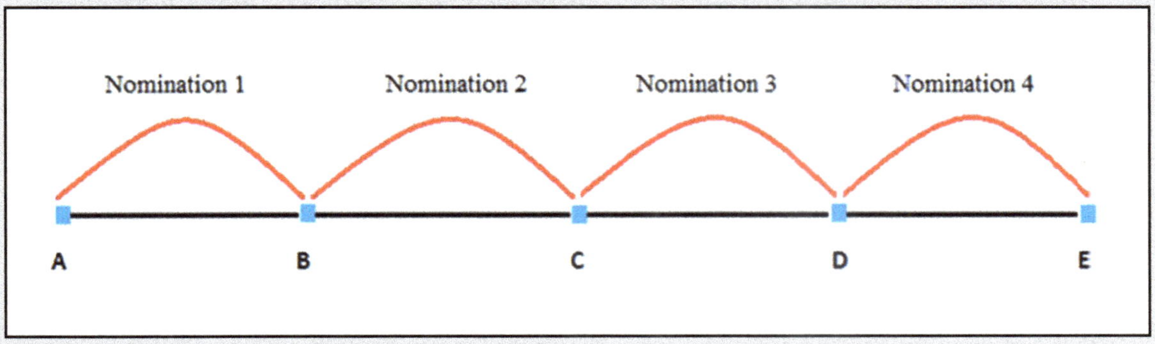

A shipper who wishes to segment its capacity through nominations might do so as illustrated in Figure 2 above. Here the shipper has elected to make four nominations, each delivering the contract's Maximum Daily Quantity (MDQ, also known as Maximum Daily Transportation Quantity or MDTQ) for a total delivered volume of four times the MDQ of the contract. This is allowed because none of the nominations overlap in any segment

Fig. 3 - Segmentation through capacity release

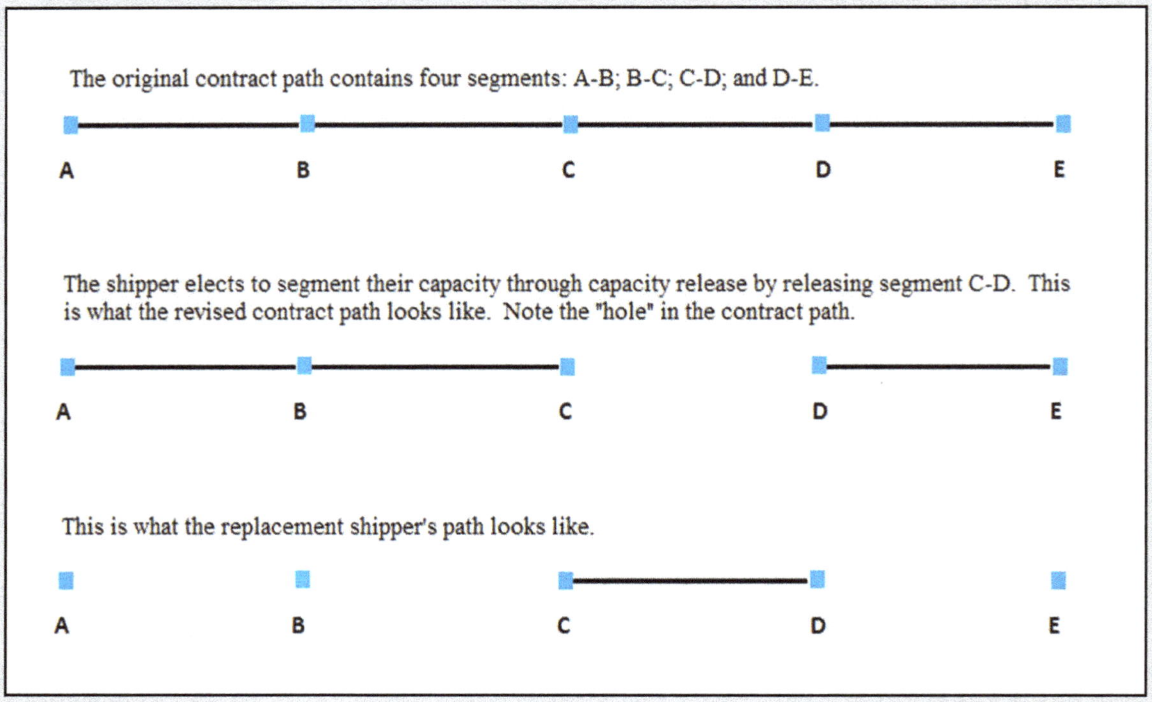

In Figure 3, the shipper has segmented its capacity through the capacity release process. It has released segment C-D to a replacement shipper. If the releasing shipper nominates its full MDQ from Point A to Point C and the replacement shipper nominates its full MDQ from Point C to Point D, then both shippers would be scheduled, since there is no overlap.

If, however, the releasing shipper nominated its full MDQ from Point A to Point E and the replacement shipper nominated its full MDQ from Point C to Point D, then the releasing shipper's gas would be cut to zero because of the overlap on segment C-D and the fact that segment entitlements for segment C-D reside with the replacement shipper's contract.

1. Pipeline Service Obligations and Revisions to Regulations Governing Self-Implementing Transportation Under Part 284 of the Commission's Regulations, Order No. 636, 57 FR 13267 (Apr. 16, 1992), FERC Stats. & Regs. Regulations Preambles [Jan. 1991-June 1996] ¶ 30,939, at 30,428, 30,420-21 (Apr. 8, 1992), Order No. 636-A, 57 FR36128 (Aug. 12, 1992), FERC Stats. & Regs. Regulations Preambles [Jan. 1991-June 1996] ¶ 30,950, at 30,559 n.151 (Aug. 3, 1992), Order No. 636-B, 61 FERC ¶ 61,272, at 61,997 (1992).

2. FERC Docket Nos. RM98-10-000 & RM98-12-000; Order No. 637 Regulation of Short-Term Natural Gas Transportation Services, and Regulation of Interstate Natural Gas Transportation Services (Issued February 9, 2000) AGENCY: Federal Energy Regulatory Commission. pp. 125-127

For contract level segmentation, the shipper has the right to modify a firm-capacity contract with a demand quantity so that the demand is divided into two or more distinct pieces of non-contiguous transportation. The shipper then has the right to release all or a portion of each of those capacities. The important aspect of this is that the releasing shipper only incurs one demand charge for the entire flow of gas.

For instance, suppose a pipeline has a continuous flow of points from A to Z and Shipper Alice has a firm transportation contract on that pipeline for 10,000 DTH per day from A to Z at a demand charge of $1 per DTH.

Figure 11.4
A representation of the described example of a single contract with firm capacity on the pipeline.

Shipper Alice can segment rights on the pipeline into 10,000 from A to L and another 10,000 from L to Z. Then, Alice can release one of those segments to another party through the capacity-release process and retain all of the rights on the second segment.

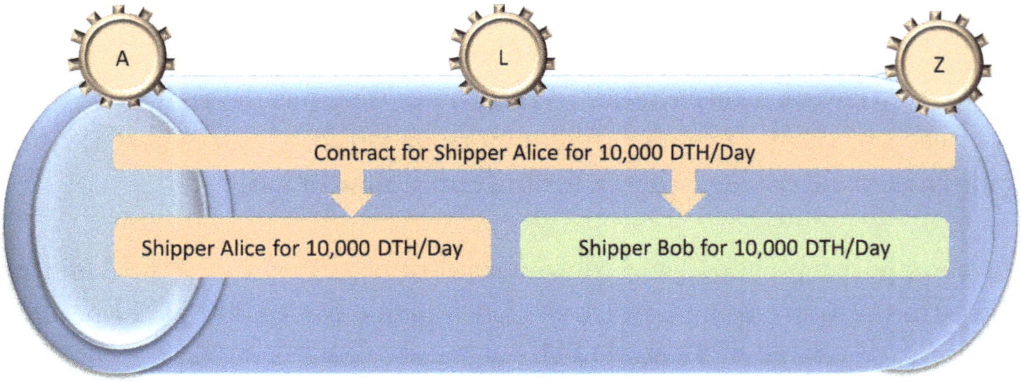

Figure 11.5
Showing, as in the example, how capacity rights may be segmented and one segment released to another shipper

In this example, Alice will release the rights for 10,000 from L to Z for a demand charge of $.80 to Shipper Bob. Alice has still retained the rights on A to L for 10,000 and now has a net rate of $.20 on that segment because she will receive a credit through the capacity release for the $.80 demand. Additionally, Alice could have released a portion of the capacity on L to Z and retained some of the transportation capacity on that segment.

There is no limit to the number of segments a shipper can create in its contract. Alice could have segmented the contract into 5,000 DTH from A to L, 5,000 DTH from L to P, 5,000 DTH from P to Z, 5,000 DTH from A to F, 5,000 from F to N, and 5,000 from N to Z. Then Alice would have six different segments to work with from a capacity-release perspective. This would still keep Alice's demand rate at the same $1/DTH for 10,000 from A to Z. As long as the sum of the overlapping segments does not exceed the original contract demand quantity, then the segmentation can proceed.

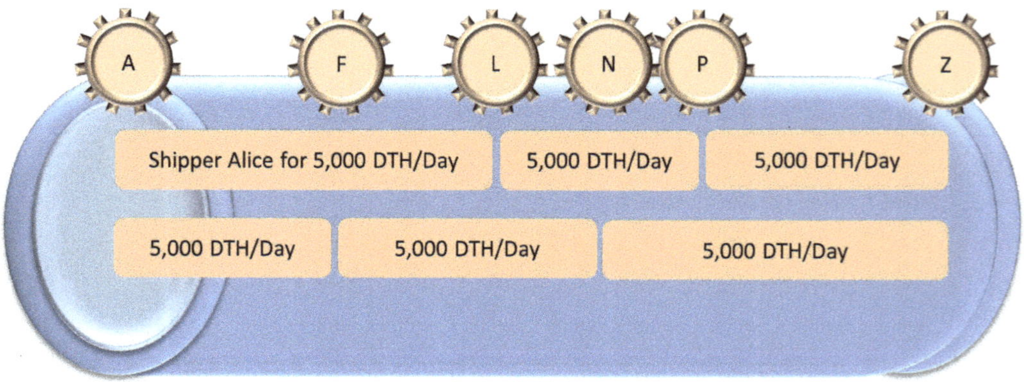

Figure 11.6
Examples of how a shipper could segment one block of capacity into multiple segments without creating overlaps

The segmentation process described here would result in multiple releases of Alice's capacity and in Alice's ability to use and re-use the same 10,000 capacity across the flow from A to Z in multiple scenarios without incurring an additional demand charge. If Alice's intent was to segment the capacity but retain the contracted quantities, then Alice could also accomplish the same actions through segmentation in the nomination process.

12. Credit

Credit is an important issue in pipeline transportation. Most often, credit is considered to be an issue associated with trading/purchasing and selling gas, but that focus has shifted to transportation. In transportation, the credit check is important in evaluation of all contracts, including capacity release. Capacity release uses the credit check to determine a pre-approved bidder in the capacity release program.

Historically, the MDQ was the determinant of a shipper's credit with a TSP. When a shipper applied for a transportation contract, the MDQ that was granted reflected the credit limit, with consideration of other adjusted calculators, for that specific shipper. This was in a time, however, when the primary transportation service contracted on a pipeline was firm (FT) service and the secondary interruptible (IT) service was a more incidental liability.

In recent years, the trend has progressed toward more IT service contracts. This shift has put an enhanced focus on credit on the pipeline. Many pipelines write their IT service contracts with an MDQ, but that MDQ is the quantity associated with a negotiated rate, while the shipper has the right for a seemingly unlimited quantity of transportation at the maximum transportation rate or some other negotiated higher rate. The unlimited quantity of transportation is, however, not realistic. The pipeline must impose some limit on the IT shipper in order to ensure that the payments are met and the liability is within the proper risk limits. A recent trend has been for pipelines to implement "real-time" credit monitoring. This means that, when an IT shipper creates a nomination on the pipeline, the pipeline has the ability to validate that the charges associated with this nomination will not cause the shipper to exceed pre-set credit limits. This also provides a validation against any outstanding balances to make sure that the pipeline does not continue to accept transportation nominations from a shipper who has outstanding balances that, coupled with current-month liabilities, will cause it to exceed the credit limit.

Credit Example for Shipper Credit Limit = $30,000	
Current Transactions:	
Transaction 1:	10,000 DTH/Day At $0.05/DTH X 31 Days = $15,500 estimated charge
Transaction 2:	5,000 DTH/Day At $0.05/DTH X 31 Days = $ 7,750 estimated charge
	Credit Remaining = $6,750
New Transaction:	5,000 DTH/day At $0.05/DTH X 31 Days = $ 7,750 REJECTED – Not enough available credit

Example 12.1
An example of transaction-based credit monitoring

At the same time that pipelines are tightening credit limits on shippers, in order to reduce financial risk, NAESB has been writing standards to help facilitate the credit-negotiation process. The credit standards set expectations on the communication of credit requirements and credit evaluation results between the pipeline, TSP, and the shipper (service requester). These standards should be reviewed as a package of standards regarding credit[37].

If a shipper does not meet creditworthiness, it may use the mechanisms of a prepayment in which the shipper pays the pipeline a certain dollar amount ahead of initiation of the transportation service and banks those funds to guarantee the payment for services. This pre-payment amount becomes the credit limit for that shipper; in credit review, the amount is treated the same as a pre-approved credit-limit amount. When the shipper exceeds the pre-payment amount, it may be required to make a mid-billing-period payment to the pipeline to reduce the liability, it may be required to reduce or stop nominations so as not to increase liability, or it may be required to pay an additional pre-payment amount to cover the additional liability.

Nominations

The nomination is the heart of the gas-transaction-business flow. A shipper can execute a contract, but no gas will flow without a nomination. The contract establishes the relationship between the pipeline and the shipper, but the nomination initiates the action on the contract. The nomination is the communication mechanism between the shipper and the pipeline in which the shipper tells the pipeline what it wants to flow for a given period of time. Often this period of time is for a month or less than a month while the contract term may be for a much greater period of time[38].

The level of detail of the nomination travels with the transaction through the entire lifecycle of the transaction. The nomination is reflected back in scheduled quantities, allocated transactions and imbalances, and, on some pipelines, on invoices.

The amount of information required in a nomination may vary greatly between pipelines. In its most basic form, the nomination tells the pipeline where the gas will come onto the pipe, where it will exit the pipe, the dates that the gas will flow, and the quantity to be expected. Additionally the nomination tells the pipeline the specific transportation contract that the shipper wants to use to transport the gas, from whom the gas may be coming, to whom the gas will be delivered, and additional information to keep the nomination distinct from other nomination transactions.

The industry considers a nomination for a single day for a single nomination model type to be a single distinct nomination. When a nomination transaction is entered for multiple days, each day is a distinct nomination.[39] When a shipper enters a nomination transaction using a model type where multiple transactions are required to convey the complete nomination information, then the industry considers each of those transactions a distinct nomination. This is an important distinction because the business practices of some pipelines have historically considered a "nomination" to be all of the transactions under a contract for a single month. This historic view of nominations is sometimes encountered in the non-interstate marketplace.

The nomination also tells the pipeline the type of transaction that is being requested, whether transportation, storage, a payback, or any of a long list of transaction types that a pipeline may support.

A shipper submits a nomination during a cycle in the nomination timeline. There are five standard NAESB cycles[40] that are the minimum requirement for an interstate pipeline. The pipeline may support additional cycles at its option.

Pipelines may choose to support one nomination model type or multiples. When multiples are used, the pipeline chooses a model type for a specific type of contract or type of service so that all nominations of that type are submitted using the same model.

13. Models

NAESB identifies three nomination model types: the pathed model (PTH), the non-pathed model (NPT), and the pathed non-threaded model (PNT).

Historically in the gas industry, when we first went from a merchant role to a transporter role, pipelines implemented a pathed model as their way of doing business. The pathed model ties all of the information upstream of a specific receipt location on a nomination for a transportation contract to all of the information downstream of a specific delivery location. Some pipelines at that same time used the non-pathed model, in which the shipper entered upstream data and downstream data in separate transactions that can be used to route portions of the shipper's gas in diverse paths. Non-pathed models only require that the receipt and deliveries be in balance before submitting the nomination. It became apparent that the non-pathed model offered customers much more flexibility in the way they transport their gas; however, the non-pathed model does not fit all pipelines because it only works in a situation where a pipeline is using a single postage-stamp rate, has no segmentation, and has a simple business process. Subsequent rule changes by the FERC made it difficult for an interstate pipeline to implement the non-pathed model for regular transportation unless that pipeline has FERC-approved exceptions to

Model Type Terms and Deadlines

Threaded: a threaded nomination ties a specific receipt location to a delivery location. A threaded nomination occurs in the pathed model type and in the pathed portion of the pathed-non-threaded model type.

Unthreaded: an unthreaded transaction does not specifically tie a source of supply to a delivery market. This method occurs in the non-pathed transaction and in the unthreaded portions of the pathed-non-threaded model type.

Pathed: the pathed model type incorporates all of the information for a transportation transaction in one single line item. The nomination includes all of the upstream information, downstream information and transportation information for one quantity of gas.

Non-Pathed: the non-pathed model type uses two transactions to inform the pipeline of all of the components of the transportation arrangement. The upstream nomination contains the supply information upstream of the receipt location and the receipt location for a quantity on a transportation contract. The downstream nomination contains the market information downstream of the delivery location and the delivery location for a quantity on a transportation contract. Total receipts must equal total deliveries on most contracts.

Pathed Non-Threaded: The pathed non-threaded model type has three components to deliver all of the transportation arrangement. The upstream nomination contains the supply information up to the receipt location. The downstream component contains the market information downstream of the delivery location. The pathed component ties the receipt locations to delivery locations for contract pathing.

those rules. The non-pathed model, within these rules, is still used successfully for pooling and storage transactions. A third model type, the pathed non-threaded model, evolved out of these processes in an effort to provide a model with the benefits of both the non-pathed and the structure of the pathed models. The pathed non-threaded model is a bit complex to describe, but it accomplishes the flexibility for the shipper that exists in the non-pathed model while providing the more exact transportation instructions from the pathed model. In the pathed non-threaded model, the pathed nomination portion ties a specific receipt location to a specific delivery location for a transportation contract while the upstream supply information is on a distinct nomination, the downstream market information is on a distinct nomination, and they are not linked. Instead, the shipper assigns ranks to supplies and markets, which allows the shipper to control which supplies of gas get cut in the event of reductions. The "non-threaded" portion of this model type indicates the supplies and markets are not directly tied to each other, while the "pathed" transactions path the receipts to the deliveries on the contract.

Why does it matter today?

Why is now any different than it has been in the last 10 years since the model types first arrived on the transportation front? The recent purchase of the El Paso pipelines by Kinder Morgan has brought model types, specifically the pathed non-threaded model, to the forefront. Kinder Morgan originated this model type and uses it in all of its pipelines. When Kinder Morgan first introduced the model type, it was the lone outlier in the nomination model arena. As the gas industry has evolved, many pipelines have adopted the pathed non-threaded model for their transportation nominations. As Kinder Morgan has grown, it has assimilated all of its pipelines into the same pipeline application and, correspondingly, the same model type. Now that Kinder Morgan has purchased El Paso, it has added major coast-to-coast pipelines into its fold and, yes, it is moving all of them to the PNT model.

A pipeline does not have to choose one nomination model to use for the entire pipeline. Each individual contract on the pipeline can have a different nomination model type. In reality, a pipeline might want to implement the path non-threaded model for entities such as marketers who are doing complex transactions for multiple shippers on the pipeline, while it uses the non-pathed model for injecting gas into and out of storage or delivering gas into and out of pools. At the same time, the pipeline may have many industrial or commercial customers who are buying the gas from one or two locations and delivering it to one or two locations. These industrial customers may not need complex abilities to aggregate and disaggregate gas, and may not use extensive pooling or storage capabilities; therefore, for their business needs, the pathed model may provide the clarity needed for the type of business that they do. The pipeline has the option of setting up different nomination models for different types of service that it offers as a way of delivering its transportation services.

Model Types

Nomination model types may seem like an extremely tedious subject. They definitely get down into the deep details of gas transportation, but they have a lot of impact. The nomination model type can open the door for a marketer to gain more flexibility out of a pipeline system and, hence, keep its customers satisfied and gain a higher margin on that very thin transportation-cost margin. When fully utilized, the model type offers a powerful tool to the shipper.

The nomination model types are one of the less-understood capabilities in the nomination process. The model types are the key to initiating the gas-flow process in the nomination, and the model type stays with the transaction throughout its lifespan until an imbalance is reported on the actual quantities. Understanding the model type and how a specific pipeline uses it can open opportunities for optimal flow management for the pipeline customer.

Look first at what the industry intends a nomination to accomplish. A shipper sends a request, in the form of a nomination, to a pipeline to tell the pipeline where the gas will be brought onto the pipeline system and where the gas will be taken off.

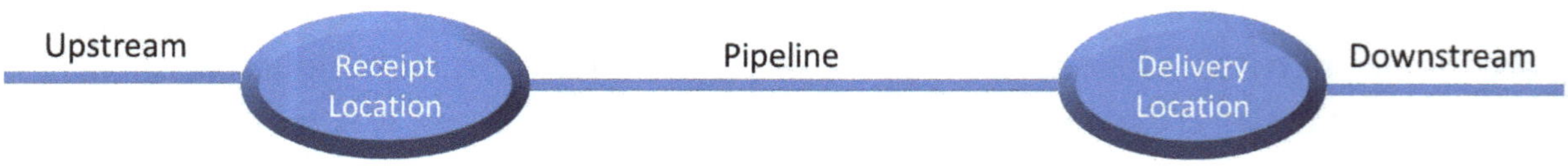

Figure 13.2
The perspective of a nomination – depicting upstream information, pipeline information, and downstream information.

The nomination contains all of the information to instruct the pipeline on how the shipper wants its gas to be treated on the pipeline:

- the pipeline's transportation contract for that shipper,
- the start and end dates, and times, if needed,
- the receipt and delivery locations,

- the upstream and downstream entities and contracts (These are the title owners of the gas before the gas enters the system for that shipper and after the shipper takes the gas off. The operator uses these parties to match up the flows of gas and to confirm the quantities. The shipper may own the gas upstream or downstream and, if this is the case, it will list itself as the upstream or downstream entity.), or
- if required to aid the operator in confirming the flow, the upstream contract under which the gas is being shipped, the downstream contract to where the gas is being delivered, or both.

The nomination may include many additional pieces of data, which are determined on a pipeline-by-pipeline basis, but these are the ones essential for this discussion.

For the total flow of gas, NAESB has defined a comprehensive list of all of the data elements that may be required by a pipeline[41]. The model type overlays this list of elements and determines which portion of data elements belongs in which of the sections of the model-type sub-structure. This document will only examine those mandatory to define the differences between the model types. Those not mandatory are another story.

The nomination tells the pipeline from where the gas is coming on the upstream side, how it is being transported on the pipeline via the shipper and shipper-contract information, and where the gas is going on the downstream side of the pipeline. Assume for the remainder of this section that any reference to a nomination transaction includes any other data required by the pipeline, plus the start and end dates/times and the required quantity information. Also, all examples and discussions will assume the pipeline retains no fuel. This keeps the calculations simple.

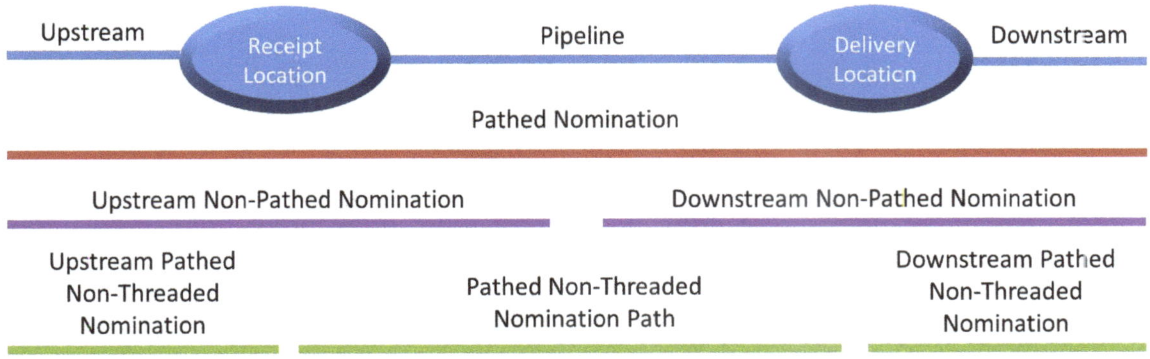

Figure 13.3
Nomination information is contained in a single nomination on the pathed model, two nominations on the non-pathed model, and three nominations on the pathed non-threaded model.

In the **pathed model type (PTH)**, the shipper conveys to the pipeline all of the nomination information, the upstream information, the transportation information, and the downstream information as one single piece of data – one single transaction. North American pipelines use this model type most often because it allows them to make an easy transition between their merchant roles and their service roles. The single transaction contains all of the information for the flow of gas. When the shipper or the pipeline looks at the gas at a delivery point, the pathed model type provides a direct view of where and from whom the gas came to get on that pipeline. This model type is an excellent choice for a shipper bringing in multiple supplies to a single delivery point on the pipeline system.

In the **non-pathed model type (NPT)**, a transaction contains the upstream information, including all of the upstream data, plus the receipt location, the shipper, and the transportation contract. A second transaction contains all of the relevant downstream data, plus the delivery location, the shipper, and the transportation contract. The NPT requires two nomination line items to move the gas from the point of receipt to the point of delivery.

With this model type, several options open up for the shipper. Because the receipt flows and delivery flows are not directly linked, the shipper could choose to enter receipts from many locations and deliver all of those receipts to a single delivery location on a single nomination line item.

Figure 13.4
The number of nominations on a non-pathed contract does not have to be the same on the receipt side and delivery side. The contractual quantity must be equal across the total of the receipts versus the total of the deliveries regardless of the number of line items.

Or, the reverse, the shipper could bring all of the gas onto the pipeline from one or more receipt points and distribute those quantities to a large number of delivery locations. The combination of shipper and transportation contract when using this model type creates a virtual pool on the pipeline where all of the receipts are brought together in one aggregate quantity and disaggregated to the deliveries.

Many pipelines use the NPT for nominations into and out of pools and for nominations to inject into and withdraw from storage. These same pipelines often use PTH or pathed-non-threaded (PNT) as the model type for throughput transportation on their system. It is difficult to effectively assess zone-based rates or segmentation when using the NPT model. Because of this, pipelines that use these features do not use the NPT model. Pipelines with a single rate or with mileage-based rates use the NPT model successfully for throughput transportation. Many pipelines successfully use the NPT model for storage, pooling, hub services, and park and loan services.

The **pathed non-threaded model (PNT)** has been increasing in popularity since its inception in 1993. A few pipelines moved to adopt it once the construct of the model type was made generally available. Pipelines have made a slow and steady progression toward the PNT model over time. Some of those moves have been made when a PNT pipeline acquired a non-PNT pipeline. Other pipelines have chosen to move to the PNT model as a form of customer service.

The PNT model, at first glance, seems to be complex but, once a shipper has taken the time to understand the model and to comprehend the options that the model offers, the shipper realizes this model makes available a significant service offering.

The PNT model requires three nomination line items to form a single complete transportation flow: the upstream unthreaded transaction, the pathed transaction, and the downstream unthreaded transaction.

Figure 13.5
Each of the components of the PNT model nominations

The upstream unthreaded transaction brings the gas from the source to the receipt location on the pipeline's system. This transaction contains the information that is used to confirm where the gas is coming from. It identifies the upstream entity, the upstream contract (when required), and other elements that the pipeline may require.

The downstream unthreaded transaction contains all of the information required to deliver the gas from the exit point on the pipeline system. This information is used to confirm the gas by the delivery operator. This transaction contains the downstream entity, the downstream contract (when required), and other possible elements depending on the requirements of the pipeline.

The pathed portion of the PNT model links the receipt location and delivery location together and assigns the requested quantity to a transportation contract. The pathed transaction contains the receipt location, delivery location, transportation contract, and other elements depending on the requirements of the pipeline. The pathed portion tells the pipeline that a specific quantity of gas being received at a receipt location should be transported to the specified delivery location.

But what does it mean, and why does it matter?

The three portions of the PNT model give the shipper virtual pools at the receipt and delivery locations. All of the receipts brought onto the pipeline at a single location are aggregated into one quantity from which the take-away gas transportation can be scheduled. The same holds true on the delivery side. All of the transportation transactions bringing gas into a single delivery side get added together into one quantity from which the deliveries out of that location can be distributed. This gives the shipper flexibility and control at both the receipt and delivery locations.

Let's look at all of this from the receipt-side perspective using the example below.

Here are four receipt nomination transactions. The upstream pipeline delivers each of these receipts to the receipt location "south 47." The shipper has ranked the receipts in order of priority from 1 to 4.

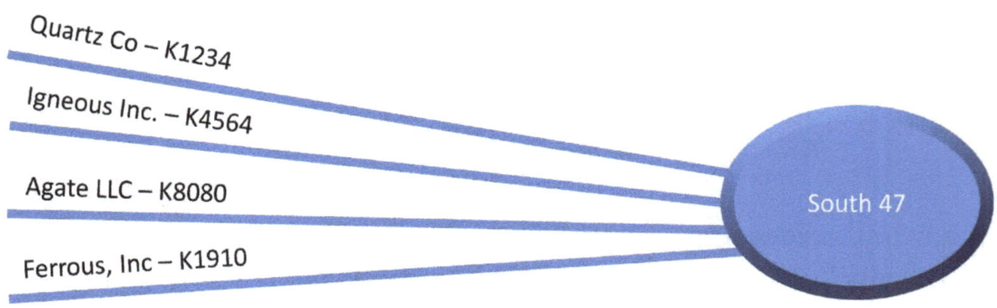

Figure 13.6
Multiple upstream nominations coming into a single receipt per the described example.

Upstream Company	Upstream Contract	Quantity	Upstream Rank	Receipt Location
Quartz Co.	K1234	100	1	South 47
Igneous Inc.	K4564	100	2	South 47
Agate LLC	K8080	100	3	South 47
Ferrous, Inc.	K1910	100	4	South 47

Table 13.1
The upstream nomination data for the described example

When the shipper enters all of these transactions on the pipeline system for receipt at South 47, the shipper has now made this bundle of gas, totaling 400, available for transportation at South 47. Each of these line items in the example is a stand-alone distinct nomination. The shipper now has 400 to schedule on the transportation side of this receipt location. Next, the shipper has to specify where the gas is going to go on the pipeline system and how it should be transported. The example below continues with three nominations to transport the gas to its destination. Two of the nominations will take the gas away from the receipt location on transportation contract F1492, and one of the nominations will take the gas away on transportation contract F1776. One of the nominations will deliver 150 to the delivery location West 142, and the other two nominations will deliver a total of 250 to East 17.

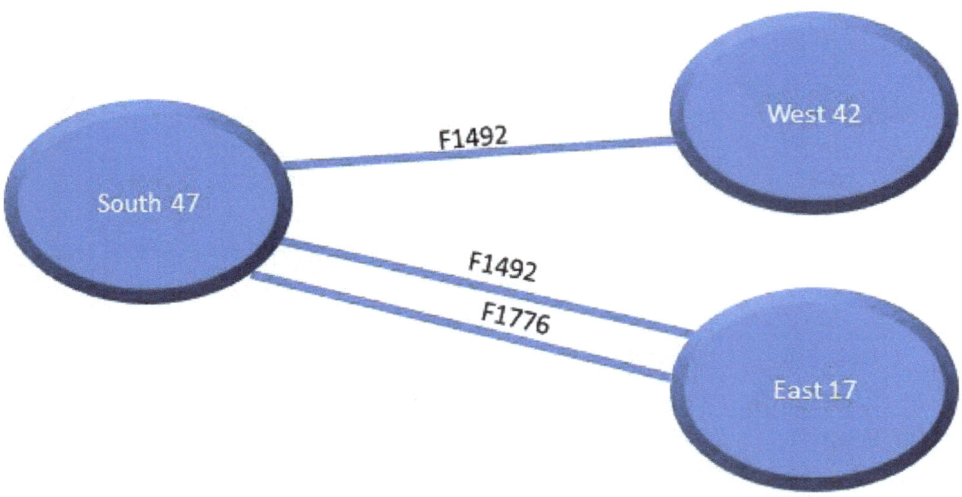

Figure 13.7
The paths for transportation between the receipt and two deliveries per the described example

Receipt Location	Transportation Contract	Delivery Location	Quantity	Receipt Rank	Delivery Rank
South 47	F1492	West 42	150	1	1
South 47	F1492	East 17	50	3	2
South 47	F1776	East 17	200	2	3

Table 13.2
The path nomination data for the described example

The last step in nominating the PNT pipeline is to add in the destinations for the gas at the delivery location. In this example, we have gas being delivered to two different delivery locations, West 42 and East 17.

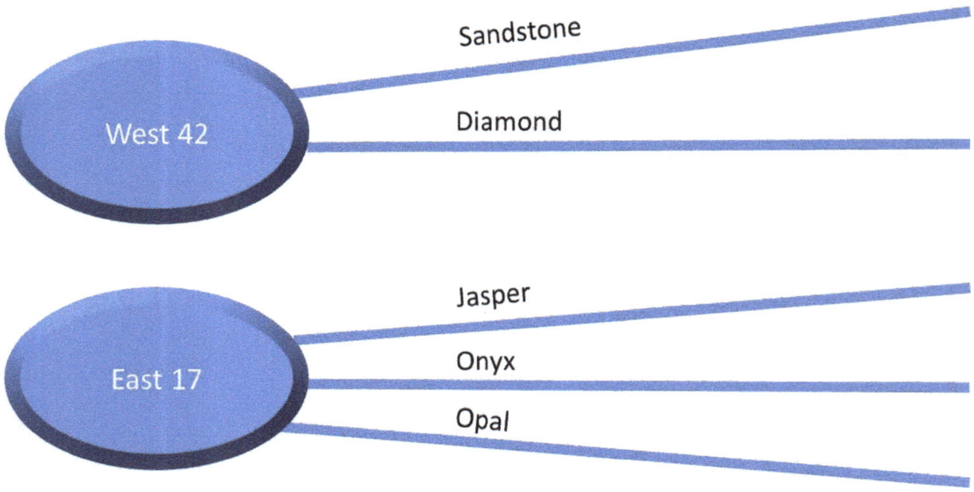

Figure 13.8
The downstream delivery nominations from the two delivery locations per the described example

Delivery Location	Downstream Party	Quantity	Downstream Rank
West 42	Sandstone	50	4
West 42	Diamond	100	2
East 17	Jasper	75	3
East 17	Onyx	50	2
East 17	Opal	125	1

Table 13.3
The downstream nomination data for the described example

In this example, because the gas is being delivered to the end user, the pipeline requires no downstream contract. The requirement for an upstream or a downstream contract depends on the business practices of the pipeline.

This last group of five nominations takes gas available at the two locations and distributes it. Of the 150 available at West 42, two nominations distribute 50 to Sandstone and 100 to Diamond. Of the 250 available at East 17, three nominations deliver 75 to Jasper, 50 to Onyx, and 125 to Opal.

The example applied to scheduling:

Once a shipper has constructed the nominations to flow the gas in the PNT model, the pipeline can schedule the gas. At this point, the benefits of the PNT model become apparent. The pipeline, using this model type, has four different scheduling ranks to utilize in the scheduling process. When cuts occur, the pipeline uses these ranks to determine the impact on the shipper's gas flow.

When a cut occurs on the receipt side, then the pipeline follows the path of gas to the affected delivery point, and uses the rank to determine which downstream nomination receives the cut. When a cut occurs on the delivery side, then the pipeline follows the path of gas to the receipt location, and uses the rank to determine which upstream nomination receives the cut.

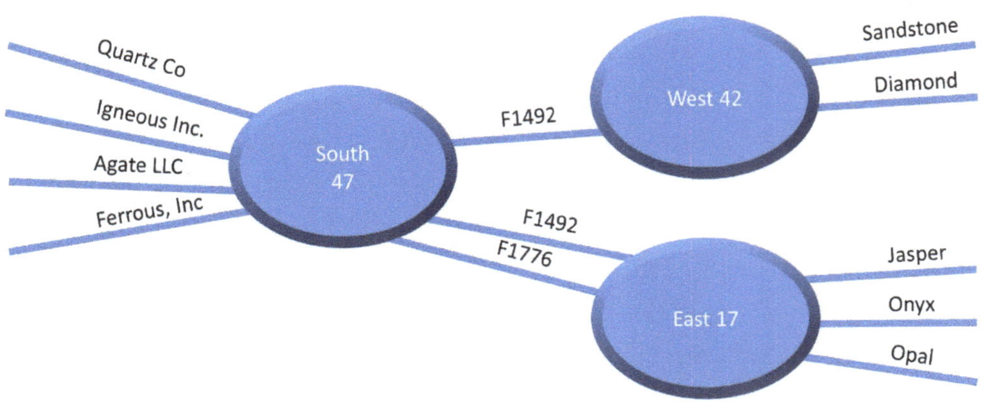

Figure 13.9
All of the nominations in the described example in a single view

In the above example, Quartz Co. loses 100 of its supply. Even though Quartz Co. is ranked as number one, the pipeline has cut its supply through the confirmation process. All of the receipts in this example come into the system at location South 47. Looking at the paths of gas away from South 47, the transaction of a nomination on contract F1776 delivering 200 DTH to East 17 has the lowest receipt rank. The pipeline will cut this nomination from 200 to 100 DTH. Next, we look at the deliveries at East 17 delivery location. The lowest ranked delivery out of East 17 is 75 to Jasper. The pipeline will cut this transaction to zero. The pipeline needs to cut a remaining quantity of 25, so it will cut Onyx, the second-ranked transaction out of East 17, to 25.

Figure 13.10
The nominations that would receive cuts per the described example

Now assume that no cuts have occurred to our original example, and let's look at what happens when a market is lost. For this example, the pipeline will cut the market of 125 for Opal to 25. Opal receives delivery at East 17, so we need to look at where the supply for East 17 comes from. South 47 supplies East 17 on contracts F1492 and F1776. Since F1776 is the lowest-ranked path delivering to East 17, we will cut the pathed portion of the F1776 contract down to 100. Then we will look at where the supply for F1776 comes from. South 47 supplies F1776, also; therefore, we will cut the lowest-ranked supply at South 47, Ferrous, Inc., from 100 down to zero. In this example, regardless of the rank of the market that is cut, because all of the supply comes in at South 47, the lowest-ranked supply, which is Ferrous, Inc., will always be cut first.

This example uses shipper-level aggregation, which means that all of the upstream nominations and the downstream nominations were associated to a specific shipper, but not to any specific contracts of that shipper. If the pipeline had used shipper-contract-level aggregation, then the transportation contract would have been identified on each of the upstream nomination transactions and on each of the downstream nomination transactions. In the shipper-contract-level aggregation scenario, the ranks and path of transaction would still have been used, but the affected transactions would have been determined first by the contract specified on the corresponding upstream or downstream nomination.

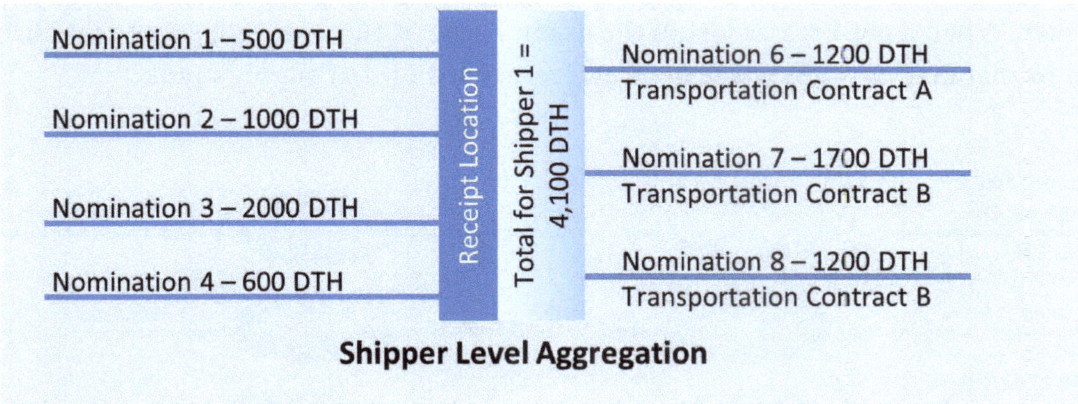

Example 13.1
An example of shipper level aggregation on Pathed Non-Threaded Model

In shipper-level aggregation, any of the supplies bringing the gas into the location can be used on any of the take-away contracts moving the gas on the transporting pipeline.

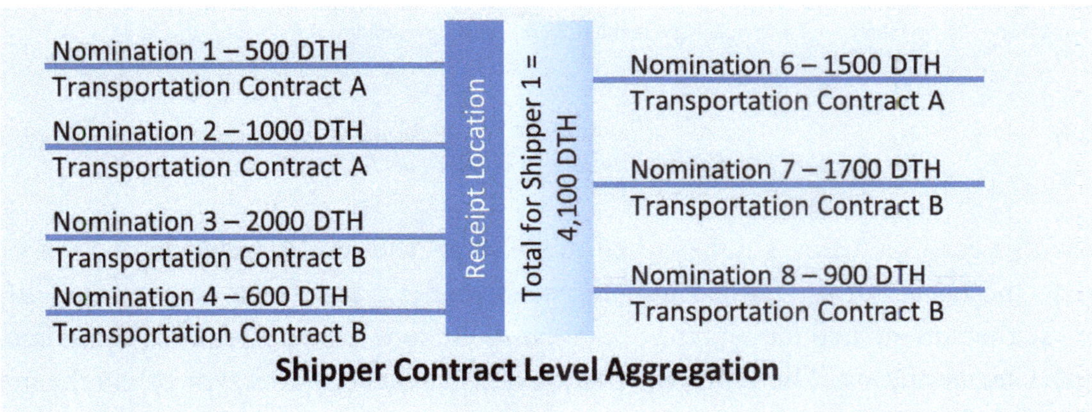

Example 13.2
An example of contract level aggregation on Pathed Non-Threaded Model

In contract-level aggregation, the supply transactions are associated with a specific transportation contract. The take-away nominations must be for the same transportation contract as specified on the supply side. Ranking is effective within the contract.

In this example, if the pipeline had used a pathed model type, then the nominations would have been entered with discrete associations between the upstream company and the downstream company. For example, one of the nominations may have looked like upstream company Quartz Co., upstream contract K1234, receipt location South 47, delivery location West 42, transportation contract F1492, and downstream party Diamond. In the pathed model, the upstream supply is tightly tied to the downstream market. When a market was lost in the example above, the upstream supply that had been tied to that market would have been cut, regardless of that supply's rank.

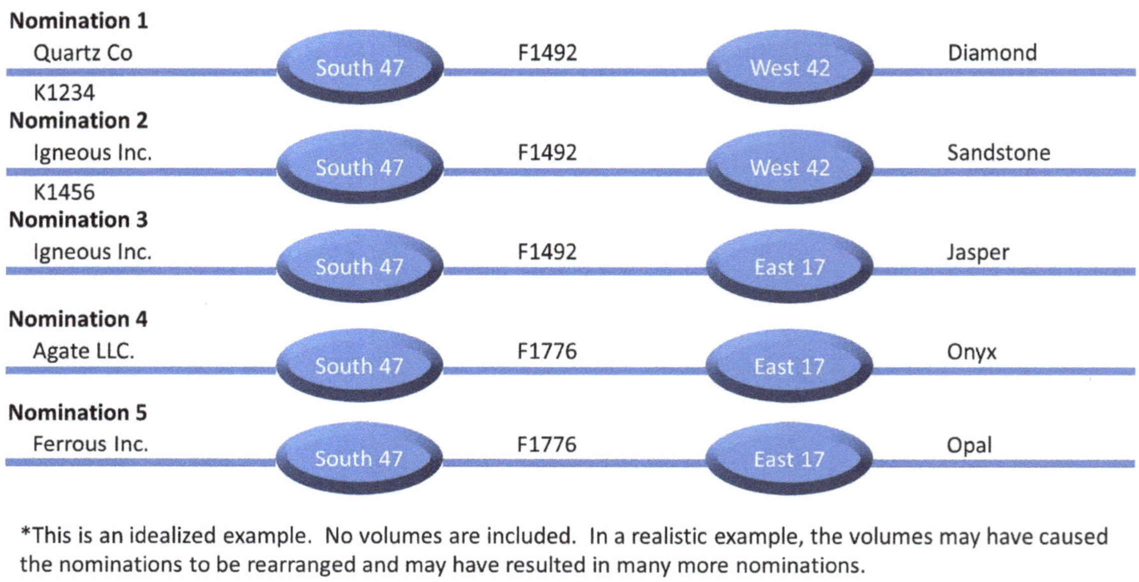

Figure 13.11
The described example nominations in a pathed model type view

To draw this example using a non-pathed model type, the results would have been very similar to the results of the pathed non-threaded model type. However, many pipelines cannot use the non-pathed model type because of their zone-based rates and requirements to support segmentation. Therefore, the pathed non-threaded model type offers the most flexibility for their shippers.

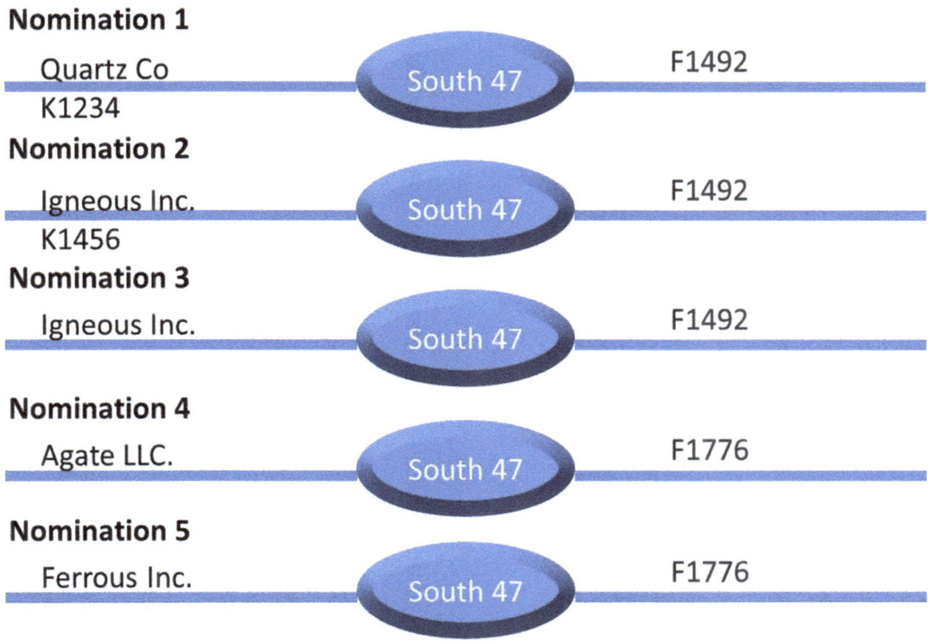

Figure 13.12
The described example **receipt** *nominations in a non-pathed model type view*

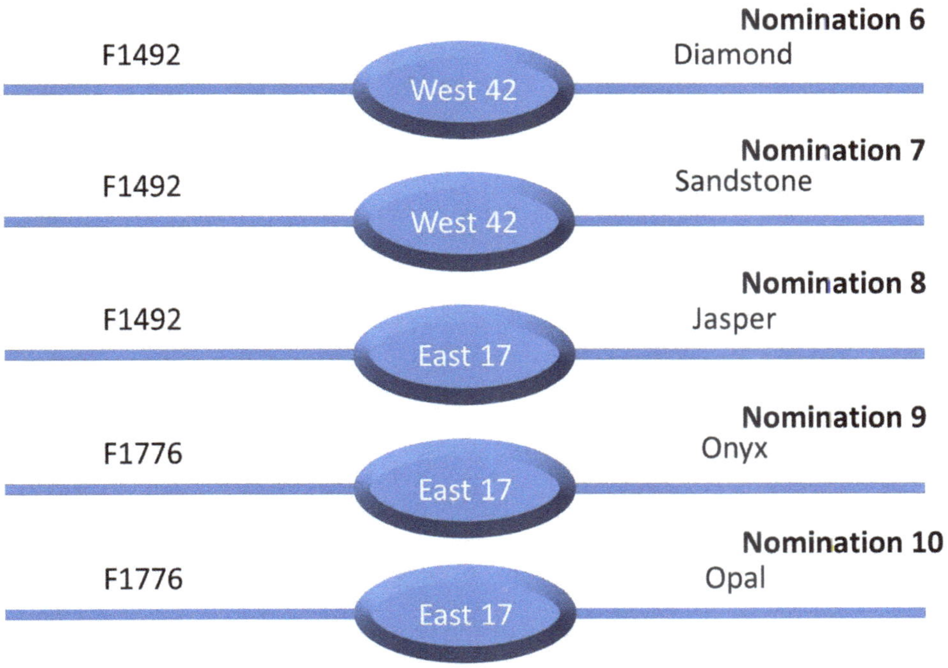

Figure 13.13
The described example **delivery** *nominations in a non-pathed model type view*

Model Types by Mike Schisler

I"m always amazed at how seemingly simple choices of the words we use to express a concept or thought can have unforeseen consequences and misunderstandings, and how what is clear for one person might not be so clear for another. We seem to have just such a case in the NAESB nomination model types, and in particular Pathed Non-Threaded. Here's the story:

In the days of NAESB's predecessor organization, GasFlow, I created and named the Pathed Non-Threaded nomination model as a way to bridge Natural Gas Pipeline of America's new nomination model and business practices to the nascent GasFlow standards. The need existed to make NGPL's radically different approach "look and feel" similar to what all other pipelines at that time were doing, and Pathed Non-Threaded was the result.

In creating this bridge, I reasoned that two concepts are in play when describing how all nominations work. First is the concept of "Pathing," describing the tangible attributes of the transportation nomination, meaning which pipeline locations and service contracts are utilized, and of course the quantities of gas involved. Second is the concept of "Threading", describing the logical attributes of the transportation, meaning the entities (title holders) involved, the title locations, the title quantities being nominated, and whether a direct tie between supply entity and market entity is established as part of the nominations.
Using these two concepts, I reasoned that any nomination model type can be fully described. A "Pathed" nomination is actually a "Pathed Threaded" nomination because (1) the physical path of the pipeline locations and service contract(s) is fully described in the nomination, and (2) the logical thread of a specific supplier entity to a specific market entity at specific pipeline locations for a specific quantity is also fully described. "Non-Pathed" nominations are actually "Non-Pathed Non-Threaded" nominations because (1) physical "location-to-location" paths are not described in the nominations, and (2) no ties of specific supply entities to specific market entities are established. And for "Pathed Non-Threaded" nominations, (1) the physical path of the pipeline locations, service contract(s), and quantity are fully described, and (2) no ties of specific supply entities to specific market entities are established.

So far this probably seems straight forward enough, but a reading of the NAESB standards for Pathed Non-Threaded may just change that for you. Reading the standards reveals that for PNT, the term "thread" is associated with describing BOTH the physical path and the (lack of) logical ties between specific suppliers and markets. So in the standards for PNT we see the "threaded segment" (code value T) describing the physical aspects of the nomination, despite the fact that the name of the model states it is non-threaded. You very well may find yourself asking "how can a "non-threaded" nomination have a thread?" And the more you read the standards with this lingering question in the back of your mind, the more you may feel you aren"t fully grasping PNT, leading to, well, fill in the blank how you may.

The history behind this seemingly inconsequential choice of standards nomenclature is that after creating and naming Pathed Non-Threaded, I was not part of the standards-making process when it came time to create the implementation materials for PNT. The good people driving the process in my absence understood how PNT worked, but didn"t fully take into account what was behind the name. As a result, the descriptions in the standards for PNT make enough sense to those who were part of the standards-creation process, but often seem to be less clear to those who weren"t involved or are new to all of this. So if you find yourself in that camp, you are not alone. But perhaps now that you have "the rest of the story", Pathed Non-Threaded and its associated standards become more clear.

14. Mandatory, Optional . . . And how the conditions are used

Before going further in understanding the nomination process, it is important to understand the use of data elements within the standards.

There have already been several references to the data-element uses. It is important to explain how they work and how the pipeline and shipper must use these. Data elements in every dataset, including Nominations, are expressed with a use code. That use code tells the sender of the transaction set what the use of each data element will be from the perspective of the sender, but there are also requirements/expectations placed on the receiver of the transaction.

The NAESB data element uses are:

- Mandatory
- Sender's Option
- Conditional
- Business Conditional
- Mutually Agreed

NAESB WGQ Standard 1.2.2[42] defines the uses of the data elements. Even though the standard is within the Nominations grouping of standards, this standard applies to all of the datasets in all of the standards groupings related to wholesale natural gas. It is important to review these definitions and understand their meanings.

Mandatory (M) seems obvious to some and confuses others. When an element is stated as mandatory, it means that the sender must provide the described information for this data element as part of the transaction. It also means that, if the data contained in the element is something that can be processed, then the receiver of the information must use or process, or use and process that data in the course of processing the dataset. In the nomination dataset, an example of mandatory elements would be the begin date and the nominator's tracking ID. The begin date tells the receiver when this sender would like for the flow of gas to begin for this nomination. The sender must validate that the date is a valid date and that it is in the future with an open nomination cycle, and the receiver must use this date as the starting date for the transaction. All of these steps mean that the receiver is processing the data that was received. In the case of the nominator's tracking ID, as discussed elsewhere, this element has no processing value to the receiver of the data. It is a tracking tool for the sender of the data and is received and sent back in subsequent transactions. This data is not processed by the receiver of the data, but is stored, tracked, and returned.

Sender's Option (SO) data element is, as stated, optional for the sender to send, but mandatory for the receiver to receive. It is only optional for the sender. When a sender uses this data element and provides data for it, then the receiver of the data must use the information in the way the data element was intended. Examples of sender's option data elements in the nomination dataset are the package ID and receipt rank. The package ID, as described elsewhere, is an element that the shipper may use to make two line items of nominations, that would otherwise be identical, unique through placement of unique data in each of the package IDs for those nominations. This element will not contain information that the pipeline will evaluate or validate. The pipeline will accept any data that the shipper provides in this element and will use it as part of the key to that nomination. The receipt rank, however, must be a valid whole number with a value between 1 and 999 when used. The pipeline will use the receipt rank in later processing of this nomination in the scheduling and allocations processes. Often, because the receipt rank is optional, a pipeline will state a default value that will be used if a receipt rank is not provided. In other cases, where a receipt rank is not provided, the pipeline will process all of the non-ranked nominations on a pro-rata basis. For more information on the use of ranks, see chapters on Scheduling and Allocations later in this book.

The **Conditional** (C) data element is dependent on the value in another data element in the same dataset or in another dataset[43]. If that data element contains information that meets the stated condition in the dataset's data dictionary, then the element becomes activated. In some cases, the condition may be that the element is sender's option when the corresponding element's condition is met. In other cases, the condition may be that the element is mandatory when the corresponding element's condition is met. In the nomination dataset, examples of the conditional data element are the receipt location and the receipt quantity. The receipt location is required if the model type is pathed or the pathed segment of the pathed non-threaded model. The receipt location is also required on nominations that are non-pathed or the receipt segment of the pathed non-threaded model when the delivery location information is not used. This second condition may appear to be circular in its instruction when viewed with the corresponding instruction for the delivery location. What the instruction conveys is that, when sending the receipt-side nomination for the non-pathed or receipt segment of the pathed non-threaded models, the receipt location is required. When sending the delivery-side nomination of these same models, the receipt location is not used and the delivery location is required. Though stated differently, the receipt quantity works in a similar way - the condition on this element states simply that at least one of the receipt quantity or the delivery quantity is required. But this must be taken in context of the use of the data element among the various nomination model types listed in the data dictionary. This element is listed as conditional on all of the Web-based model types. On the EDI Dataset Cross Reference, where the model types are detailed for EDI, it shows that this element is either not used or mutually agreed for all of the model types.

The use of **Business Conditional** (BC) means that the receiver of the transaction will, through the communication of its business practices, tell the sender whether this element is used and, for this receiver, whether this element is mandatory or sender's option for this receiver's business practice. If a marketer wishes to create a gas-management system to record the nominations that it conducts on five different pipelines then, in building the nomination transaction, the marketer must evaluate if each business conditional data element is used on one or more of those pipelines. If it is used, it must be included. Additionally, the marketer may find that the same business conditional data element is used by different pipelines in a different way. All of these variables must be considered by the marketer building this system.

One important aspect of the business conditional use is that, if a sender provides information in a business conditional data element that the receiver of the data does not support, then the receiver of the data must respond with a warning message that the data was not processed. This means that, in the nomination dataset as an example, any time a company requests and is granted a new business conditional data element, then all receivers of nominations must update their systems to process the data to the extent that the warning message can be created and returned to the sender when the unused business conditional element is received.

Mutually Agreeable (MA) is somewhat confusing. NAESB WGQ Standard 1.2.2[44] states that "...Mutually agreeable (MA) means that the data element is mutually agreed to between trading partners. ... It does not, by its definition, create a NAESB WGQ standard business practice. Usage of this element in no way can be mandated for inclusion by either trading partner in order to achieve a level of service." This description seems to state that the data element will always be optional for the sender, and, if not sent by the sender, then the same level of service can be obtained as if the sender has chosen to send the data. However, this is often not the case. The best implementation of mutually agreeable is where the receiver of the data states that it supports a mutually agreeable data element and, if not provided, the default value is declared. In this scenario, the sender has the true option of sending the data and, if not sent, it is aware of the result.

Unlike the business conditional data element, when a sender provides data in a mutually agreeable element that the receiver of the data does not support or process, then the receiver of the data has no obligation to collect the information, store it, or process it.

It is important to note the impact of business conditional and mutually agreeable data elements on the nomination key. The key is made up of data elements in all of the data-element use types. The Nomination Key chapter of this section describes the use of the key.

15. Nomination Key

NAESB WGQ Standard 1.3.27[45] describes the contents of the nomination key. The nomination key is the group of data elements in a nomination that, when a value in one or more elements is different, causes a new nomination to be created. It is important to understand the key and how it works in the nomination process. The list of elements that comprise the key are those that, when combined, create a unique line item of a nomination. When an element is not part of the key, then the value of that element does not contribute to the uniqueness of the nomination and may be changed without creating a new nomination. When an element is part of the key, then a change in the value of that element will result in a new nomination being created.

Start with three elements, the service requester contract, transaction type, and upstream party. If these three elements were the only key elements used in a set of two nominations, then only one of the elements would have to be different from the other in order to keep the two line items with unique keys.

Nomination	Service Requester Contract	Transaction Type	Upstream Party
Nomination 1	K1234	01	143243343
Nomination 2	K1234	01	555666777

Table 15.1
The nomination data for the described example
where the upstream party data creates two distinct nominations

In this example, Nomination 1 and Nomination 2 are unique because the upstream parties are different on each of the nominations.

But this example is simple in that it only refers to three data elements. In reality, Version 3.0 of the NAESB Standards, contains 18 data elements that comprise the key. If any one of these elements has a distinct value between two submitted nominations, then those two nominations are unique.

Of course, it would not be fun if it were as simple as that. The three elements listed in the example above are all mandatory data elements. Many of the data elements in the key are business conditional or mutually agreeable, and one very important element is sender's option.

The sender's option data element is the package ID. This one is easy because the package ID is designed to give the service requester a place to put information unique to that service-requester nomination; it can be used to make a nomination unique that would otherwise be the same key as another nomination. The package ID can be used to solve any potential problems of nomination uniqueness if the service requester chooses to use this data element. The important note here is that it is up to the service requester to use the data element to achieve uniqueness.

The other two conditions, business conditional and mutually agreeable, are not as easy to explain. When provided in a nomination but not used or processed by the receiving pipeline, both the business conditional and mutually agreeable data elements are discarded and not considered to be part of that nomination on that pipeline. When these elements are part of the nomination key and are discarded, it could mean that the elimination of that data element makes one nomination for a shipper appear to be identical to another nomination for that same shipper. If this happens, the first nomination will be replaced by the second nomination as a new nomination even though the shipper intended for the two nominations to be distinct and separate.

It is essential for the shipper to know which of the business conditional and mutually agreeable data elements are used by a pipeline; otherwise, the shipper could send two or three nominations to the pipeline that are distinct to the shipper because of the data contained in the BC or MA field but, since the pipeline does not process this data, the pipeline regards this as one nomination that is updated by two subsequent nominations.

A classic example of this scenario is using the pathed nomination model and the upstream contract. The upstream contract is a business conditional data element. If a shipper is receiving gas from one upstream party, but that gas is being provided on two different upstream contracts, then the shipper will naturally create two nominations: one nomination for the package of 500 DTH of gas from upstream contract 1, and the second for the package of 400 DTH of gas from upstream contract 2. Other than these two pieces of data and the quantity, the nominations are the same. When the shipper sends these two nominations to a pipeline that does not utilize the business conditional field of upstream contract, then the pipeline will discard this information. From the processing-pipeline point-of-view, a second nomination with the same key for 400 DTH immediately follows the first nomination for 500 DTH. The nomination for 400 DTH replaces the nomination for 500 DTH, and the shipper is now requesting one package of gas for a total of 400 DTH when the original intention was for two packages of gas totaling 900 DTH.

In this example, the shipper could have used the package ID element to create uniqueness in order to prevent this problem. In that case, when the receiving/processing pipeline discarded the upstream-contract information, the two nomination line items would have remained unique due to the package ID.

Example Nomination 1 –

- Transportation Contract = K9 for Shipper Blue
- Upstream Party = Agent Cloud
- Receipt Location = Receipt A
- Downstream Party = Rocky Creek
- Delivery Location = Delivery Q
- Transaction Type = 01 (Current Business)
- Package ID = (blank)
- Upstream Contract = CC24
- Quantity = 400 DTH

Example Nomination 2 –

- Transportation Contract = K9 for Shipper Blue
- Upstream Party = Agent Cloud
- Receipt Location = Receipt A
- Downstream Party = Rocky Creek
- Delivery Location = Delivery Q
- Transaction Type = 01 (Current Business)
- Package ID = (blank)
- Upstream Contract = STR55
- Quantity = 500 DTH

Note – the only difference between Nominations 1 and 2 is the value in the Upstream Contract field. Upstream Contract is a Business Conditional data element. This means that its usage is dependent on the business practices of the receiving pipeline.

PIPELINE A	PIPELINE B
• Receives the two nominations from Shipper Blue. • Pipeline A requires Upstream Contract on the nomination. • Pipeline A processes and stores two distinct nominations giving Shipper Blue a total nominated quantity of 900 DTH.	• Receives the two nominations from Shipper Blue. • Pipeline B does not use the Upstream Contract on the nomination. • Pipeline B processes and stores the first nomination for 400 DTH. The first nomination has a key with a null value in the Upstream Contract because the pipeline discarded the value. • Then Pipeline B processes the second nomination. When the Upstream Contract is discarded on the second nomination, the key becomes identical to the first nomination. The second nomination's value of 500 DTH is stored as a replacement for the first nomination giving Shipper Blue a total nominated quantity of 500 DTH.

Example 15.1
An example of how two different pipeline rules treat the same nominations depending on the pipeline configuration.

16. Elements

The data elements that make up a nomination are intended to give the TSP enough information to effectively confirm and schedule the gas on the pipeline. The NAESB nomination dataset, Version 3.0,[46] offers 72 possible data elements to comprise the nomination. Of those 72 data elements, 14 are mandatory. From this a shipper could consider that, in optimum conditions, the minimum number of elements to identify a nomination would be 14; in a worst-case condition, the shipper may have to use all 72 data elements. The good news is that, within the 58 data elements between the minimum and maximum requirement, many of them are mutually exclusive. The nomination dataset provides a comprehensive data dictionary that defines each data element in the nomination[47].

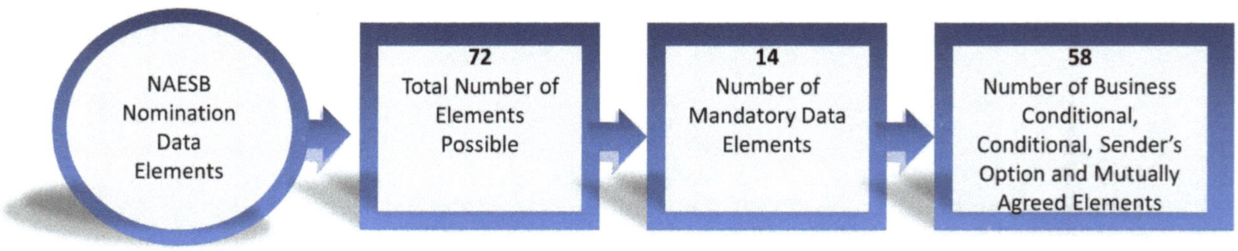

Figure 16.1
The number of different types of nomination elements

Note: In the NAESB datasets, what would naturally be one data element is sometimes portrayed as several data elements because of the different electronic delivery mechanisms that may be employed to deliver the information. For instance, the downstream party is displayed in the nomination dataset as three separate data elements under the heading of Downstream Identifier Data. These three elements are the Downstream Identifier, Downstream Entity Name, and Downstream Identifier Proprietary Code[48]. Current practice uses the common code identifier, Downstream Identifier, to represent the downstream party, while the Downstream Entity Name is the pipeline's representative descriptive name of the downstream party, and Downstream Identifier Proprietary Code is the pipeline's own code assigned for that downstream party. In current NAESB rules, Version 3.0[49], the proprietary code is only used in the situation where the common code is not available. NAESB version 2.1[50] eliminated the requirement to use the common code for locations and now requires only the pipeline proprietary code or the name. In any case, there must be enough information either transmitted or displayed to the shipper for the shipper to make the correct decision in choosing the downstream party. The dataset contains each of the separate data elements that can be conveyed for each of the data elements listed below. The data elements listed below will be described at the summary level, such as downstream party. Refer to the NAESB WGQ Standard 1.4.1 Nominations[51] dataset for a complete list of the detail data elements.

Below is a look at the data elements, grouped by their functional area. The detail element proper names, definition, and use options of the data element are not provided here. Instead, there is a description of ways in which the element is used in the business process:

	Pathed	Non Pathed		Pathed Non-Threaded		
Data Element		**Receipt**	**Delivery**	**Receipt**	**Path**	**Delivery**
*Transportation Service Provider	M	M	M	M	M	M
*Begin Date	M	M	M	M	M	M
*Begin Time	BC	BC	BC	BC	BC	BC
*End Date	M	M	M	M	M	M
*End Time	BC	BC	BC	BC	BC	BC
Shipper Contract	M	M	M	M	M	M
Transaction Type	M	M	M	M	M	M
Package ID	SO	SO	SO	SO	SO	SO
Associated Delivery Location	BC	BC	BC	BC	BC	BC
Associated Receipt Location	BC	BC	BC	BC	BC	BC
Delivery Location	M	Not used	M	Not used	M	M
Downstream Contract	BC	Not used	BC	Not used	Not used	BC
Data Element		Receipt	Delivery	Receipt	Path	Delivery
Downstream Party	M	Not used	M	Not used	Not used	M
Downstream Transaction Type	BC	Not used	BC	Not used	Not used	BC
Imbalance Period	BC	BC	BC	BC	BC	BC
Receipt Location	M	M	Not used	M	M	Not used
Route	BC	BC	BC	BC	BC	BC
Upstream Contract	BC	BC	Not used	BC	Not used	Not used
Upstream Party	M	M	Not used	M	Not used	Not used
Upstream Transaction Type	BC	BC	Not used	BC	Not used	Not used

* These elements are not listed as "key" elements in the NAESB standards but they are inferred in context.

Table 16.1
The usage types of the nomination data elements

Contracts:

Service Requester Contract identifies the shipper's contract that will be used to transport this package of gas. The contract may identify a transportation contract, a storage contract, a contract for parking/loaning or balancing, or other services on the pipeline. The pipeline's tariff specifies contract terms associated with the service requester contract. The contract terms identify the service level, the locations available for transportation, and the rates for the contract. The service requester contract on the nomination informs the pipeline that the shipper elects to use this contract's set of terms to move this package of gas.

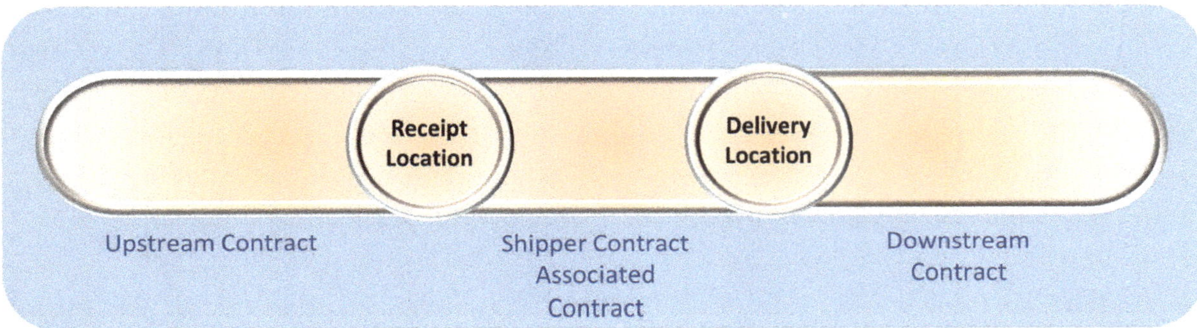

Figure 16.2
The contracts associated with a nomination

Downstream Contract Identifier identifies the service-requester contract to which the shipper is delivering this package of gas. If the pipeline delivers the gas at an interconnect location, the downstream contract identifier will identify a contract on the pipeline downstream of that interconnect. If the pipeline delivers the gas at the pool or other point on the current TSP, then the downstream contract will be a contract on that pipeline. If the pipeline delivers the gas for this nomination to a storage facility on the pipeline, then the downstream contract may indicate the contract number of the title holder of the gas in the storage facility. In this case, the identification of the storage contract in the downstream contract field will inform the pipeline of the injection of the gas into the storage facility. Some pipelines require a discrete nomination separate from the transportation nomination to inject into storage. On other pipelines, a single transport nomination with the storage contract as the downstream contract is sufficient for the injection.

When the downstream contract identifier in combination with the downstream shipper indicates that the receiving party is different than the party transporting the gas in this transaction, then the information tells the pipeline that the transfer of title of the gas is taking place at the delivery location from the service requester (shipper) to the downstream party.

Upstream Contract Identifier denotes the service-requester contract under which this package of gas was serviced prior to (upstream of) the title being held by this shipper. If the gas is received at an interconnect location, the upstream contract identifier will indicate a contract on the pipeline upstream of the interconnect. If the gas is received at a pool or other point on the current TSP, then the upstream contract will also be a contract on this pipeline. If the gas for this nomination is received at a storage facility on this pipeline, then the upstream contract may indicate the contract of the title holder of the gas in the storage facility. In this case, the identification of the storage contract in the upstream contract field will inform the pipeline of the withdrawal from the field. As with the downstream contract process described above, a pipeline may offer the service that the upstream contract from a storage facility, when included with a transportation nomination, will denote a request to withdraw gas from that storage facility. Other pipelines may require a discrete nomination to request the withdrawal of the gas from the storage facility separate from the transportation of the gas.

Associated Contract is used to identify a contract important to this transaction other than the shipper's transportation contract. On some pipelines, the associated contract may identify a storage contract or other contract to be used to keep this transaction in balance in the case of an out-of-balance situation. On another pipeline, the associated contract may be used to identify an in-state contract that guarantees the firm supply. The pipeline determines the use of the associated contract; there is no industry-standard requirement on how this data element is used to enhance the information in the nomination stream.

Dates:

Beginning Date indicates to the pipeline the date that the service requester wishes for the flow of gas to begin for this transaction. If it provides the beginning date without the associated beginning time, then the flow of gas will begin at the pipeline's next available nomination cycle on the indicated day. If the service requester submits the nomination prior to the start of the gas day, the beginning time of the flow of gas will be at the start of the gas day. If the service requester submits the nomination as an intraday nomination, the pipeline will determine the next available cycle for the flow of gas to begin. Additionally, if the pipeline permits, a service requester may request a specific cycle in which the gas should begin to flow. This would utilize the cycle indicator data element on the nomination.

Beginning Time depends upon the business practices of the pipeline. If a pipeline allows the use of beginning time, then it may require that the service requester select one of a set of beginning times that the pipeline permits to be requested on the pipeline. One pipeline may allow the start of the gas day as the only available value for beginning time, depending upon the business practices of that pipeline. Another pipeline may permit shippers to indicate the cycle start time in the beginning time field. Yet another pipeline may allow the shipper to indicate any start time in the beginning time field, and that pipeline will accommodate that elected start time on a best-efforts basis.

Ending Date tells the pipeline the date that the service requester wishes for the flow of gas to cease for this transaction. Generally, the service requester provides the ending date without an associated ending time. When no ending time is provided, the pipeline assumes the end of the gas day to be the time at which the flow is to cease.

Ending Time is optional for the pipeline to support and if supported, is either required or optional for the sender to send. If the pipeline business rules support the ending time, then it may only allow the ending time provided to be the same as the end of the gas day, or the pipeline may allow an ending time that is different than the end of the gas day. The business practices of the pipeline will determine how the ending time is used for that specific pipeline. If the shipper does not provide an ending time on the nomination, then the pipeline will assume the end of the gas day is the ending time.

The beginning date/time and the ending date/time comprise the date range for a nomination. This date range may be for a partial day, a single day, or a span of days. The span of days may be within a single month, or may span multiple months. Generally a pipeline validation will require that the date range is within the terms of the contract. This means that the date range for the nomination cannot begin before the contract begin date and cannot end after the contract end date.

Cycle Indicator is not required by the shipper, and it may not be used by the pipeline. When used by the pipeline, it gives the shipper the ability to elect the cycle in which it wishes to begin the flow of gas. If a pipeline supports the cycle indicator, this field creates an opportunity for the shipper to submit nominations for future cycles in the current open cycle. For instance, a shipper may indicate during the timely cycle that it is making a timely nomination of a quantity of 2,400 for the following day. The shipper may then submit a second nomination, with the same nomination key, with a cycle indicator of Intraday-1 for a quantity of 3,600. This would indicate to the pipeline that, for the first eight hours of the gas day, the pipeline should transport 2,400 per day. A nomination of 2,400 DTH per day implies that a pipeline will flow 100 DTH per hour through that location. When a nomination quantity changes mid-day, then the pipeline must estimate the quantity that has flowed based on the number of hours of flow that has already occurred. This would have, effectively, provided the shipper a quantity of 800 during that eight–hour period. For the next 16 hours of the day, the shipper is requesting 16/24ths of 3,600 – or 2,400. This 2,400 is in addition to the 800 that flowed in the first eight-hour period, giving a total of 3,200 for the gas day for this shipper.

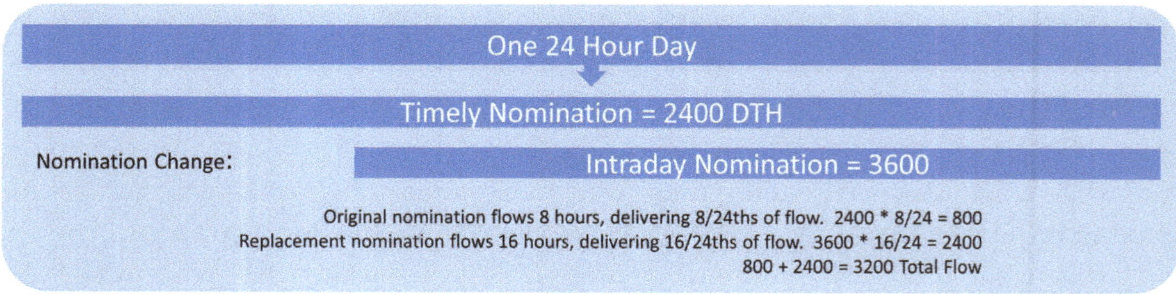

Figure 16.3
The described example of nominated quantity versus delivered quantity for an intraday nomination request

Nomination Subsequent-Cycle Indicator gives the shipper the ability to have the original nominated quantity re-nominated in each cycle of the day, if the original nominated quantity is not fully confirmed or scheduled in the previous cycle. By using this indicator, the shipper tells the pipeline that, if the requested quantity is not confirmed or scheduled, then the shipper wishes the pipeline to treat the nomination as a new nomination in each cycle and to continue to attempt to confirm and schedule the desired quantity. This indicator is neither required for the shipper nor required for a pipeline to support.

Timestamp is a system-generated time created by the pipeline when it receives the nomination. The time a shipper enters a nomination in the pipeline's server on the web determines the nomination timestamp and provides a view of that timestamp back to the shipper. The timestamp is important to the shipper because it indicates whether the nomination was received within the boundaries of the expected nomination cycle. When a sending server enters a nomination via Electronic Data Interchange (EDI), the pipeline server assigns a timestamp at the receipt of the EDI transmission and provides that timestamp back to the sending server so that the shipper, via the sending server, has an indication of whether the nomination was received within the boundaries of the expected nomination cycle. In either case, the important note is that the pipeline server assigns the timestamp and that the timestamp determines the cycle in which the nomination was received.

In an EDI nomination, the pipeline requires the submitter of the nomination, the shipper, to provide the timestamp. This timestamp informs the pipeline of the time that the shipper recorded as the submittal time, but is not the official timestamp of the nomination. The pipeline determines the official timestamp of the nomination and provides it back to the shipper at the completion of the sending of the nomination via EDI.

Rates:

Bid Transportation Rate may be used by a pipeline to offer the shipper the ability to indicate the rate it is willing to pay for transportation on this specific nomination. A scenario where the bid transportation rate would be used could be: A pipeline offers a shipper a negotiated rate that is significantly less than the maximum rate. The pipeline's scheduling process utilizes the value of the transportation in determining which nomination flows if there are more nominated quantities than the pipeline can support. The shipper recognizes that its nomination may not flow because its negotiated rate is low, and the quantity is near capacity flowing through the pipeline route the shipper wants to use. By using the bid transportation rate, the shipper can indicate to the pipeline that it is willing to pay a higher price, the bid price, in order to get its transportation to flow. This is one example of how the transportation rate may be used.

Bid-Up Indicator may be used with or without the bid transportation rate. Used alone, the bid-up indicator tells the pipeline that the shipper is willing to pay a higher rate than the negotiated rate in order to obtain a scheduled quantity of transportation. Again, the shipper may be in a situation where it had a low negotiated rate on the pipeline, but the pipeline is near capacity, and the shipper wants to indicate to the pipeline that it wishes to increase its transportation rate incrementally until it is assured that its requested quantity will be scheduled. On one pipeline, use of the bid-up indicator may signify an incremental increase in the transportation rate until the gas reaches a rate at which it will flow. On another pipeline, the use of the bid-up indicator may signify that the shipper is going to pay the maximum tariff rate for this transportation.

Maximum-Rate Indicator is another data element that a pipeline can use to allow the shipper to indicate to the pipeline that it is willing to pay a higher rate in order to get its transportation to flow. A pipeline may use a combination of the bid-transportation rate, the bid-up indicator, and the maximum-rate indicator as a service for its shippers. It is important for shippers to understand which of these services, if any, the pipeline offers.

Example 1: Using a Bid Rate

- Nominate from Receipt Location A to Delivery Location Q on Transport Contract I42
- Include a Bid Rate of $0.31
- Tariff Rate Range for Commodity Charge is $0.01-$0.69

The only rate this shipper is willing to pay for this transaction is $.31/DTH. If the pipeline schedules on an economic basis, any nomination with a rate greater than $.31 will be scheduled before this one.

Example 2: Using a Max-Rate Indicator

- Nominate from Receipt Location A to Delivery Location Q on Transport Contract I42
- Contract has an existing negotiated rate of $0.48
- Include a Max-Rate Indicator = YES
- Tariff Rate Range for Commodity Charge is $0.01-$0.69

This shipper has a negotiated contract rate of $0.48 but knows that it is likely to be bumped by other shippers with higher transportation rates. The shipper is informing the pipeline that, for this transaction, it is willing to pay the maximum tariff rate of $0.69 in order to get the gas scheduled.

Example 3: Using a Bid Rate plus a Bid-Up Indicator

- Nominate from Receipt Location A to Delivery Location Q on Transport Contract I42
- Include a Bid Rate of $0.31
- Include a Bid-Up Indicator = YES
- Tariff Rate Range for Commodity Charge is $0.01-$0.69

This shipper has indicated a starting rate of $0.31 for this transaction. The shipper has also informed the pipeline that it is willing to increase the transportation rate until it is assured the transaction will be scheduled.

Example 4: Using a Bid-Up Indicator

- Nominate from Receipt Location A to Delivery Location Q on Transport Contract I42
- Contract has a negotiated rate of $0.24
- Include a Bid-Up Indicator = YES
- Tariff Rate Range for Commodity Charge is $0.01-$0.69

This shipper has a negotiated contract rate of $0.24 but knows that it is likely to be bumped by other shippers with higher transportation rates. The shipper has also informed the pipeline that it is willing to increase the transportation rate, until it is assured the transaction will be scheduled.

Example 16.1
Examples of transactions using the Bid Up Indicator, Bid Transportation Rate, and Maximum Rate Indicator

Locations:

Delivery Location informs the pipeline of the end point for the transaction. The delivery location may indicate the point on the pipeline where the shipper is delivering the gas for it to be received at a pool, received by another shipper, injected into storage, or delivered to some other service provided by the pipeline. The delivery location may also indicate the exit point for the gas on the pipeline by delivering the gas to a downstream pipeline.

Receipt Location informs the pipeline of the beginning point for this transaction. The receipt location may indicate the point where the gas enters the pipeline, or it may indicate the point on the pipeline where this shipper is taking title to the gas and will begin its transportation transaction for the gas. The receipt point, if on the pipeline, may be at a storage-withdrawal location, at a pool where the gas is received from another shipper, or at another location on the pipeline where receipt from another service is provided.

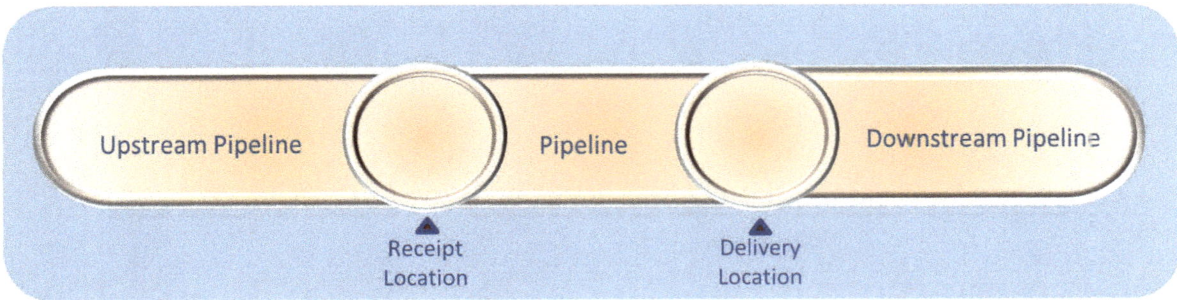

Figure 16.4
The locations associated with a nomination

Ranks:

Multiple ranks may apply to a nomination line item.

- Delivery Rank
- Downstream Rank
- Receipt Rank
- Upstream Rank
- Path Rank

The use of ranks in the nomination can be confusing. There is the receipt-and-delivery-rank combination, the upstream-and-downstream-rank combination, and the path rank. It would not make sense to use all of the ranks in all of the locations where they can occur. The shipper requires clarity from the pipeline to understand which rank to use under which condition for that pipeline. Generally, the upstream and downstream rank applies only to the un-threaded portion (upstream and downstream nominations) of the pathed non-threaded nomination model. The non-pathed model uses the receipt rank on the receipt-focused nomination and the delivery rank on the delivery-focused nomination. The shipper specifies both receipt and delivery rank on the pathed model and on the pathed portion of the pathed non-threaded model to indicate how it wants the nomination to be ranked in the case of a receipt or delivery cut, respectively. The path rank is intended, optionally, in place of receipt and delivery ranks, on the threaded portion of the pathed non-threaded model.

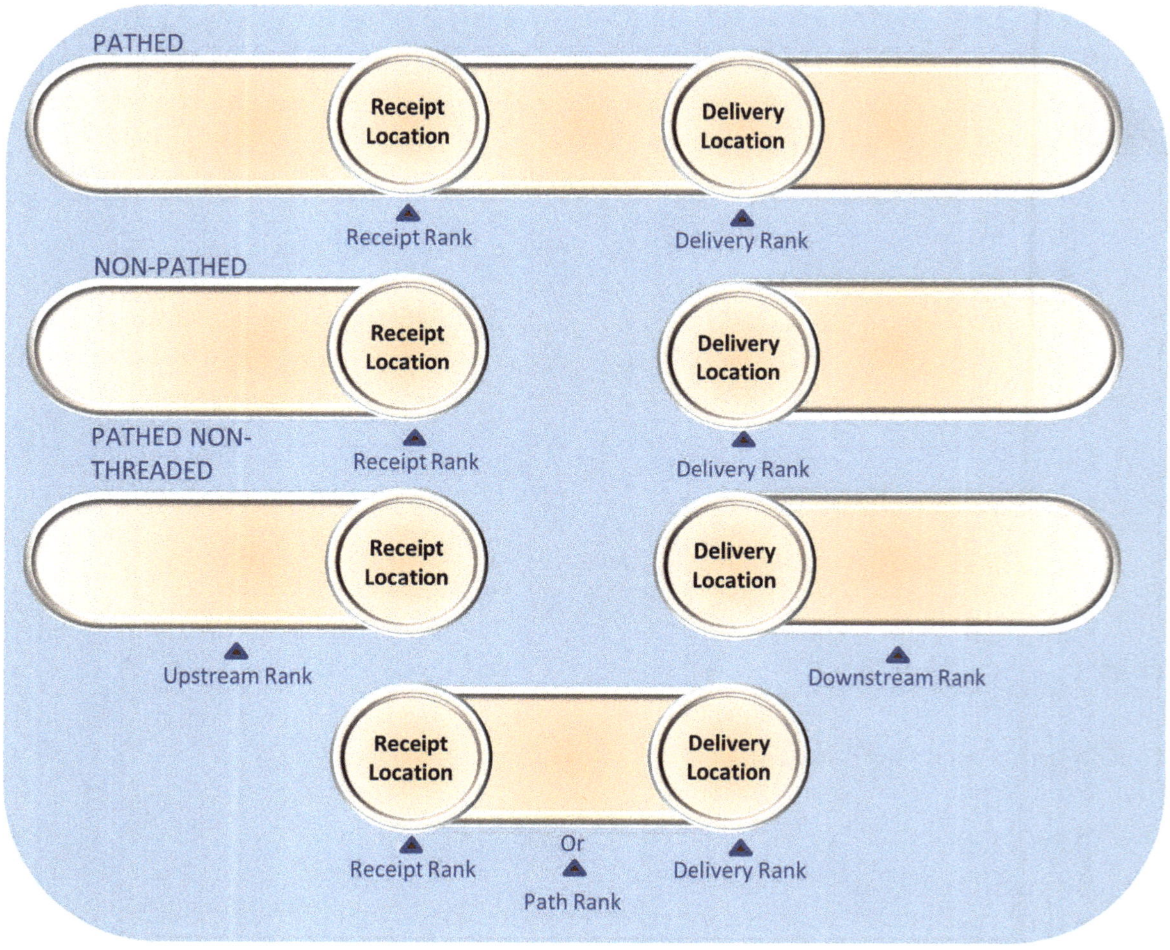

Figure 16.5
The ranks associated with a nomination depending on the model type used

Parties:

The parties in NAESB transactions are identified using common codes. The Dun and Bradstreet (DUNS)[52] number for a business entity is the common code used as the mandatory identifier for a party. On web screens, the party name may be displayed. If a DUNS number is not available for a business entity, then the pipeline may use its own proprietary identifier as a temporary measure until the common code is available.

Transportation Service Provider (TSP) is the proper name for the entity providing the service on the pipeline. The term Transportation Service Provider is used instead of pipeline because this entity may perform many services in addition to traditional transportation service, such as gathering, storage, processing, and distribution of gas. The nomination names this party as the addressee for the request for nomination service.

Service Requester is the proper name for the shipper on the pipeline. Just like the Transportation Service Provider, the term service requester identifies many different roles of parties that may request service on the pipeline. The service requester may represent the shipper holding the transportation contract or other service contract, or it may represent the designated agent for that shipper. It may also identify the operator holding the OBA. Additionally, the service requester may identify an asset manager or other party providing service to the shipper, who is representing that shipper for this transaction on the pipeline.

Upstream Identifier is the party delivering gas to the TSP for the service requester in the nomination. The upstream party may be a party on the pipeline if the service requester initiates the nomination at a point on the pipeline system, or it may be a party on the upstream pipeline if the service requester initiates the nomination at an interconnect with another pipeline. Because of this, the upstream identifier may be an entity known to the pipeline, when the upstream flow of gas is on the pipeline, or it may be an unknown entity when the upstream flow of gas is on an interconnected pipeline.

Downstream Identifier is the party receiving gas from the TSP for the service requester in the nomination. The downstream party may be a party on the pipeline if the nomination is delivering to a point that continues on the pipeline system, or it may be a party on the downstream pipeline if the nomination is delivering to a point that is an interconnect with another pipeline. Because of this, the downstream identifier may be an entity known to the pipeline, when the downstream flow of gas is on the pipeline, or it may be an unknown entity when the downstream flow of gas is on an interconnected pipeline.

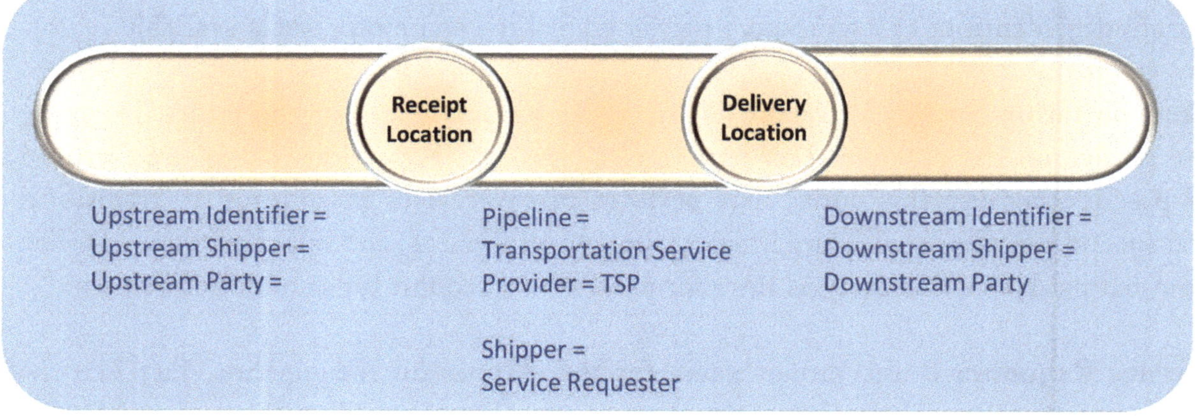

Figure 16.6
The parties associated with a nomination

Packages:

Package ID is used by a service requester to create a distinction in a nomination that allows one nomination to be different from another when all of the other key identifying fields in that nomination would otherwise be the same. If all the data elements in two nominations are equal, but the shipper wishes to keep two nominations distinct, the shipper will use the package ID to identify this distinction between the two transactions. The shipper determines the use and the content of the package ID. The pipeline does not validate or edit the information in the package ID other than to use the content to distinguish one nomination transaction from another. One shipper may use identifiers such as "1", "2", or "4" as package IDs while another shipper may put deal or market information in the package ID field in order to transmit with the nomination the shipper's own information that is meaningless to the pipeline but meaningful to the shipper that provided the information.

The **Upstream Package ID** identifies a shipper's unique package of gas from which the gas is delivered at the receipt point for this nomination transaction. The upstream package ID tells the pipeline which package of gas can be matched to this package of gas for confirmation purposes. During the confirmation process, the upstream package ID would be matched to the nomination on the upstream pipeline. (The confirmation process is described later in this book.) Few pipelines use the upstream package ID in the nomination.

The **Downstream Package ID** identifies a shipper's unique package of gas that is receiving the gas at the delivery point for this nomination transaction. The downstream package ID tells the pipeline which package of gas can be matched to this package of gas for confirmation purposes. During the confirmation process, the downstream package ID would be matched to the nomination on the downstream pipeline. (The confirmation process is described later in this book.) Few pipelines use the downstream package ID in the nomination.

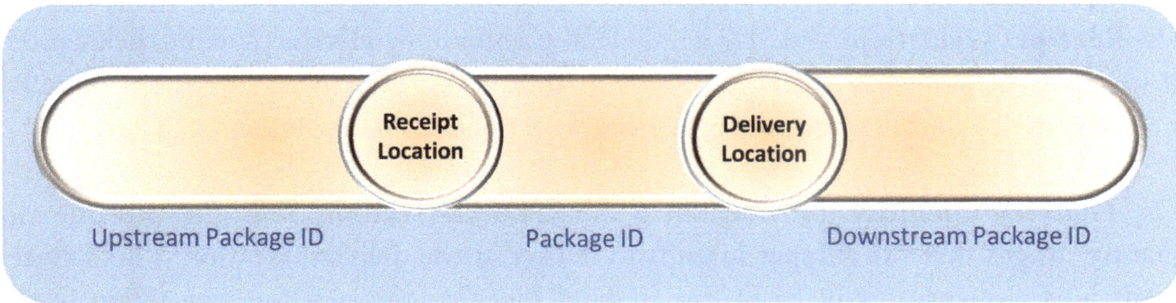

Figure 16.7
The package IDs associated with a nomination

Quantities:

There are multiple quantities that may be used in a nomination. Most pipelines require only one quantity.

The **Quantity** is used on a nomination transaction where the model type requires only one quantity to be provided. This use applies only to the EDI-nomination format. On an EDI-submitted nomination, this is the only quantity provided for each nomination line item. All web-submitted nominations are identified as either a receipt quantity or a delivery quantity. The service requester uses the data element in conjunction with a quantity-type indicator, which tells the receiver of the information that the quantity is either a receipt quantity, delivery quantity, or both. On the receipt nomination for the non-pathed and pathed non-threaded models, the quantity indicates the receipt quantity and should be accompanied by a receipt quantity-type indicator. On the delivery nomination for the non-pathed and pathed non-threaded models, the quantity indicates the delivery quantity and should be accompanied by a delivery quantity-type indicator. On the pathed model and the pathed nomination of the pathed non-threaded model, the quantity may be the receipt quantity, the delivery quantity, or both. The quantity-type indicator will provide the distinction. When only one quantity is provided on a pathed nomination, the pipeline will calculate the other quantity based on contract terms.

The **Quantity Type Indicator** informs the pipeline, in an EDI transaction, that the quantity provided is either a receipt quantity or a delivery quantity or both when the

Quantity, described above, is used to identify a single volume.

The **Delivered Quantity** may be used by a pipeline for EDI purposes to allow the shipper to provide both the receipt quantity and the delivered quantity in the nomination transaction. For the delivered quantity to be used, the quantity-type indicator must be "R", and the quantity contained in the quantity element is the receipt quantity.

The **Receipt Quantity**, provided in a non-EDI nomination, tells the pipeline the quantity of gas that the shipper intends to receive at the receipt location. The receipt quantity includes any in-kind fuel that the pipeline may retain in the nomination process.

The **Delivery Quantity**, provided in a non-EDI nomination, tells the pipeline the quantity of gas that the shipper intends to deliver at the delivery location. The delivery quantity is a quantity reduced by any in-kind fuel that the pipeline may retain in the nomination process.

A pipeline may choose to support the **Minimum Delivery Quantity**. When used, the minimum delivery quantity tells the pipeline that the shipper will accept a scheduled quantity less than the nominated quantity if the pipeline is unable to provide the entire quantity the shipper has requested. The pipeline may reduce the quantity as low as the minimum delivery specified. If the pipeline decides to schedule the shipper's nomination below the minimum delivery quantity, then the shipper has elected to have the resulting scheduled quantity reduced to zero.

A pipeline may choose to support the **Minimum Receipt Quantity**. When used, the minimum receipt quantity tells the pipeline that the shipper will accept a scheduled quantity less than the nominated quantity if the pipeline is unable to provide the entire quantity the shipper has requested. The pipeline may reduce the quantity as low as the minimum specified. If the pipeline decides to schedule the shipper's nomination below the minimum receipt quantity, then the shipper has elected to have the resulting scheduled quantity reduced to zero.

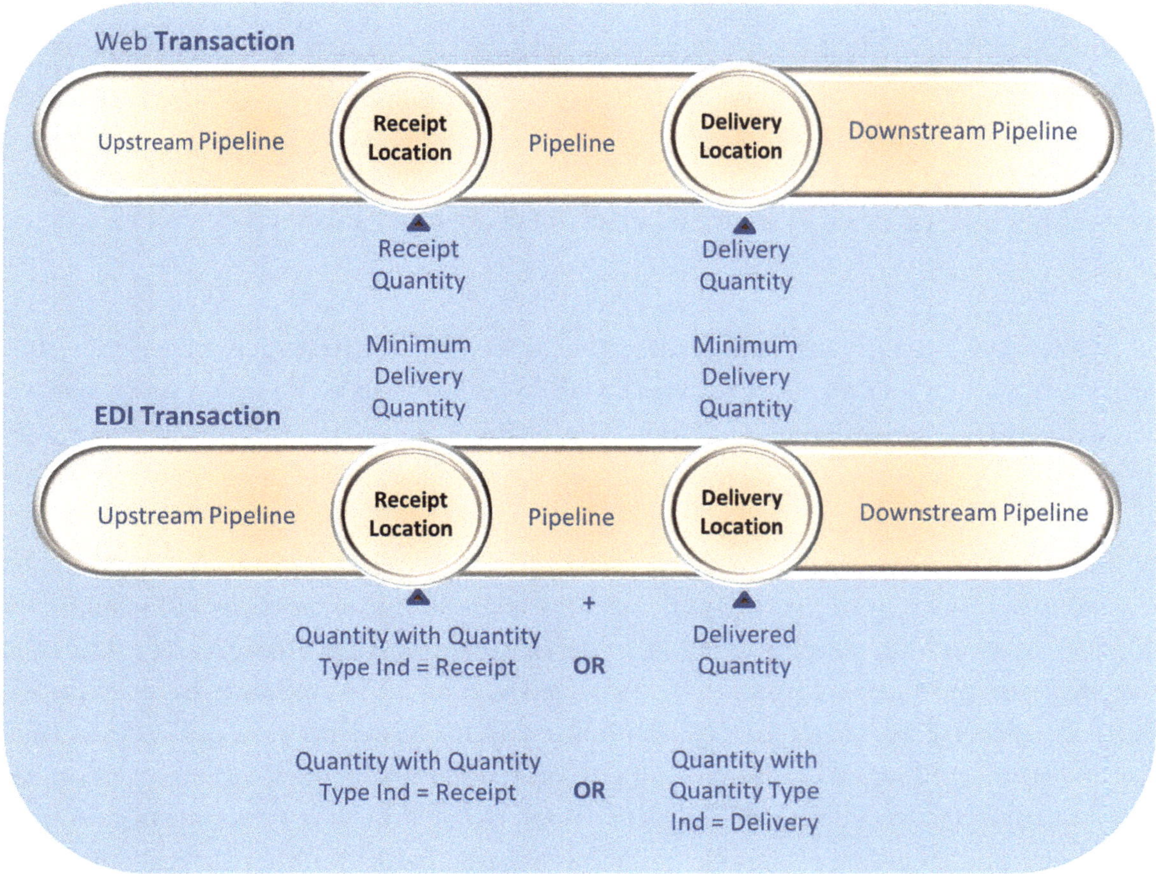

Figure 16.8
The quantities associated with a nomination and the difference in requirements between a web based nomination and an EDI nomination

Other:

Data elements are contained in the "Other" category when they do not belong to groups of associated data elements, but work independently. This does not mean that these data elements are of lesser importance. Several data elements contained in this category are critical, mandatory, or both in the nomination process.

The **Capacity Type Indicator**, when supported by the pipeline, tells it that the locations on this nomination are using specific capacity rights. For instance, the capacity type indicator may indicate primary-to-primary-rights, primary-to-secondary rights, etc. The code values for the capacity type indicator provide a list of capacity-right combinations that may be used for this element.

A pipeline may support the **Deal Type** data element, and the shipper may use it. The data dictionary provides an excellent description of the uses for the deal type. Individual pipelines provide the values for the deal type. There is no predefined set of code values for this data element. The deal type is used to specify pre-negotiated arrangements between the shipper and the pipeline.

The **Export Declaration** is an element used for transportation that is crossing the border from Canada into the United States. Canadian transportation service providers use this element.

The **Model Type** data element indicates the model type with which this nomination conforms. Another chapter in this section extensively describes the use of and examples of model types. The valid values for this data element are: pathed, non-pathed, pathed non-threaded - pathed segment and pathed non-threaded - unthreaded segment.

The **Nominator's Tracking ID** was originally created to provide a unique identifier for each nomination line item in an EDI dataset transmission. The pipeline will validate the tracking ID, which has no restriction. The service requester may assign any numbering or naming scheme to the nominator's tracking ID. The TSP provides the tracking ID back to the service requester in the nomination quick response (on EDI transactions only) and in the scheduled quantity. The tracking ID is not part of the nomination key and is not used by the pipeline to indicate or determine a unique nomination line item. The information is provided by the service requester solely for the service requester's informational purposes. Some pipelines allow a shipper to enter a nominator's tracking ID on their website so that the shipper has the same tracking ability on a web-generated nomination as it has on an EDI-generated nomination. Other pipelines automatically generate a nominator's tracking ID on a nomination entered in through the website for the same purposes. Pipelines that do not associate a nominator's tracking ID to a web-entered nomination will not have a nominator's tracking ID to provide with the scheduled-quantity in the scheduled quantity transaction set.

If a shipper submits a nomination for the first time and assigns a tracking ID of "123" to that nomination, and then decides to change that nomination, then the shipper may assign the same nominator's tracking ID of "123" to the replacement nomination or may assign a new nominator's tracking ID of "456" to the replacement nomination. Additionally, shippers may reuse the nominator's tracking ID in different batches of nominations sent to the pipeline. Because there is no validation on the nominator's tracking ID, there is no requirement that the tracking ID be unique.

Nomination User Data 1 and **Nomination User Data 2** are data elements that have been provided in the nomination dataset so that a service requester may include data in a nomination that travels with that nomination for its own informational business purposes. The data in these two data elements is not processed or validated in any way by the TSP. The TSP provides the use of these two data elements as a service for the service requester. The TSP is not required to offer this service nor is the service requester required to use this service.

The **Processing Rights Indicator** may be used by TSPs that offer processing services on their system. The processing rights indicator tells the pipeline whether this shipper has elected to use those rights. The use of this indicator is one way to communicate processing services. Other pipelines may use other contractual terms to provide this service.

Different pipelines use the **Service Provider's Activity Code** in different ways. One pipeline uses the service provider's activity code as an alias for the nomination key. This service allows its shippers to nominate for a gas day, using the service provider's activity code, the date, and the quantity instead of all of the data elements required to identify a nomination on its system. Another pipeline with multiple distinct pipelines that are connected to each other uses the service provider's activity code for the shipper to identify that the nomination on one pipeline flows onto the nomination on another pipeline. This use ties into one package of gas the nominations across the different pipelines within the same company. Other pipelines may use the service provider's activity code in a different way. There is no industry standard on how this data element must be used.

The **Transaction Type** is a mandatory data element in every nomination. The transaction type tells the service provider the type of service the shipper wishes to utilize within the selected transportation contract. General transportation is most often indicated by the "01" code, indicating current business. The transaction type may also indicate a request for authorized overrun, imbalance payback, or one of many other services. There is a long list of transaction types available in the code values dictionary of the NAESB WGQ Standard 1.4.1[53] Nomination dataset, and a pipeline will choose which of the transaction types to support for the types of service offered.

The transaction type is an important tool in the nomination. Other than "current business" mentioned above, there are important transaction types that a pipeline may employ to provide services within a shipper contract.

The "authorized overrun" transaction types are used by a shipper to request transportation in excess of the contractual MDQ (contract level, location level or path level). Shippers are required to use the "authorized overrun" to request to transport above the MDQ on interstate pipelines[54]. These transaction types give a shipper the ability to distinguish this type of service from "no notice" types of service.

A pipeline may use the "flow-day diversion" transaction types as one of the methods of implementing the flow-day diversion requirement[55]. A pipeline may choose other methods to meet this requirement without using the transaction type. Flow-day diversions are explained in more detail in the chapter on Flow-Day Redirects in the Scheduling section.

A shipper may use the "backhaul" transaction type to indicate to the pipeline that the delivery location for a nomination is physically upstream of the receipt location and that the shipper wishes to use displacement capacity to transport the gas. A backhaul transaction does not really flow gas backwards on the pipeline. Instead, the pipeline will schedule less physical gas to be delivered at the backhaul receipt location and less gas to be received at the backhaul delivery location such that the backhaul transaction displaces gas that would have actually flowed on the system. Some pipelines have specific charges that would apply to this service. Figure 16.8, below, gives an example of a backhaul transaction and the impact on the pipeline physical gas flow.

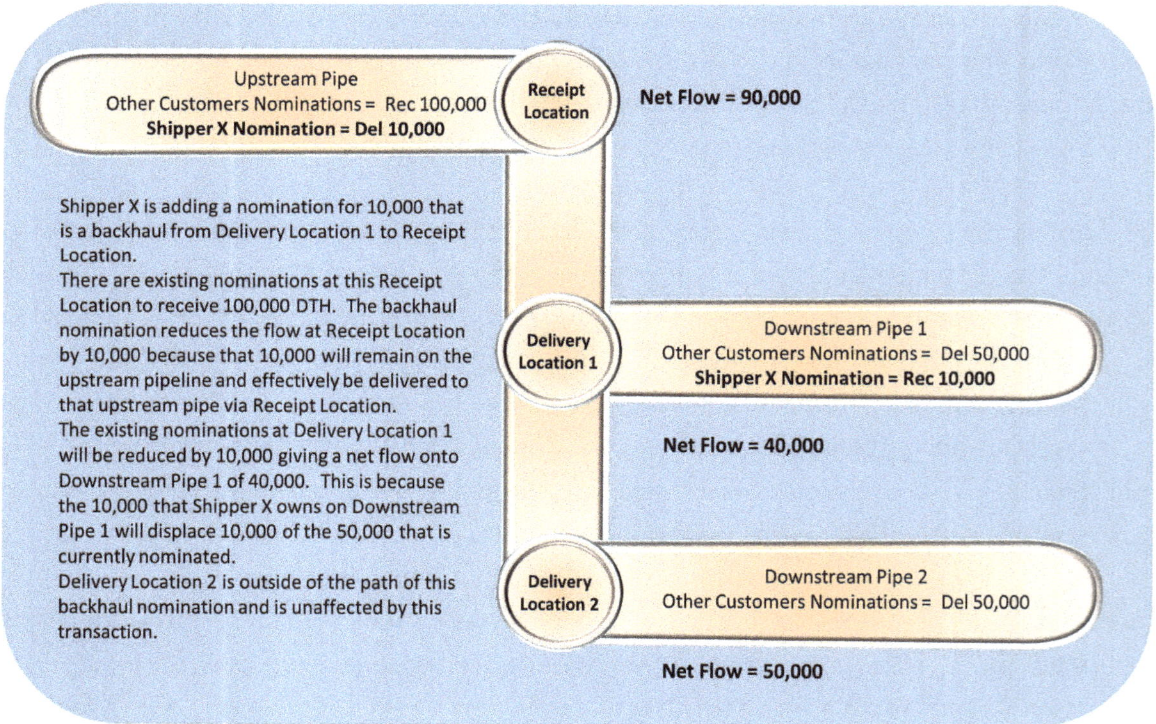

Figure 16.9
An example of a backhaul nomination and the impact on the pipeline physical gas flow

"Imbalance payback" transaction types inform the pipeline that the shipper nomination will be returning gas to the pipeline or receiving gas from the pipeline to resolve an outstanding imbalance.

"Segmented" transaction types inform the pipeline that the shipper nomination being submitted is used to segment the shipper capacity on the contract through the nomination process. Again, this is one way that a pipeline may implement this requirement. A pipeline may implement the nomination segmentation requirement without using the "segmented" transaction types.

Shippers may use "storage injection" and "storage withdrawal" transaction types to indicate the use of a storage contract in the nomination and the action to be taken.

Numerous transaction types exist for the service of "parking" and "loaning" gas. On some pipelines, the term may also use the "bank" transaction type.

In some cases, a transaction type will cause type-specific validation to occur on a nomination. In other cases, the transaction type will cause specific charges to be incurred. In yet other cases, the transaction type will indicate a scheduling priority that is being incurred. There are many transaction types that a pipeline may work with to identify service-level transactions. A pipeline will utilize a small subset of the transaction types that are available.

17. Code Values

Many of the data elements in the NAESB WGQ Standard 1.4.1 Nomination[56] dataset have an assigned list of acceptable code values. In some of the cases, the pipeline may utilize a subset of the code values, and, in other cases, the pipeline must offer all of the code values as an option for its shipper(s). Additionally, some of the data elements with code values are mandatory, some conditional, etc. Additional clarity will be helpful in this area:

Data Element	Code Value Rules
Bid-Up Indicator	One code – Must be used if the element is used.
Capacity-Type Indicator	All of the codes are supported if those service levels are supported and apply to the pipeline and the element is used.
Cycle Indicator	Use of the standard nomination cycles is required to be supported if the data element is used. Use of the additional cycles for a pipeline is optional.
Export Declaration	These code values must all be used if the element is used.
Maximum-Rate Indicator	These code values must all be used
Model Type	Only the code values supported by the pipeline must be used.
Nomination Subsequent Cycle Indicator	These code values must all be used if the element is used.
Processing-Rights Indicator	These code values must all be used if the element is used.
Quantity-Type Indicator	These code values must all be used
Transaction Type	This is a master list of code values from which a pipeline will choose which codes to use. A shipper may only use codes from the list of code values that the pipeline supports

Table 17.1
The code value rules associated with different data elements

Among these code-value-related data elements, the most important is the transaction type. This element is used to inform the pipeline of the type of service, within the service contract, that the shipper is requesting for this nomination line item. This list continues to grow as pipelines add new service offerings or variations on service offerings. The maintenance of the codes in all of the code-value sets is an ongoing process within NAESB through which it is simple to request changes[57].

18. Validation

Validation of the nomination may occur in one of several ways.

For the EDI transaction, the validation of the nomination transaction occurs when the pipeline has received the nomination file; the pipeline validates the terms of the nomination and then provides the nomination quick response dataset back to the service requester. The nomination quick response dataset either informs the shipper that the nomination was validated, found to be correct, and was accepted; or informs the shipper through a series of pre-approved error codes that the pipeline found errors or warnings in the nomination line item.

For the web-based nomination transaction, there is a general assumption that all nomination validation occurs in the real-time interaction of entering and submitting the nomination. There are, however, no rules that require a pipeline to validate the nomination in real time. Additionally, the amount of information validated on the web at the time of the transaction entry varies from pipeline to pipeline. Some pipelines provide at the time of the nomination entry or change extensive validation, including contract capacity being exceeded, credit validation, or location availability, for example. Other pipelines provide during the confirmation and scheduling process the contract capacity validation, credit validation, and location-availability validation. As part of the general assumption on validation of the web-based nomination transaction, shippers assume that, when entering in a nomination on the web, the nomination quick-response warnings and error codes that apply to the transaction will be displayed back to the shipper during the nomination entry. If a pipeline chose to allow nomination entry on the website with no validation, it would be technically correct for the pipeline to provide a second web screen for the nomination quick response that showed any validation error and warning messages for the transaction. This however is not a customer-friendly mode for a pipeline and does not provide good representation of the pipeline's services.

The error codes and messages provided in validation are the same whether they are provided through a web interaction or through EDI. The nomination quick-response dataset provides the validation response to the EDI dataset and provides error codes with messages and warning codes with messages that are to be used to communicate to the shipper issues with the nomination transaction in both the EDI communication and the web communication. The pipeline can augment both by additional informational data provided to the shipper.

When the pipeline provides a nomination quick response via the EDI dataset, the nominator's tracking ID becomes an important data element. The pipeline organizes communication of error and warning codes and messages by tracking ID in the quick-response datasets. The pipeline does not send back to the shipper the entire originating nomination, and it utilizes the tracking ID to identify the nomination in error. The assignment of the tracking ID becomes important at this point. If a shipper or its computer system assigned a tracking ID value of "1" for 10 different nominations in an EDI nomination file, and there was one nomination in error, then the quick response dataset would identify the error message pertaining to tracking ID "1." The shipper would have no method to determine which of the nominations were in error.

Example 1 – EDI file usage:

Nomination File 101 contains:

1st Nomination	with Tracking ID = 10101
2nd Nomination	with Tracking ID = 10102
3rd Nomination	with Tracking ID = 10103

Quick Response (validation file) on Nomination File 101:
File Status = OK, with errors
Error: Invalid receipt location for Nominator's Tracking ID = 10102

This is a good and useful response. The shipper knows that the second nomination in the originating file was not accepted but that the first and third nominations were processed and accepted with no errors. The shipper can correct the second nomination and re-submit that transaction while leaving the first and third transactions in place.

Example 2 – EDI file usage:

Nomination File 102 contains:

1st Nomination	with Tracking ID = 999
2nd Nomination	with Tracking ID = 999
3rd Nomination	with Tracking ID = 999

Quick Response (validation file) on Nomination File 102:
File Status = OK, with errors
Error: Invalid receipt location for Nominator's Tracking ID = 999

This is a bad use of the Nominator's Tracking ID. There is no way for the shipper to identify which of the 3 nominations had an invalid receipt location and which nominations were accepted. The shipper's only option is to log onto the pipeline's web page and search to determine which nominations were accepted and deduce which nomination was in error.

Example 18.1
Examples of the use of the nominator's tracking ID

19. Segmentation in Nominations

Nomination-level segmentation works in much the same way as contractual segmentation from a capacity-utilization perspective. Nomination-level segmentation occurs for the same shipper inside the same contractual rights. In our previous example for contract segmentation, suppose Shipper Bob acquired the released capacity from Alice for 10,000 DTH from L to Z. In traditional transportation, Shipper Bob could nominate 10,000 DTH from L to Z or from M to Z, etc., and that would fully utilize the contractual capacity. With nomination-level segmentation, Shipper Bob can submit one nomination from L to P for 10,000 DTH, another nomination from Q to W for 10,000 DTH, and a third nomination from X to Z for 10,000 DTH. All three of these nominations would be subject to the applicable commodity rate for each transaction, but Shipper Bob is charged the original contracted demand charge of $.80 from L to Z.

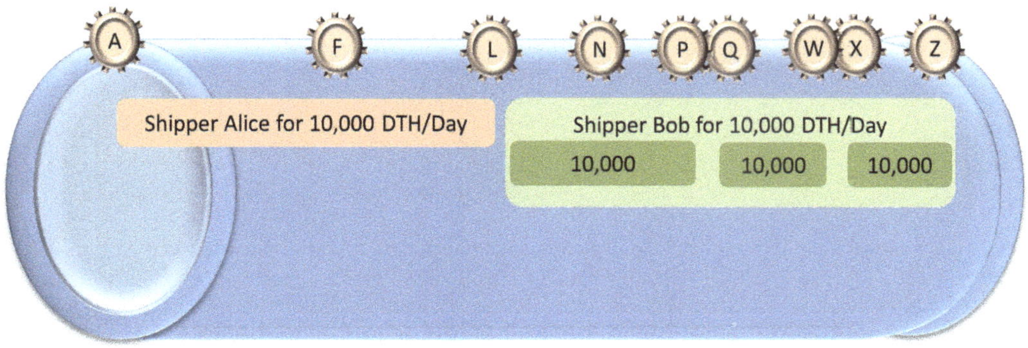

Figure 19.1
The described example of a segmented contract using nomination-level segmentation to optimize flow

As in contract-level segmentation, the nomination-level segmentation may overlap as long as the sum of the nomination quantities in any given overlap does not exceed the quantity rights of the contract. Continuing with the example of Shipper Bob, this would mean that Shipper Bob could submit one nomination for 2,000 DTH from L to Z, a nomination for 4,000 DTH from L to P, a nomination for 4,000 DTH from Q to W, and a nomination for 4,000 DTH from N to Y. This would consume the contractual rights from N to P and from Q to W. If Shipper Bob tried to submit an additional nomination from P to Z for 1,000, then the contract quantity would have been exceeded.

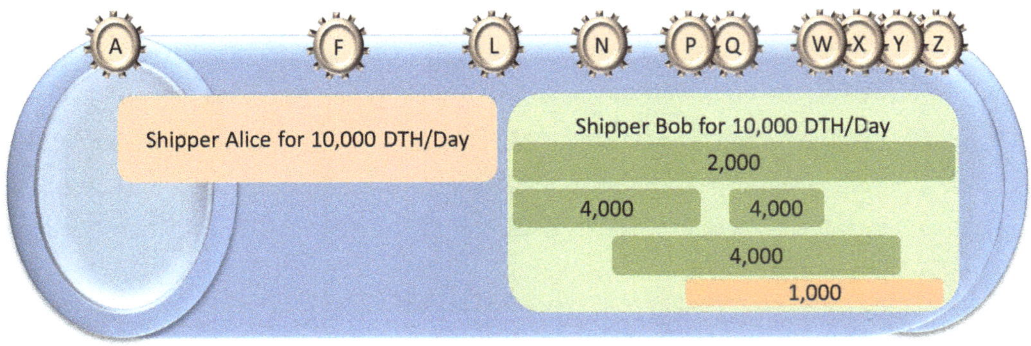

Figure 19.2
The described example of a segmented contract using nomination-level segmentation and exceeding the contract MDQ

The scenario can get much more complicated than these limited examples. It is important to note that overlapping capacities cannot exceed the capacity rights, and capacities cannot be segmented so that the flow of gas is not contiguous.

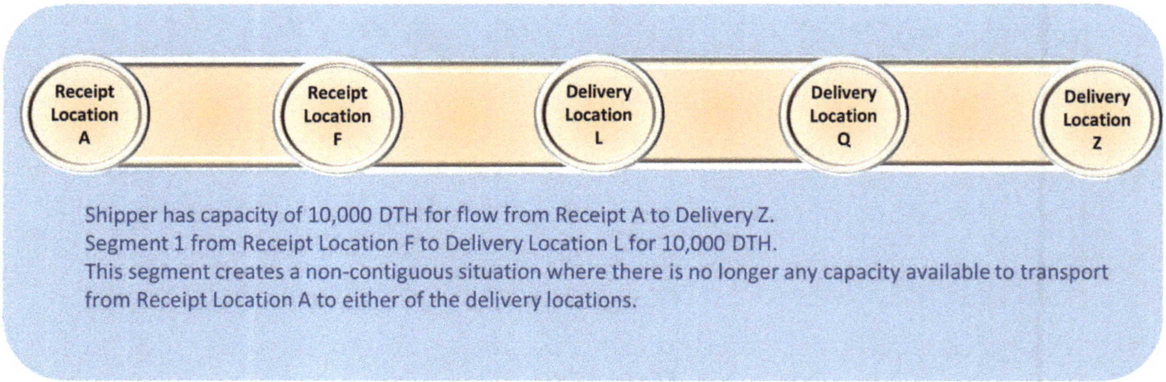

Figure 19.3
An example of segmentation resulting in non-contiguous capacity

For instance, if a pipeline has two receipt locations and three delivery locations in a straight line, and the shipper releases capacity between the second receipt and the first delivery, then the shipper has no continuous capacity remaining between the first receipt and any of the remaining deliveries. In this example the capacity between the first two receipts and the remaining two deliveries is unusable or stranded.

The ability to segment capacity both contractually and through the nomination process adds flexibility to the firm contract for the shipper on the pipeline and for the party acquiring the shipper's released capacity.

20. Storage, Transport Pools

In addition to nominations transactions for transportation, nominations may be used for other services provided by the TSP, such as storage, pooling, parking and loaning, hub services, etc. The model type and the method for handling these ancillary transactions will differ among pipelines.

On many pipelines that use the pathed nomination model or the pathed non-threaded nomination model, the pipeline will use the non-pathed model for transactions that occur at a single location. Some pipelines offer a service where the shipper does not have to create a separate stand-alone transaction to move gas from transportation into one of these location-specific services or to move gas out of one of these location-specific services onto a transportation-service agreement. On these pipelines, the transportation nomination will list, for example, the location as the delivery point, the target agreement as the downstream agreement and, without a discrete nomination for the service, the pipeline will infer that the transportation transaction is delivering the gas into the downstream-service agreement for the designated downstream shipper. Some pipelines will require a second nomination from the shipper to contain this information; on other pipelines, the single transportation nomination is sufficient. In essence, the pipeline is offering two transactions on one nomination line item: both the transportation transaction and the receipt into the downstream contract.

Method 1 – Using two nominations

Nomination 1

From Receipt A to Delivery S

Where Delivery S is the storage injection meter

Nomination 2

Non-Pathed nomination (generally)

Delivery S with downstream owner information and storage injection as the transaction type

Method 2 – Using one nomination

From Receipt A to Delivery S

Where S is the storage injection meter

Downstream contract is the shipper's storage contract

By providing the storage contract in the downstream contract field, the pipeline interprets that this is a storage injection with no secondary nomination required.

Method 3 – Using a Pathed Non-Threaded nomination model

From Receipt A to Delivery S

The downstream unthreaded nomination is a combination of Method 1 and 2 above. It is a separate line item and indicates the injection into storage with the storage injection as the transaction type and with the storage contract in the downstream contract field.

Example 20.1
Different methods to accomplish a storage-injection nomination

The reverse process occurs where the shipper uses the upstream information to receive from a contract on the pipeline into the transportation contract. In this scenario, the upstream contract or upstream party reference will identify the source of the gas on the pipeline for the transportation.

Method 1 – Using two nominations	Nomination 1 Receipt portion of a Non-Pathed nomination (generally) Receipt W with upstream owner information and storage withdrawal as the transaction type
	Nomination 2 From Receipt W to Delivery Z Where Receipt W is the storage withdrawal meter
Method 2 – Using one nomination	From Receipt W to Delivery Z Where Receipt W is the storage withdrawal meter Upstream contract is the shipper's storage contract And by providing the storage contract in the upstream contract field, the pipeline interprets that this is a storage withdrawal with no secondary nomination required.
Method 3 – Using a Pathed Non-Threaded nomination model	From Receipt W to Delivery Z The upstream unthreaded nomination is a combination of Method 1 and 2 above. It is a separate line item and indicates the withdrawal storage with the storage withdrawal as the transaction type on the upstream-unthreaded nomination and with the storage contract in the upstream contract field.

Example 20.2
Different methods to accomplish a storage withdrawal nomination

When a pipeline offers this service, it must also have a provision for shippers who wish to transfer ownership of gas at a pool or storage facility without physically moving the gas. In this instance, the pipeline may utilize a transportation transaction or a non-pathed transaction to accomplish the communication of the deal.

Storage by Steve McCord

In some cases, pipelines operate a series of physical storage facilities across their asset as a single location for the purposes of nominating and scheduling gas. These physical facilities may be in close proximity to one another, or may be physically positioned across a large geographic area. In such cases, the Storage team will work closely with Operations and Gas Control to manage the physical aspects of injecting and withdrawing gas into and from the individual storage fields, and the customers will only be required to manage injections and withdrawals on their individual storage contract(s). This arrangement provides flexibility to the pipeline for use in balancing the pipeline system, and for day-to-day system operations, while allowing shippers the ease of business to nominate quantities on their storage contract(s) without impediment.

This ability of the pipelines to manage the physical aspects of flow to and from storage has become more critical and challenging over the past several years as national flow patterns have shifted from conventional supply sources to the newer shale plays. Pipelines, especially those in the Northeastern area of the United States, are no longer receiving gas at the traditional supply locations for which they were originally designed. As the bulk of pipeline supply shifts further from conventional sources, pipelines are operating and modifying their systems in new ways in order to provide reliable service to their customers while prudently managing their physical storage facilities.

21. Nomination Aggregation

In the chapters on the nomination key and the data-element uses, it is clear that the service requester must be careful when creating nominations to different pipelines so that the business conditional and mutually agreeable data-element uses of the pipelines do not create unexpected results.

In a previous example, where a marketer is nominating on five different pipelines, it is important that the marketer's gas information system can identify which of the business conditional or mutually agreeable (or both) data elements are used for each pipeline and for which types of contracts and model types. A single pipeline may support multiple model types and may require a different group of data elements for different types of service on the same pipeline.

With all of these variables in play for the service requester, there may come a time when the service requester has to aggregate its detail nominations to the level that is required by the pipeline, or the service requester may have to disaggregate nominations from a pathed model type to a non-pathed or pathed non-threaded model type. Both of these scenarios could occur in one interaction between a service requester and a pipeline.

For the first scenario of aggregation, suppose that a shipper records nominations at a purchase-deal level that equates to multiple upstream contracts for one upstream shipper and, consequently, equates to multiple nominations. But, the pipeline on which the shipper is submitting the nominations does not support the use of the upstream-contract data element. In this scenario, the shipper will have to summarize the distinct nominations into a nomination that is at the level of detail supported by the pipeline. Then, when the shipper receives scheduled quantities, allocated quantities, etc., from the pipeline, the shipper will need a process, such as ranking or prorating, to disaggregate the nominations from the pipeline level back to the shipper's level of detail.

Marketer's nominations for internal usage versus the nominations required by the pipeline from the marketer. The marketer may need to aggregate nominations before sending them to the pipeline OR the marketer may need to use a Package ID to keep the nomination line items distinct.

Example:

Purchase Deal 99 - From Receipt A to Delivery Q on Transportation Contract X - For Sales Deal 101

Purchase Deal 88 - From Receipt A to Delivery Q on Transportation Contract X - For Sales Deal 101

Purchase Deal 77 - From Receipt A to Delivery Q on Transportation Contract X - For Sales Deal 101

From the marketer's perspective, this may be captured as three separate nominations, each for a different purchase deal, to fulfill the sales deal # 101.

From the pipeline's perspective, the pipeline does not carry deal information and the nominations will look the same from the pipeline point of view. Therefore, the marketer can 1) aggregate all three nominations into a single nomination to submit them to the pipeline system or 2) the marketer can use the Package ID data element to provide information to keep the three nomination line items distinct.

There is a risk with both options.

The first option requires that any scheduling or allocation variances from the original nomination be distributed among the three purchase deals in some allocation method. The method that the marketer uses will be determined by the terms of the deals that supplied the gas.

The second option gives the pipeline the ability to determine which of the nomination line items are changed to accommodate any scheduling or allocation variances. In this case, ranking of the nominations by the marketer becomes very important so that the pipeline distribution of quantities provides the results that the marketer desires.

Example 21.1
How a marketer's internal nominations may differ from the level of detail required by a pipeline

For the next scenario of aggregation, suppose that a marketer has a gas transaction management system that is modeled only in the pathed model type. One of the pipelines onto which the marketer needs to submit nominations uses the pathed non-threaded model for regular transportation. When the marketer transfers nominations from the gas transaction management system to the pipeline, either through that pipeline's website or through EDI, then the marketer must split the pathed nomination from its system into three distinct nominations required by the pipeline. The marketer can approach the disaggregation of the nomination as breaking each nomination into three distinct nomination line items; however, it is likely that the marketer will quickly run into a problem where there are multiple threaded segments that appear to be identical. The marketer must either develop a strategy using a tool such as the package ID to keep each of those nomination line items unique, or the marketer must aggregate the transactions together where they would otherwise be identical. If the marketer chooses the aggregation method, then it must also have a disaggregation method planned so that, when the scheduled quantities and allocated quantities are returned by the pipeline, the marketer will be able to distribute those quantities back to the original nomination.

Marketer's nominations for internal usage versus the nominations required by the pipeline from the marketer. If the marketer stores nominations in a pathed model and the pipeline requires nominations in a pathed non-threaded or non-pathed model, then the marketer may need to disaggregate nominations before sending them to the pipeline. Unlike the previous example, this scenario cannot be solved by adding data to the nomination line item. Splitting the marketer nomination from one into multiple nominations is not terribly difficult but it does create several risks. The marketer must make sure that each nomination line item is kept unique or is summarized if there will be duplicates created. Additionally, when response information, such as scheduled quantities and imbalances are provided by the pipeline, the marketer must devise a way to re-aggregate the information back into their system.

Marketer's Example:

Nomination 1: From Receipt A to Delivery Q on Transportation Contract X

Nomination 2: From Receipt A to Delivery S on Transportation Contract Y

Nomination 3: From Receipt C to Delivery Q on Transportation Contract X

If the marketer enters the three nominations above for business on a pipeline and the pipeline's nomination model type is non-pathed then the marketer will need to enter these transactions as 5-6 separate nominations on the pipeline.

Non-Pathed Pipeline's example:

Nomination 1: From Receipt A on Transportation Contract X

Nomination 2: From Receipt A on Transportation Contract Y

Nomination 3: From Receipt C on Transportation Contract X

Nomination 4: To Delivery Q on Transportation Contract X

Nomination 5: To Delivery S on Transportation Contract Y

Nomination 6: To Delivery Q on Transportation Contract X

Note: For nominations 4 and 6 – they need to be either combined into one nomination or made into distinct nominations using a package ID or other data value.

Example 21.2
An example of a marketer's nomination that is recorded as pathed when the pipeline nomination is recorded as non-pathed and pathed non-threaded

Another consideration that the same marketer must face is that the pipeline will return a scheduled quantity for the upstream portion of the pathed non-threaded model, and for the receipt quantity on the threaded segment of the pathed non-threaded model. This will give that marketer two scheduled quantities for the receipt quantity on the transaction, and it may provide difficulties in determining which quantity to store. The same scenario, of course, holds true on the downstream and delivery side of the same transaction.

22. Cycles and Intraday

Cycles are a very important part of the Nominations process and gas-transportation scheduling. Cycles identify the times in a day when a shipper may submit nominations on the pipeline. In NAESB terms, there are five standard cycles for a gas day, but an interstate pipeline may elect to provide more cycles than the five minimum ones defined. Non-interstate TSPs are often not required to support all of the cycles. In most cases, they support the first cycle, the Timely cycle, but their support of the additional cycles may be on a best-efforts basis[58].

Most non-interstate providers support the Timely nomination cycle because it is a time to synchronize transportation requests across the pipeline grid. For this same reason, many of the non-interstates that connect with interstate pipelines will also support the other standard cycles in order to provide a true-up synchronization time with those interconnecting pipelines.

A nomination is submitted before transportation of gas. On the interstate day-ahead scenario, a nomination is submitted as a Timely nomination by 1:00 p.m. of the day before the gas will flow on the next business day. It is important to understand that a nomination may be submitted at any time prior to this deadline. A nomination may be submitted a month or even several months ahead of the expected flow. The cycle timelines are actually deadlines when the nomination must be entered into the system in order for the request to be considered for the next day's beginning of gas flow. Nominations for dates in the future, beyond the next day's flow, may be entered at any time of day.

Whether a nomination is created two months or five days or one minute before the deadline for the Timely nomination cycle at 1:00 p.m., it is created as equal to all other nominations with regard to the timing of that cycle. All of the nominations received before the Timely nomination deadline are considered to be timely for that cycle and are treated under the same set of scheduling rules for that pipeline. All of these nominations will begin gas flow at the beginning of the next gas day.

Some non-interstates offer the Timely nomination cycle, then offer continuous scheduling throughout the remainder of the nomination period on a space-available basis and based on their ability to confirm the receipts and deliveries of the gas. This second, continuous scheduling service is often referred to as being offered on a best-efforts basis meaning that, as long as the gas can be confirmed and the capacity is available for gas flow, then the nomination can be scheduled and supported.

Interstates, which are required by FERC to support all five of the standard cycles, support the Timely, Evening, Intraday-1, Intraday-2 and Intraday-3 cycles. The Timely cycle has a nomination deadline of 1 p.m. for gas to flow at the start of the next day. The Evening cycle has a nomination deadline of 6 p.m. for gas to flow at the start of the next gas day. The Intraday-1 cycle has a nomination deadline of 10 a.m. on the day of the gas flow, and the flow of the gas will begin at 2 p.m. during that gas day. This means that a nomination entered into the pipeline's system at 10 a.m. on the subject gas day, and beginning flow at 2 p.m., will have a partial day of flow during the gas day rather than the full 24 hours of flow. The Intraday-2 cycle has a nomination deadline of 2:30 p.m. on the day of the gas flow, and the flow of the gas will begin at 6 p.m. during that gas day. This means that the intraday nomination entered into the pipeline's system that begins flow at 6 p.m. will have a partial flow during the gas day. Intraday-3 cycle has a nomination deadline of 7 p.m. on the day of gas flow, and the flow of the gas will begin at 10 p.m. during that gas day. Intraday-3 gas will also have a partial day of flow during the gas day. The table below can be used to determine the percentage of a gas day that will flow when the intraday nomination is for a number of hours less than 24 hours of a whole gas day.

Number of Hours that Gas Has Flowed	Percentage of Scheduled Quantity that Has Flowed	Number of Hours Remaining to Flow	Percentage of Flow Remaining
0	0.00	24	100.00
1	4.17	23	95.83
2	8.33	22	91.67
3	12.50	21	87.50
4	16.67	20	83.33
5	20.83	19	79.17
6	25.00	18	75.00
7	29.17	17	70.83
8	33.33	16	66.67
9	37.50	15	62.50
10	41.67	14	58.33
11	45.83	13	54.17
12	50.00	12	50.00
13	54.17	11	45.83
14	58.33	10	41.67
15	62.50	9	37.50
16	66.67	8	33.33
17	70.83	7	29.17
18	75.00	6	25.00
19	79.17	5	20.83
20	83.33	4	16.67
21	87.50	3	12.50
22	91.67	2	8.33
23	95.83	1	4.17

Table 22.1
The percentage of a gas day of flow based on the number of hours of flow

Evening cycle nominations are for an entire day's flow of gas, but they are scheduled after the timely nomination cycle. This means that, if a pipeline has capacity constraints, nominations submitted in the evening cycle may not receive the capacity that is being requested. Evening cycle nominations must compete for the remaining available capacity. If a shipper has a firm transportation contract, then that shipper may submit an evening cycle nomination that bumps any previously scheduled interruptible transportation. But that shipper may not bump any firm transportation capacity that has already been scheduled in the timely nomination cycle.

Intraday nominations are for one day[59]. The quantity nominated for an intraday nomination is for a full day of flow, and the pipeline will calculate the quantity available to be delivered in the remaining hours of flow for the day. Because the flow of gas is for a partial gas day, the pipeline requires that a separate nomination, for a full-day flow, must be submitted for subsequent days if additional flow is requested.

Also, in Intraday nominations, gas may be pro-rated to accommodate the available flow for a partial day. There is an important calculation to consider in Intraday nominations and that is for Elapsed Pro-Rated Scheduled Quantity, EPSQ[60]. The EPSQ is that calculated quantity of gas that could have flowed during the period that has already passed. Nominations are submitted as a whole-day quantity. When a shipper submits a Timely nomination for 10,000 DTH and then decides to reduce that quantity to 2,000 DTH in Intraday-2, the EPSQ calculation determines the number of hours that gas has already presumed to have flowed, calculates the percentage of gas that has flowed and determines that the flow of gas cannot be below that calculated level. In the example above, assume that the gas day begins at 9 a.m. The Intraday-2 cycle flow begins at 2 p.m., giving a total number of flow hours of five. Using the table above, the pipeline can see that five hours of flow equates to 20.83 percent. The EPSQ calculation is:

EPSQ = Scheduled Quantity * (Number of Hours that Have Flowed / 24).

In this case, the Number of Hours / 24 = 20.83 percent. 10,000 DTH * 20.83% = 2,083 DTH. This is the lowest quantity to which the pipeline will allow the shipper to reduce the nominated flow. The calculation must take into account the beginning time of the gas day in relationship to the beginning flow of the intraday cycle that the shipper is requesting in order to determine the number of hours that the gas has flowed.

Many pipelines show this calculation and use it as part of the validation in the nomination entry/maintenance screens. Other pipelines use this calculation in the scheduling process to modify the requested nominated quantity. A pipeline may determine that its operational flexibility affords it the ability to bypass EPSQ enforcement. That determination must be made by the pipeline.

The nomination deadline is only one part of the nomination cycle. Several other times are important in each of the nomination cycles.

The Timely cycle, which has a nomination deadline of 1:00 p.m., considers that the nomination may be submitted via EDI or via a flat-file as a form of communication. If the nomination is submitted via EDI, then the pipeline must receive that nomination file within 15 minutes. This 15-minute window allows for communication of the file from the shipper's system to the pipeline's system. The pipeline and its servers determine whether to designate the nomination as received on time. The pipeline assigns a timestamp to the package of nominations at the end of the receipt of the nomination file. This timestamp is then provided back to the sending party (in this case, the shipper or its agent) to inform it of the timestamp that the pipeline has assigned to the transmission. This tells the sending party if the nomination was received in the timely cycle or if it will be considered in the next open cycle.

The pipeline is required to send a Quick Response transaction within the next quarter hour period, for a nomination file[61]. This means that, when a shipper has submitted a timely nomination at 1:00 p.m., the Quick Response must be provided to the shipper by 1:30 p.m. If the nomination was submitted by the shipper prior to 1:00 p.m. for the timely cycle, then that quick response should have been sent during the subsequent quarter-hour period; it is not held until 1:30 p.m. and then sent.

After the pipeline receives all nominations for a given cycle, it begins the confirmations and scheduling process. This process, in the timely cycle, takes place between 1:30 p.m. and 4:30 p.m. There is no prescribed process or method for the timing of the confirmation and scheduling processes within that time period. The pipeline may choose to schedule the flow of gas and then confirm with the interconnecting parties, or the pipeline may choose to confirm flows with the interconnecting parties before scheduling the flow of gas. Some pipelines use an iterative approach during this window, where they confirm the gas on the receipt and delivery sides, balance the transactions, schedule the pipeline, then confirm the flows again. Some pipelines run many of these iterations in this timeline in order to ensure that the best available quantity of gas is resolved at the end of the confirmations/scheduling period. At 4:30 p.m., the last confirmation takes place between the pipeline and the interconnecting parties. Then, in the next half hour, the pipeline must finalize any scheduling cuts and provide a report of the scheduled quantities to both the shipper and to the operators of points interconnecting with the pipeline. The scheduled quantities provided to shippers are provided at the same level of detail as the original nomination[62] while the scheduled quantities provided to operators are provided from a point perspective and are at the level of detail of the confirmation transaction.

Nominations received after the timely nomination cycle deadline may be processed in the timely cycle but must be processed after those nominations that were received before the nomination deadline. [63]

The four additional nomination cycles that occur after the Timely nomination cycle work in much the same manner as the timely cycle. There is a deadline for the EDI transaction to be received by the pipeline; there is a deadline for the Quick Response; there is a deadline for confirmations to be complete and a deadline for when the scheduled quantity must be provided to the shipper/agent and the operator. NAESB WGQ Standard 1.3.2[64] fully describes each of these timelines. For a simple view of these deadlines, refer to the table below:

Cycle	Nominations Due to Pipeline	Nominations via EDI Received	Quick Response due to Shipper	Confirmations Completed by Pipeline	Scheduled Quantity provided to Shipper and Operator	Gas Begins to Flow
Timely	1:00 p.m. on day prior to gas flow	1:15 p.m. on day prior to gas flow	1:30 p.m. on day prior to gas flow	4:30 p.m. on day prior to gas flow	5:00 p.m. on day prior to gas flow	9 a.m. start of next gas day
Evening	6:00 p.m. on day prior to gas flow	6:15 p.m. on day prior to gas flow	6:30 p.m. on day prior to gas flow	8:30 p.m. on day prior to gas flow	9:00 p.m. on day prior to gas flow	9 a.m. start of next gas day
Intraday-1	10:00 a.m. on day of gas flow	10:15 a.m. on day of gas flow	10:30 a.m. on day of gas flow	12:30 p.m. on day of gas flow	1:00 p.m. on day of gas flow	2:00 p.m. on day of gas flow
Intraday-2	2:30 p.m. on day of gas flow	2:45 p.m. on day of gas flow	3:00 p.m.on day of gas flow	5:00 p.m. on day of gas flow	5:30 p.m. on day of gas flow	6:00 p.m. on day of gas flow
Intraday-3	7:00 p.m. on day of gas flow	7:15 p.m. on day of gas flow	7:30 p.m. on day of gas flow	9:30 p.m. on day of gas flow	10:00 p.m. on day of gas flow	10:00 p.m. on day of gas flow

Table 22.2
Nomination cycle deadlines

The standard cycles are mandatory for interstate pipelines. Pipelines may choose to offer cycles in addition to the five standard cycles, so any other cycles must be in addition to those five minimum cycles. When a pipeline chooses to offer additional cycles, the standards contain code values to support the additional cycles identified by the pipeline[65]. The pipeline must, however, provide all of the deadlines within those custom cycles.

23. Title Transfer Tracking (TTT)

The standards for Title Transfer Tracking (TTT) are complex, but the process is relatively straightforward. Historically, TTT was referred to as "daisy chaining" the gas. This meant that the exchange of the title of gas was chained together with the flow of gas to determine who were the ultimate receipt party and ultimate delivery party[66].

TTT is the process by which the TSP tracks the exchange of ownership of gas when it is bought, sold, or exchanged between two or more parties at a location. Interstate pipelines offer TTT services at all pools on the pipeline.

A shipper may receive gas at a receipt point and deliver the gas to a pool on the pipeline, and then sell the gas to a second shipper at the pool. This second shipper at the pool is often a marketer that is managing gas for several clients. The purchasing shipper then sells the gas to a third shipper that becomes the party to transport the gas from the pool to a delivery point on the pipeline. The intermediate shipper that purchases and then sells the gas at the pool may record a TTT transaction on the pipeline.

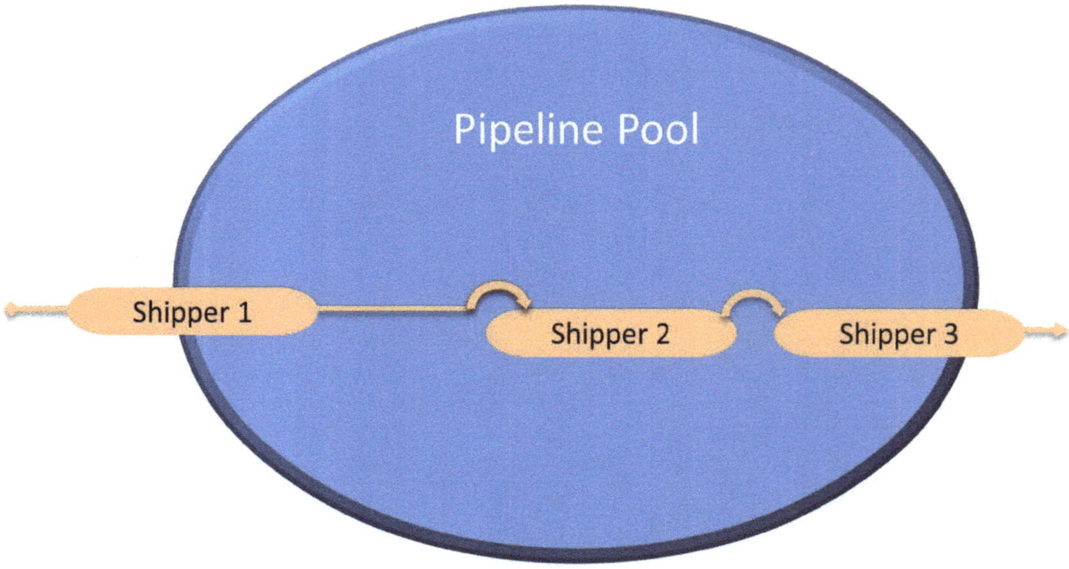

Figure 23.1
Shows title transfers between multiple shippers in a pool

The transporting shipper that delivers the gas to the pool and the transporting shipper that receives gas from the pool are both known entities on the pipeline and therefore receive scheduled quantity and confirmation updates through the normal nomination process. Without the use of a TTT transaction, the shipper at the pool that was buying and selling the gas would receive no scheduled quantities, confirmations, or other communication transactions from the pipeline. Without a TTT transaction, how else would the pipeline match the quantity of gas to all these shippers? If shipper A puts 100 DTH into a pool, but never takes it out and shipper B takes 100 DTH out of the pool that it never put in, how would the pipeline connect these two 100 DTH of gas?

The service of TTT enhances the pipeline's ability to confirm the transfer of gas ownership on the pipeline and to confirm the parties in an expected flow of gas. If all of the parties in the purchase and sale within the flow of gas submit either transportation nominations or TTT nominations to the pipeline, then the pipeline has a complete picture of the ownership of the gas as it travels through the pipeline and has the relationship in place so that it can communicate the status of the flow of gas to all of the parties involved. The TTT nomination is the same type of nomination as a transportation nomination with a nomination transaction type that indicates it is a title transfer. Without the TTT transaction, the pipeline often has to guess at the exchange of ownership of gas at the pool, or the parties have to give the upstream and downstream information pertaining to the ultimate upstream and downstream party as part of the transaction rather than their own information so that the pipeline can confirm the gas.

Pipelines are allowed to charge for the TTT service. They may charge a flat fee for each TTT transaction, or they may charge a volumetric fee tied to the number of DTH in the transaction. When a pipeline does not charge a TTT transaction fee, then it is always in the best interest of the buy/sell party to record the TTT transaction on the pipeline so that it receives its own independent transaction status information for the confirmation, scheduled quantity, allocation, and imbalance of the gas. Many parties do not enter TTT transactions because they are optional, and there are so many other transactions to provide in the gas process. But there is value to both the shipper and the pipeline when these transactions are provided.

There is a requirement that the ability to perform TTT is accessible for all supply-receipt locations. If the supply-receipt location does not have a pool available to it, then the pipeline must provide the ability to conduct TTT at a location.[67]

The TTT Standards

There is a long list of standards that compose the TTT group. The NAESB process for developing the standards was long, arduous, and fraught with peril. The standards can be very confusing when read for the first time. One of the first terms in the TTT standards is that of the title transfer tracking service provider and the third-party account administrator. These two terms are unique to and specific to the TTT standards. The title transfer tracking service provider (TTTSP) is a party that may contract and offer services to buy/sell parties so that those buy/sell parties can submit their nominations to the TTTSP, instead of to the pipeline. This service, theoretically, gives the buy/sell party anonymity in the transaction. The TTTSP has the right to collect and aggregate multiple buy/sell transactions at a pool so that the nomination between the TTTSP and the pipeline is at a higher, summarized level. In this instance, the pipeline will provide the scheduled quantity and subsequent volumes to the TTTSP, and the TTTSP will distribute those reported volumes to the buy/sell parties that it supports. This may mean that the TTTSP has to perform a secondary allocation or other distribution of quantities for the buy/sell parties that it supports.

The third-party account administrator (3PAD) is another term introduced in the TTT process. The 3PAD's role is that of a service provider to the pipeline to provide TTT transaction collection and aggregation services for that pipeline. If a pipeline were to contract with a 3PAD to perform TTT services for it, then buy/sell parties who wished to submit TTT transactions to the pipeline would submit them through the 3PAD instead. This 3PAD service would become a type of operator for the pipeline at that location.

Term	Abbreviation	Description
Title Transfer Tracking	**TTT**	The ability to track the ownership gas through multiple purchase and sale transactions at a single location.
Title Transfer Tracking Service Provider	**TTTSP**	A party who offers a service to shippers whereby the shipper submits its TTT transaction to the 3PAD, and the 3PAD aggregates the transactions into one transaction to submit to the pipeline. The 3PAD transaction, if used by multiple parties, allows intermediate parties to remain undisclosed to the pipeline.
Third Party Account Administrator	**3PAD**	A party who offers the service of managing the TTT process for a pipeline at a location.

Table 23.1
Shows party roles unique to title transfer tracking

When this set of standards was enacted, pipelines elected to conduct TTT services themselves rather than contract with a third party to administer the service. Additionally, as of this writing, there are no known TTTSPs performing TTT service on behalf of buy/sell parties. This means that today buy/sell parties that wish to enter a TTT transaction enter that transaction directly onto the pipeline's system, and pipelines perform the TTT service for themselves.

This gives permission for parties implementing the standards to overlook or bypass the requirements for the TTTSP and the 3PAD roles. [68]

Confirmations

In the history of the natural gas industry, the terms confirmations and scheduling have been used interchangeably. When standards were being written for confirmations and scheduling, the lack of distinction between these terms caused confusion. Participants agreed on which terms would be used in which process. "Confirmations" was selected to designate the interchange between the pipeline and an operator to communicate and confirm transactions that are expected to flow and their associated volumes of gas. "scheduling" was chosen to designate a process whereby the pipeline accumulates all of the quantities that have been nominated and determines, through capacity scheduling and confirmations, which quantities will be able to flow in the next open cycle. The scheduling process for capacity may occur on a pipeline before or after the confirmation process, depending on the operational configuration of that pipeline. In all cases, the culmination of both the confirmation process and the scheduling process results in the scheduled quantity.

Each nomination cycle includes a period of time between when the nomination is due to the pipeline and when the scheduled quantity must be provided back to the shipper and operator. This period of time is set aside for the pipeline to conduct the confirmation process and to schedule the flow of gas on the pipe. There is no rule on how the pipeline segments this block of time. Some pipelines schedule the pipe, confirm with interconnecting parties, and then run the scheduling process again. Other pipelines conduct multiple confirmation iterations and then schedule the pipeline. The only restriction is that the process must be complete in order to provide the scheduled quantities to the shippers and operators at the end of the time allotted.

The confirmations process takes place between a pipeline and an operator at a location. The operator may be the other interconnecting pipeline at that location or may be a third-party contracted to operate the location. The confirmation process allows operators to compare transaction information and to determine the gas that can and should flow across the location. When transactions are confirmed, this means that the delivery of gas on the upstream side of the location has been matched to the receipt of gas on the downstream side of the location. This is often a multi-part match in that there may be multiple transactions on the upstream side that match to a single transaction on the downstream side; or, the reverse, there may be one transaction on the upstream side that matches to multiple transactions on the downstream side. Unless TTT services are performed at the location, the downstream parties listed on the delivering pipeline should be the same parties listed as shippers on the receiving pipeline, and the upstream parties listed on the receiving pipeline should be the listed shippers on the delivering pipeline.[69]

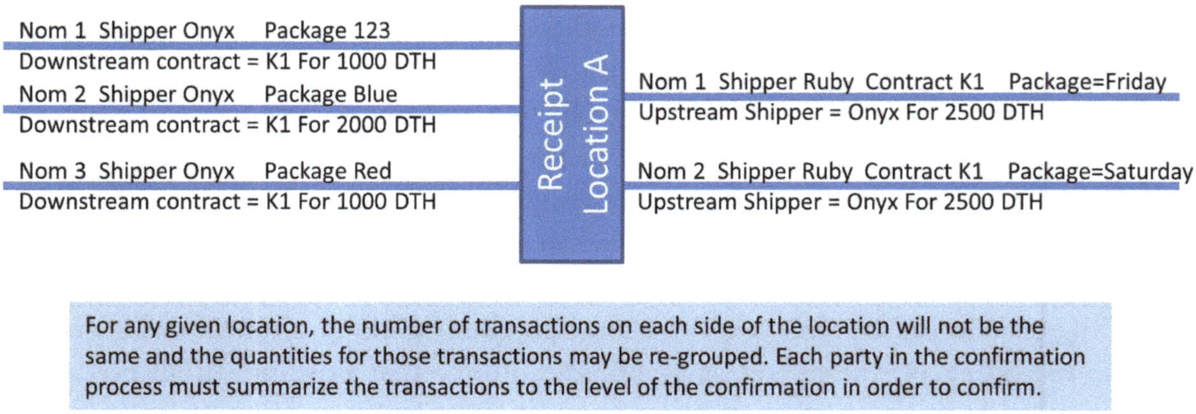

Figure 24.0
How the number of nominations on each side of an interconnect location may not perfectly align

24. Datasets

The NAESB WGQ standards 1.4.3, 1.4.4, and 1.4.7[70] contain the supporting transaction sets for the confirmation process.

Standard 1.4.3[71] contains the Request for Confirmation. This dataset is used to initiate the confirmation process from one of the parties at the interconnected point. The request for confirmation may be initiated by either of the interconnected parties at a location. It is the responsibility of both of the parties to initiate the confirmation process if there is not mutual agreement on which party will initiate the process. In most cases, two pipelines agree that one of the pipelines will always be the initiating party, and the other will always be the confirming party. In the absence of an agreement, both parties are responsible to initiate the process.

The request for confirmation dataset contains the data elements related to both the receipt side and the delivery side of the nomination. Since the confirmation process takes place at a location, the confirmation requester, in initiating the transaction, will send information on the delivery side of the nomination when the gas is being confirmed at a delivery location for that party, and will send information on the receipt side of the nomination when the gas is being confirmed at a receipt location for that party. The request for confirmation does not contain all of the information in a nomination; however, it may contain information as detailed as the package ID number. The operator initiating the confirmation process must determine the level of detail of the confirmation at that location.

Standard 1.4.4[72] contains the confirmation response, which the confirming party sends in response to a request for confirmation. The confirming party may also send an unsolicited confirmation response when it needs to initiate a change in the confirmation. The confirmation response contains the same level of detail as the request for confirmation or is sent at a predetermined level of detail when the confirmation response is unsolicited. The confirmation response tells the confirmation requester the quantity that the confirming party expects to deliver or to receive (depending on the point of view) at the location for each of the transactions that the request for confirmation contained. The confirming party may also add new line-item transactions into the confirmation response that were not part of the original request for confirmation. This occurs when transactions are mismatched or when a nominating party on one side of the location has entered in nominations that do not have a matching nomination on the other side of the location.

Standard 1.4.5[73], in EDI, contains the confirmation quick response. This dataset captures any validation errors or messages between the parties and conveys those validation errors or messages to the other party. The confirmation quick response performs much like the nomination quick response. It provides validation error and warning codes and messages that tell the sender of the information that one or more pieces of data contained in the transmission were unable to be processed. The only information returned in the confirmation quick response is either a reference to the confirmation tracking ID saying that it was accepted, or a reference to the confirmation tracking ID saying that it was rejected or had warnings followed by the relevant error and warning information.

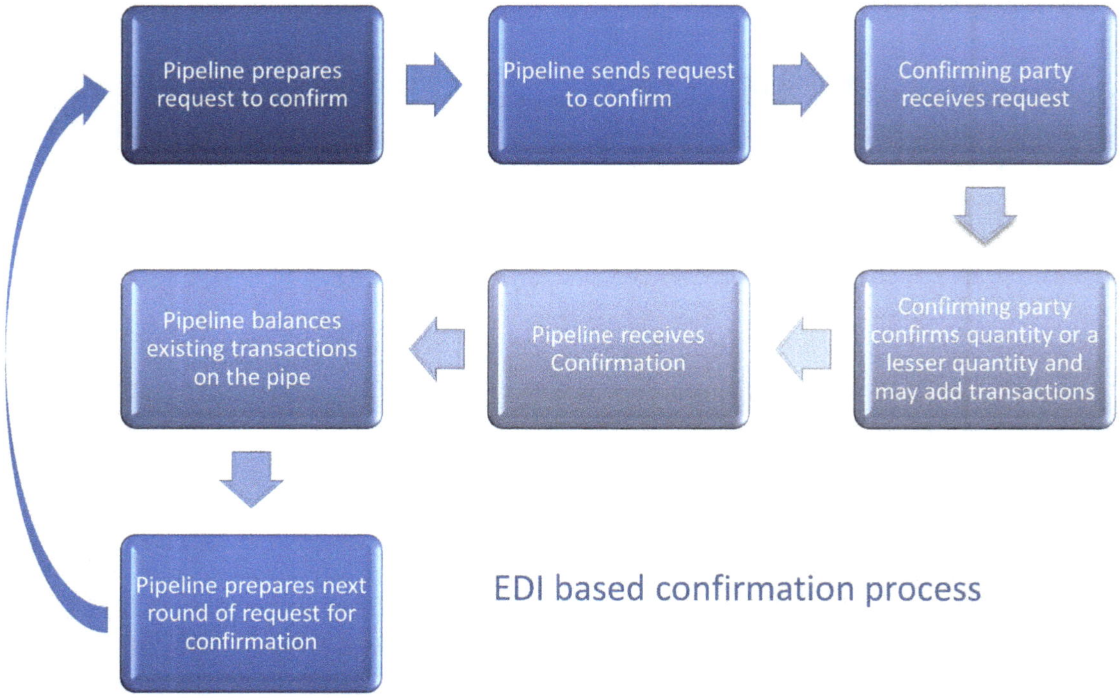

Figure 24.1
The flow of the EDI-based confirmation process

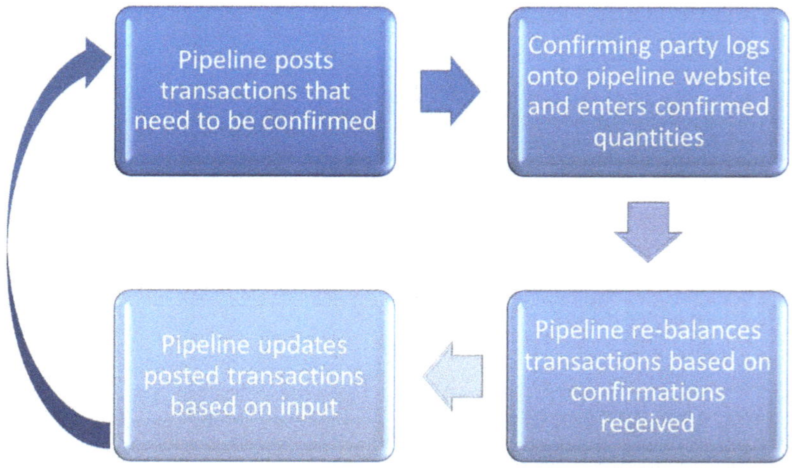

Figure 24.2
The web-based confirmation process flow where the pipeline is the confirmation requester

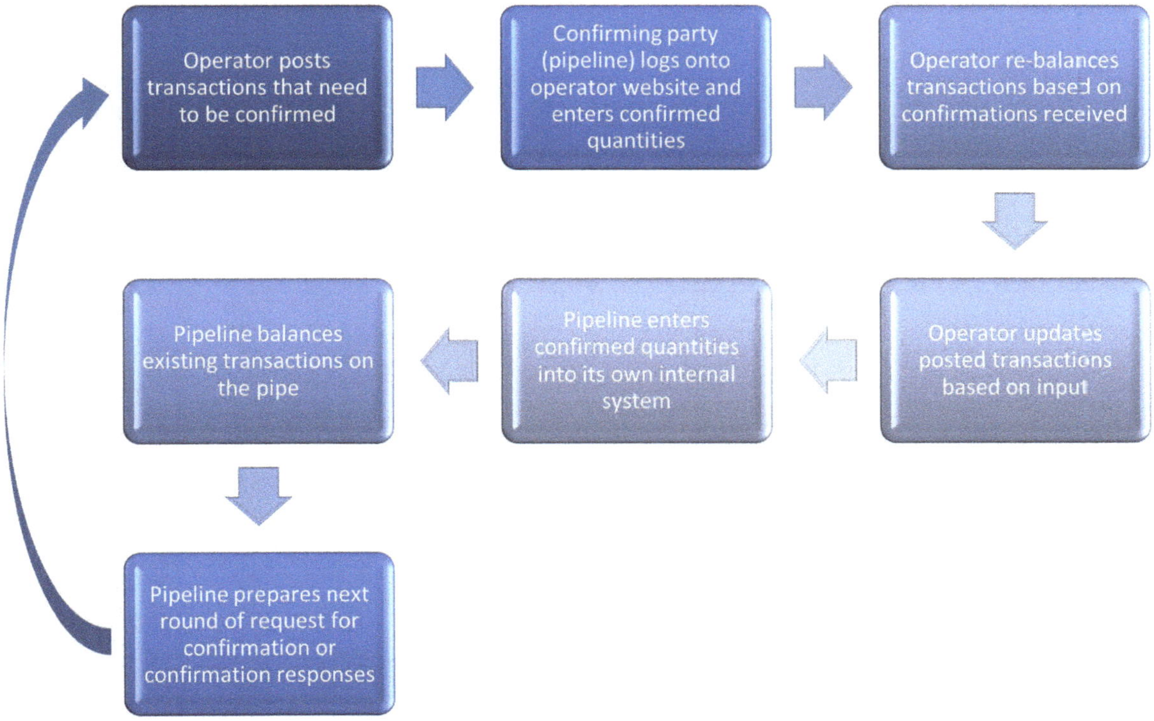

Figure 24.3
The web-based confirmation process flow where the pipeline provides the confirmation response

Confirmations conducted on a web screen are generally resolved in one interaction between the pipeline and the operator. A pipeline seeking confirmation from an operator will present the list of transactions that it has received for a location in a view on a web screen, and the operator will confirm the nominated quantity or a lesser quantity for the transaction. Additionally, the pipeline should allow the operator the opportunity to enter confirmation line items into the web screen for an equivalent process to the unsolicited confirmation transactions described above. The pipeline and operator accomplish the same business process transactions as those described in the three EDI datasets above by the pipeline presenting the view of the confirmable transactions on a web view for the operator, and by the operator providing the confirmed quantities and submitting them to the pipeline. Note that when an operator provides the confirmed quantities on a pipeline's web site, then the operator will have to maintain those same quantities in the operator's system for the operator's subsequent processes to proceed. The EDI process described above resolves this by having the computers of each party communicating the information already contained in those party's systems. In either case, the end result should be that each party at the location contains the same total quantities for the transactions on its side of that location.

El Paso Confirmation Case Scenario by Mike Stender

With the adoption of the NAESB 1.4 Standards by the FERC, El Paso Natural Gas (EPNG) was required to make available the EDI X12 Confirmation process to its interconnecting pipelines. EPNG already had an X12 team in place, so it was not an unknown to them. That was not the case for all of the interconnecting pipelines. It was the case for all the interconnecting parties. The federally regulated pipelines have a process in place for receiving and sending X12 documents because of prior regulation.

The standards also changed the timeline for the confirmation process. The process needed to be completed in four hours. Before this, the nomination/confirmation process for one day's gas flow was a multiple-day routine.

One of the benefits was that EPNG could confirm with the interconnecting without logging on to the interconnecting party's website to confirm. EPNG had a file transfer process in place before this time so the concept was not new to them.

EPNG started working with its western interconnects some regulated and some non-regulated. The first process was to establish communications. The communications used the HTTP protocol. Not everyone interpreted them the same.

Using the X12 datasets created by GISB had some challenges. The standards were not "hard" standards. Confirmation could be processed at different levels. One level, entity, was not a standard as to what the data was other than customer identification. EPNG could confirm at the entity/contract/package level. Some interconnects used only the entity/contract level and others only the entity level. The standards allowed interconnect to use the higher levels so those using the multiple levels needed to sum up to the higher level.

Because entity was a key data element in making a confirmation unique, the entity data needed to be the same when the matching was completed. Different methods were used. Some interconnects ignored the data element. Others created a substitution process. Later GISB defined "entity"as a DUNS number (need footnote). It also became an education process for the nomination customer. The customer entered the data on both pipelines. They needed to enter the same data on both pipelines. The entity and contract entered for the delivering information needed to be same on both pipelines and the receiving information needed to be the same information on both pipelines.

There were multiple datasets used in the confirmation process. Request for Confirmation (RQCF), Confirmation Response (RRFC), and Scheduled Quantities for Operators (SQOP). Later the Confirmation Quick Response (CRQR) was added. The interconnecting parties needed to determine which party sent which dataset. Some parties could only send or receive one type of dataset. EPNG had interconnects that could only send the RRFCs and receive nothing. It was a process of learning what capabilities the interconnecting party had and what they wanted. Working through those first years was a challenge.

NNG Confirmation Case Scenario by Micki Hoffee

As mentioned in the EPNG scenario, the initial years of EDI confirmations were certainly a challenge. While the process is now more familiar and commonplace amongst interconnecting parties, there are two major questions to answer before pursuing the exchange of data.

Which party will initiate the process? And at what level of detail will we transact?

In the case of Northern Natural Gas (NNG), the Request for Confirmation (RQCF) is an inbound transaction, meaning the confirmation process is initiated by the interconnecting pipeline, such as EPNG.

The preferred level of detail for NNG is entity/contract level. While this has been fairly standard and readily available for most interconnecting pipelines, there have been a few for which some creative data entry and data mapping has been necessary to capture the necessary level of detail.

By using three ANSI ASC X12 datasets, the EDI confirmations process is virtually seamless. Through the RQCF, the initiating party communicates its desired detail and quantities. The confirming party first responds with Confirmation Quick Response (CRQR) to communicate any data failures, followed by the Confirmation Response (RRFC) to communicate desired quantities, including any operational reduction reasons. The initiating party may then choose to communicate any data failures or errors relevant to the RRFC back to the confirming party via CRQR.

While the initial setup and testing can sometimes be tricky, for NNG the outcome is well worth the effort. Transacting confirmations electronically via "EDI" has proven to be an accurate, efficient, and time-saving venture.

25. Business Flow

On a single pipeline, that pipeline may have the role of confirmation requester on some locations and confirming party on other locations. From a website perspective, when the pipeline is the confirmation requester, then it presents on its website all of the transactions that the operator should be prepared to confirm; the expectation is that the operator will log onto the pipeline's website and confirm or cut the transactions that the pipeline has received. In this scenario, the pipeline should also offer the capability for the operator to enter an unsolicited confirmation onto the pipeline.

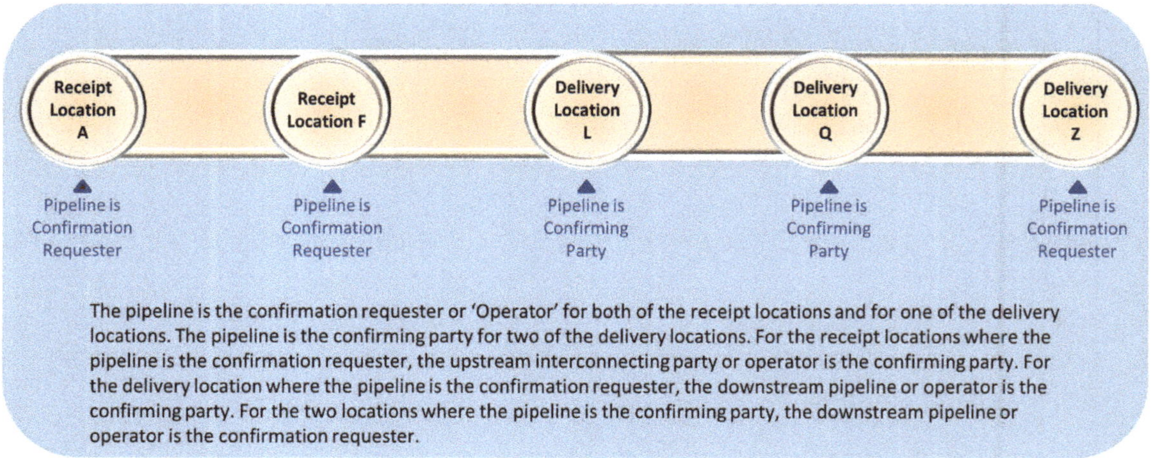

Figure 25.1
A pipeline may be the confirmation requester or the confirming party at different locations on the pipeline.

The operator receives the information on all of the entered transactions to be delivered-to and received-from a single location. This information may be at a very detailed level of information, equivalent to a nomination level of detail, or it may be at a higher level of detail, such as shipper contract, depending on the terms of confirmation for that operator. The operator then matches the transactions on each side of the location to determine which transactions have corresponding transactions on the other side of the location.

Unmatched transactions can be cut to zero by the operator because the pipeline receiving the unmatched transaction does not want to receive gas from an unknown shipper, and the pipeline delivering the unmatched transaction does not want to deliver gas where there is no one to receive it.

Mismatched quantities at a location, that are not confirmed, are reduced to their lowest common quantity. This is explained more thoroughly in the lesser-of-rule process described in a later chapter of this section.

The confirmation process may be an iterative process. During the confirmation and scheduling window of a cycle, a pipeline operator may issue the request for confirmation multiple times because the request for confirmation is sent out at the same time for both receipt and delivery points on transactions, and, when responses are received, they will cause adjustments to the nominations that now need to be reconfirmed at those locations. Some pipelines issue the request for confirmation at the beginning of the confirmation window and only send a new request for confirmation when there is a change in the quantity expected. Other pipelines have a schedule where they send the request for confirmation at scheduled intervals in the confirmation cycle. The decision on whether to conduct iterative confirmations is made by the confirmation requester. The confirming party always has the right to submit an unsolicited confirmation during the confirming and scheduling window of the open cycle.

Confirmations Example:

Nominations	From	Contract	To	Qty
Nomination 1	Rec A	K1	Del Q	1000 DTH
Nomination 2	Rec A	K2	Del S	5000 DTH
Nomination 3	Rec B	K3	Del Q	2000 DTH
Nomination 4	Rec B	K4	Del S	3000 DTH

Quantities to be Confirmed:

Rec A	1000 DTH for K1
	5000 DTH for K2
Rec B	2000 DTH for K3
	3000 DTH for K4
Del Q	1000 DTH for K1
	2000 DTH for K3
Del S	5000 DTH for K2
	3000 DTH for K4

Note: This scenario could be shown with the pipeline as the initiator of the confirmation process or with the pipeline as the responder (aka confirming party) to the confirmation or a combination of the two. For this example, we will show the pipeline as the initiator on the delivery side and the respondent on the receipt side.

Example 25.1
An example of the confirmation data exchanged between two parties

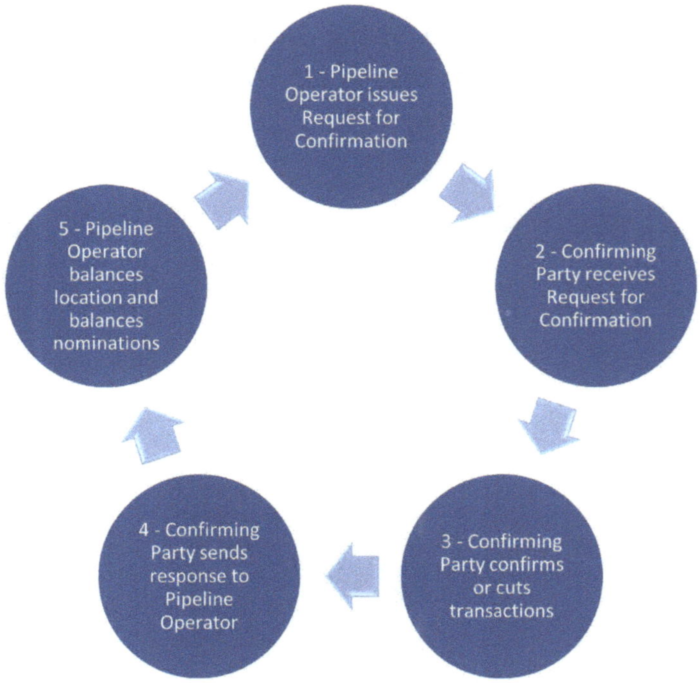

Step 1- When the pipeline operator issues the request for confirmation, the request is for both the receipt-location confirming party and the delivery-location confirming party.
Step 3 – If the delivery location confirming party responds with a reduction on a transaction, then the pipeline operator will balance the nomination in Step 5 and may issue a new request via Step 1 to the corresponding receipt-location confirming party.

Figure 25.2
The business process flow of the iterative confirmation process

This is an example of a simple confirmation cycle process. A true confirmation cycle would contain many more combinations of receipt/delivery locations and many more transactions.

Step 1 – Pipeline posts transactions for Del Q and Del S on website for the confirming party to confirm.

Step 2 – Pipeline accesses web site for Rec A and Rec B to confirm the quantities.

Rec A confirmation request contains:
900 DTH for K1 as the Downstream
5000 DTH for K2 as the Downstream
Pipeline confirms 900 DTH for K1 and 5000 DTH for K2

Rec B confirmation request contains:
2000 DTH for K3
3000 DTH for K4
Pipeline confirms both original quantities.

Step 3 – Pipeline balances Nomination 1 to reduce quantity from 1000 DTH to 900 DTH per the confirmation.

Step 4 – Pipeline re-posts transaction for Del Q with a revised number for the delivery for K1 to 900 DTH.

Step 5 – Pipeline receives confirmation for Del Q and Del S

Del Q confirmation contains:
1000 DTH for K1 as Upstream
2000 DTH for K3 as Upstream

Del S confirmation contains:
4000 DTH for K2 as Upstream
3000 DTH for K4 as Upstream

Step 6 – Pipeline balances Nomination 2 to reduce receipt quantity from 5000 DTH to 4000 DTH per the confirmation.

Step 7 – Pipeline re-confirms Rec A with updated quantities per the confirmation.

Example 25.2
The confirmation data in Example 25.1 applied to the business-process flow in Figure 25.2

There is always a chance that the confirmed quantity will change at the last minute of the confirmation and scheduling window, and the parties will not have enough time in the timeline to confirm the transaction again. In this case, the operator and the shippers will rely on the pipeline's scheduled quantity for the final result. The last quantity that a confirmation requester or confirming party receives in the confirmation process cannot be assumed to be the final quantity.

26. Confirmation Method Options

Pipelines may use several different confirmation methods. At a single location, a pipeline may use an explicit confirmation, an auto-confirmation, a confirmation-by-exception, or a standing confirmation method.

The explicit confirmation method[74] is the one that has been used in the examples above in this chapter. An explicit confirmation is used by an operator that supplies a confirmed quantity in response to a confirmation request.

Some pipelines offer a confirmation-by-exception service[75] which is an agreement between the two interconnected parties where any nomination that is entered for that location is automatically assumed to be confirmed so that the pipeline may proceed with the scheduling process. This process is often used at a location that is a receipt point from a single producer or a delivery point to a single consumer. In this case, the assumption is that the nomination comes from that same party; therefore, that same party does not need to enter a secondary transaction to confirm the gas. The confirmation-by-exception service allows the operator to come onto the pipeline and provide a different quantity than was nominated. In this case, the operator is monitoring the nominations that were entered and confirmed but only has to take action when the operator's quantity should be different than what was nominated.

Many pipelines offer the capability for an operator to enter in a standing confirmation. This standing confirmation is often associated with production points where the flow is expected to be relatively constant and there are contracted parties that will be taking the gas on a long-term basis. This standing confirmation is entered on a prospective basis for a period of time in the future agreed to between the pipeline and the operator. In the case where there is a change in the flow or the parties, the operator can provide that change to the pipeline within the confirmation window of the open cycle.

27. The Lesser of-Rule

The lesser-of-rule outlines the decisions that a pipeline and operator must make when the quantities in the confirmation process do not match or there is no confirmation received for a transaction[76].

In the timely nomination cycle, when the confirmation process is complete, if the two quantities do not match, then the lesser quantity is the quantity that becomes the confirmed quantity. In this same cycle, when no response to the request for confirmation is received, then the lesser of either the confirmation quantity or the previously scheduled quantity should be the new confirmed quantity. This assumes that, at a minimum, the previously scheduled quantity gives a valid indication of the next day's expected gas flow.

Example 1

	Nominated	Confirmed
Nomination 1 at Receipt Location A	1000 DTH	1200 DTH
Nomination 2 at Receipt Location A	2000 DTH	1400 DTH

In this example, using the lesser-of rule, the pipeline will cut Nomination 1 to the original nominated quantity of 1000 DTH, and the pipeline will cut Nomination 2 to the confirmed quantity of 1400 DTH.

Example 2

	Nominated	Confirmed
Nomination 1 at Receipt Location A	1000 DTH	none
Nomination 2 at Receipt Location A	2000 DTH	none

In this example, where no confirmation is received, the pipeline will use the previous day's scheduled quantity as the confirmed quantity for these transactions.

Example 27.1
Examples of the lesser-of rule applied

In the confirmation process on the intraday cycles, there are separate rules for requests for increases and requests for decreases in quantity. For requests for increases, the same lesser-of-quantity choice applies when a confirmation is received, and, when no response to the request for confirmation is received, the previously scheduled quantity is retained. For requests for decreases, the same lesser-of-quantity choice applies when a confirmation is received with the exception that the elapsed-prorated-scheduled quantity should be the minimum resolved quantity if it applies. This rule applies in the case of a received confirmation and in the case of no response.

The elapsed-prorated-scheduled quantity is that quantity which is presumed to have flowed on a pro-rata basis during the hours of the gas day that have elapsed prior to this change in flow. This calculation is explained in more detail in the Chapter for Cycles and Intraday.

When a nominated quantity is cut because of the confirmation process, the pipeline is required to provide the shipper, via the schedule quantity document, with a reduction-reason code/explanation of the reason. There is a standard list of required values for these cuts when the cuts are the result of a party's failure to perform in the confirmation process.

Lesser Of Rule by Jim Buccigross

Flow Day Redirects generally affect pipelines that have no excess capacity and have a constraint at a point on the pipeline. Shippers requested that pipelines allow them to change either the delivery point or the receipt point and maintain their capacity on the pipeline. In response, pipelines agreed to a new standard that allowed an exception to the NAESB standard that requires that any change to a nomination be considered a new nomination.

In most cases that the firm shipper requires redirected flow, his circumstances have changed. The shipper needs to change his nomination for a number of reasons: loss of supply, changes in supply, new requirements to deliver gas to his city gate, or to inject excess gas into storage. In any case, the shipper could incur an imbalance penalty on the pipeline by not receiving or delivering gas in accordance with the original nomination. Additionally, the shipper could be penalized for not delivering gas in the contracted quantities.

Any change to a nomination is considered a new nomination per NAESB Std. No.1.3.7. A new nomination does not have the same priority because it is not considered timely. The Redirect standard (NAESB Std. No. 1.3.80) allows an exception to Std. No. 1.3.7. This redirect standard is useful in the following conditions:

1. Pipeline has a constraint at point on the pipeline and will allow no increases in volume through the constraint point.
2. There is no additional capacity on the pipeline and there is no interruptible capacity that could be bumped by the firm shipper with a new nomination.
3. The shipper already has firm capacity through the constraint point and changes to either the delivery point or the receipt point would not increase the capacity through the point or cause operational problems for the pipeline.
4. The change in the nomination will not increase in volume through the point, the shipper's contract MDQ is not exceeded, the pipeline can operationally accommodate the change in point and the new receipt or delivery point operator confirms that shipper's quantity is available.

28. Confirmations and the EDI process

The EDI process of confirmations is different because, unlike the other transactions, the confirmation process takes place between two interconnected pipelines or between a pipeline and an operator instead of between a pipeline and its customers. Because this is considered a pipeline-to-pipeline exchange of information, pipelines are required to be able to support the process, if requested, but a pipeline is not mandated to contact another pipeline and ask it to engage in the EDI transaction. As EDI processes have evolved and matured, pipelines have now begun implementing the confirmation process between each other as an efficient means of communication. By implementing the EDI process, pipelines can develop an automated process, using the confirmation rules, to set and respond to the confirmation request without the need for personnel at one pipeline company signing on to the website of the other pipeline company and manually entering the confirmed response. This is one of the few processes in the standards where the pipelines can take advantage of the EDI processes to make their own business processes and interactions more efficient.

Scheduling

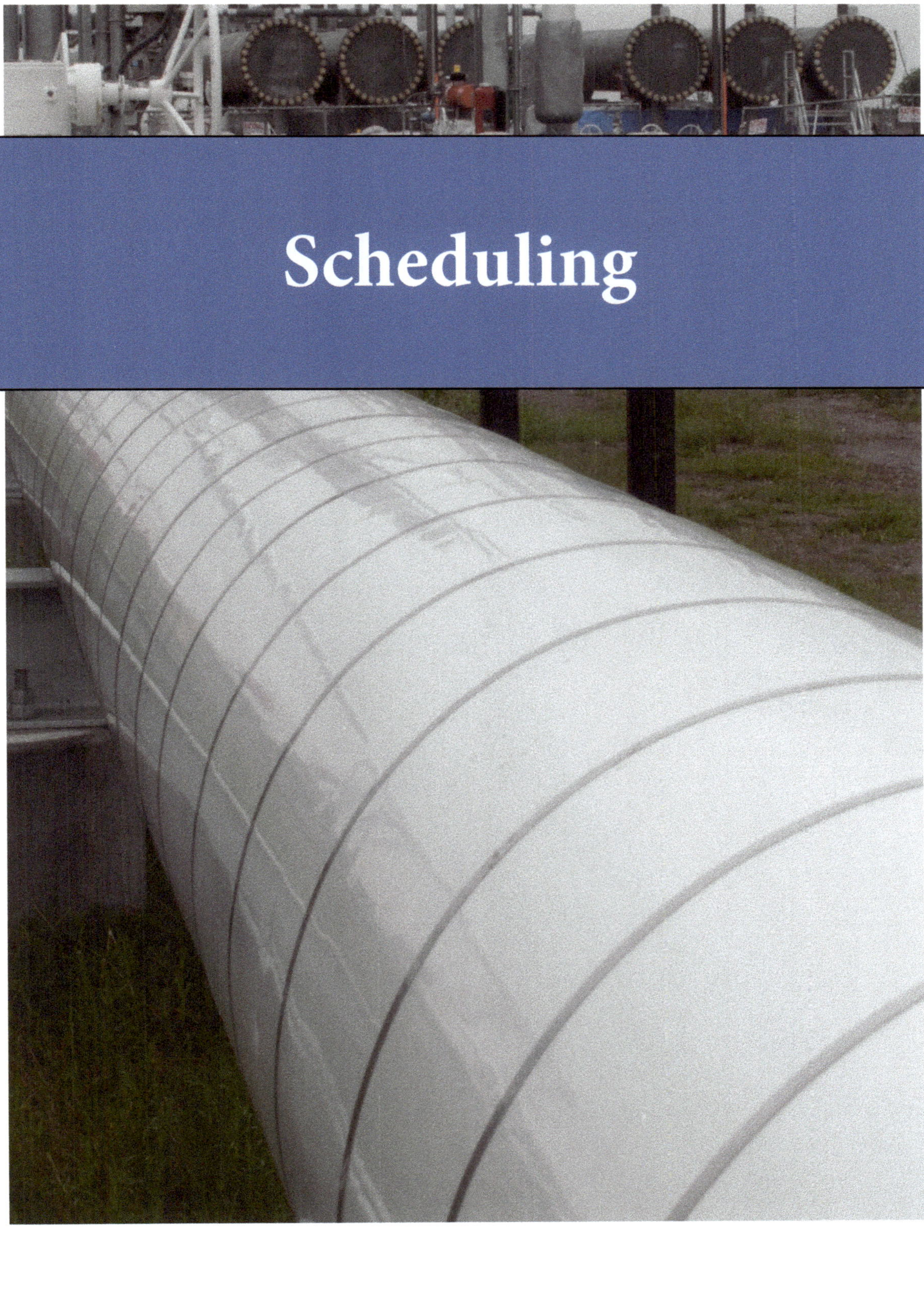

Scheduling is one of the most important business processes on a pipeline system. The scheduling process determines how much gas can flow through each location and through each section of pipe for a given cycle. The scheduling process takes place when the pipeline compares the available operational capacity to the nominations that were confirmed and determines which and how much of those requested quantities will be able to flow. The pipeline must employ rules from its tariff, regulatory rules, and information from the operator and shipper in order to conduct the scheduling process[77].

The scheduling process draws on the rules for scheduling that each pipeline provides in its General Terms and Conditions of its tariff. Within those rules, the pipeline will state that firm service is scheduled ahead of interruptible service and which transaction priority it gives to authorized overruns, imbalance paybacks, and other transactions. In addition to the tariff rules, the pipeline needs the following information to conduct the scheduling process:

- Nominations and nomination ranks
- Confirmed quantities
- Contract terms
- Meter outages
- Pipeline capacity
- Capacity constraints
- Nomination model type
- Operational priorities

A pipeline uses the constraints of operational priorities to determine whether it will schedule receipt locations first and push the results, via the nominations, down to the delivery points; or it will schedule the delivery locations first and push those results up to the receipt points; or it has other locations on the pipeline scheduled first, such as critical constraints or junctions, and then the results are pushed upstream to the receipts and downstream to the deliveries. Each pipeline, on an individual basis, must determine these operational priorities for scheduling.

The scheduling process results in the determination of balanced nominations and their associated scheduled quantities that are provided back to the nominating parties at the end of the scheduling process. It also results in the determination of balanced locations and their associated scheduled quantities that are provided back to the operating parties at the end of the same scheduling process.

The scheduling standards[78] address, primarily, the treatment of the quantities and transactions after the pipeline's gas scheduling process has been completed.

29. Cut Method Rules and Ranks

Each pipeline tariff has a stated list of the classifications of services and the order that is used to fill the pipeline capacity in the scheduling process. The general overarching order is that firm transportation goes first and interruptible transportation goes second. Within these two simple boundaries, the pipeline must consider a host of service levels. The pipeline determines how these services are scheduled. When all other services are equal, the pipeline sometimes needs to make cuts within a classification. Examples of different methods for scheduling inside of a class include:

- The oldest contract start date takes priority over newer contracts.
- The highest price for the transportation takes priority over lower prices.
- The nomination with the earliest timestamp takes priority.
- The nomination with the highest quantity is cut first (to reduce the number of cuts).
- All nominations are cut pro-rata.

There are other methods, and these are representative examples. Once the scheduling process has taken the transactions down to a shipper-contract level, the shipper may have multiple nominations at this location for this contract. If the shipper has provided ranks, then the pipeline will use the shipper-provided ranking to determine which of the shipper's nominations to cut first (lowest rank) or to cut last (highest rank). Often, there are so many layers and rules within the pipeline's scheduling priorities that the shipper-provided ranks are not used in the scheduling process because the transaction level cut is resolved before the ranks are utilized.

30. Model Considerations

The chapter on Nominations extensively describes use of the nomination model types. The model types also play an important role in the scheduling process of the pipeline.

When a pipeline determines that a cut must occur at the delivery point, whether that cut is through the confirmation process or through a scheduling constraint, then the pipeline must determine which of the nominations at that point will receive the reduction. Once the reduction has been narrowed down to a shipper-contract combination, the pipeline must determine which of the nominations associated with that shipper-contract combination will be cut.

When nominations are submitted using a pathed model type, then the nominations associated with this shipper-contract can be reviewed and the ranks assigned by the shipper will be used to determine which nomination gets cut first, meaning which nomination has the lowest rank. If the shipper has not provided ranks, then the pipeline uses the default method, of a pro–rata cut.

If the shipper submits its nominations using a non-pathed model type, then the nominations associated with this shipper-contract can be reviewed and the ranks assigned by the shipper on both the receipt side transactions and delivery side transactions will be evaluated separately and the lowest ranked receipt nomination and delivery nomination will be cut first. Like the pathed model, if the shipper has not provided ranks then the pipeline will use the default method of pro-rata to make the cut.

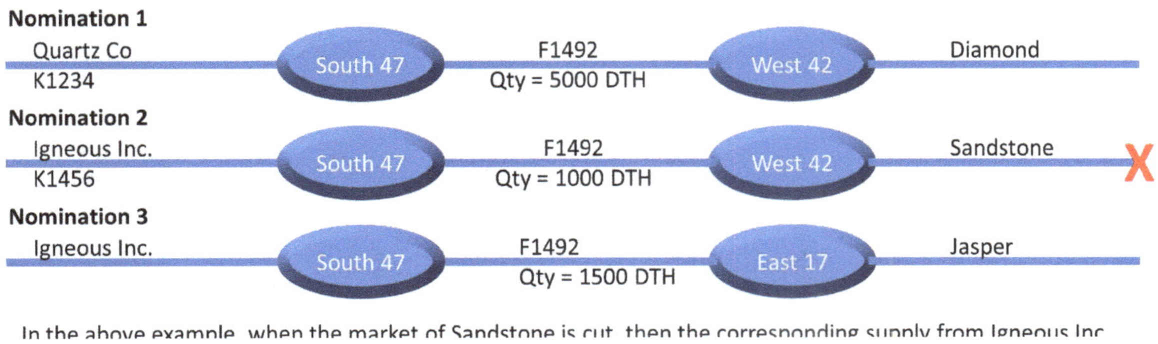

Figure 30.1
The results of a scheduling cut on a pathed model nomination

In the above example, when the market of Sandstone is cut, then the corresponding supply from Igneous Inc for 1000 DTH is also cut.

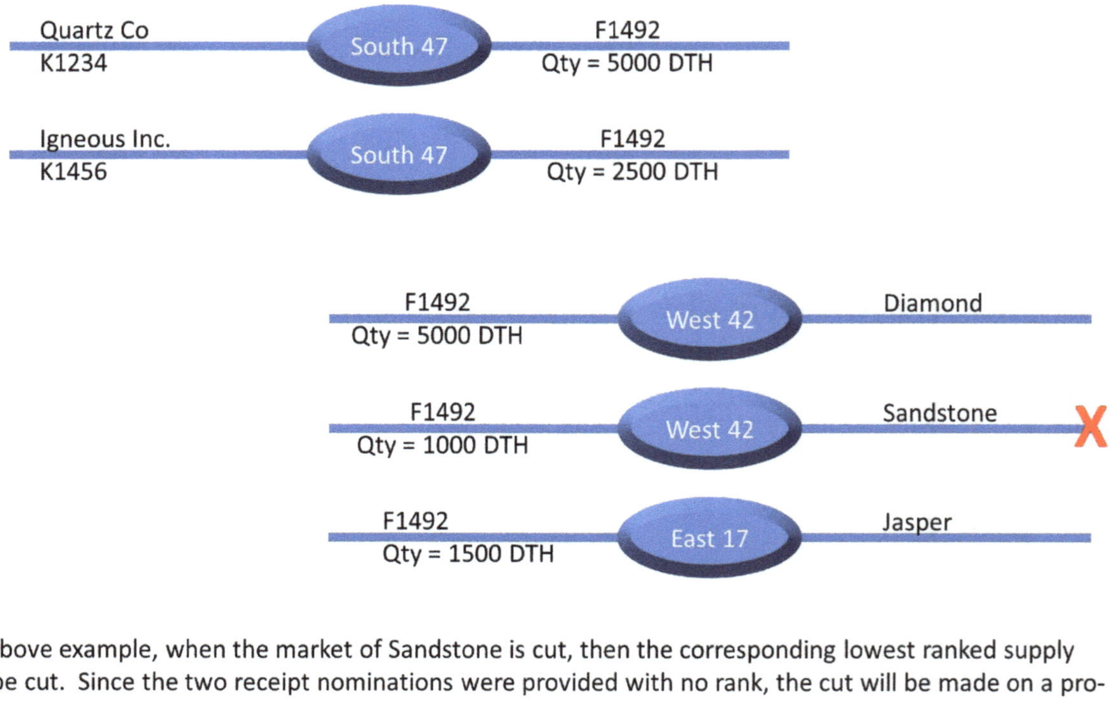

Figure 30.2
The results of a scheduling cut on a non-pathed model nomination

In the above example, when the market of Sandstone is cut, then the corresponding lowest ranked supply would be cut. Since two receipt nominations were provided with no rank, the cut will be made on a pro-rata basis. Quartz will be cut by 667 and Igneous will be cut by 333.

If the shipper submits its nominations using a pathed non-threaded model, where the downstream-market transactions and the upstream-supply transactions are not directly associated with the contract, then the ranks of those upstream and downstream transactions are used. It is important to note that the ranks across the contracts are being cut, and the transactions are not directly associated with the contract. Again, the chapter on nomination model types explains this thoroughly and has a comprehensive example of the PNT model results in the scheduling process.

31. Flow-Day Redirects

NAESB WGQ Standard 1.3.80[79] refers to "flow-day redirects."[80] This single standard carries with it a very large processing requirement. In a flow-day redirect, a shipper will submit an original nomination and receive a scheduled quantity assigned to that nomination. With this nomination, the pipeline and shipper recognize that the flow of gas travels through a point of constraint on the pipeline. When the shipper decides to change the nomination, in a subsequent cycle, to move the current receipt point to a new receipt point or to move the current delivery point to a new delivery point, the shipper must ensure that the capacity that was previously scheduled through the point of constraint is retained as scheduled capacity and not rescheduled.

The standard instructs the pipeline that the shipper has a right to retain this capacity if it moves either the receipt location or the delivery location on the existing nomination. A shipper cannot change a nomination key without creating a new nomination, and the receipt and delivery locations are both part of the nomination key. When the key remains the same, all nominations are considered to be new nominations that replace the previous nomination. In this instance, when a shipper chooses to change the receipt location, and resubmits the nomination, the pipeline will not recognize the nomination as a change to the previous nomination because the keys do not match as the receipt location has been changed. In order to support the capability of the flow-day redirect, the pipeline must recognize that, when the shipper changes the quantity to zero on an existing nomination through the point of constraint and then creates a new nomination going through the same point of constraint with the same or lesser quantity, it must consider the new nomination a "flow-day redirect" of the original scheduled nomination. A pipeline uses a mechanism based on its business practices to determine that this service is being requested. Some pipelines may use the nomination-transaction type[81] to identify the redirect nomination. Other pipelines may choose to calculate a scheduled inventory for each shipper through the point of constraint and limit the total of the shipper's nominations through the point of constraint to that scheduled inventory so that shipper can re-nominate freely through the point of constraint and safely retain its scheduled capacity rights.

Shipper Original Timely Nomination:

Receipt Location	Transport Contract	Delivery Location	Nomination Quantity
D	K1234	Q	3000

Scheduled Quantity – Timely Cycle:

D	K1234	Q	2800

Note: This gives the shipper an allocated scheduled capacity of 2800 at Location

Shipper replacement nominations:

D	K1234	Q	0
A	K1234	Q	2800

Note: Because the shipper had allocated scheduled capacity through the point of constraint, Location L, the shipper is granted the change. The shipper could also have reduced the quantity from Location D to Q and moved a portion of the nomination to Location A

Example 31.1
An example of nominations entered during a flow-day redirect transaction

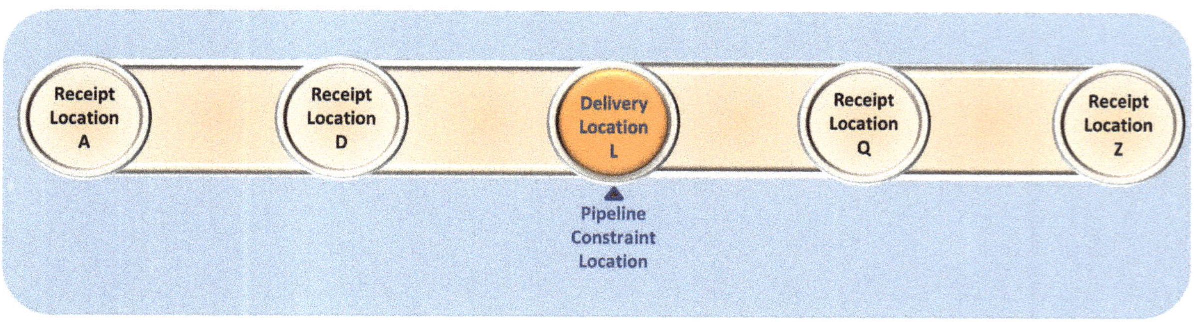

Figure 31.1
A constraint at a location on the pipeline for the described example

For example, suppose the shipper submits a nomination receiving gas at point D to deliver at point Q on the pipeline. In this example, point L is a flow constraint on the pipeline. Now the shipper wants to re-nominate the scheduled capacity and receive the gas at point A, upstream of point D, instead of point D. When the shipper re-nominates from point A, he retains his scheduled capacity through point L, and redirects that scheduled capacity right from the original nomination to the new nomination.

Flow Day Redirects by Kathryn Burch

Flow Day Redirects generally affect pipelines that have no excess capacity and have a constraint at a point on the pipeline. Shippers requested that pipelines allow them to change either the delivery point or the receipt point and maintain their capacity on the pipeline. In response, pipelines agreed to a new standard that allowed an exception to the NAESB standard that requires that any change to a nomination be considered a new nomination.

In most cases that the firm shipper requires redirected flow, its circumstances have changed. The shipper needs to change its nomination for a number of reasons: loss of supply, changes in supply, or new requirements to deliver gas to its city gate or to inject excess gas into storage. In any case, the shipper could incur an imbalance penalty on the pipeline by not receiving or delivering gas in accordance with the original nomination. Additionally, the shipper could be penalized for not delivering gas in the contracted quantities.

Any change to a nomination is considered a new nomination per NAESB WGQ Standard 1.3.7. A new nomination does not have the same priority because it is not considered timely. The Redirect standard (NAESB WGQ Standard 1.3.80) allows an exception NAESB WGQ Standard 1.3.7. This redirect standard is useful in the following conditions:

1. Pipeline has a constraint at point on the pipeline and will allow no increases in volume through the constraint point.
2. There is no additional capacity on the pipeline, and there is no Interruptible capacity that could be bumped by the firm shipper with a new nomination.
3. The shipper already has firm capacity through the constraint point and changes to either the delivery point or the receipt point would not increase the capacity through the point or cause operational problems for the pipeline.
4. The change in the nomination will not increase in volume through the point, the shipper's contract MDQ is not exceeded, the pipeline can operationally accommodate the change in point, and the new receipt or delivery point operator confirms that shipper's quantity is available.

32. Segmentation in Scheduling

Segmentation is an important part of the scheduling process because, when a shipper segments its capacity through nominations, the pipeline must consider how much of the shipper's contract capacity is being used and may use the scheduling process to monitor and evaluate the capacity use.

The Contracts and Nominations sections in this book describe the process to initiate segmentation.

Scheduling a segmented contract is the same as scheduling any other contract because the segmented contract reflects the reduced contract capacity in the terms of the agreement. Scheduling a segmented nomination is more difficult. When scheduling segmented-nomination transactions, the pipeline must be able to determine the contract use on each portion of the pipeline that the shipper has used in order to monitor the contract MDQ for that portion. The pipeline must be able to recognize when a portion of the transportation MDQ has been fully utilized so that the shipper does not exceed the MDQ. There are many ways that a pipeline can accomplish this calculation in a scheduling system.

Shipper Contract Capacity

Receipt Location	Transport Contract	Delivery Location	Nomination Quantity
A	K1234	Z	5000

Contract capacity includes secondary locations in the path of the A-Z capacity giving rights for the shipper to nominate using locations D, L and R.

Example 1

Scheduled Non-segmented nomination:

A	K1234	Z	4800

Example 2

Shipper segmented nominations:

A	K1234	D	3000
A	K1234	L	2000
R	K1234	Z	5000

Segmented nominations cannot overlap capacity. The shipper could not have a nomination from A to D for 3000 and a second nomination from A to Z for 5000. It would result in a nominated quantity of 8000 on the segment from R to Z.

Example 3

Shipper segmented nominations:

A	K1234	Z	3000
A	K1234	D	2000
R	K1234	Z	2000

Segmented nominations can include a mixture of non-segmented nominations and segmented nominations within one contract capacity. The MDQ of the contract cannot be exceeded on any one segment where the nominations overlap.

Example 32.1
Examples of segmented nominations

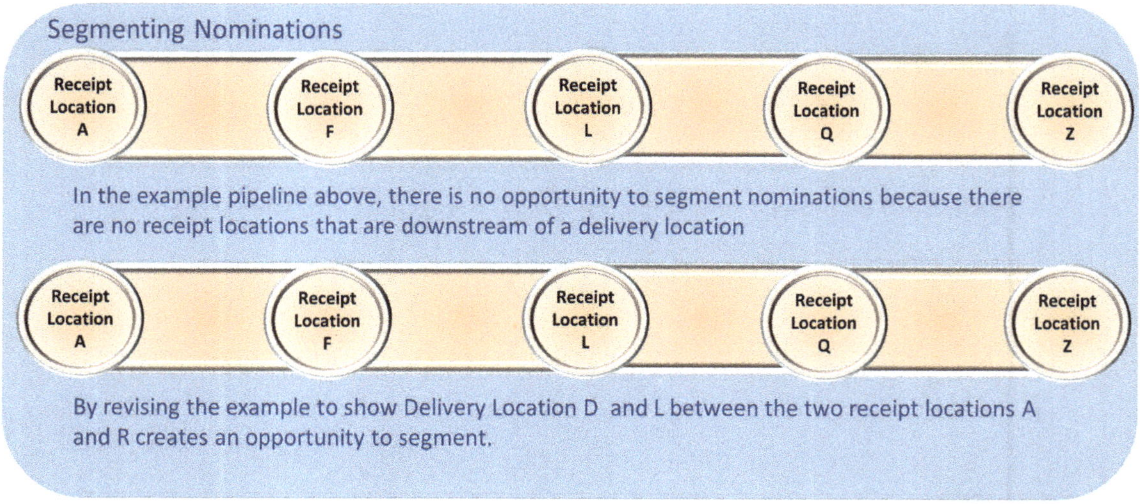

Figure 32.1
Nomination segmentation for the corresponding example

33. Sequencing of Flow

In scheduling the pipeline, the sequencing of the evaluation and the scheduling of the locations is critical. At first glance, each location can be viewed as independent and evaluated for its capacity versus nominations. However, in scheduling, a cut at one receipt location will impact the nominations that can flow through another delivery location, reducing the flow of the associated nomination through that delivery location. The cut at the receipt location may permit other nominations to flow through the delivery location when there may otherwise have been a constraint.

The pipeline's operational priorities determine the sequencing of the scheduling process. The sequence may be market-focused so that its objective is to maximize the deliveries to the market and end-use locations; it may be supply-focused, so that its objective is to maximize the supply from the receipt locations; it may be based on physical constraints of the pipeline where compression or a junction of pipes causes a reduced flow; or it may be a combination of all three.

The understanding of how a pipeline's scheduling may be sequenced is best explained by an example, using the following diagram as a sample pipeline:

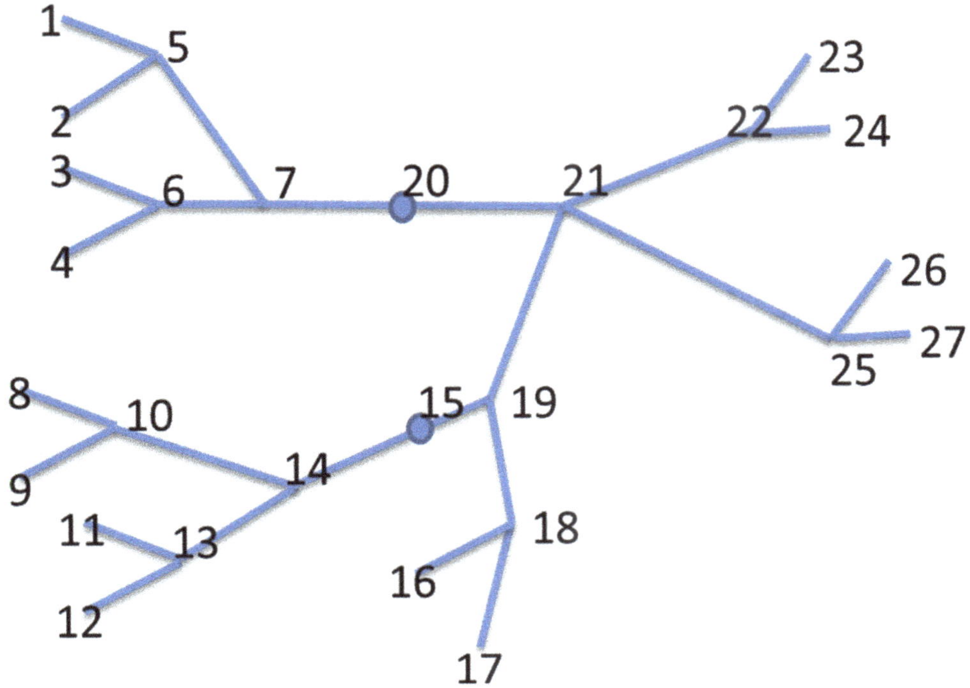

Figure 33.1
Receipt locations labeled 1,2,3,4,8,9,11,12,16 and 17 and delivery locations 23, 24, 26, and 27.

Locations 15 and 20 are mid-point constraint points on this pipeline.

Considerations for a supply-focused pipeline: A supply-focused pipeline is scheduling to maximize the receipts flowing into the pipeline.

- Receipts are the priority, and cuts are pushed downstream to the delivery side of the pipeline.
- Locations 1, 2, 3, 4, 8, 9, 11, 12, 16, 17 are all of the initiating receipt points, which we refer to as Supply Level 1.
- All receipt points can be scheduled simultaneously. There is no reason or need to schedule them separately or in any specific order because, in this scenario, they are equal in scheduling priority.
- After the receipt locations are processed, all of the scheduling locations that they supply can be scheduled. Locations 5, 6, 10, 13, and 18 will be viewed as equal in scheduling priority and referred to as Supply Level 2.

- In many pipelines, the flow of gas has no restrictions at this level. The sum of the receipts feeding gas into a Supply-Level-2 location is all that is needed to schedule the gas. This step is still important to include because, on occasion, one of the locations may have a reduced flow capacity because of maintenance or an outage, and the pipeline will need to be able to reduce the nominated receipt quantities based on this restriction.
- Supply Level 3 is comprised of the next set of downstream interconnects. This group is composed of locations 7 and 14. At first glance, it looks like location 19 can be included in this group, but it has predecessors upstream that must be scheduled first.
- The next level, Supply Level 4, will include only locations 15 and 20. This is not because they are the constraint points and must be evaluated together. In this example, they just happen to fall into the same level when approaching the scheduling from the supply side.
- Supply Level 5 contains only location 19 because the next downstream location cannot be evaluated until 19 is complete, and 19 was dependent on location 15 from Supply Level 4 and location 18 from Supply Level 2.
- Supply Level 6 contains only location 21, which is the first junction of all of the upstream flows in this sample system. From this point forward, the system branches outward toward the market. Some pipelines may continue to have receipts added into the system during this phase. It depends on the configuration of the pipe.
- Supply Level 7 contains locations 22 and 25.
- The final Supply Level is Level 8, which contains locations 23, 24, 26, and 27.

Supply-Focused Scheduling Levels

Locations	Level 1	Level 2	Level 3	Level 4	Level 5	Level 6	Level 7	Level 8
	• 1 • 2 • 3 • 4 • 8 • 9 • 11 • 12 • 16 • 17	• 5 • 6 • 10 • 13 • 18	• 7 • 14	• 15 • 20	• 19	• 21	• 22 • 25	• 23 • 24 • 26 • 27

Table 33.1
The locations associated with each level in supply-focused scheduling

- At each of the supply levels, the quantities that can flow though the location are compared to all of the nominations in that group for that supply level. At some point on the pipeline, the fuel must be applied to these quantities. The receipt quantity at Supply Level 1 will always be the whole receipt quantity, and the delivery quantity at Supply level 8 will always be the delivery quantity, which, on a balanced nomination, is the receipt quantity less fuel. Between those two groups, the determination of when to deduct the fuel in the calculation is based on the business practices of the pipeline. It may be that the pipeline compares the available capacity to the delivery quantity beginning with Supply Level 2. It may be that the pipeline begins using the delivery quantity at Supply Level 4, because this may be the point on the system where compression occurs and fuel is consumed. The pipeline may determine to use the receipt quantity all the way to Level 7 and only use the delivery quantity in level 8. A pipeline could elect to reduce the fuel on an incremental basis so that, if Level 3 was a zone demarcation, then the pipeline calculations would include an intermediate quantity with Level-3 zone fuel removed. Then, if Level 6 was the second fuel demarcation, the pipeline would revert to using the delivery quantity at or after Level 6 because it has both fuels deducted beyond that level.
- Once all of the Supply Levels have been established for the pipeline, the scheduling process can occur quickly during the scheduling cycle.
- For this scenario, Supply Level 1 is the first group of locations to be evaluated. Each of the locations is evaluated independently and, therefore, can be evaluated simultaneously through multiple processing streams. Inside Supply Level 1, consider Location 2 as an example. Location 2 has five nominations initiating at that point. Of the five nominations, three are for firm service and two are for interruptible Service. Location 2 has a capacity of 2,500 DTH, and the nominations total 3,000 DTH. The two confirmed Interruptible nominations are for 500 DTH each, and are from separate shippers, so they will bear the entire cut amount of 500 DTH. The three firm nominations can be resolved with a current scheduled receipt quantity equal to their confirmed quantity. Now, based on the cut-method rules of the pipeline, the two interruptible nominations must be cut. If the default cut method at this level is pro-rata, then each will receive a 50-percent reduction from 500 DTH to 250 DTH. If the default cut method is highest revenue, then the IT contract that is paying the highest transportation rate for this nomination will receive the entire 500 DTH, and the pipeline will cut the other nomination to zero. There is a long list of the cut methods described in the Cut Method Rules chapter of this section. For this example, we will move forward using the pro-rata cut method option.

Supply-Focused Scheduling			
Location 2 Capacity = 2,500 DTH			
Results for Location 2 Nomination 2 of 3,000 DTH			
Nomination 1	Interruptible	500 DTH	Shipper 1
Nomination 2	Interruptible	~~500 DTH~~ 250 DTH	Shipper 2
Nomination 3	Firm	~~500 DTH~~ 250 DTH	Shipper 1
Nomination 4	Firm	1000 DTH	Shipper 3
Nomination 5	Firm	500 DTH	Shipper 4

Table 33.2
The described example of a cut in supply focused scheduling

- The continuing process is pretty clear and simple until the process reaches Supply Level 6 for Location 21. Until this point on the sample system, all of the gas has been being received onto the pipeline and the quantities have been cumulative. Now, at this junction, the quantities must begin to be dispersed. The pipeline must evaluate each of the nominations flowing through Level 6 - which, in this example, is all nominations - and determine whether the nominations will proceed on the segment of the pipeline toward Location 22 or on the segment of the pipeline toward Location 25. There are many ways to approach this task through logical processing.
- Once the process completes Supply Level 8, the scheduling process on this sample pipeline is complete.
- It is important to note that this sample pipeline could be a view of Zone 1 of a huge pipeline system where one or more of the delivery locations is the receipt location into Zone 4 of that system, and two other systems, Zones 2 and 3, also deliver into Zone 4. In a case such as this, the systems for Zones 1, 2, and 3 could be scheduled simultaneously since they are all independent until they reach Zone 4. There could also be corresponding multiple systems on the distribution side of the pipeline that are scheduled simultaneously.

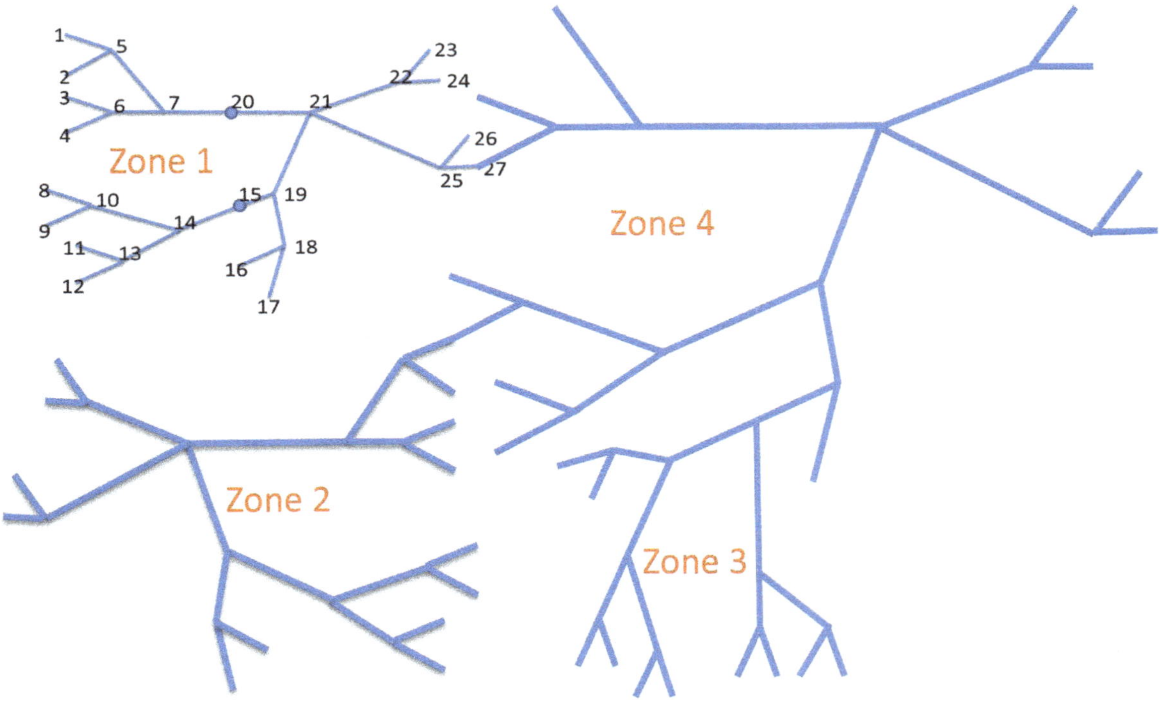

Figure 33.2
The network of locations in each of four zones

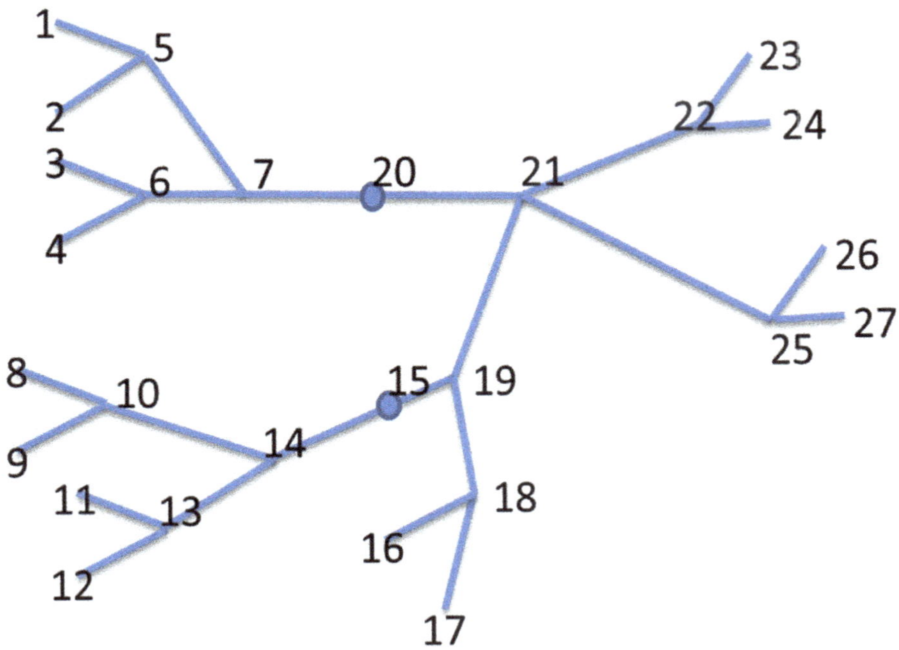

Figure 33.3
The pipeline for the described example

Considerations for a market-focused pipeline: A market-focused pipeline is scheduled to maximize the deliveries flowing out of the pipeline to the market area.

- Deliveries are the priority, and cuts are pushed upstream to the receipt side of the pipeline.
- Locations 23, 24, 26, and 27 are the market-focused deliveries, which we refer to as Market Level 1.
- All deliveries can be scheduled simultaneously. There is no reason to schedule them separately or in a specific order. All of the deliveries are equal.
- After the delivery locations are processed, then all of the scheduling locations that supply these deliveries upstream, can be scheduled. Locations 22 and 25 are the two supplies immediately upstream of the Market Level 1 locations. These locations are an aggregation of the locations downstream. Locations 22 and 25 can be scheduled simultaneously and will be referred to as Market Level 2.
- Market Level 3, the next in the flow for a market-focused pipeline, is Location 21. This location is the next upstream level from Market Level 2 and is where all of the upstream supplies are merged to supply the market locations.
- At Market Level 4, the pipeline could process location 19 so that it is merged with the upstream flow on the next level, or it could choose to process 19 and 20 together. For this example, the pipeline will process location 19. At this point in time, the pipeline can also process the two locations upstream of location 19 and consider that supply chain complete.
- Market Level 5 branches out the supply to locations 20 and 15. These are important locations because they are constraint points, but there is no aggregation or disaggregation of the gas occurring at these two locations.
- After Market Level 5 is scheduled, Market Level 6, for locations 7 and 14, is scheduled.
- Continuing upstream, Market Level 7 addresses locations 5, 6, 10, 13 and 18 simultaneously.
- The final level, Market Level 8 schedules each of the receipt locations.

Market Focused Scheduling Levels

Locations	Level 1	Level 2	Level 3	Level 4	Level 5	Level 6	Level 7	Level 8
	• 23 • 24 • 26 • 27	• 22 • 25	• 21	• 19	• 15 • 20	• 7 • 14	• 5 • 6 • 10 • 13 • 18	• 1 • 2 • 3 • 4 • 8 • 9 • 11 • 12 • 16 • 17

Table 33.3
The locations associated with each level in market focused scheduling

This picture with Supply Levels and Market Levels does not address a second component to scheduling the pipeline. This occurs when cutting gas because of a constraint at one location frees up capacity at another location where a cut may have otherwise occurred. Using the Market Scenario as an example, let's look at more detail for locations 23, 24, 26, and 27.

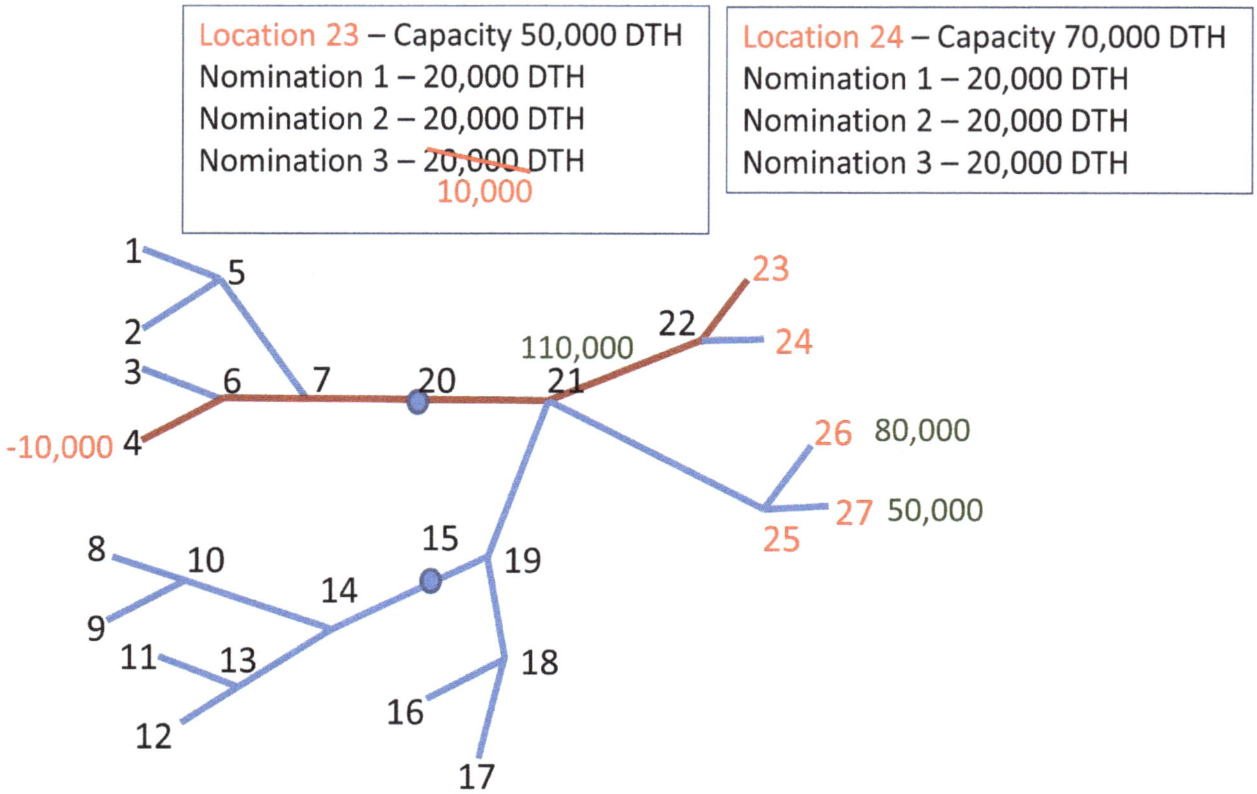

Figure 33.4
The cut process for the described example

Delivery location 23 has a capacity of 50,000 DTH. There are three nominations delivering to this location for 20,000 DTH each, giving a total of 60,000 DTH nominated at the location. 10,000 DTH must be cut at this location. Using the scheduling rules of the pipeline, the pipeline will determine if all three nominations are cut on a pro-rata basis, or if the cut quantity is divided in a different way. For this example, the third nomination will take the cut and be reduced to 10,000 DTH.

Delivery location 24 has a capacity of 70,000 DTH. It also has three nominations delivering to the location for 20,000 DTH each, giving a total of 60,000 DTH nominated at the location. Because the total nominated quantity does not exceed the location capacity, then the pipeline will schedule all of the nominations to flow at this location.

Location 22, where locations 23 and 24 combine, has no capacity constraints and all of the 110,000 DTH now scheduled for locations 23 and 24 can flow.

Assume that location 26 has nominations of 80,000 DTH and a capacity of 80,000

DTH. Location 27 has nominations of 50,000 DTH and a capacity of 80,000 DTH. Both of these locations will be able to flow all of the nominations, and location 25 will be able to handle this capacity.

Now, back to location 23, where 10,000 DTH was cut from the third nomination. When the pipeline makes this cut, it must look at the source of the gas and make corresponding cuts upstream of the location to balance the nomination. In this example, the third nomination was supplied by receipt location 4, and the pipeline will cut the supply at location 4 by a corresponding 10,000 DTH plus any fuel that had been removed in the transaction.

By cutting transactions and the total flow at locations as the scheduling process moves upstream, there may be constraint locations, such as 15 and 20 that are freed because of the scheduling cuts that have occurred at the location level prior to the constraint locations in the scheduling process.

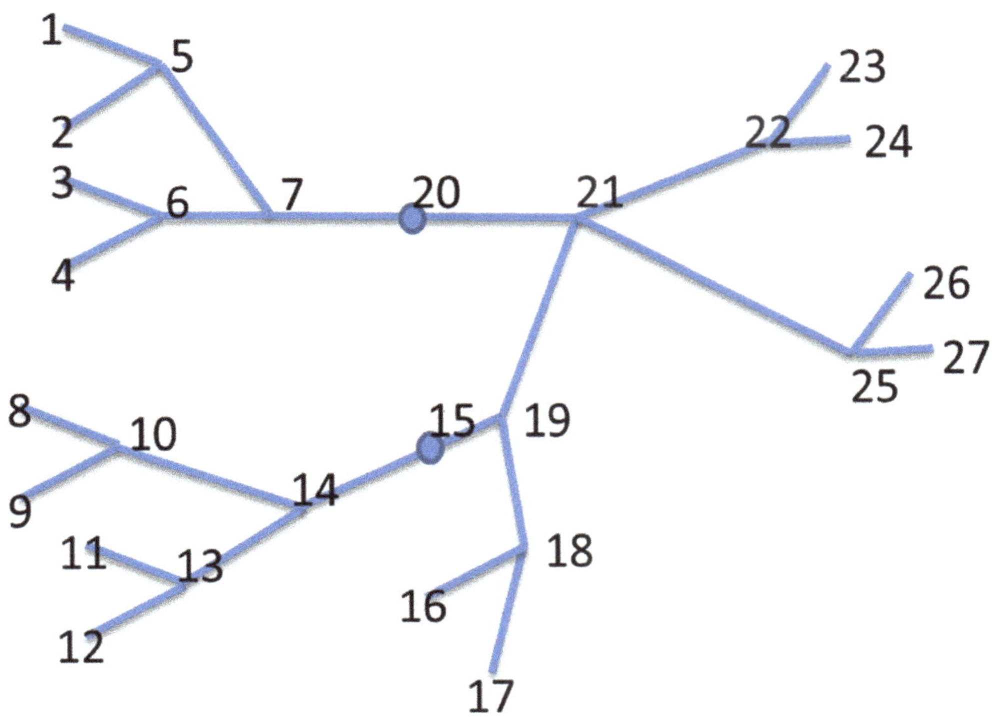

Figure 33.5
The pipeline for the described example

Considerations for a constraint-focused pipeline: On a constraint-focused pipeline, critical constraint points cause the supply or market focus of the pipeline to shift to address those constraints first in the scheduling process. In the same example, locations 15 and 20 are constraint locations on the pipeline. In the constraint-focused scheduling process, the pipeline will evaluate all of the nominations requested to flow through the points of constraint and make any required cuts. These cuts will flow to the receipt and delivery locations on the cut nominations. At that point, the pipeline will shift the focus of the scheduling process to either a supply focus or a market focus, depending on the business priorities of that pipeline.

A Day in the Life of a Scheduler by Jeff O"Block

On a good day, schedulers have completed their daily tasks by 10 a.m. On a bad day, they work around the clock. Seasoned schedulers learn the nuances of the parties with whom they deal and understand that the interruptible gas of some parties is more reliable than the firm of others. Pipeline cuts and outages can also make a long day for schedulers.

The perspective of a scheduler depends on where the business lies in the marketplace. There are two distinct groups that schedule natural gas:

1. Producers such as Shell, Apache, and Devon or producer services, such as Southwest Energy, that market the gas for such producers.
2. Consumers, both commercial (power plants such as Duke and fertilizer manufacturers such as Rentech) and residential suppliers (such as Centerpoint), LDCs (local distribution companies), and consumer services that manage the purchase of gas for such consumers.

Producers look at natural gas-producing fields and yield curves, maintenance schedules, new production, and production coming off line to estimate how much natural gas will be available to be sold in the future.

Consumers look at weather or estimated production demands to evaluate the need for natural gas in the future.

Both groups have a schedule that contains three items:

1. Date, as natural gas is usually traded on a daily basis
2. Location, which is usually an industry-named point where gas is traded
3. Volume, as almost all gas in the U.S. is traded in MMBTUs

Traders for both producers and consumers attempt to buy and sell as much of their demand as they feel comfortable with into the futures market. Futures-market natural gas is bought and sold on indices such as Inside FERC. These indices settle on an average price at the Henry Hub in Erath, Louisiana, the official delivery location for futures contracts of New York Mercantile Exchange. Natural gas that is not at Henry Hub has added to it a basis differential, which is the difference between the price of the gas at Henry Hub and the price at another specified location. Historically, demand farthest from the hub had the highest positive differentials, and production farthest from the hub had the highest negative differentials. The market has evolved, and this is no longer the case.

The futures market is at least one month ahead. The current month is called the prompt month, or cash market. Traders scurry during the cash month to balance futures supply and demand against actual values that are being produced and consumed during the cash month. Gas is bought and sold during the cash month on indices such as Gas Daily.

A normal scheduler's day starts early with a position report by location, usually from the company's ETRM (Energy Trading and Risk Management) system. The position report should show long and short positions by location for tomorrow's business. From this position report, the scheduler has the following responsibilities:

1. Verify with each shipper the exact location (pipeline and meter) where the gas is to be sourced or delivered. Most traders didn"t know this information at the time the trade was executed.
2. Verify that one or more transportation contracts are available with adequate MDQ (Maximum Daily Quantity) to move the required volume. A scheduler has many tools in the scheduling toolkit to use in placing the gas. In addition to transportation contracts, the scheduler may use storage, park and loan, and balancing agreements to schedule the deals the traders have made.
3. Gather all the necessary information required by each transportation service provider, including nomination data:
    a. Pipeline/meter
    b. Service contract
    c. Date
    d. Volume

And confirmation data, including:

a. Upstream/Downstream parties
b. Upstream/Downstream transportation contracts

4. Use either EDI, or pipeline websites to enter nominated volumes
5. Verify the nominations were accepted by the pipeline
6. Work closely with traders to make adjustments based on any cuts

Other tasks may include:

1. Releasing excess capacity on firm transportation contracts
2. Managing storage injection and withdrawal volumes
3. Maintain fuel and rate charges on transport contracts
4. Negotiating transportation rates on interruptible transport contracts
5. Keeping the system in balance throughout the day
6. Getting estimated volumes back into the ETRM system to help traders with imbalances

7. Working closely with trading desks to manage deal fulfillment.

34. Scenarios

Another factor in scheduling the pipeline in addition to the business focus of that pipe is the operational configuration. Because of the business focus, the pipeline may schedule with a marketing priority, a scheduling priority, or other priority. Because of the operational configuration, the pipeline may have to factor in special processing for reticulation, pools, or other operational considerations.

Reticulated

A reticulated pipeline system exists when the gas at certain locations on the system has the option of flowing more than one direction in order to get to the same delivery location on that same system, like when a river splits into two or more sections and then merges back together downstream. There are many versions of reticulated systems, and each of those versions has its own unique operating constraints.

Additionally, there are pipelines where the flow of gas on one section of the pipeline never comingles with the flow of gas on another section of the pipeline; there are pipelines where certain sections of pipe that connect sections of the pipeline together may be bidirectional based on the scheduled flow in the upstream or downstream sections of that pipeline. These pipelines must have special scheduling scenarios to fit these conditions.

Pools

The placement of pools in the scheduling process is strategic. Most pipelines keep pools whole, meaning that a reduction on the upstream side of the pool flows through the participating transactions in the pool and reduces the flow on the downstream side of the pool, and vice versa. In this case, the deliveries into the pool and receipts from the pool can be scheduled first, directly in the flow of the scheduling scenario and then the affected parties may be determined as a secondary step in the scenario.

Revenue-Based

A revenue-based pipeline scheduling scenario is a special case where the pipeline's scheduling priorities are based on the projected revenue of the transportation transactions. The goal of the scenario is to maximize the revenue on the pipeline.

This revenue calculation may focus, as a determinant, on the total charge per DTH for the gas being transported, or it may take a more complex approach to determine selected flow and evaluate the transactions that will flow based on the "rate times charge times distance traveled = revenue" to reflect overall revenue. The pipeline may implement the revenue-based calculations many ways, and these options must be coupled with the operational and business focus of the pipeline.

In one revenue-based scenario, the pipeline may choose to cut a group of nominations rather than turn on an additional compression facility because the cost of turning on another compression engine is exceeded by the amount of revenue collected by those additional transactions. This situation would only occur with interruptible transportation. In a firm transportation scenario, the pipeline would be obligated to turn on the additional compression engine.

Maximize Throughput

The pipeline with a scheduling scenario focused on maximizing throughput has determined that the pipeline operates most efficiently when it has the most available volume flowing through. While the revenue-based scenario may elect to cut requested quantities because the cost of moving those quantities is not cost-efficient, the throughput-based pipeline has determined that these factors do not meet its operational needs. Thus, the requirement for additional compression does not become a determinant in the scheduling process.

35. Scheduled Quantities - Operator versus Shipper

The culmination of the scheduling process is a scheduled quantity at the nomination line-item level whereby the pipeline provides the nominating shipper a scheduled receipt quantity and a scheduled delivery quantity at the same level of detail as the original nomination. In addition, the pipeline provides to the operator these same scheduled quantities at each location at the same level of detail in which the confirmation process was conducted.

Because they are reported at the same level of detail as the nomination and confirmation transactions, the pipeline is able to report both the scheduled quantity for shipper and the scheduled quantity for operator using the corresponding nominator's tracking ID or confirmation tracking ID. If a nominator's tracking ID or confirmation-tracking ID has been assigned to a transaction, then the pipeline, when reporting these scheduled quantities to the shipper and operator, must provide the tracking ID. The pipeline has the option of providing only the tracking ID and the scheduled quantities for a transaction line item instead of all of the elements that identify a transaction in addition to tracking ID quantities. Most pipelines elect to provide all of the data rather than this abbreviated form. The same option holds true on the confirmation side. The pipeline has the option of providing only the confirmation tracking ID and the scheduled quantity for a confirmation line item instead of all the additional data elements to identify that confirmation transaction. Again, most pipelines elect to provide all of the data rather than the abbreviated form on the confirmed scheduled quantity.

The scheduled quantity for shipper and for operator are reported at the culmination of each nomination cycle and at the end of each gas day.

36. Scheduled Quantity Data

The scheduled quantity report[82], when provided back to the shipper or operator, is for a single day and for a single nomination cycle. The scheduled quantity datasets support the ability for a pipeline to provide scheduled quantities for a broader period of time, such as multiple days or a month; however, that information would have to be continuously updated every day based on the required processing of the nomination cycles. Therefore, pipelines most often report the scheduled quantities for a single business day.

Scheduled quantities are required to be provided back to the shipper at the same level of detail as the nomination. This means that, when scheduled quantities are reported back to the shipper, a scheduled quantity is associated with each nomination line item from the original nomination for that cycle.

One important sideline to this requirement is the requirement that the nomination stay in its same form, in the same model type, from the nomination through imbalances. Historically, some pipelines provided a service where shippers nominated in a non-pathed model, and the pipeline determined the best-fit path for the gas. The premise was that the pipeline was giving the shipper the best value on the transportation through this method. But shippers were clear, in creating standards, that this was not a service that they wanted. Shippers preferred to be able to provide the nomination in one model type and receive the scheduled quantities and imbalance quantities back at the same level of detail. The shippers made it clear that, when the pipeline provided this information back at a different level of detail, it made it difficult, and sometimes impossible, to place the quantities back into their internal gas-management systems because the pipeline algorithms used to path the gas varied by pipeline.

On the scheduled quantity for operator dataset, the scheduled quantities are provided back to the operator at the same level of detail as the confirmation. If the confirmation was conducted at a high level of detail, such as shipper-contract, then the scheduled quantities will be provided to the operator at the shipper-contract level; if the confirmation was conducted using upstream parties, upstream contracts, and package IDs, then this same level of detail must be the level of detail that is reported for the scheduled quantity for the operator.

If the quantity that is provided in the scheduled quantity is reduced from the original nominated quantity, then the pipeline must include with the scheduled quantity a reduction-reason code. A pipeline may provide one single or multiple reduction-reason codes, but must provide at least one code even if it has the value of "AOK." The pipeline can provide these reduction-reason codes at the header level, detail level, or line-item level in the data. In some cases, the pipeline may provide reduction-reason codes at all of these levels in the data at the same time. Like other situations, the pipeline may support a sub-group of the reduction-reason codes that are available.

Scheduled Quantity Report

First American Pipeline Company January 1, 2000

Nomination:

Receipt Location	Transportation Contract	Delivery Location	Nominated Quantity	Scheduled Quantity
A1492	FK4242	Z1476	1000 DTH	900 DTH
Reduction Reason:	*Upstream Confirmation Reduction*			
A1492	FK4242	Q1776	4000 DTH	3500 DTH
Reduction Reason:	*Downstream Confirmation Reduction = 100 DTH* *Scheduling Reduction = 400 DTH*			

Example 36.1
An example of a paper scheduled quantity report with reduction-reason codes

There is an explicit list of reduction-reason codes that must be used by pipelines. The datasets describe these reduction-reason codes for the scheduled quantity for shipper[83], and provides codes for the scheduled quantity for operator[84].

Measurement

Measurement involves the recording of the active flow of the gas on the pipeline at a given time or interval on that pipe. Measurement is often reported as estimates during the gas-production month and as an actual quantity a few days after the close of the production month. It includes the quantity of gas flow as well as gas quality information.

Pipeline measurement systems may receive data from electronic-flow devices, manual entry, gas-quality lab results, and weather data during the month to determine the calculated measured quantity.

Information that comes into the pipeline measurement system may be from measurement devices owned and operated by the pipeline or may be received from interconnecting parties acting as the operator for a specific location[85].

37. Meters and Locations

Physical measurement takes place at a meter. A meter is a physical device on the pipeline that measures the flow of gas at a rate, and is affected by temperature, pressure, and many other factors.

One location on a pipeline may have one or multiple meters that, when summed together, provide the total flow for that location. The location in this instance may also be referred to as a point. A single location may not have a measurement device on it because the location is an aggregation point for multiple meters. This could be where multiple receipt meters come into a single location, or it could be where multiple delivery meters are delivered off of the single location. In either instance, the total flow at that location is the sum of the upstream or downstream locations that it supports.

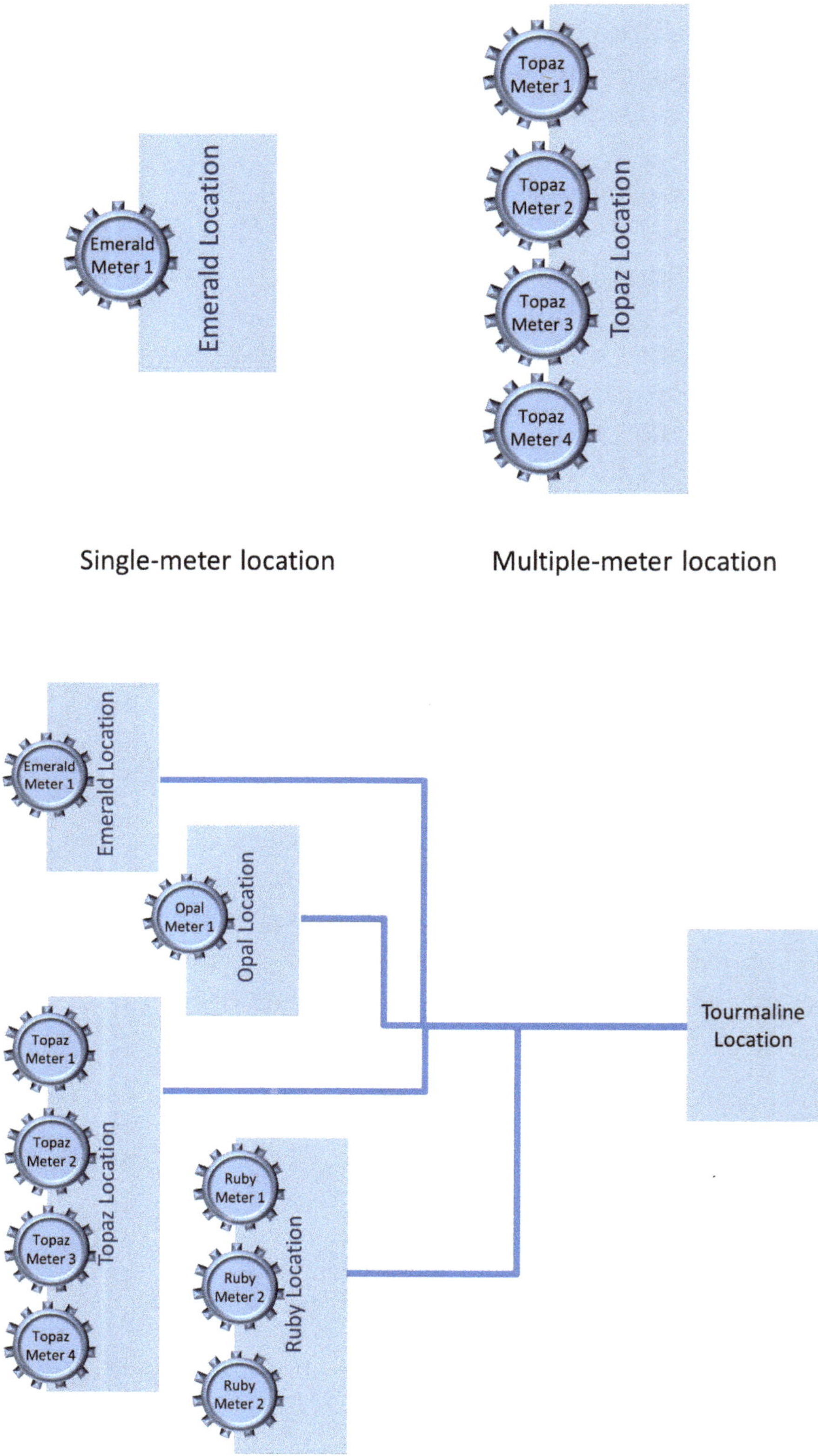

Figure 37.1
Multiple meters may comprise one location and multiple locations may add up to a single location on the pipeline.

Some pipelines divide their locations into groups. A group may define all of the locations in a segment, zone, operational impact area, or other category on the physical pipeline. Often a location will be associated with multiple different types of groups. A pipeline may associate all receipt locations into one group, all throughput locations into another group, and all delivery locations into a third group. At the same time, that same pipeline may group all pool locations into a group, all storage injections into a group, etc. There are many ways that pipelines can group the locations on the pipeline into processing groups that are used for the business processes throughout the transaction lifecycle.

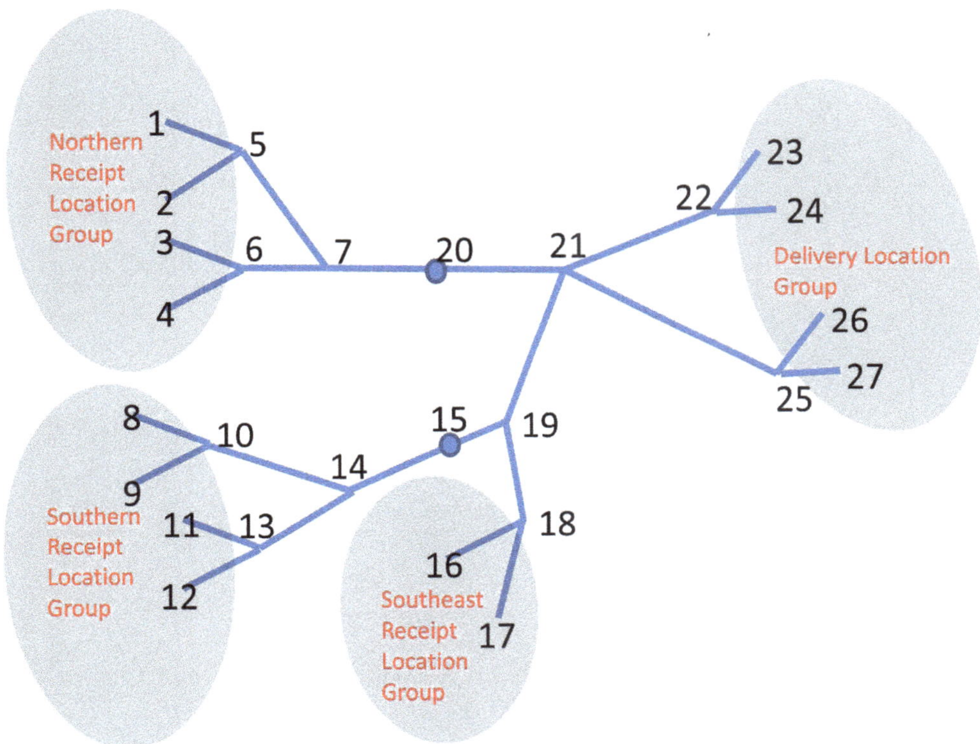

Figure 37.2
Pipelines may place locations into groups for ease of reference.

Zones and segments may also be used to identify physical boundaries such as the transition from offshore to onshore transportation, gathering versus mainline versus distribution transportation. The pipeline determines and includes in pipeline maps and tariffs the boundaries for zones on the pipeline. Segments identify specific sections of a pipeline that operate in the same manner. A pipeline may identify many segments separated by operational constraints, points of connection, or locations where pipe size changes or where compression causes the operational capacity to vary.

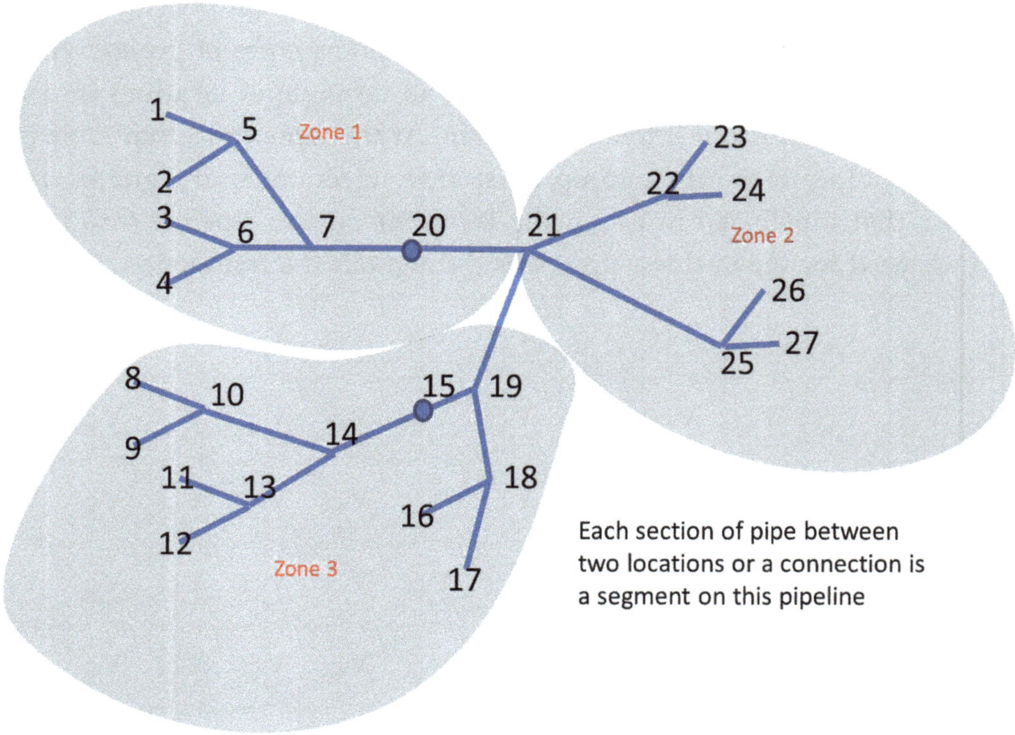

Figure 37.3
Pipelines may group locations into zones

Meters

The term **meter** most often refers to the physical measurement device that measures the flow of gas. There may be one or more physical meters at a location. The sum of the gas measured at the physical meters gives the total flow of gas for the location. If there is only one meter at a location, often the meter and the location carry the same identifier. Gas analysis, which is the information gathered to determine gas quality, is associated with the meter. The gas analysis at one meter usually determines the gas quality for all of the meters at a location. The gas analysis for one meter location may be the same gas analysis used for many locations in a geographic area. Additionally, several gas-analysis data may be averaged or prorated to determine the gas quality for a gathering location that has no gas-analysis device.

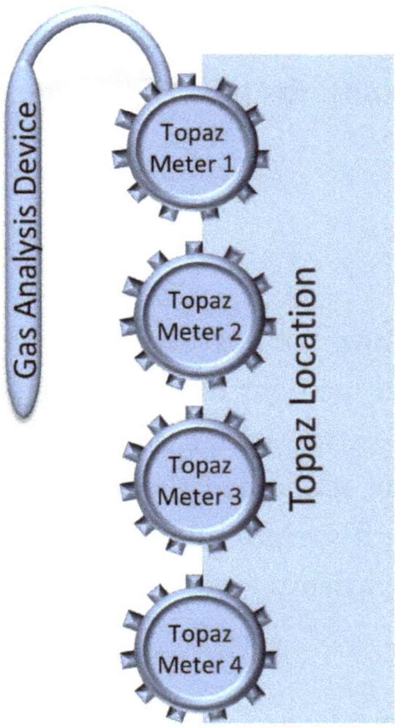

Figure 37.4
Gas Analysis at a location is tied to one of the meters though it represents all of the meters at the location

Metering devices range from high-end real-time telemetry devices that can be controlled electronically to paper charts on manual devices to estimated flows based on pressures and temperatures. Often, the higher the volume of flow at a device, the higher the technology of the measuring device, but this is not always true.

Measurement meters are not able to be controlled in a precise manner. The measurement itself is precise, but the control of the valve to turn the meter on and off at an exact flow is not. Imagine turning on the faucet in your bathtub at full force and trying to fill a juice glass with water from that faucet without spilling any water. It's not going to happen. Now imagine a 36-inch pipeline at 600 pounds of pressure and trying to turn a valve on or off to measure an exact cubic foot of gas. Again – it's not going to happen. Even with advanced flow control devices, there will always be overages and underages in gas measurement. The question becomes, what to do with those differences in amounts. If the delivery is to an end user, then the end user pays for whatever is delivered. If the measurement is at an interconnect, there is usually one designated party to take the overage or underage. In some instances, there may be a party who will take the excess amount and a different party who will take the shortage. This is where PDAs, allocations and Operational Balancing Agreements come into the business flow. These are discussed in the Allocations chapter later in this book.

With measurement, if you schedule for 100,000, you might get 102,000 or you might get 99,800. If there is not a party who absorbs the differences, the allocation rules determine who gets which quantity.

38. Gas Control

After gas has been scheduled to flow, the next step in the business process is for the gas to begin flowing at the start of the next gas day. Quantities that have been scheduled to flow are communicated to Gas Control, which then creates a plan to set the valves for meters on the pipeline so that the scheduled flow can be received and delivered. This plan may include turning on and off various compressor stations on the pipeline, setting pipeline-segment pressures, and confirming with upstream and downstream operators to coordinate operational deliveries.

39. Intervals – Hourly, Daily, Weekly, Monthly

Two things are important to note here. First the measurement basis for gas, which is often referred to as the unit of measure. Second, the interval of measurement for gas.

The measurement basis or unit of measure, in North America, is DTH or Thousand Cubic Feet (MCF). Measurement in MMCF stands for millions of cubic feet of gas and is a volumetric measurement. Measurement in DTH stands for the quantity of gas in relationship to its heating value. 1000 MCF equals one MMCF and is equal to one DTH when that DTH has a heating value of 1.00. The heating value reflects the quality of the gas. If a gas is of low quality, having water or other compounds, then it will have a heating value of less than one. When gas is of a higher quality, meaning that it has little or no water or inert materials, and may contain other heavier hydrocarbons, then the heating value of that gas may be higher than one. Gas that is considered "wet" or unprocessed often may have a high or low heating value. For a full understanding of gas quality, see the chapter on gas quality. The measurement basis for gas in Mexico and Canada is different than in the United States and must be measured in or converted to gigajoules for Canada and gigacalories for Mexico.[86]

Gas may be measured on a sub-hourly basis, an hourly basis, a daily basis, a weekly basis (or some other interval less than one month), or a monthly basis. Most gas is measured on a daily basis using electronic measurement devices. Most contracts for gas are for daily measurements of gas. Some gas that does not have electronic measurement devices is available only on a monthly or sub–monthly basis. In some instances, pipelines will contract for gas on an hourly or sub-hourly basis. Most often, these contracts are associated with deliveries to industrial customers or electric-generation facilities. There are many locations on the gas-gathering side of the business where gas is not measured using a physical meter device, but is measured using periodic pressure measurements in a calculation including temperature and time. Often these locations are aggregated together and measured through a metering device further downstream. Differences between the calculated measured quantity and the metered measured quantity are resolved through allocation rules.

40. Gas Quality

Natural gas is composed of methane. Methane is a single-carbon gas with the scientific formula of CH4. Pure methane has a BTU factor of 1.0.

Natural gas, when it comes out of the ground, may not be pure methane and is referred to as "wet gas." It will either have a low BTU factor because it has impurities such as water, sulfur, oxygen, bacteria, solid matter, dust, gums, and other components, or it will have a high BTU factor because it is mixed with higher carbon gases such as propane and butane. The gas may be of a quality that it does not have to be processed before being transported under high pressure or, in the case of a high or low BTU factor, the gas is processed through a gas-processing plant to remove the other components and bring the gas back as close to a BTU factor of 1.0 as is practicable. Even after processing, the gas may have impure components, but it may only have components that are not harmful to the pipeline when the gas is under compression. Examples of non-harmful components are oxygen, carbon dioxide, and water, though all of these must still be in very limited quantities. Even sulfur and hydrogen sulfide may still exist in the gas in some scenarios, but these must be limited to extremely small amounts.

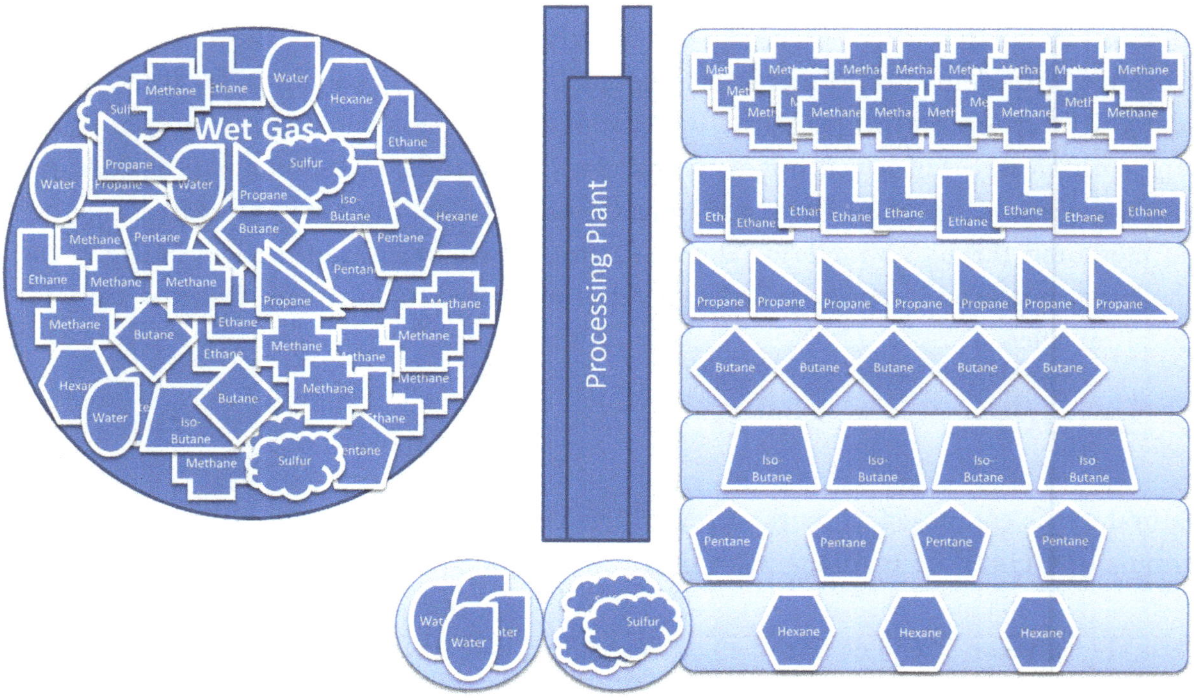

Figure 40.1
Wet gas is broken into components of methane plus other hydrocarbons and byproducts.

Natural gas with a low BTU factor must be cleaned of its impurities before it can be compressed to a high compression for pipeline transmission. A gas-processing plant is used to extract the water, sulfur, and other non-methane contents. In most cases, the products that are extracted can be sold. For example, sulfur is sold for production of fertilizer. The revenue from the sale of the extracted ingredients is allocated back to the owners of the gas based on their contract with the plant processor and based on their percentage of ownership of the product.

Natural gas with a high BTU factor contains additional heavier carbons. These carbons often consist of: ethane, propane, iso-propane, butane, iso-butane, pentane, iso-pentane, hexane, heptane, and octane. The highest content is usually the lower carbon gasses such as ethane and propane. The lowest content is often pentane. Hexane, heptane, and octane are found in minor quantities, if at all. These heavier carbon gasses are referred to as Natural Gas Liquids (NGLs). The sale price of NGLs often far exceeds the sale price of the methane and causes NGLs to be a sought-after commodity. Trading, selling, transporting, and processing NGLs are popular topics in natural gas.

Gas Quality by Jeff O"Block

The quality of the gas can also vary greatly from one MCF to another. The more "bigger" carbon molecules in the gas, the more heat it will create when burned. So one MCF is not the same as another. This is kinda unfair when you are buying gas. This is why Natural gas in not usually bought and sold by volume (MCF), but rather converted to MMBTu, which is a heat quantity. MMBtu is 1,000,000 BTU Units.

Btu (British Thermal Unit) - A Btu is defined as the quantity of heat that must be added to one pound of pure water to raise its temperature from 58.5 degrees Fahrenheit to 59.5 degrees Fahrenheit under standard pressure. A Btu is generally thought of as the heat required to raise the temperature of one pound of water one degree Fahrenheit.
So not only do we have to measure the gas flow, we have to measure the heating value and multiply the two together to get the "quantity" of gas that we are buying, selling, or transporting.

To measure the flow of gas, most meters use an orifice plate, a small piece of metal inside the pipe that acts like an airplane wing. The "meter", will measure the pressure above and below the plate, and using the Bernoulli equation, the flow rate is displayed.
The Btu value for gas is usually determined using a gas chromatograph.

Gas Chromatography - Gas chromatography is a physical method of separating a gas into its components and then measuring the quantity of each component in the gas mixture to determine its molecular composition. Once the molecular composition is determined the heating value of the gas is determined by calculation. In practice the gas chromatograph is composed of a sample injection system with a regulated carrier gas supply, thermally stabilized separation columns, a detector, and a recorder. The analytical results from the gas chromatograph can be used to calculate super compressibility, specific gravity, gallons per thousand cubic feet of liquids, and heating value. The gas chromatograph is calibrated using a natural gas standard with a certified molecular composition for each component in the gas.

What is the energy value of 1,000 cubic foot of gas with a heating value of 1050 Btu per cubic foot?

Energy value = (1,000 ft^3) (1050 Btu/ft^3) = 1,050,000 Btu = 1.05 MMBtu = 1.05 Dekatherms

Thermal Correction Factor Using Volume and Btu - The thermal correction factor for a gas at standard temperature and pressure is calculated by dividing the measured heating value per cubic foot by a base of 1,000 Btu per cubic foot. Standard conditions are 60 degrees and 14.73 PSIA.

Canadian and European natural gas is measured in Metric units. Metric Units are E3M3 (Cubic meters) and GJs (gigajoules).

---

41. Gas Quantity

Natural gas in North America is measured in MCFs. An MCF is a thousand cubic feet. However, the pressure and temperature of this gas can vary. Each state in the United States has a "state pressure base" for measuring an MCF. Most states measure at a standard barometric pressure of 14.73 PSI. This information can be found on the internet for specific states. When using an MCF measurement, the numbers will need to be converted when moving from one state pressure base to another.

Gas may have a BTU factor above or below 1.0. This depends on the quality of the gas produced, operating priorities and, if the gas is processed, performance of the plant. Because of this, the BTU factor is combined with the MMCF, volumetric measurement of the gas to give the MMBTU measurement. The MMBTU quantity is a caloric quantity that ensures all of the participants in the flow of gas on a pipeline are treated equally from a heating-value perspective. With this measurement, regardless of whether a shipper provides gas with a BTU of 0.89 or a shipper provides gas with a high BTU of 1.13, the heating value of the gas they receive at the delivery of the product will be the same as the heating value they provided to the pipeline.

MMCF * BTU = MMBTU

1042 MMCF * 1.062 BTU = 1107 MMBTU

1159 MMCF * 0.891 BTU = 1033 MMBTU

Example 41.1
Examples of an MMCF-to-MMBTU conversion

Allocations

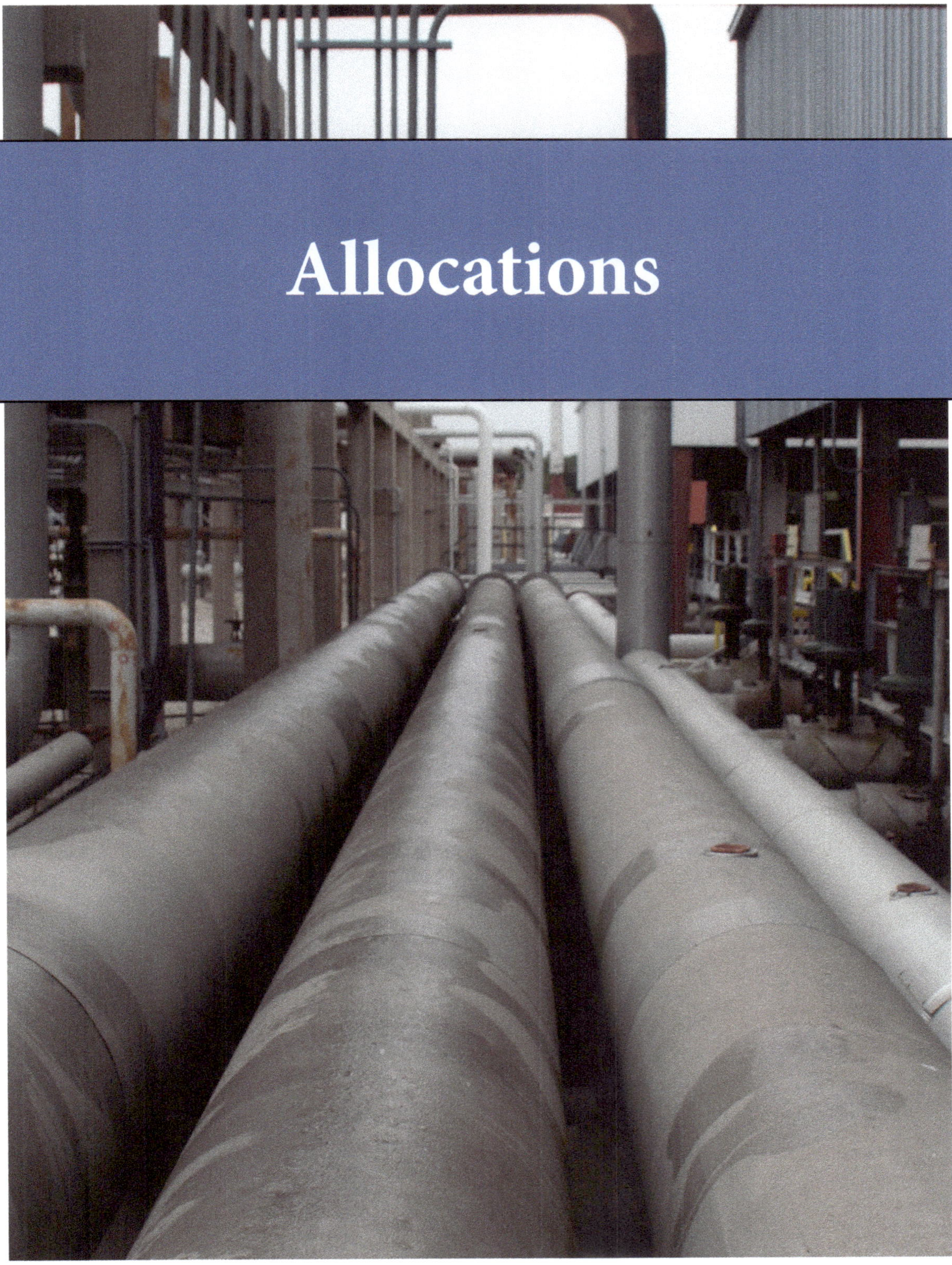

In the business-process flow, the flow of gas is now complete. Estimated or actual measurement is complete. It is time to determine how much gas each of the parties at a location really flowed versus what was scheduled. The total quantity of gas flow is allocated back to the parties and transactions in that flow.

Once gas has been measured, whether it is for one hour, one day, or one month, then the gas can be allocated. Allocations is the process where the quantity of gas that is measured is compared to the quantity of gas that was scheduled, and the measured quantity is distributed to the transactions that participated in that quantity at that location. These transactions are the scheduled nominations and, if it exists, the operational balancing agreements at that location. Remember, the scheduled quantity on a nomination is that quantity that was confirmed and scheduled by the pipeline after the nomination was submitted. Until now, the scheduled quantity is the best quantity available.

There are specific allocation methods that must be supported by a pipeline[87] . The allocation methods are: pro-rata, rank, percentage, swing, and operator-provided-value.

42. Pre-Determined Allocations

The allocation occurs at a location on a pipeline. The operator, producer, or shipper of the location, depending on the levels of allocation provided by the pipeline, will provide allocation instructions to the pipeline through the Pre-Determined Allocation (PDA) dataset.[88] The pipeline may have allocation rules specified in its tariff that identify allocation steps that will occur before the PDA and may identify allocation steps that will occur after the PDA on that pipeline. Additionally, the pipeline may accept levels of PDAs where the operator provides shipper-to-shipper level allocations at the location, the shipper provides shipper-to-contract level allocations, and the producer provides contract-to-line-item level allocations. These practices depend to a great extent on the operational configuration and business practices of the pipeline. Most pipelines accept a single PDA from the operator at the location. Note that if the operator has an operational balancing agreement with the pipeline, the PDA may not be required. That PDA may provide allocation instructions at the shipper level, the shipper-contract level, or a more detailed level. Again, the level of detail that the operator provides in the PDA is determined by the business practices of the pipeline. The combination of the PDAs at a location plus the allocation rules of the pipeline provide enough information for the pipeline to determine an allocated quantity for each of the transactions flowing through a single location.

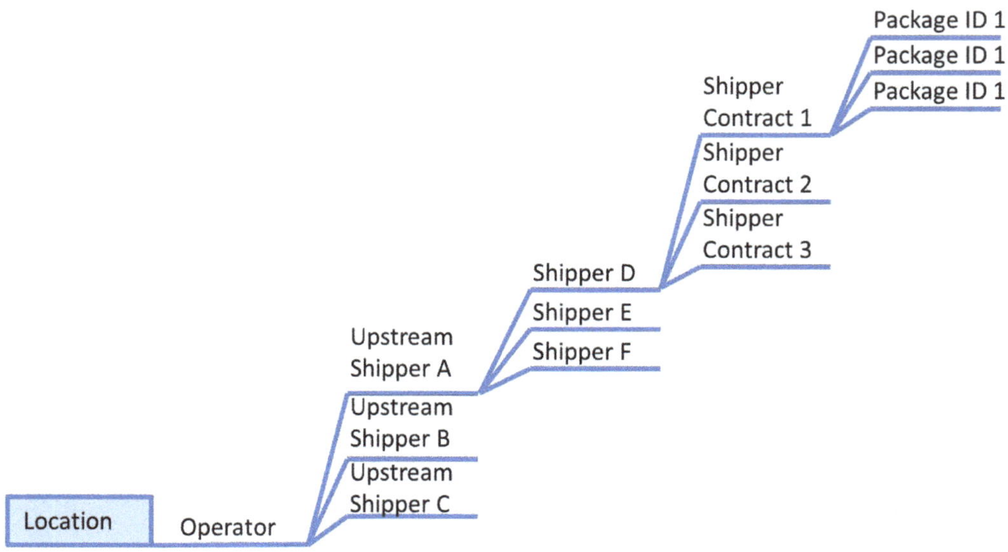

Figure 42.1
A possible hierarchy of multi-tiered PDAs at a location

In NAESB 2.4.1 Pre-determined Allocations dataset[89] the PDA Transaction Type Matrix[90] reflects the level of PDA for a transaction so that the PDA submitter may inform the pipeline of the level of PDA that is being provided. The level that a submitter may select comes from a set of the levels that is permitted by the pipeline. The matrix level is included in the PDA transaction type code. There are 18 different levels that may be used to conduct a PDA from which a pipeline may choose. Some of the levels are specific to a PDA at a receipt location and some are specific to a PDA at a delivery location. For instance, one of the levels, Code Value = "7" would be used by an operator at a receipt location that is confirming at the shipper-shipper level. With this level, the operator would provide the service requester ID for the party on the pipeline and the upstream party ID for the party on the upstream pipeline.

43. Allocation Rules

If the measured quantity at a location is higher than the total scheduled quantity for that location, then one or more parties at that location will receive more gas allocated than they requested. If the measured quantity at a location is lower than the total scheduled quantity for that location, then one or more parties at that location will receive less gas allocated then they requested. The allocation scenario determines which of the parties are affected.

Within the business-process flow for the pipeline, the pipeline may have an operational balancing agreement (OBA) as a standing contract on the pipeline with the operator at a location. If an OBA is in place, the pipeline business practice may preclude the use of a PDA, and the OBA will accept any differences in flow.

When a PDA is used, the operator or other parties at a location submits the PDA prior to the beginning of the flow of gas. This means that it may be submitted as a "standing PDA" for a period of time, or it may be submitted daily during the nomination, confirmation, or scheduling cycle. It must be in place before gas begins to flow for a gas day. Once gas flow has occurred and a quantity is available, the pipeline can allocate the gas. After the pipeline has performed the allocation process, it will provide the results of the allocation process, via EDI, a web screen or a report to the operator and all other parties from which the pipeline accepted a PDA. The pipeline may also provide the allocation statement to other affected parties, such as the shipper. The pipeline must provide either the allocation statement or the imbalance statement to a shipper. The imbalance statement will show the same information but from a nomination point of view rather than a location point of view.

The pipeline determines the level of detail to which it allocates. A pipeline may allocate at a service-requester level or service requester/contract-level and provide allocated quantities at that level to the interconnected parties. The level of detail to which the pipeline allocates also determines the level of detail required for the PDA. If the pipeline allocates to only the shipper level, it is not required to accept instructions in the PDA at a lower level of detail. When the reverse happens, that a pipeline allocates to a lower level of detail than the PDA provided, then the pipeline will use its tariff rules to determine the method for allocating the gas to the lower level of detail.[91] Once the pipeline has utilized the PDA and any other tariff allocation rules, if it must employ additional steps to divide quantities to the nomination transaction line-item level, then it may use shipper-provided nomination ranks.

In the Allocations[92] dataset the Allocation Transaction Type Matrix[93] reflects the level of allocation that the pipeline is providing. There are 27 different levels that may be used to report an allocation level in the allocation transaction type code. Some of the levels are specific to an allocation at a receipt location and some are specific to an allocation at a delivery location. The level that a pipeline may report to an individual party will be dependent on the level of detail in that party's PDA or will be dependent on the rights of that party in the allocation process. For instance, in the previous example of a PDA level, the operator provided the PDA at the shipper-shipper level using a PDA transaction type code value = "7." When this same operator receives an allocation statement, it will be at the shipper-shipper level from a receipt location point of view. For this allocation statement the pipeline will report using the value of "5R" for the allocation transaction type code.

It is important to review the standards and to understand how they work together in order to understand the allocations process. These standards explain the relationship of the operator and the allocating party and explain the expected outcome of the allocation process. [94]

44. OBAs

The OBA plays an important role in the allocation process. When an OBA is in place, the transactional parties on either side of the location are kept whole and any differences between the scheduled quantities and gas flow is assigned to the OBA between the interconnected operating parties per the terms of that agreement. In this situation, it is the responsibility of the pipelines on each side of the OBA location, to allocate their own gas. Generally, when an OBA is in place, the shippers on each of the interconnected pipelines receive their scheduled quantities as the resulting allocated value. In this case, the shipper does not incur any cuts or overages. All differences are added to the balance of the OBA.

Without an OBA in place, one of the pipelines is the allocating party for the location and the other pipeline/interconnect party receives the results of the allocation process.

45. Scenarios

When pipelines are establishing the allocation rules for locations on the pipeline, the pipeline may group locations into those of a similar type. For instance, there may be one set of allocation rules for receipt locations and another set of allocation rules for delivery locations. In reality, though, a pipeline is not as simple as that and will have many groups of locations that employ specific allocation rule schemas. Examples of these groups include all receipts from processing plants, all receipts from an interstate interconnect, all receipts from a non-interstate interconnect, all receipts from gathering locations, and other receipts, deliveries to an interconnect, deliveries into storage, deliveries into a pool, deliveries to an industrial end-user. The list could be extensive depending on the operational configuration of the pipeline. In establishing these groups of locations, a pipeline does not have to create unique allocation rule schemas for every location on the pipeline, but may create a master set of allocation rule schemas from which to work according to the type of the locations.

Pipelines may have services where the nomination must be kept in balance through the allocation process. For these services, a pipeline may be required to allocate one location, such as the receipt side of these transactions, and then push the allocation results to the delivery side of the transaction. In this case, the pipeline's allocation of locations would need to be sequenced so that the receipt locations were allocated, the transactions were balanced, and then the delivery locations were allocated. Or the pipeline could approach the allocation process as an iterative process so that the affected locations were reallocated after the transactions were balanced. In another scenario, the pipeline allocates the locations independent of each other and the resulting difference on the nomination between the allocated receipt quantity and allocated delivery quantity becomes an imbalance quantity on that nomination.

NAESB WGQ Standard 1.3.71[95] includes an important note for the allocations process. For allocations performed at a pool, if the pipeline operates the pool such that allocated quantities are always the scheduled quantities into and out of the pool, then the pipeline does not have to accept PDAs from the TTT parties. Most pipelines in North America operate in such a manner and do not "allocate" the pool but, instead, assign the pool transactions an allocated quantity based on the transaction's scheduled quantity.

Pipelines may perform allocations on an hourly, daily, or monthly basis. A pipeline may have the physical capability to measure gas flow on an hourly basis but a contractual obligation to provide allocated quantities on a monthly basis. Whether a location is allocated on a daily or monthly basis impacts subsequent processes in the pipeline's business cycle. If a pipeline performs monthly allocations, then it can only monitor and access imbalances on a monthly basis.

Some pipelines provide daily allocations throughout the month as an estimated quantity in order for the shipper to be able to track its balances and imbalances on the pipeline system. These quantities are then reallocated at the end of the month to provide a final allocated quantity using the actual quantities from that pipeline's measurement system. A pipeline could provide daily estimated allocated quantities throughout the month even though it has the contractual obligation to provide an actual allocated quantity from a monthly perspective at the end of the month. When a pipeline provides these daily allocations as estimates, NAESB WGQ Standard 2.3.21[96] requires that the operational allocations are provided within one business day after the end of the gas day so that the shipper receives the allocated quantities in a timely manner to affect future nominations.

46. Allocation Methods/Types

The allocation methods are: rank, pro-rata, swing, percentage, and operator-provided-value. An operator may provide more than one allocation method in a single PDA. For instance, the operator may identify one transaction as an operator-provided-value, and then rank the remaining transactions, or an operator may identify several transactions as a percentage and then the remaining transactions are pro-rata.

The rank method means that the transaction is assigned a numeric priority in order from highest, 1, to lowest, 999. A transaction that is ranked number 1 would receive the first distribution of the measured gas, and would be cut last in the allocation process. A transaction that is ranked number 2 would receive the second distribution of gas and would be cut second-to-last in the allocation process. Transactions that carry the same rank are considered equal and are cut on a pro-rata basis.

Pre-Determined Allocation

First American Pipeline Company — January 1, 2000

Location 59

Shipper	Transportation Contract	PDA Method	Method Value
Blue Horizon	TK1433	Rank	1
Red Dawn	TK9845	Rank	2
Green River	TK3368	Rank	3

Example 46.1
An example of a PDA using the rank method

The pro-rata method, when used, instructs the pipeline that the quantity of gas distributed to each party is determined by that party's percentage of the original overall scheduled quantity for the location. For instance, if the original total scheduled quantity for a location was 1,000 DTH and the measured quantity for the location was 800 DTH, then each of the transactions that were marked as pro-rata would receive 80 percent of their original scheduled gas flow. When pro-rata is used on the remaining gas at a flow, then the pro-rata calculation is the percentage of the total scheduled quantity of those remaining transactions versus the remaining gas flow.

Pre-Determined Allocation

First American Pipeline Company January 1, 2000

Location 59

Shipper	Transportation Contract	PDA Method	Method Value
Blue Horizon	TK1433	Rank	
Red Dawn	TK9845	Rank	
Green River	TK3368	Rank	

Example 46.2
An example of a PDA using a rank method with pro-rata results

The swing method designates one or more transactions at the location as the transactions that will receive the differences in the measured flow of gas. The operator may designate one or more transactions as the swing transactions when the measured quantity is "high." This means that these transactions will absorb the excess quantity when the measured quantity is greater than the total scheduled quantity. The operator may also designate one or more transactions as the swing transaction when the measured quantity is "low." This means that these transactions will absorb the deficient quantity when the measured quantity is less than the total scheduled quantity. In addition, a swing transaction may include a maximum quantity that the transaction will absorb. For example, in the case of a high swing, a transaction may have a limit of 1,000 DTH and, when the excess quantity exceeds that 1,000 DTH, then the remainder of the swing quantity will fall to another transaction at the location. When an OBA is in place at a location, the OBA is the swing transaction for all over- and under-deliveries of gas. No further instructions are required in the PDA.

Pre-Determined Allocation

First American Pipeline Company — January 1, 2000

Location 59

Shipper	Transportation Contract	PDA Method	Method Value
Blue Horizon	TK1433	Rank	1
Red Dawn	TK9845	Swing Low	
Green River	TK3368	Swing High	

Example 46.3
A PDA example with a swing-high designation and a swing-low designation

The pipeline uses the percentage method when the operator wants to distribute the quantities measured at a location based on the shipper's percentage rights rather than on the quantity that was originally scheduled. Use of this method could cause a shipper to receive a significantly different quantity than the original scheduled quantity because the pipeline will not rely on the scheduled quantities for the allocation decision. The percentage specified by the operator will rule. For example, suppose there were two nominations at a location, each for 500 DTH, totaling 1,000 DTH, and the operator provides a PDA giving the first nomination 80 percent of the flow and the second nomination 20 percent of the flow. In this case, the pipeline would allocate 800 DTH to the first nomination and 200 DTH to the second nomination, regardless of the nominated quantity.

Pre-Determined Allocation

First American Pipeline Company — January 1, 2000

Location 59

Shipper	Transportation Contract	PDA Method	Method Value
Blue Horizon	TK1433	Percent	50
Red Dawn	TK9845	Percent	30
Green River	TK3368	Percent	20

Example 46.4
A PDA example using percentages

The operator-provided-value method gives the operator the ability to assign a fixed volume to one or more transactions at the location. When the operator uses this method, it generally uses another allocation method for the remainder of the gas flow. It is possible that an operator using this method will assign operator-provided-values that exceed the flow of gas at the location. In this case, the designated swing contract, such as an OBA, at that location would absorb the difference.

Pre-Determined Allocation

First American Pipeline Company — January 1, 2000

Location 59

Shipper	Transportation Contract	PDA Method	Method Value
Blue Horizon	TK1433	Operator Value	10,000 DTH
Red Dawn	TK9845	Rank	2
Green River	TK3368	Rank	3

Example 46.5
A PDA example using operator-provided value and rank

Pre-Determined Allocation

First American Pipeline Company — January 1, 2000

Location 59

Shipper	Transportation Contract	PDA Method	Method Value
Blue Horizon	TK1433	Operator Value	10,000 DTH
Red Dawn	TK9845	Percent	30
Green River	TK3368	Rank	2

Example 46.6
A PDA example using operator-provided value, rank, and percent

As discussed, there can be combinations of allocation methodologies on one PDA. When this occurs, the pipeline will employ a set of priorities to the allocation methods such that one method is evaluated first, another second, etc.

Examples of combinations of allocation methods are shown below. These are some of the combinations that could be employed.

Below are six examples of multiple allocation methods used in one PDA transaction. There is a set order of evaluation of the allocation methods resulting in consistent and predictable results. The six examples are based on the basic example data in the table below:

Order of processing of allocation methods when multiples are used:

1 – Operator-Provided Value
2 – Percent
3 – Rank
4 – ProRata
5 - Swing

Basic Example of nominations at one location:

Loc 1	Qty	Loc flow
Nom1	1000	4500
Nom2	1000	
Nom3	1000	
Nom4	1000	

Loc 1	PDA Ex 1	Extras	Process Sequence	Result
Nom1	OPV	1000	1	1000
Nom2	Pro Rata		3	1250
Nom3	ProRata		3	1250
Nom4	Rank	4	2	1000

Loc 1	PDA Ex 2	Extras	Process Sequence	Result
Nom1	Swing		4	1375
Nom2	Rank	1	2	1000
Nom3	Rank	2	3	1000
Nom4	Percent	25%	1	1125

Loc 1	PDA Ex 3	Extras	Process Sequence	Result
Nom1	Swing		4	1500
Nom2			1	1000
Nom3			1	1000
Nom4			1	1000

Loc 1	PDA Ex 4	Extras	Process Sequence	Result
Nom1	Rank	1	1	1000
Nom2	Rank	2	2	1000
Nom3	Rank	3	3	1000
Nom4	Rank	4	4	1500

Loc 1	PDA EX 5	Extras	Process Sequence	Result
Nom1	OPV	1200	1	1200
Nom2	ProRata		2	1100
Nom3	ProRata		2	1100
Nom4	ProRata		2	1100

Loc 1	PDA Ex 6	Extras	Process Sequence	Result
Nom1			1	1000
Nom2			1	1000
Nom3			1	1000
Nom4			1	1000
	SWING	OBA K	2	500

Example 46.7
Several examples of PDAs using a combination of allocation methods in one PDA

In any of the methods described above, when an OBA is in place, the results of the allocation process could be that more gas is allocated than was measured or less gas was allocated than was measured. In each one of these cases, the OBA will be assigned the difference. If an OBA is not present, then the order of evaluation of the methods used plus any ranks provided will determine which of the transactions are assigned the difference.

47. Inventory

When the pipeline has completed the allocation process, then the quantity in a shipper's account on that pipeline is known. The shipper's account reflects the differences between the allocated quantity the shipper delivered onto the pipeline at the receipt location and the allocated quantity that the shipper received off of the pipeline at the delivery location. The pipeline may track imbalance quantities, quantities into accounts such as storage, parking, and loaning, or other quantities relevant to the shipper.

Inventory

A pipeline may maintain four distinct types of inventory for shippers" accounts: contractual, storage, park and loan, and imbalance. For an operator, the pipeline manages the inventory in the OBA, discussed elsewhere. In addition, the pipeline operations group must maintain the balance across all shippers on the pipeline to manage the operational pressures on that pipeline.

48. Contractual

A pipeline may maintain an inventory balance on a contract for several reasons or in certain scenarios. The first, most common is the monitoring of the contractual MDQ. The MDQ will always be maintained at the contract level, but also may be maintained at the path level, the location level, or both path and location levels on any given contract. As the shipper nominates on a contract, each nomination uses a portion of the MDQ for that contract or one of the lower levels of MDQ. The pipeline must monitor that use to be able to inform the shipper that the MDQ at one or more of the levels has been exceeded during the nomination process.

Contract TKF13769

Terms:		
	Contract MDQ	20,000 DTH / day
Locations:		MDQ:
	Receipt Location A	3,000 DTH/ day
	Receipt Location C	12,000 DTH/ day
	Receipt Location D	10,000 DTH/ day
	Delivery Location N	10,000 DTH/ day
	Delivery Location Q	14,000 DTH/ day
	Delivery Location S	4,000 DTH/ day
Path Restrictions:		
	Receipt Location A to Delivery Location N = 2,000 DTH/ day	
	Receipt Location D to Delivery Location N = 4,000 DTH/ day	

Example 48.1
An example of the contractual MDQs that must be monitored for inventory balance

The pipeline also uses the contract-inventory method of minimum-performance requirements for the contract. These minimums may be for monthly use or may span several months. These minimums may be to require a certain level of performance to qualify for the contract to remain in place, may impose minimum charges, may give credits back on underutilized demand charges when they are used in a subsequent periods, and many other scenarios. These contract-level accounts or accumulators are identified in the shipper's contract with the pipeline and in the General Terms and Conditions of that pipeline.

Contract TKF13769

Terms:

Contract MDQ	20,000 DTH / day
Contract Minimum Take	10,000 DTH/ day

Rates:

Demand Rate	$0.20 / DTH / day
Commodity Rate	$0.08 / DTH / day
Underutilization Rate	$0.12 / DTH / day

Example:

Contract Usage for January 14 = 20,000 DTH	
Charges =	
Demand at $0.20 * 20,000 DTH	$4,000
Commodity at $0.08 * 20,000 DTH	$1,600
Contract Usage for January 15 = 12,000 DTH	
Charges =	
Demand at $0.20 * 20,000 DTH	$4,000
Commodity at $0.08 * 12,000 DTH	$ 960
Contract Usage for January 16 = 7,000 DTH	
Charges =	
Demand at $0.20 * 20,000 DTH	$4,000
Commodity at $0.08 * 7,000 DTH	$ 560
Underutilization at $0.12 * 3,000 DTH	$ 360

Example 48.2
An example of contract terms of MDQs and rates applied to create charges for underutilization

49. Storage

Storage inventory means the quantity of gas in a shipper's contracted storage account. The balance in inventory is the sum of all of that shipper's injections and withdrawals on the storage facility. On a single storage facility, a pipeline will have accounts for each of the shippers with contracts to store gas at that facility. Shippers may use a nomination transaction to transfer ownership of gas, via buying and selling, to another shipper in that same facility. If a shipper desires to buy or sell gas to a shipper in another facility, then one of the shippers must enter a transportation transaction to move the gas from one facility to the other.

As discussed in Contracts, a storage contract will usually have a period of time for injecting gas into storage and a period of time for withdrawing gas from storage. Some pipelines will allow a shipper to inject during the withdrawal period, withdraw during the injection period, or both. This is determined by the operational constraints of the pipeline. In the United States pipeline grid, the time for switching between these periods is usually November 1 and April 1 of each year. On April 1, a contract may require that the storage-inventory balance is a zero.

Ratchets

Storage contracts often have storage contract ratchets which manage the injection and withdrawal limits during peak periods of the inventory season. Some storage facilities base the ratchet percentage on the overall field inventory as a sum of all shippers while other storage facilities base the ratchet percentage on the contracted shipper's inventory level.

When the levels in the storage field are low, during the injection season, it is easy for the field to accommodate 100 percent of the contract MDQ for injection. When the storage field is nearing capacity, at the end of the injection season, it is more difficult for the field to accommodate 100 percent of the contracted injection MDQ. The storage ratchet for injection will allow full MDQ capability when the storage field is at a low capacity and will limit the injection to a percentage of the MDQ when the field is close to full. An example of a storage ratchet would be that, when inventory is between 0 and 50 percent, then injection can be at 100 percent of MDQ, when inventory is between 50 percent and 75 percent, then injection can be at 75 percent of MDQ, and, when inventory is between 75 percent and 100 percent, then injection can be at 50 percent of MDQ.

The storage ratchets for withdrawal work in a similar manner. When the levels in the storage field are high, during withdrawal season, it is easy for the field to accommodate 100 percent of the contract MDQ for withdrawal. When the storage field is getting close to zero in inventory, at the end of the withdrawal season, it is more difficult for the field to accommodate 100 percent of the contracted withdrawal MDQ. The storage ratchet for withdrawal will allow full MDQ capability when the storage field is at a high inventory level and will limit the withdrawal to a percentage of the MDQ when the field is low in inventory. An example of a storage ratchet for withdrawal would be that when inventory is from 100 percent down to 50 percent, the withdrawal can be at 100 percent of MDQ, when the inventory is from 50 percent down to 20 percent, the withdrawal can be at 60 percent of MDQ, and when the inventory is below 20 percent, the withdrawal can be at 30 percent of MDQ. Another example of the storage ratchet percentage would be a pro-rata calculation of the customer's inventory level versus contract quantity.

This practice gives the storage operator the ability to manage the injections and withdrawals during prime periods so that customers are given equal and fair access to the capabilities of the storage facility.

50. Park and Loan

Pipelines with the operational capacity may offer a park and loan (PAL) service[97]. The service operates much the same as storage service, utilizing injection and withdrawal transactions to manage the balance. The shipper is charged a fee for the balance in inventory on a daily or monthly basis, depending on the terms of the contract. There is generally no seasonal cycle to PAL that is equivalent to the seasons in storage. Because this service is an interruptible service, the pipeline may retain the right to require the shipper to withdraw any parked gas on very short notice. If the gas is not withdrawn, the shipper will be subject to cash-out terms in the agreement, where the pipeline will automatically purchase the parked gas from the shipper in order to meet its operational needs. The reverse is true on the loan side of the contract. If the pipeline needs the quantity paid back in a short period of time to maintain operational integrity, the pipeline may give notice to the shipper to permit it to provide the gas or may force the shipper into purchasing the gas from the pipeline as a cash-out.

51. Imbalance

The first and most important thing to know about imbalances is that there are a host of ways that companies calculate imbalances. There are many different types of imbalances, and there are many different ways to resolve imbalances. This chapter will cover the most common forms and methods, but it will not be able to cover all of the forms, and there will always be new variations found in the industry.

The most common type of imbalances start as the difference between a planned receipt and a planned delivery. Generally, this occurs between a receipt location and a delivery location on a nomination.

A shipper imbalance is the difference between what a shipper delivered onto the pipeline and what the shipper received off of the pipeline. This imbalance may be maintained on an hourly, daily, or monthly basis. It may be maintained at the nomination level or at one of many aggregate levels that are described below.

Some pipelines calculate the imbalance as the difference between scheduled receipt quantity and scheduled delivery quantity. This situation most often occurs on pipelines that have an OBA at both the receipt and delivery location and, therefore, keep the shipper's scheduled volumes whole. Other pipelines calculate the imbalance as the difference between the allocated receipt quantity and allocated delivery quantity. In this situation the pipeline performs an allocation of the measured quantity at a location to determine the shipper's portion of gas that flowed.

An operator imbalance at a location is the difference between what was scheduled to flow through a location and what actually flowed. This imbalance is maintained and resolved at the location level through an OBA.

The imbalance may be managed and resolved through several mechanisms. The imbalance-resolution mechanisms that a pipeline offers depend on whether the pipeline is interstate or non-interstate and on the services of that pipeline.[98]

OBAs

One of the first imbalance-management mechanisms to understand is the OBA. When an OBA is in place at both the receipt and delivery locations of a shipper's transportation, then the shipper's actual quantity is the same as the shipper's scheduled quantity, and the shipper is immune to variations in the flow of gas. The pipeline and the operators at the receipt and delivery locations absorb the variations in flow into their OBA agreements, keeping the shipper's flow "whole", and allocate to the shipper the entire quantity that was scheduled.

Pipelines and operators can manage OBAs through make-up of gas, through cash-out, by rolling the imbalance from month to month or, in some instances, by trading the imbalance. When the operator resolves an OBA through makeup of gas, this means that, when the flow of gas through a point is from Pipeline A to Pipeline B and the measured gas is less than what is scheduled, then on a subsequent gas day(s), the operator will increase the flow of gas to more than what was scheduled to make up the deficiency on the previous day(s). If the flow of gas through the location is more than what was scheduled then, on a subsequent gas day(s), the operator will reduce the flow of gas to less than is scheduled to resolve the overage on the previous day(s). When an OBA uses only the make-up of gas to resolve balancing differences, then the make-up may occur on a next-day basis or in subsequent months, depending upon whether the operational flow information is exchanged between the parties on a daily basis or on a monthly basis. Some pipelines require the OBA make-up/payback of gas to be entered into their nominations system as a make-up/payback type nomination. In these instances, the interconnected pipeline submits the nomination with the number of the OBA contract for the quantity being resolved. In some OBA contracts, an intentional make-up process is not used on a daily or monthly basis. Instead, there is an occasional true-up where the two parties determine if there are any imbalance trends that need to be reconciled. When an OBA is resolved through cash-out, each month's balance difference is either bought or sold to the other party at the end of the billing month. In some cases, operators holding OBA agreements participate in imbalance trading with the shippers on that pipeline. The operator may use a long or short position on their contract to offset the imbalance quantity on the pipeline held by a transportation shipper. More information on imbalance trading is discussed in a later chapter.

Long versus Short

An imbalance where a shipper has delivered more gas than was received is considered as a "balance-due shipper" because there is still gas remaining on the pipeline that belongs to the shipper. An imbalance where a shipper has received more gas than was delivered is considered a "balance-due pipeline" because the shipper has taken more gas off the pipeline than it provided, and the shipper owes the pipeline the difference. Historically, pipelines used the terms "long" and "short" to describe these positions, but there was often confusion on whose point of view the long and short positions described. "Balance-due shipper" and "balance-due pipeline" are intended to provide clarity on which party has the shortage versus the overage.

Levels

At the most detailed level, the imbalance must be calculated at the same level of detail as the original nomination[99] or the allocation must be provided at this level of detail. Most pipelines provide allocations at a higher level of detail and provide imbalances at the nomination line-item level of detail.

Additionally, a pipeline may summarize imbalances to a higher level of detail to effectuate a resolution via make-up/payback, trading, or cash-outs. The level of summarization that a pipeline uses will vary according to the operational constraints and tariff provisions of that pipeline. This summarization level is often referred to as the Operational Impact Area (OIA). Depending on the pipe, OIA may be for a zone, a group of locations, a path, a segment, or for the entire pipeline. The pipeline may have a shipper account in which to summarize the imbalances across contracts to this OIA on the pipeline, or the pipeline may designate a contract to hold the summarized imbalances. The goal of a pipeline in establishing the OIA is to create an area that is as large as operationally feasible for the resolution of imbalances. The summarization of imbalances is also referred to as imbalance netting[100]. By netting imbalances, a balance that is due to the shipper on one contract may offset a balance that is due to the pipeline on another contract to minimize the quantity that the shipper has to resolve and to minimize the shipper's exposure to a potential penalty assessment.

Imbalance Resolutions

Most pipelines resolve inventory imbalances on a quantity basis. Some pipelines use an imbalance valuation method to determine the value of the imbalance at a point in time, and the imbalance resolution method seeks to resolve the value rather than the quantity of gas. The imbalance valuation resolution method is very pipeline-specific.

There are several different mechanisms that a pipeline may provide to resolve imbalances. Make-up/payback nominations, balancing agreements, cash-outs, and imbalance trading are the most common tools.

Make-up and payback nominations[101] are made by the shipper or operator to either bring gas onto the pipeline when the party is in a "balance-due pipeline" position or to take gas off of the pipeline when the party is in a "balance-due shipper" position. The make-up/payback nomination is most often provided during the production month in which the imbalance occurred. Some pipelines permit shippers to submit make-up/payback nominations in the subsequent production month for a limited time period.

Some pipelines offer their shippers balancing agreements as a tool to ensure that the minimum imbalance exists. There are two forms of balancing agreements. The shipper can specify the first type of balancing agreement on the nomination as an associated contract to indicate to the pipeline that, should the nomination have an over- or under-delivery, then the difference should be placed on the balancing agreement. A storage contract is often used for this balance agreement so that the over- or under-delivery is made up by the quantity in storage. The pipeline may designate the second type of balancing agreement to hold a summary-level imbalance for this shipper. As discussed above, this summary-level agreement permits over deliveries to offset under deliveries for this shipper.

Cash-outs are a method where, at the end of the imbalance period, the pipeline either sells the "balance-due pipeline" to the shipper from pipeline inventory or the pipeline buys the "balance-due shipper" from the shipper into pipeline inventory. This is a monetary transaction rather than a quantity transaction to reduce a quantity imbalance.

Imbalance trading is a method where, after the end of the production month but before the cash-out process, shippers and, in some cases, operators are given the opportunity to trade imbalance positions on the pipeline. The pipeline hosts this process, which is revenue-neutral from the pipeline point of view. Imbalance trading is discussed in more detail below.

Trading

The transportation pipeline hosts the imbalance trading process. The pipeline posts imbalances that are available for trade, accepts requests for trade and confirmation of trade from the two parties affecting the trade, and approves or rejects the trade. At the end of the trading process, the imbalance quantities that were traded are used to reduce the imbalance amount for each of the parties in the transaction[102].

The goal of imbalance trading is to allow the shippers who are due gas from the pipeline or owe gas to the pipeline to trade any imbalances that are subject to penalty with other parties on the pipeline who have the opposite position. This imbalance off-setting process permits the affected parties to resolve their imbalance quantities and avoid being subject to cash-out or penalty assessments.

Imbalance trading takes place after the accounting period for the active operational period has closed. The pipeline offers a trade window during which imbalances may be traded. NAESB defines a minimum window for this trading period. [103]

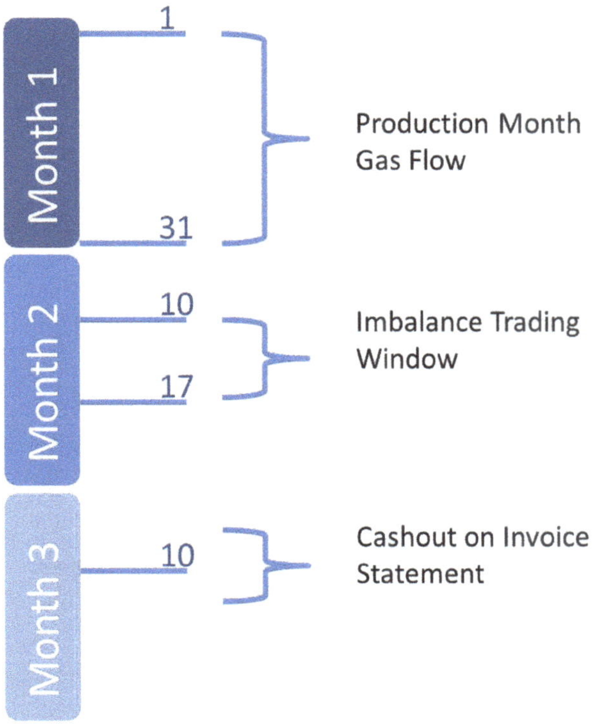

Figure 51.1
The imbalance trading window within the business calendar

The shipper's goal in imbalance trading is to reduce the imbalance quantity to a level that it either minimizes the quantity to be cashed out or is not in the range for penalties to be assessed. Some pipelines offer a shipper the option to trade beyond their imbalance as long as they stay out of the penalty range. An example of this would be where a shipper has a scheduled quantity of 1,000 DTH and an allocated quantity of 1,200 DTH. The pipeline's penalty levels begin at +/-10 percent. The shipper is in the penalty range because the allocated quantity is 20 percent higher than the scheduled quantity. The shipper finds an opportunity to trade 250 DTH, but the counterparty will not take a lesser amount. If the pipeline in this example allows the shipper to trade past zero, then the shipper can trade the entire 250 DTH, giving a new allocated quantity of 950 DTH. This new allocated quantity is less than the shipper wanted, but is within the +/-10-percent penalty range and therefore removes the shipper from the risk of incurring penalties.

Nomination:

Receipt Location	Transportation Imbalance Contract	Delivery Location	Nominated Quantity	Scheduled Quantity	Allocated Receipt	Allocated Delivery
A1492	FK4242 +200 DTH	Z1476	1,000 DTH	1,000 DTH	1,200 DTH	1,000 Dth

Imbalance Penalty at +/- 10% of transaction: 200/1000 = 20% imbalance for this transaction

Imbalance Trade – Sell 250 DTH to the other party: +200 DTH -250 DTH= -50 DTH
New, adjusted imbalance = -50 DTH: 50/1000 = 5% imbalance –> no penalty

Example 51.1
An example of a statement with an imbalance penalty assessed

The shipper who has incurred imbalances on the pipeline has the option on whether or not it wants its imbalances posted for other shippers to view as being available for trade. A shipper elects to post or discontinue posting through the Authorization to Post Imbalances[104] transaction. This transaction informs the pipeline that the shipper, as of the authorization date, wishes for its imbalances to be posted on the pipeline's website. The Authorization to Post is effective until a subsequent Authorization to Post is received.

Regardless of whether the shipper posts imbalances, the shipper may participate in the imbalance-trading process. Shippers who desire to trade imbalances must contact each other independent of the pipeline to determine the quantity and price that they wish to trade. Once this transaction is agreed, one of the shippers in the trade will submit the transaction to the pipeline to initiate the trade process through the Request for Imbalance Trade.[105] The other shipper in the trade is then responsible to either confirm the trade through the Imbalance Trade Confirmation[106] with the pipeline or to have in place a standing agreement with the pipeline to automatically confirm the trade. Once the trade is entered and confirmed, the trade is complete. The pipeline will then reduce the imbalance quantities of each of the trade parties to reflect the quantities they traded. The pipeline will also notify both of the trading parties that the trade is complete.

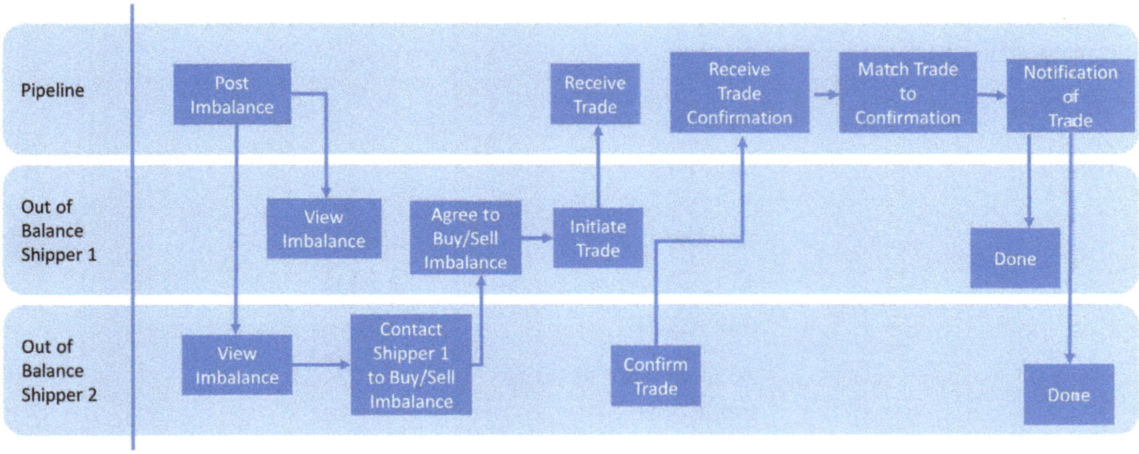

Figure 51.2
The flow of information in the imbalance trading process

In some instances, a pipeline's OIA for trading may include multiple rate zones. If this case occurs, the pipeline may also require one of the shippers to transport the quantity being traded to the zone of the other imbalance for the trade. Otherwise, if a shipper traded an imbalance between two different rate zones, the pipeline would lose the transportation revenue between those two zones and create an opportunity for manipulation of the pipeline system.

Cash-outs

The dollar amount that a pipeline charges or pays in the cash-out process is specified in the pipeline tariff or SOC. Often, the cash-out price is based on a market-index price or a factor of multiple market-index prices. When a pipeline has to buy the gas from the shipper, the pipeline will pay a percentage less than or equal to the market price. When a pipeline has to sell the gas to the shipper, the pipeline will charge a percentage equal to or greater than the market price. Cash-outs may be used on shipper imbalances or operator OBA imbalances.

Combination Rates		
Cashout Rates		
Zone 2	Rate Basis = Average of Zones 1,2 & 3 First of Month Index Rate	
	Zone 1 First of Month Index Rate	$3.146
	Zone 2 First of Month Index Rate	$3.25
	Zone 3 First of Month Index Rate	$3.3146
	Resolved Rate Basis = Average (Zone 1, Zone 2, Zone 3)	$3.2369

Combination Rates		
For Imbalance Due Pipeline :		
	If Imbalance Quantity </= 5% then Rate = Rate Basis	Resolved Rate = $3.2369
	If Imbalance Quantity > 5% and </+ 10% then Rate = Rate Basis + 20%	Resolved Rate = $3.8843
	If Imbalance Quantity > 10% and </= 30% then Rate = Rate Basis + 40%	Resolved Rate = $4.5317
	If Imbalance Quantity > 30% then Rate = Rate Basis + 50%	Resolved Rate = $4.8554
For Imbalance Due Shipper:		
	If Imbalance Quantity </= 10% then Rate = Rate Basis	Resolved Rate = $3.2369
	If Imbalance Quantity > 10% then Rate = Rate Basis - 30%	Resolved Rate = $2.2658

Example 51.2
Cash-out rates that are a combination of formulas

Some pipelines cash out the entire imbalance quantity each month. Other pipelines cash out any quantity in excess of the minimum tolerance. For instance, if a pipeline has an imbalance tolerance of +/-5 percent and, within that 5 percent, the pipeline will not charge any penalties but will cash out at the 100 percent index price, then the pipeline may offer that the cash-out will only be to the tolerance of 5 percent and will not be for the entire imbalance. This practice gives the shipper the opportunity to make up or pay back the imbalance during a subsequent cycle. An example of this would be where a shipper had a nominated quantity of 1,000 DTH and has an allocated quantity of 1,100 DTH. This shipper has an imbalance of 10 percent. In the pipeline scenario described above, the pipeline would cash out the quantity of 50 DTH to bring the shipper's quantity down to the 5-percent tolerance rather than cashing out the entire 100 DTH imbalance.

Nomination:

Receipt Location	Transportation Contract	Delivery Location	Nominated Quantity	Scheduled Quantity	Allocated Receipt	Allocated Delivery	Imbalance
A1492	FK4242	Z1476	1,000 DTH	1,000 DTH	1,100 DTH	1,000 Dth	+100 DTH

Imbalance percentage = 100/1000 DTH = 10%
Pipeline cashout process cashes out any imbalance quantity greater than 5%.

Pipeline cashout tolerance quantity = 1,000 DTH * 05% = 50 DTH.
Cashout Quantity = 100 DTH – 50 DTH = 50 DTH

Example 51.3
An example of a statement where the shipper is cashed-out to a tolerance

Penalties

The pipeline does not retain revenues that it collects from imbalance cash-outs because the pipeline is not allowed to make money in the cash-out process. This is why incentives such as make-up/payback and imbalance trading exist to give the shipper the opportunity to resolve imbalances before the cash-out penalty is used. The pipeline must distribute penalties that it collects during the cash-out process back to the other shippers on the pipeline that were impacted by the imbalance. Each pipeline's tariff's General Terms and Conditions will describe the method that the pipeline uses to distribute these penalties back to the affected parties. The determination of how these penalties are distributed is often based on the pipeline's definition of operational impact areas (OIA) for imbalances. If the OIA for a pipeline is a zone, then the distribution of penalties could be to all parties who had cut transactions in that zone during that period or it could be to all parties who transported gas in that zone during that period.

Penalty Tiered Limits

As described earlier, a pipeline most often uses market-index rates to determine the basis for a cash-out price. In addition to these index rates, the pipeline will list a tiered price to include the penalties based on the percentage of overage or underage of the imbalance. An example of a tiered cash-out rate would be:

For Balance-Due Pipeline	
Imbalance quantity < 10%	Rate = Index Price
Imbalance quantity 10% - <20%	Rate = 110% of Index Price
Imbalance quantity 20% - <40%	Rate = 130% of Index Price
Imbalance quantity 40% +	Rate = 150% of Index Price

For Balance-Due Shipper	
Imbalance quantity <10%	Rate = Index Price
Imbalance quantity 10% - <20%	Rate = 90% of Index Price
Imbalance quantity 20% - <40%	Rate = 70% of Index Price
Imbalance quantity 40% +	Rate = 50% of Index Price

Example 51.4
An example of a tiered cash-out rate

In some cases, pipelines permit agents and asset managers for shippers to summarize imbalances incurred across the shippers that the agent represents, and then the agent or asset manager will cash out on their own account rather than at the individual-shipper level. The individual pipeline determines this practice.

Accounting

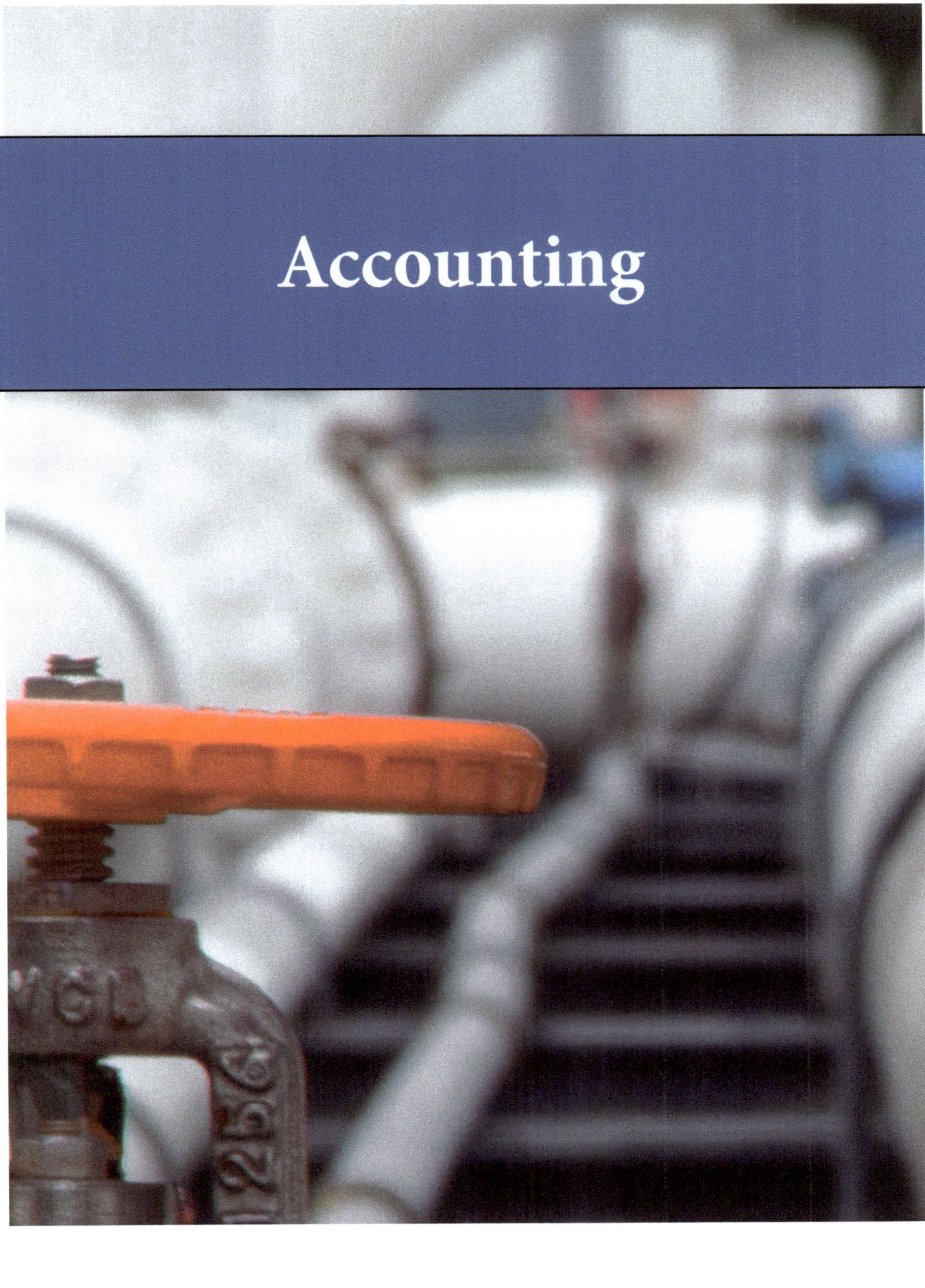

General accounting principles from the Council of Petroleum Accountants Society (COPAS)[107] provide a comprehensive and solid foundation for accounting. In addition, requirements for Sarbanes-Oxley (SOX)[108] compliance cause many specific accounting practices to be in place to ensure compliance. Regular audits of accounting practices in the industry provide information quality assurance.

In addition to requirements that pipelines must resolve the charges they are assessing customers for transportation, penalties, and other tariff services, the pipelines must also resolve the quantities of gas exchanged at interconnects that impact their OBAs with the interconnected pipeline operator. These checks and balances are part of a pipeline's regular accounting business process.

52. Taxes

Some pipelines are required to collect state and local taxes on transportation when they are the ultimate delivery for a flow of gas or, in some cases, the initial receipt of gas. The shipper contract with the pipeline defines the taxes to be collected. The pipeline assesses the taxes based on the rules of the state, county, city, or other local authority, and disburses those quantities with accompanying reports to those authorities. Interstate pipelines do not have to collect taxes on interstate transportation.

53. Non-Volumetric Charges

At times in the business process, a pipeline may assess non-volumetric charges. Generally these charges are a one-time or a limited-term occurrence.

Some pipelines have flat-fee charges that may be assessed at the contract level or at a shipper level. These charges are usually associated with some type of regulatory settlement. The flat-fee charges are not use-based, meaning that they are not multiplied by a quantity of gas transported, nor are they zone- or location-based, so the amount of the charge is not associated with any location or distance traveled. These fees are a single charge applied to a service on the contract. In some instances, these charges may be in the form of a refund where a regulatory settlement has determined that the pipeline should return some portion of a previously collected fee to the shippers. This refund may be based on a pro-rata share of a prior invoice or service of the pipeline.

A pipeline may assess another contract or shipper-level charge, which is an interest charge on an unpaid balance from a previous invoice.

54. Fuel

Fuel is another type of charge. When gas is received onto a pipeline, the pipeline will, in most instances, retain a percentage of the gas as fuel to be used in operating the pipeline. This quantity is referred to as fuel in-kind. The retained quantity includes not just the fuel used, but may also include a calculated percentage of pipeline unaccounted for gas and other pipeline operational quantities.

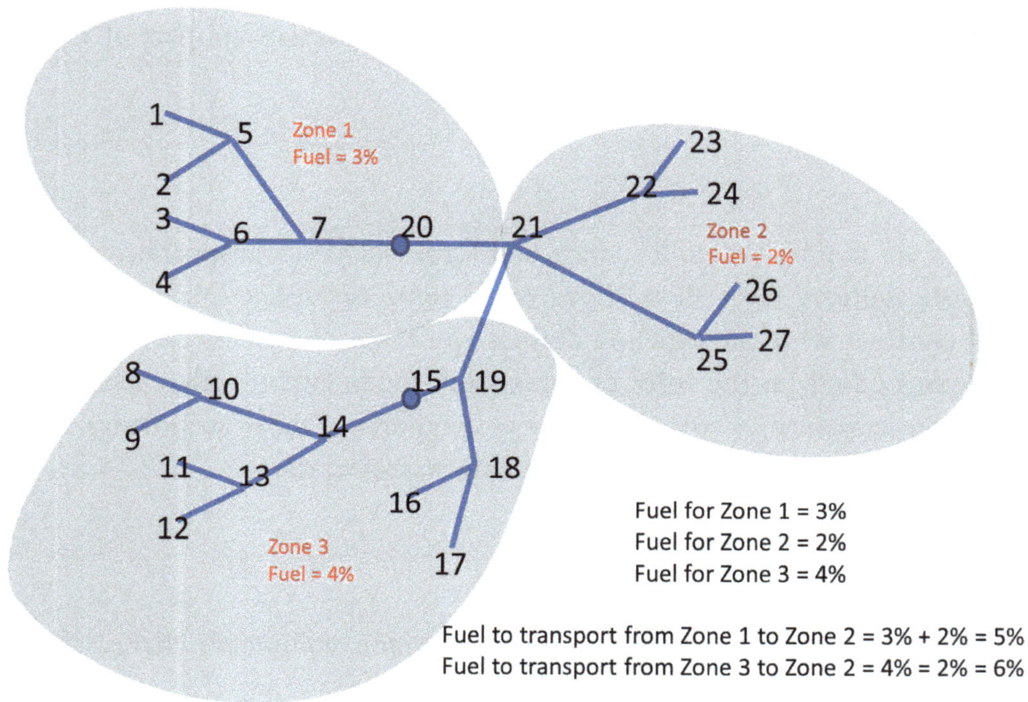

Figure 54.1
Cumulative fuel rates when crossing multiple zones

A pipeline may offer the shipper the ability to pay a fee for fuel rather than have a quantity retained from the transportation quantity. When this is offered by a pipeline, the pipeline tariff, contract with the shipper, or both will state the fuel-related charges.

55. Charges

Each individual pipeline tariff explains charge calculations. The charges assessed on an invoice are those charges for each of the charge types specified in the shipper's contract/ service agreement. The chapter on Contract Rates discussed the various charge types that a pipeline may include in a shipper contract.

Pipelines use the basic charge calculation of a rate * quantity for natural gas transportation, the rate being the stated charge in the agreement, and the volume being the best available quantity of gas that was transported during the billing period. There are, of course, exceptions to every rule.

One of the first exceptions is that some rates are stated as daily rates, and some are stated as monthly rates. When transportation is measured on a daily basis, but the rate is a monthly rate or if the transportation is for a partial month, then the pipeline must convert the rate from a monthly to a daily charge. NAESB WGQ Standard 5.3.22[109] provides the calculation rules for converting a daily rate to a monthly rate and for converting a monthly rate to a daily rate. By using these calculations instead of using one of several different approaches for conversion, participants in the industry are given a consistent result, and shippers can more accurately predict the invoice charges that will come from the pipeline.

Charges may be added together into one rate and multiplied by the total quantity, or the invoice may list each of the charges as separate charges applied to the quantity. A common scenario where charges are added together is when the transportation passes through multiple rate zones. A pipeline may summarize the commodity charges for all of the zones that were utilized into one rate.

Storage charges are a special situation. A pipeline tariff may include charges for injection of the gas into storage, withdrawal of the gas from storage, or a daily charge per quantity for keeping the gas in storage. These are the most common charges. In addition, there are many variations of storage services and the charges that may be incurred. For example, some pipelines have a rule that all gas must be withdrawn from storage by a specified date in spring and, if there is any gas remaining in the storage account, then the gas may be assessed an additional cycling fee or may be assessed a charge as though the gas is withdrawn from storage and re-injected on that date. Some pipelines assess storage charges based on performance, meaning that there are expected quantities or percentages of gas to be injected into storage by a certain calendar date. This is to encourage shippers to inject gas on a regular basis throughout the injection cycle rather than trying to force the target storage quantity into the storage facility in a short period of time immediately prior to the deadline and causing operational issues on the pipeline and at the storage facility. Similar fees and rules apply on the withdrawal side of these same storage facilities.

The pipeline applies credits to a releasing shipper's contract during the capacity-release process. When payments are received from the replacement shipper in the capacity-release transaction, the pipeline applies those payments as credits to the releasing-shipper's contract. See Charges under the Capacity Release chapter for more information.

The cash-out section of the Imbalances chapter discusses cash-out rates and charges. Cash-outs are generally index-based charges with associated cash-out formula prices. The cash-out may be a tiered charge based on the percentage of the imbalance. The cash-out may include a penalty assessment if the quantity of the imbalance exceeded the tariff- or contract-level tolerance.

The charge calculations, charge codes, and rates specified in a pipeline tariff determine the charges that are assessed on an invoice, which are agreed to or modified by the shipper contract.

56. Charge Calculations

Pipelines may assess charges at a shipper level, at a service-contract level, at a path level, at a zone or segment level, or at a point level depending on the pipeline tariff and shipper-contract terms. Most charges are assumed to be quantity-based charges, meaning that they are based on a rate * quantity calculation.

The quantity used in transaction-based calculations is the best available quantity for that transaction. The final quantity for a transaction may be the actual allocated quantity. For transactions that are made whole by an OBA, there may be no allocation and the best available quantity may be the scheduled quantity. The best available quantity hierarchy or the contract terms determine which quantity will be used in calculations.

When the pipeline assesses charges at a path level, this means that a contract or tariff states the charge that will be assessed from a stated receipt location to a stated delivery location. Such a contract often identifies multiple paths.

Charges assessed on a zone level may be stated at the contract level or in the pipeline tariff. When zone-based charges are applied, the transportation from one receipt to one delivery is evaluated and each of the zones that the transportation path travels through are multiplied by the quantity of gas that traveled through that zone.

Pipelines apply segment charges much the same as zone-based charges. It may assess segment charges in addition to a zone-based charge. Some pipelines implement general zone-based rates, but assess an additional charge if the transportation travels through those certain specified segments on the pipeline. The use of segment charges and zone charges, though somewhat similar, are not mutually exclusive.

A recent trend in transportation has been charges based on index pricing. Index-based pricing has been used for many years for the purchase and sale of gas, but it has not been used for the pricing of transportation. When index pricing is used for transportation, the pipeline usually bases the charge on the difference between an index price that is indicative of the price of gas at the receipt location on the pipeline and an index price that is indicative of the price of gas at the delivery location on the pipeline. This difference is then multiplied by a percentage factor, modified by the addition or subtraction of a flat amount, or both. The use of index pricing in transportation is required to be supported in capacity release and is optional on other transportation services[110]. Index-based pricing allows the pipeline, the shipper holding firm service on that pipeline, or both to recognize the value of the transportation service as the difference between the two market prices rather than transferring all of that value to the purchase and sale of the gas.

Complex Charge Formula Examples

Example 1:

Transportation Rate = Diff (Chicago Hub Month Average, Henry Hub Month Average) * 80%

This example sets the transportation rate at 80 percent of the difference between the receipt market sales price and delivery market sales price for gas.

Example 2:

Zone 1 Transportation Rate = Rate = (Zone 1 Index * 20%) + $0.60

This example sets the transportation rate as a small percentage of a zone index rate plus a fixed charge.

Example 3:

Tariff Commodity Rates		
Zone 3	0-5,000 DTH	$0.14
	5,001-10,000 DTH	$0.11
	10,001-30,000 DTH	$0.09
	30,001 + DTH	$0.08

This example shows tiered rates within a zone.

Example 56.1
Examples of complex charge formulas

Example 4:
The example below shows cashout rates for a tariff. The rates are tiered using an index as the basis. There are different tiers depending on whether the cashout quantity is due the pipeline or the shipper.

Combination Rates		
Cashout Rates		
Zone 2	Rate Basis = Average of Zones 1,2 & 3 First of Month Index Rate	
	Zone 1 First of Month Index Rate	$3.146
	Zone 2 First of Month Index Rate	$3.25
	Zone 3 First of Month Index Rate	$3.3146
	Resolved Rate Basis = Average (Zone 1, Zone 2, Zone 3)	$3.2369
For Imbalance Due Pipeline :		
	If Imbalance Quantity </= 5% then Rate = Rate Basis	Resolved Rate = $3.2369
	If Imbalance Quantity > 5% and </+ 10% then Rate = Rate Basis + 20%	Resolved Rate = $3.8843
	If Imbalance Quantity > 10% and </= 30% then Rate = Rate Basis + 40%	Resolved Rate = $4.5317
	If Imbalance Quantity > 30% then Rate = Rate Basis + 50%	Resolved Rate = $4.8554
For Imbalance Due Shipper:		
	If Imbalance Quantity </= 10% then Rate = Rate Basis	Resolved Rate = $3.2369
	If Imbalance Quantity > 10% then Rate = Rate Basis - 30%	Resolved Rate = $2.2658

Example 56.1 (continued)
Examples of complex charge formulas

In charge assessment, a hierarchy determines which charge is used on a transaction. A pipeline will publish a tariff rate for a specific charge, for example, a commodity charge. This rate may be stated as a single rate or as a minimum/maximum rate range. The shipper may then negotiate a contract commodity charge that is within the terms of the tariff. In addition, the shipper may negotiate a rate that is specific to one path on the contract. When assessing charges, the lowest level of rate provided is the one that is selected. If a shipper has a negotiated path rate, that rate will supersede a path, contract, or tariff rate. If a shipper has a negotiated location rate, that rate will supersede a contract rate but not a path rate. If a shipper has a negotiated contract rate, that rate will supersede a tariff rate but not a path or location rate. If no contract level rate is provided, then the tariff rate will prevail.

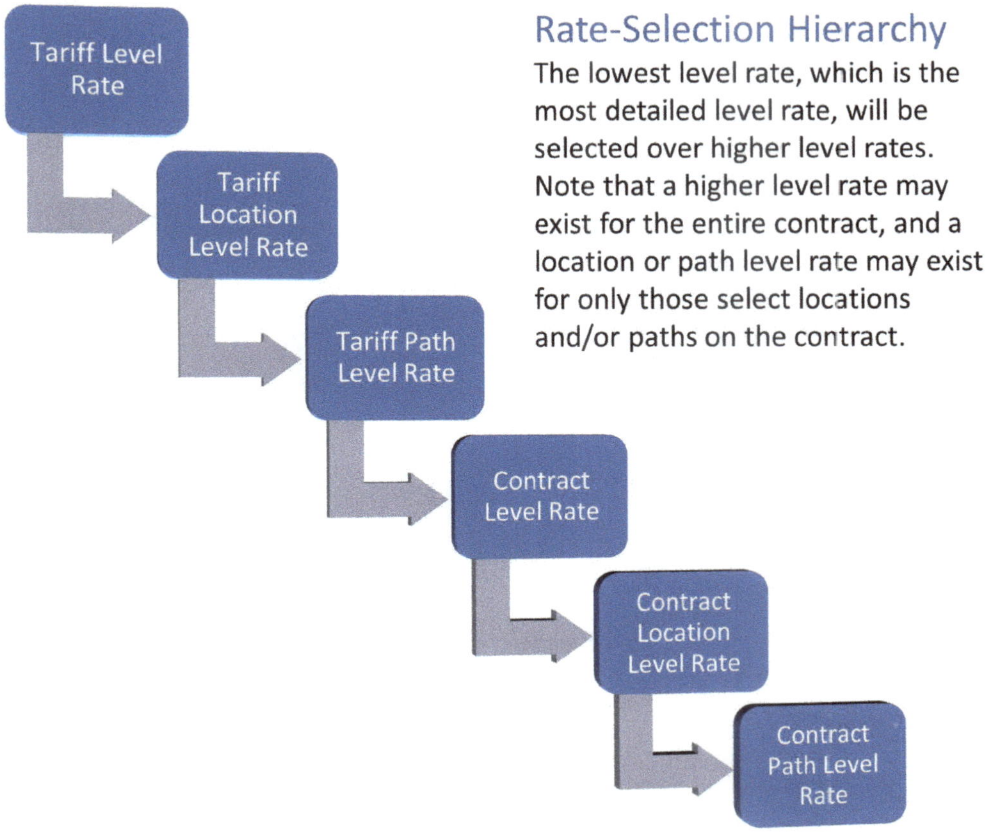

Figure 56.1
The rate selection hierarchy between tariff and contract level rates

57. Adjustments

Prior-period adjustments are common in natural gas. This happens for many reasons but the most common reason for a prior-period adjustment is that the final actual measured volume, and consequently the actual allocated quantity, was not available for the previous month prior to invoice calculations. Once the actual volume is available, then the pipeline issues a prior-period adjustment (PPA) to correct the volume from the estimate value to the actual value. This correction will cause either an additional charge to be assessed on the current-month charge statement or a refund to be issued by the pipeline.

PPAs are applied back to the production month in which they occurred. For example, if gas flowed in the month of March and was given an estimated flow of 1,000 DTH, then the shipper would be charged for the quantity of 1,000 DTH on the April statement for the March activity. Later in April, the actual flow for March is determined to have been 1,050 DTH. The May statement for that shipper would include an additional charge of 50 DTH to reflect the actual flow in addition to the activity for the April production month. The charge that is assessed in May will use the charges that were in effect for March to calculate that amount of the charge/refund.

March Activity Invoice # 20000301			April 10, 2000
Transportation Flow	1,000 DTH	Rate = $0.21	**Total Charge = $210**

April Activity Invoice #20000401			May 10, 2000
Transportation Flow	2,000 DTH	Rate = $0.24	Charge = $480
PPA for March	50 DTH	Rate = $0.21	Charge = $10.50
			Total Charge = $490.50

Example 57.1
Two invoices. The first is a straight invoice and the second contains a prior period adjustment against the first invoice.

Additionally, any inventory accounts and their associated charges must be adjusted based on the March values. All of these adjustments will be reflected on the May charge statement. [111]

There is a time limit on PPAs. PPAs may only be assessed for six months after the original transaction is invoiced. In addition, when a PPA is issued, the customer has a three month time period in which to evaluate and dispute the PPA.

58. Close Cycle

The accounting cycle is a process that can span several months. Generally, transactions that occur in a calendar production month are settled in the subsequent month. There are, of course, exceptions. Imbalance trading occurs in the month following production and therefore is not settled until two months after the production month. Prior period adjustments may occur for several months after the production month. There are general accounting principles employed by pipelines to determine the accounting close cycle. These must be coupled with any NAESB standards to see an entire accounting close picture. [112]

59. Invoice

Invoicing is more than the generation of the bill to the customer. The invoicing process includes gathering the charges that have been assessed for an accounting period and providing them along with all of the backup statements and documentation to support the invoiced charges. The charges on the invoice may be provided at a contract level, or any of a number of summary levels between the contract and the original nomination line item[113].

The documents that accompany an invoice will include any required measurement statements, allocation statements, imbalance statements, inventory-account statements, storage-account statements, imbalance-resolution statements such as cash-outs or trading results, or any combination of these statements.

Pipelines often issue an invoice statement for a contract that is concise and provides the details in the accompanying statements.

There are no industry best practices related to invoicing. Invoicing is a very important part of the face that a pipeline presents to customers; therefore, it is a very important part of business. Pipelines often do not present the invoice and invoice details on their websites. Instead, they provide a link to the invoice via the website for the customer to download the invoice and accompanying documents as a PDF or HTML. NAESB[114] requires that the supporting documents for the invoice should be prepared and presented prior to or with the invoice. This means that the invoice should be accompanied by any of the statements described above that the shipper will need in order to be able to validate and understand the components of the bill. These accompanying documents may be presented as links either on the invoice statement page as subordinate documents to the invoice, or PDF-generated invoice will include a link to the supporting statements so that the shipper can expand and access the statements at will. The pipeline may provide an invoice document that includes all of these supporting statements in the invoice itself.

The invoice will include information on when the invoice payment is due to the pipeline and how the shipper may remit the payment.

60. Receipt of Payments

A shipper submits payments to the pipeline according to the instructions in the contract, the invoice statement, or both. When a shipper submits a payment, it may be for multiple invoices. If a shipper submits a partial payment for the outstanding invoices, the pipeline needs to know to which invoices or partial invoices the payment should be applied. The Payment Remittance[115] provides a mechanism via EDI or via the pipeline website where the shipper may inform the pipeline of any invoices that are not being paid, any partial payments, and any reasons for the differences between what was invoiced and what is being paid.

Payment Remittance			April 15, 2000
	Invoice Amount	Payment	
Invoice 20000301	$210	$200	
Dispute: Invoiced Quantity is incorrect			

Example 60.1
An example of a payment remittance with a disputed amount

61. Statement of Account

The Statement of Account[116] may accompany an invoice or may be provided by the pipeline separate from the invoice. The statement of account reflects the invoices that have been issued, the payments that have been received, and any outstanding balances that are due the pipeline.

Statement of Account			May 10, 2000
	Invoice Amount	Payment	Due
Invoice 20000301	$210	$200	$ 10.00
Invoice 20000401	$490.50		$490.50
Total Due	$500.50		

Example 61.1
An example of a statement of account

62. Accounts Receivable/Payable and General Ledger

General accounting practices govern the recording of accounts receivable/payable and General Ledger. These practices are thorough and complete. For more information on accounting of accounts receivable/payable and general ledger, refer to the COPAS[117] guidelines that are used throughout the energy industry.

From wellhead to burner tip, many players have a hand in transporting natural gas to the end consumer. We have touched on that journey in this book, but the end of this story doesn't mean an end to everything there is to learn in this ever-changing industry. As soon as this book is sent to press, something will be changing that will be the first step to the next update of the book. The constantly changing environment with new technologies, new regulations, and new business practices are just some of the ways of keeping all the contents under pressure.

Your questions, comments and additions are welcome. For up-to-the-minute industry information or to ask questions, visit **ContentsUnderPressureBook.com.**

Thank you.

Appendices

Appendix A: Names in Regulation

A-1: FERC

The Federal Energy Regulatory Commission (FERC) is the United States" organization that sets the rules and governance of all of the energy sector including oil, electricity, hydropower, and natural gas. For natural gas transportation, the focus of the FERC is on interstate gas transportation (transportation that spans state boundaries), but the FERC also has influence in all areas of gas transportation where interstate transportation is involved.

The FERC governs/manages the market with four primary mechanisms. Each interstate pipeline must file with the FERC its tariff of operations. This tariff informs the FERC and the pipeline customers of the service offerings, the rates, and the business operation rules and procedures for that particular pipeline. Through the FERC process, the tariff is posted and customers are given the opportunity to comment, question, and appeal the tariff before the FERC rules on the final tariff that will be approved.

FERC also utilizes a second mechanism: the process of a Notice of Proposed Rulemaking (NOPR) and rulings. FERC staff makes the NOPR filing on one or more issues that they have observed in the market/industry where they perceive a change needs to be made. The NOPR is posted, and industry participants are given an opportunity to comment on how the proposed change will impact their business in either a positive or a negative manner. Once all of the comments have been filed, the FERC will either hold a technical conference where different sides of the issues can be expressed by participants or will evaluate the comments and issue a ruling.

The third mechanism is the Code of Federal Regulations. This publication contains Section 284, which is specific to energy. The rules stated in this document are mandatory and establish the framework for pipeline operations in the interstate market.

A fourth mechanism is the authorization of certificates for construction of facilities. All new interstate-related pipeline construction must go through an application filing, review and approval process before construction can begin.

In the mid-90s, the FERC made a huge shift in the way it governs the interstate market. The FERC issued a NOPR that identified five areas of major changes that needed to be explored. Along with that, it formed working groups for each of the areas, and industry participants met to discuss and develop consensus on the issues. Out of those working groups was formed the Gas Industry Standards Board (GISB)[118], which later became the

NAESB. The FERC utilizes NAESB as a mechanism to bring together, on a voluntary basis, representative members of the gas industry into a consensus-building process to develop standards and implementation instructions for transactions in the industry.

The FERC has an excellent website where information on the natural gas transportation business can be researched. The website is at www.ferc.gov.

A-2: States

At the state level, each state has a governing body to regulate the natural gas that originates and/or terminates in that state. The state regulatory commission (it may be called by other names in certain states) sets safety, rates, transmission, and permits within that state. Some state commissions have adopted some of the NAESB standards, but, at this time, no state commission requires use of all of the standards in that state.

Beyond the state level, there may be local, city, or county commissions that govern the production or delivery of gas in a certain area.

All of these levels of regulation coupled together must be considered when transporting natural gas from its point of origin to its point of consumption.

State	Web Address:
Alabama	www.psc.state.al.us
Alaska	rca.alaska.gov
Arizona	www.azcc.gov
Arkansas	www.arkansas.gov/psc
California	www.cpuc.ca.gov
Colorado	www.dora.state.co.us/puc
Connecticut	www.state.ct.us/dpuc
Delaware	www.depsc.delaware.gov
Florida	www.floridapsc.com
Georgia	www.psc.state.ga.us
Hawaii	www.puc.hawaii.gov
Idaho	www.puc.idaho.gov
Illinois	www.icc.illinois.gov
Indiana	www.in.gov/iurc
Iowa	www.state.ia.us/iub
Kansas	www.kcc.state.ks.us
Kentucky	www.psc.state.ky.us
Louisiana	www.lpsc.org

Maine	www.state.me.us/mpuc
Maryland	www.psc.state.md.us
Massachusetts	www.mass.gov/dpu
Michigan	www.michigan.gov/mpsc
Minnesota	www.puc.state.mn.us
Mississippi	www.psc.state.ms.us
Missouri	www.psc.mo.gov
Montana	www.psc.mt.gov
Nebraska	www.psc.state.ne.us
Nevada	puc.nv.gov
New Hampshire	www.puc.state.nh.us
New Jersey	www.bpu.state.nj.us
New Mexico	www.nmprc.state.nm.us
New York	www.askpsc.com
North Carolina	www.ncuc.commerce.state.nc.us
North Dakota	www.psc.nd.gov
Ohio	www.puco.ohio.gov
Oklahoma	www.occeweb.com
Oregon	www.oregon.gov/puc
Pennsylvania	www.puc.state.pa.us
Rhode Island	www.ripuc.org
South Carolina	www.regulatorystaff.sc.gov
South Dakota	www.puc.sd.gov
Tennessee	www.state.tn.us/tra
Texas	www.puc.texas.gov
Utah	www.psc.utah.gov
Vermont	www.psb.vermont.gov
Virginia	www.scc.virginia.gov
Washington	www.utc.wa.gov
West Virginia	www.psc.state.wv.us
Wisconsin	www.psc.wi.gov
Wyoming	psc.state.wy.us

Table A.1

A-3: Local Governance

Often there are taxes associated with delivery of gas at a local level. These taxes may be cumulative where there are county, city, school, water district, or other taxes applied to the delivery of the gas.

APPENDIX B: NAESB

Introduction to NAESB

Understanding NAESB is an important factor in understanding natural gas transportation. The following section is provided to give an introduction to NAESB, how the NAESB process works, how to use the standards, and how to use the implementation guides. This section will also explain the rules and standards pertaining to the Informational Postings Website, the Customer Activities Website, and the use of EDI in exchange of transaction information.

B-1: The NAESB process and how it works

The North American Industry Standards Board (NAESB) is a membership-supported organization that works hard to maintain an unbiased and balanced position in the energy industry. There are three parts to the organization, referred to as quadrants. The quadrants represent wholesale and retail electric and gas businesses. The Wholesale Gas Quadrant (WGQ)sets standards for natural gas transportation, such as those mentioned in this book.

To create or modify a standard, a request must be submitted to NAESB. That request can come from any participant in the gas industry, and the requester does not have to be a member of NAESB in order to make a request. The request is then assigned to one of the standing committees of NAESB to investigate further. If the request is of a nature that it has large impact, will involve other quadrants, or is of an urgent nature, then there may be a temporary committee created to address the request. The committee will meet to determine a recommended solution to the request. The solution must receive a passing vote through that committee's balanced voting process before being approved. The committee to which the request is assigned may pass the request to several committees before it is complete. Once complete, the recommendation is posted for comment before it is presented to the Executive Committee for vote. The Executive Committee balanced voting process includes representatives from each segment of the WGQ and has voting rules to protect the rights of each of those segments. In order for a standard to pass, it must obtain 17 votes from the 25 members and there must be at least two in-favor votes from each of the five segments. Once a standard has been approved by the Executive Committee, it must still be ratified by the overall membership of the organization before being adopted. Once a standard is adopted, it is scheduled into the next publication of the NAESB standards manuals.

There are publications on the NAESB website that further describe the organization, the balanced voting processes, and the other quadrants of NAESB.

B-2: Navigating the NAESB website

The NAESB website is available at www.NAESB.org. The organization works hard to maintain this website with industry-relevant information. The site contains thousands of documents.
The information for natural gas transportation is part of the WGQ on the website. While there is a lot of useful information available to the public for viewing, a lot of information available can only be viewed by NAESB members or by a party who has paid for website access.

B-3: NAESB Overview

The NAESB WGQ[119] standards are related to natural gas transportation. In NAESB terms, transportation includes movement of gas on the pipeline as well as storage transactions and buy-sell transactions that are communicated to the pipeline. These standards are divided into a series of books. Each book contains a category of information that has been grouped together for relevance. The books are:

- Additional Standards
- Nominations
- Flowing Gas
- Invoicing
- Quadrant Electronic Delivery Mechanisms
- Capacity Release
- Contracts
- Internet Electronic Transport
- eTariff.

The **Additional Standards** book contains standards that apply generally to one or all of the other books in the NAESB standards, and contains standards that do not comfortably fit into any of the other categories.

The **Nominations** book contains standards for the processing of the nominations transactions. This book contains the nomination transactions, the confirmation transactions, and the reporting of scheduled quantities. All of the datasets in this book are related to transactions that occur before gas flows.

The **Flowing Gas** book contains information about transactions related to gas flow and the distribution of gas after it has flowed. This book contains pre-determined allocations, allocations, imbalance reporting, and imbalance trading datasets.

The **Quadrant Electronic Delivery Mechanisms** (QEDM) book contains instructions for the electronic exchange of data in the NAESB process. These instructions cover EDI, flat file, and web-based transactions. On the web-site, the instructions cover the design and posting of data for the Informational Postings Website, and for the Customer Activities Website. The Informational Postings Website is in the public domain of a pipeline's system and is generally available for anyone to view. The Customer Activities Website is the section on the website that is secured by login and contains data available only to that specific customer login. The Customer Activities Website is where transactions occur to initiate and manage the flow of gas.

The **Capacity Release** book contains all of the transactions related to the posting and trading of released contractual capacity, along with supporting datasets. In the capacity-release-process flow, there is the creation of the offer, posting of the offer, creation of the bid, posting of the bid, and execution of the award, along with recalls and re-puts of capacity, and withdrawal of capacity. The accompanying datasets also support the request for the download of datasets, posting of transactional reporting, and system-wide notices.

The **Contracts** book contains model and standard contracts for use in the natural gas industry. These contracts include the short-term purchase and sale of natural gas, the purchase and sale of natural gas liquids, and a trading partner agreement for electronic exchange of data. The NAESB contracts addressee areas of the business that are outside of the focus of this book.

The **Internet Electronic Transport** book contains standards for data exchange and communication that apply to all NAESB standards, not just the WGQ-related standards. These standards pertain specifically to the electronic exchange of information through EDI or flat files.

The **eTariff book** contains the instructions for an interstate pipeline to file its periodic tariff updates in an electronic mechanism with the FERC. This book is very specific to that transaction. The WGQ Quadrant Electronic Delivery Mechanism book contains instructions for public view of the interstate pipeline tariff on the web-site, via the Informational Postings.

B-4: How to read the Standards

The NAESB WGQ standards were written sequentially within each category. Because of this, the standards within a category are not grouped inside of a standards set. There may be a small group of standards that are sequentially placed in a category because they were written and adopted together, but there may be additional standards further down in the categories, adopted later, relating to that original group. [120]

The numbering pattern for standards is often referred to as "x.y.z" where X is the number of the standards category; Y identifies the standard as a Principle, Definition, Standard, Dataset, or Model; and Z is the sequential number assigned to the specific standard.

The values for X are:

0 - Additional Standards
1 - Nominations
2 - Flowing Gas
3 - Invoicing
4 - Electronic Delivery Mechanisms
5 - Capacity Release
6 - Contracts
7 - Interpretations
10 - Internet Electronic Transport
11 - eTariff

The values for Y are:

1 - Principles
2 - Definitions
3 - Standards
4 - Datasets
5 - Models

B-5: What the sections of the standards mean

If you look at the Table of Contents of each of the NAESB books you"ll see a consistent pattern:

- Table of Contents
- Version Notes
- Executive Summary
- Business Process and Practices

- Related Standards
- Sequential Datasets

After the Table of Contents is the Version Notes. The Version Notes contains a list, for each version of the NAESB standards that identifies all of the changes that occurred to this particular book in that version release. There is a subsection identified in each version of the NAESB standards that identifies the **Version Notes** that pertain to that specific version so that the reader does not have to sift through all of the previous notes to determine the ones that are relevant to the current version.

The **Introduction** and **Executive Summary** contain a brief description of the business function that is accomplished in this book of NAESB standards. For instance the Nominations book has Introduction and Executive Summary that identifies that the Nominations Related Standards encompasses The Nomination Transaction Set, The Confirmation Transaction Sets, and the Scheduling Transaction Sets.

The next section is labeled **Business Process and Practices**. This section contains a description in more detail of the business processes that are covered in the book and the interrelationship of the datasets covered in the book. Inside this section you will also see all of the NAESB standards that are related to this book. Using the Nomination Book as an example again, all Nomination standards begin with the number "1." But in The Business Process and Practices section of standards you will see standards with the number beginning with "0" for General Standards, "1" for Nominations Related Standards, "4" for any Electronic Delivery Mechanism Related Standards that are associated to the Nominations process, and "7" for any Interpretations that are related to Nominations. All of these are contained in this Business Process and Practices section. As previously discussed, note that, when looking at the standards for a specific book, the standards appear and are numbered in the sequential order in which they were created. This means that standards relating to a specific topic such as the confirmation, may occur interspersed throughout the long list of standards. Standards are not grouped numerically according to the type of standard except within the large categories into which the books are divided.

Additionally within the standards, there are three different types: principles, definitions, standards, followed by datasets and models. Principles are considered to be a guiding concept that should be used in determining business direction. Often a principal is written to support standards that are subsequently developed. Definitions are self-explanatory: They define terms that are unique to NAESB and the natural gas industry that are used in the NAESB standards. The standards are the core source of instruction in each of the books. Datasets and models will be discussed later.

The **Related Standards** section of every book identifies standards outside of the NAESB standards that are important to the NAESB process. This is where you will see described the common codes that are used EDI, the ANSI ASC X12 dataset use, HTTP, etc.

The heart of the book begins in the next section. Following these introductory sections, are the datasets themselves. Each dataset has its own section in the book, and each dataset may have multiple sub-sections. Continuing with our example of the Nominations book, the first dataset in the Nominations book is the Nomination dataset itself.

The Nomination dataset has five sections:

- Technical Implementation of Business Process
- Sample Paper Transaction
- Data Dictionary
- Code Values Dictionary
- EDI Subtab

Other datasets may contain additional sections if there are special circumstances for a dataset. Some datasets may not contain the EDI subtab if there is no EDI implementation of that dataset.

The first section, the **Technical Implementation of Business Process** (TIBP) describes the interrelationship of the data elements inside the nomination dataset. It contains descriptions of elements and the use of elements to enable the user of the transaction to use it successfully.

The TIBP is followed by the Sample Paper Transaction which gives a paper-document representation of how the dataset could be used if the dataset was exchanged in a paper format. The sample paper transaction is not intended to use all of the data elements available in the dataset or all of the permutations and combinations of data elements that are available in the dataset. It is meant to be a very simple example to show how the information could be used. The important part about the sample paper transaction is that it corresponds to the sample EDI document in the EDI sub tab. This gives the viewer a visual representation of the EDI data and how it is translated.

The **Data Dictionary** contains all of the data elements that are related to this dataset. It also identifies the uses of the data elements for the various electronic communication formats that are appropriate for the dataset. In the case of the nomination, there are multiple nomination model types, so the data element use also covers the use of these data elements across the model types and across the communication formats.

The Data Dictionary is followed by the **Code Values Dictionary**. Many of the data elements in NAESB transactions contain an explicit list of code values that may be used for that data element. Where a set of code values exists, there will be a Code Values Dictionary listing the code values that may be used. In many of these code values sets, an implementer is not required to use all of the code values, but the code values may give a list of the values that the implementer may select from. In some situations the implementer must support all of the code values. The language in either the dataset for the associated standards, will give clarity to whether all or a subset of the code values may be used.

The Code Values Dictionary is followed by the **EDI Subtab**. The EDI Subtab contains four sections:

- Data Element Cross Reference
- Sample ASC X12 Transaction
- ASC X12 Mapping Guidelines
- Transaction Set Tables

The **Data Element Cross Reference** is the first section of the EDI Subtab. This grid format contains a list of all of the data elements in the Data Dictionary presented in the order that they appear in the EDI mapping. From this cross reference, the implementer can see the level at which the data element appears in EDI; whether it appears in the header, the detail, or the sub detail of the transaction set. This will give the implementer an indication of whether the data element appears once, multiple times per header, or multiple times per detail in the dataset. This cross reference is also useful in determining the exact name of the data element when trying to locate the elements in the data dictionary.

The next section of the EDI Subtab is the **Sample ASC X12 Transaction**. This section contains a sample EDI translation of the same information contained in the Sample Paper Transaction. This is to be used as a tool for the implementer to get a visual representation of what the X12 data would look like for the sample that is provided.

The third section of the EDI Subtab is the **ASC X12 Mapping Guidelines.** These guidelines use the ANSI ASC X12 standards, but contain only the NAESB segments, data elements, and code values that are relevant to the NAESB implementation. These guidelines are generated using the EDISIM product by Foresight[121] Technologies.

The last section of the EDI Subtab contains the **Transaction Set Tables**. Where the data element in the EDI mapping contains more than one value, NAESB has formatted that data into a transaction set table for that data element to give the implementer a clear representation of the values that should be used for each of the elements. In most cases, the Transaction Set Tables give detailed implementation instructions for the code values that are found in the Code Values Dictionary.

B-6: Business Standards and their use

Many of the standards in NAESB are business-related standards which pertain directly to the interaction of shippers and transporters. The x.3.standards of each of the NAESB books contains these business-related standards. Some of the standards refer to an overarching business practice, such as the definition of a gas day. These standards are available to implement as business practices by the affected business parties. Often there will be a reference to a specific transaction set or required transaction process.

NAESB x.4.z standards refer to a transaction set. These standards reference all data elements in the transaction, the use of that transaction overall, or business practices relating to the transaction. The next section titled "EDM" discusses the electronic exchange of these standards.

It is important to recognize that the NAESB standards are written in a consensus-building process whereby one company may present an idea or concept and the participants in the process will edit and hone the concept until all of the participants in the process can agree on it. Because of this, the standards language may at time appear awkward or vague. This intentionally vague resulting language provides an opportunity for participants to reach consensus and meet the needs of their individual business requirements.

The NAESB standards language uses the terms "may" or "should" instead of the terms "must" or "shall." This is because, from a NAESB point of view, all standards are voluntary. A regulatory agency such as the FERC or a state regulatory body may adopt the standards and make them mandatory, but NAESB does not make that decision.

B-7: Electronic Delivery Mechanisms

When groups in NAESB beyond the WGQ began setting standards for exchange of information, it became clear that the work that was begun in Wholesale Gas should be the starting point. NAESB determined that the standards in the Electronic Delivery Mechanisms (EDM) section should be split into two groups, with one book, comprised of standards beginning with the number 10[122], containing those EDM standards that applied to all segments of the industry. The other book, comprised of those standards beginning with the number 4,[123] contains those standards that are specific to Wholesale

Gas. This book is not intended as a technical instruction, and the instructions contained in those NAESB manuals are very thorough with comprehensive examples. Refer to NAESB Quadrant Electronic Delivery Mechanism Related Standards (QEDM) and NAESB Internet Electronic Transport Related Standards (IET)[124] for understanding and information on the technical aspects. The business side of the EDM standards will be covered here.

NAESB WGQ EDM refers to three standard mechanisms for the exchange of transactional information: EDI (EDI/EDM), web transaction pages (EBB/EDM), and flat files (FF/EDM). Of these, flat files may be exchanged via the same communication methods as EDI or may be uploaded via a web page. The use of the flat-file formats is optional, and the pipeline offering the optional service determines the communication method. Interactive Flat File describes flat files loaded via a browser. [125]

EDI transactions are those datasets that have been identified to be exchanged through formatted EDI files in the internet through secured communication protocols. For exchange of EDI, the standards direct the parties to exchange data over the public internet using secure connections and encrypted files. The specific transaction enveloping, exchange protocols, and security requirements are discussed in detail in those manuals. The NAESB instructions for EDI are comprehensive and complete. This book will not describe those standards in further detail.

Informational Postings is a web-based mechanism that the pipeline must use to provide public information to customers and potential customers. Customer Activities is a web-based mechanism that the pipeline must use for secured transactions with existing customers. There are standards that pertain specifically to Informational Postings Website (IPW), Customer Activities Website (CAW), and to web interaction in general. The general web-interaction standards apply to both the IPW requirements and to the CAW requirements.

Note: One of the terms that you will see in the NAESB standards, particularly those related to the web, is the reference to the EBB. EBB is the term that was originally applied to the requirements for posting of information in a public manner prior to the use of the public internet. This was in the days of using dial-up modems to access a company's site. EBB refers to Electronic Bulletin Board. No one uses this technology today, but the term still appears in standards, rulings, etc. Any time the term EBB is used, it should be construed as applying to either the Informational Postings or the Customer Activities. In most cases, it will refer to the CAW.

B-8: Web - Informational Postings

Informational Postings describes a set of required, optional, and pipeline-specific information that a pipeline makes available in a public, unsecured area of its website. The FERC requires Informational Postings, as defined by NAESB, for interstate pipelines. Many non-interstate pipelines offer a subset of IPW on their website. The standards prescribe very specific rules about the defined postings, but allow for the pipeline to offer more than the minimum requirement[126].

NAESB WGQ_Standard 4.3.23[127] lists the items that should be included in the IPW navigation and the order in which the items should appear.

Most of the items required in the IPW can be described as "reports" of information. This means that the information presented is static as of the time that it is posted and, when the item is selected, the view of the information presented does not contain search, sort, or selection capabilities. There are, of course, exceptions.

The first section of the IPW contains Operationally Available and Unsubscribed Capacity[128]. The Additional Standards manual specifies datasets and data requirements under WGQ_Standard 0.4.2[129] - Operationally Available Capacity and WGQ_Standard 0.4.3 - Unsubscribed Capacity[130]. These two postings of information are required to be provided and updated each time the operational capacity, unsubscribed capacity, or both changes. Most pipelines update this information at the end of each nomination/scheduling cycle.

Operationally Available Capacity is a report of the operational capacity at locations on the pipeline versus the scheduled quantity at those same locations. This information is provided to give the potential shipper an indication of where capacity may be available for scheduling on the pipeline.

Unsubscribed Capacity is a report of the quantity of gas at locations and segments on the pipeline that has not been contracted for firm transportation service. This information gives the potential shipper an indication of the quantities that may be available for firm transportation contracting.

The combination of Operationally Available Capacity and Unsubscribed Capacity at a location tells the shipper how much of the capacity is committed to firm transportation, how much is utilized through interruptible transportation, and how much is available for firm and interruptible negotiations with the pipeline.

Operationally Available Report January 1, 2000

First American Pipeline Company

Location	Direction of Flow	Operational Capacity	Available Capacity
R123A	R	50,000	12,000
R453A	R	60,000	40,000
D687B	D	80,000	40,000
S078V	D	40,000	22,000

Unsubscribed Capacity Report January 1, 2000

First American Pipeline Company

Location	Direction of Flow	Operational Capacity	Unsubscribed Capacity
R123A	R	50,000	0
R453A	R	60,000	60,000
D687B	D	80,000	60,000
S078V	D	40,000	10,000

Analysis and Observations of the two reports:
1 – All of the locations have available capacity to nominate interruptible transportation.
2 – Locations R123A and S078V have firm capacity that is subscribed but not being used in the quantity of 12,000 DTH. This may be an opportunity to obtain capacity release.
3 – Location R123A does not have any capacity available for a new firm capacity contract.
4 – Locations R453A and D687B have more interruptible transportation flowing and have a lot of room for a firm contract to be subscribed.

Example B-8.1
A pictorial example of the contents of an Operationally Available Capacity Report and an Unsubscribed Capacity Report with examples of how the data may be analyzed to provide decision making information.

The next section of the IPW is Gas Quality information. This information has specific standards accompanying it that require the information to be able to be selected for specific dates or date ranges and for all or specific locations. This is one of the few Informational Postings items that requires the ability to select and filter the information that is presented, rather than presenting a straight "report" of information. The NAESB WGQ 4.3.z[131] standards contain the requirements for Gas Quality.

The FERC's Code of Federal Regulations[132] fully describes the Index of Customers posting and provides instructions on the heading titles, format, etc., for this posting.

The Notices section of the IPW is a very active section. The information made available there must be divided into a list of categories, and this information must be provided multiple ways in addition to the Informational Postings website. The chapter of this book titled Notices will cover the different types of notices and the different mechanisms for providing those notices to customers. The NAESB WGQ 4.3.z and NAESB WGQ 5.3.z standards contain the standards for Notices. [133]

Posted Imbalances, Regulatory postings, and Standards of Conduct follows the Notices section. These areas have a prescribed set of rules that govern their content and refresh rate. The NAESB WGQ 2.3.z[134] standards contain Instructions for Posted Imbalances. The Imbalance Trading section of this book also describes them.

The Tariff section of the IPW is another interactive section of the requirements. The standards have several requirements for this section that direct the tariff to be searchable, downloadable, to have navigation to the previous and next sheets, and to have a table of contents that links to each section. The NAESB WGQ 4.3.z[135] standards contain the standards related to the posting of the Tariff on the IPW. NAESB WGQ eTariff Related Standards[136], which spells out e-tariff filings to the FERC, also contains tariff-related standards. These have no direct relationship to the Tariff posting section on the IPW, except that the information is the same and must be kept in sync.

The last section in the IPW is for Transactional Reporting. This section contains select firm, interruptible, and capacity-release contract information that is required to be posted by the pipeline when a contract is executed or changed. The NAESB WGQ 5.4.20, 5.4.21, 5.4.22[137] standards contain the Transactional Reporting datasets.

On both the IPW and the CAW, the pipeline is allowed to provide additional links for information that it is either required to provide or has chosen to provide. The instructions are that these additional links should appear after the NAESB-required links in the relevant category.[138]

Additionally, it is important to note that all documents that are posted on a Transportation Service Provider's web-site should be downloadable[139]. The Appendix of the NAESB WGQ Quadrant specific Electronic Delivery Mechanism[140] standards lists the acceptable download formats, and NAESB WGQ Standard 4.3.5[141] describes the requirement for this ability.

Notices

Notices covers two distinct areas of the NAESB process. Both of these areas need to be addressed in chorus because there is a huge amount of overlap between the requirements of the two areas[142].

The first area of notices is the System Wide Notices dataset, NAESB WGQ Standard 5.4.16,[143] which is required for pipelines to make available as part of the Capacity Release standards requirements via EDI. The second area of notices covers those notices required to be posted on the public IPW. The NAESB WGQ QEDM Standards, 4.y.z[144] contains these standards. There are a group of these standards, listed below, that must be considered for posting and categorization of these notices. The third area of notices is Notifications. This label concerns selected information the pipeline is required to send via email to parties on selected occasions. The Notifications section is part of notices because pipelines must post some notifications as notices, and must distribute some notices as notifications.

System Wide Notices are a required process. Pipelines are required to make system-wide notice information available for download via the NAESB WGQ EDI format provided with that dataset. Pipelines are also required to post this same information on the IPW as part of the Notices category of postings. The easiest assumption is that all items posted on the IPW must also be included in any EDI System Wide Notice download. If a pipeline takes this approach, it eliminates any confusion and ensures that comparability between the EDI offering and the web offering is maintained. NAESB WGQ Standard 4.3.23[145] identifies four categories of notices that a pipeline should support on the website:

- Critical
- Non-Critical
- Planned Service Outage
- Waste Heat

The critical and non-critical categories should provide a list of the notices for that category when the category is selected.

Correspondingly, the System Wide Notices dataset has a Critical Notice Indicator that informs the recipient of whether the notice is a critical notice or a non-critical notice. The two categories of Planned Service Outage and Waste Heat are identified using the notice type. While the System Wide Notices[146] uses the notice type to classify the notice being sent and the Informational Posting[147] depends on the column labeled Notice Type to classify the notices being displayed, it is important to note that the lists are the same and, while the groupings of the data may be slightly different between the EDI dataset and the Informational Postings groupings and requirements, the information conveyed is the same between the two datasets. The Notice Type in 4.3.29[148] can appear under the Critical or the Non-Critical label in the same manner that the indicator, in the 5.4.16 [149] dataset can indicate any of the Notice Types to be critical or non-critical.

The third area to be addressed in Notices is that of notifications sent from a pipeline to an individual service requester or to a group of service requesters. These notifications are sent via email, unless the two parties mutually agree to another mechanism. There are several situations that require the pipeline to send an email notice to a shipper:

- Credit standards require sending a notice to a shipper when that shipper has credit actions, the pipeline has asked for additional credit information, or the shipper is denied a credit request. [150]
- Intraday Bumps are situations where either a scheduling scenario has occurred or a capacity recall has occurred that causes a shipper's previously scheduled quantity to be reduced or "bumped." The pipeline is required to provide email notification to affected parties in the case of an intraday bump. [151]
- Operational Flow Orders are notices by pipelines to one, a group, or all shippers notifying them of an operational condition on the pipeline that requires action by the shipper(s), the pipeline, or both. The Operational Flow Order contains instructions and compliance timelines for the order. [152]
- Critical Notices are notices that the pipeline has qualified and designated as being of a critical nature. [153]
- The Capacity Release section of this book describes Capacity Release Recalls and Reputs. Notices to the affected parties in the case of a recall and/or a reput are covered under a group of recall- and reput-specific standards. [154]
- Capacity Release status information must be emailed to the releasing shipper in the case of non-performance by the replacement shipper. The specific conditions require a status email[155].

The use of an email notice does not replace the need for a System Wide Notice or an Informational Posting Notice. For any given situation, the need to provide one of the notices is evaluated independently of the other notices. There are situations where all three notices may be required and others where only one may be required.

One additional posting required in the System Wide Notices of the IPW is that of the potential replacement shipper's request to purchase released capacity. This requirement is for a pipeline to post instructions, on the System Wide Notice, for the mechanism that a potential replacement shipper should use to electronically submit a request to purchase capacity. The pipeline will then post the Offer to Purchase Capacity that it receives on the same System Wide Notice platform with a notice type indicating such request[156].

B-9: Web - Customer Activities

The CAW is primarily for transactional data related to a specific shipper, operator, or its agent. The CAW requires a login for security access, and the party can only have access to its own or authorized specific data. The pipeline and the party's agreement with the pipeline determines control of which web-screens and the data that the party can access[157].

NAESB WGQ_Standard 4.3.42[158] lists the high level navigation categories of the CAW as:

- Nominations
- Flowing Gas
- Invoicing
- Capacity Release
- Contracts
- Informational Postings
- Site Map

Each of these categories then has subsequent EDM standards that identify the breakdown of that high-level category into more detailed transactions. For instance, the Nomination link is later divided into Nomination, Confirmation, and Scheduled Quantity in NAESB WGQ_Standard 4.3.43[159]. An individual pipeline may want to break down one or more of those categories even further. For instance, the Nomination category may be split into non-pathed nomination and pathed non-threaded nomination or the Scheduled Quantity category may be split into scheduled quantity for shipper and scheduled quantity for operator.

The initial categories of the CAW coincide with the NAESB books and divisions of standards. The Nominations category belongs to the 1.y.z standards,[160] the Flowing Gas category belongs to the 2.x.y standards,[161] the Invoicing category belongs to the 3.y.z standards,[162] the Capacity Release category belongs to the 5.x.y standards,[163] and the Contracts category belongs to the 6.y.z standards.[164] The Informational Postings category provides a quick link back to the public Informational Postings site described above. The Site Map link provides a quick reference to all of the links on the CAW and IPW for ease of navigation.

On both the IPW and the CAW, the pipeline is allowed to provide additional links for information that it is either required to provide or has chosen to provide. The instructions state that these additional links should appear after the NAESB-required links in the relevant category. [165]

A specific set of standards within the 4.3.z[166] standards governs how the web pages in the CAW should be designed. These standards do not dictate a specific format or technology for use in developing the screens. The standards identify certain sections that must exist on every web page and, in some instances, designate the types of web pages that must exist for a function.

Nine Important Standards

One of the biggest conundrums for a company undertaking the building of a NAESB-compliant CAW is the layout of the information on the page. The designer wants to create something that will provide the customer with the best experience possible. The pipeline wants to be compliant. The NAESB EDM standards contain a host of standards related to the technological and visual data-exchange experience. Most designers, upon first viewing these standards, see them as limiting, restrictive, and requiring a formulaic approach that will result in a cookie-cutter type of design. The good news is that this is not true. There are EDM standards that direct how the CAW will appear, how it will perform, and how the data and code values will interact. Within these standards for appearance lie a handful of standards that offer permissions rather than restrictions. These permission-granting standards are the most important standards to take into consideration when designing the web page because they grant opportunities to vary from what would otherwise appear to be a restrictive approach. Though the general term of "standard" is applied to all of these in the discussion, it is important to note that the standards with a format of x.1.z are NAESB Principles and are not mandated for implementation by the FERC while the standards with a format of x.3.z are NAESB Standards and are part of the FERC requirements.

A later discussion will cover the rules and guidelines specific to NAESB web page design. The discussion here is to understand the nine standards that provide modifiers or catalysts to the design rules.

These standards examine two considerations. The first is the arrangement of the data on the page, and the second is the specific data that may be displayed on the web page.

Prior to NAESB WGQ Version 2.1[167], NAESB prescribed the groups of data into which the data on the web page would be arranged and the order of the data within the groups. NAESB WGQ Version 2.1[168] eliminated these standards; there is no longer a requirement for the order of the data elements on the web page.

NAESB WGQ Standard 4.3.72[169] refers to the creation of "alternate views" of web pages. This standard says that the NAESB "basic view" is required, but that the pipeline may provide "alternate views" in addition to the basic view. If the designer finds the standards to be so restrictive that a basic view cannot be constructed that gives the level of service to the customer that the pipeline needs to provide, then there is the option to create alternate views that give the preferred layout of data. The catch is that the alternate view must offer the same business result. This means that a customer could use the basic view and achieve the exact same transaction, though the interaction may be more cumbersome or less friendly. The other catch is that, when an alternate view is offered, it must be offered to all applicable users.

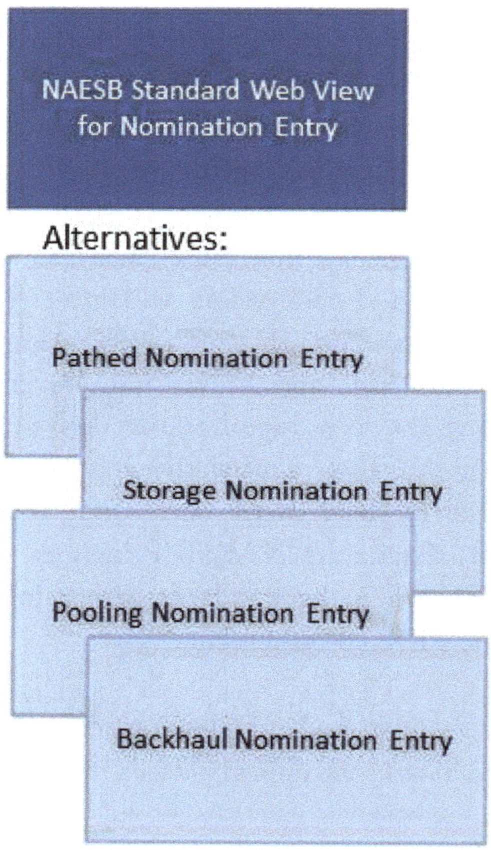

Figure B-9.1
Example showing a standard NAESB web view
with examples of alternative web views that a pipeline might offer

Example: In addition to the standard basic view, a pipeline decides to offer a nomination entry page specific to storage shippers. For this pipeline, storage shippers nominate using the NPT type (see section on Nomination Model Types for more information on the non-pathed model). In that view, the required entry fields may be arranged in a different order or grouped in a different way than the basic view, which meets the requirements for all nomination models and all nomination-service types.

NAESB WGQ NAESB Principle 4.1.30[170] is considered a Principle, in NAESB terms (see "What the sections of the standards mean" for discussion of the difference between a principle and a standard), but is an important consideration in designing the web page. This standard addresses the fields that have "default values" and how they can be moved from their prescribed placement. When a field has a default value, the assumption, with this principle, is that the customer entering data will most likely accept that value and leave it as-is. In this case, the principle allows the designer to place this element at the end or "last" in the web view so that it is out of the way of the customer and to minimize the data in the primary view on the web page. This principle should be used cautiously, and the customer's use of the data field must be thoroughly considered before implementing this option.

Example A: A pipeline has a default value of "Current Business" for the Nomination Transaction Type field but has a code value subset of 10 possible values for the Transaction Type. Those possible values include transaction types that may be used in general business use such as "Storage Injection." In this example, it is likely that a customer will choose a Transaction Type other than "Current Business" as part of the normal course of business. Therefore, it would not be a good idea to implement this principle and place the Transaction Type at the end of the view so that it possibly is not visible in the primary view but must be accessed using scrolling, because the customer needs access to the cue to change this Transaction Type to the desired value.

Example B: A pipeline has a default value of "Current Business" for the Nomination Transaction Type field but has a code value subset of three possible values for the Transaction Type. Those possible values include transaction types that the pipeline expects will be used on an exception basis only. In this example, it is likely that the customer will leave the "Current Business" Transaction Type as the selected value in the normal course of business. Moving this field to the end of the view so that it does not take up space on the primary view would be a good decision.

NAESB WGQ Standard 4.3.58[171] has a similar effect on the placement of data on the web page. This standard refers to "informational display fields" on the web page and how they may be placed. First, what is an "informational display field"? The term is not distinctly defined in NAESB terms, but if reference is made to the other places in the standards where the term is used, the definition can be derived. An "informational display field" could be either a) a field that is not part of the current dataset but has been included in the current view from another dataset as a piece of data to enhance the information displayed on the screen,[172] b) a field that is not defined in any dataset but that the pipeline has selected to provide as a service to the customer,[173] or c) a field that is part of the current dataset but that has a single value available because this pipeline only supports that single value or because the fields on the screen that the customer has already selected have filtered the available values down to a single value so that there is no selection to be made by the customer.[174] Thus, the field is rendered on the web page as an "informational display" because the field is required by the dataset but there is no choice available to the customer.

In either case, this standard provides the option for the pipeline to move the field from the prescribed position on the web page so that it is displayed with the related information that resulted in it being a display value. This movement is at the option of the pipeline. The pipeline is not required to move the field to place it adjacent to the related field(s).

In this group of standards, two refer to the placement of fields in the Header of the web page.

NAESB WGQ Standard 4.3.50[175] addresses the filtering of data on the web page. The first part of the standard states that "navigation for input data lookups . . . should be placed near the field being looked up." An example of a frequent use of this standard in web-page design is where the down-arrow icon is placed beside a data-entry field so that the customer can click on that down-arrow and see a list of possible values to select from to populate the field. An improper placement of a data lookup would be to have a location elsewhere on the web page, for instance at the bottom, in a side-bar work area or in a pop-up, where the value for the field could be searched and retrieved, requiring the customer to find the desired value and then return to the primary web page to enter the desired value.

The second part of this standard refers to "informational lookups." An informational lookup is an added-value offering that the pipeline has offered to the customer.

An example of an informational lookup would be where the shipper could retrieve specific zone, segment, township, or zip code information about a receipt or delivery point. This could be used on a contract-maintenance view or on a nomination-entry view. The retrieved information will aid the customer in its selection of a specific receipt or delivery location, but the retrieved information does not become part of the transaction. Only the selected receipt or delivery location identifier would move forward to become part of the transaction. In this example, the standard directs the web designer to place the "informational lookup" in the Header area of the web page.

NAESB WGQ Principle 4.1.29[176] presents another option for placing information in the Header area of the web page. This principle refers to "constants" in the field values and specifies that they may be moved to the Header portion of the page view. In NAESB dataset design, there are no constants defined in the datasets. A constant may result from one or more selections in the data that filters the set of available values down to one possible value and thus resulting in a "constant." This would be the same result as is described in the example of 4.3.58[177] c) above. In this principle, however, the designer is given permission to move the single value to the Header portion of the web page. In Standard 4.3.58[178], the designer is given permission to move the single value adjacent to related information.

The remaining standards in this section are directed toward the data that is included on the web page rather than the arrangement of the data on the web page. The placement of this included data is governed by the preceding standards in this section.

NAESB WGQ Standard 4.3.68[179] begins the next group with a simple statement that permits data that is not part of the NAESB dataset's data dictionary to be displayed on the CAW. The standard may appear, at first, to give wholesale permission to add anything to a web page. The key word here is "information." The standard does not grant the ability to add data entry fields to the web page. Data entry fields are not informational to the customer; they are added value to the provider of the service. Some examples of that information permitted include:

1. Data fields that further describe the selections made by the customer. An example would be a brief description of the selected "Contract 1234" may be followed by the description "Firm Transportation Contract from Southeast Region."
2. A general message regarding the pipeline schedule such as "The current open nomination cycle is 'Timely.' There are three hours and 15 minutes remaining in this open cycle", or regarding the pipeline business, such as a link to a news release.
3. A current-information status update that pertains to one or more of the data fields selected on the web page. For example "Location abcd is scheduled for routine maintenance on February 14th and may experience a reduced available capacity on that day."

NAESB WGQ Standard 4.3.48[180] addresses totals on the web page. The datasets do not contain totals, and totals are a valuable tool to the customer. The assumption, in the dataset design, is that, when the data is exchanged electronically through an electronic file transfer, the use of totals is redundant[181]. The party receiving the data will be presenting the data to its company's staff through either a screen view or a report and will have the ability to generate any totals through that tool.

When a dataset is presented by the data provider (the pipeline) in a web view, it is useful and friendly to include totals so that the customer can use the data. This standard instructs the web designer to place the totals in the content area and to make them distinct so that they stand out from other transactional data on the web page. This distinction can be made through visual cues such as bold, color change, font change, or other tools.

NAESB WGQ Standard 4.3.44[182] refers to any data that is contained in another NAESB dataset. This information is allowed to be presented on a web page even though the data field is not included in the current dataset. Remember that the datasets are designed to be efficient for electronic transmission of data from computer-to-computer. An example of use of this standard would be on the Scheduled Quantity web page. On this web page, the pipeline is instructed to display the scheduled quantity for each nomination that a shipper has provided, along with any reasons that the scheduled quantity was reduced from the original nominated quantity. The dataset does not include the original nominated quantity. The nominated quantity is part of the Nomination dataset. With this standard, the pipeline web designer may elect to present the original nominated quantity on the same line item with the scheduled quantity and the reduction reasons so that the shipper sees, in one view, what was requested and what was scheduled.

NAESB WGQ Standard 4.3.55[183] takes the offering of NAESB WGQ Standard 4.3.44 one step further. First, it states that the data presented on the web page does not have to be directly obtained from another EDI dataset, but may be obtained from other uploads or downloads on the pipeline's website, such as the location download or the pipeline tariff. Second, it states that the information may be "derived" from that data.

Therefore, the dataset being displayed on the web page may not include a Location Description to go with the Location Code, for example. The Location Description may be included in the Location Download file that the pipeline provides elsewhere on the web-site. Because this information is included in that download, the pipeline is permitted to include the data for display purposes on the web page.

Additionally, the Informational Postings dataset for Operational Capacity may elect to include a data element, for a location, for "Scheduled Capacity." This data element is not found in the Operational Capacity dataset but is one that the pipeline has created to contain information derived from other data that is available. From this, the pipeline may elect to total the calculated remaining available capacity for a location on the nomination page for the shipper to see what is available at a location. This information is not required for a pipeline to display, nor is it required for a pipeline to calculate on a real-time dynamic basis and make it available to its customers. It is the customer's responsibility to utilize all of the sources of information that a pipeline is required to provide and use that to determine the actions it wants to request from the pipeline. However, this standard gives the pipeline permission to exceed the minimum expectations and to offer such features and services on the web page.

One last noteworthy standard in this group is **NAESB WGQ Standard 4.3.34**[184]. While the other data-related standards are directed toward allowing additional data on the web page, this standard allows data to be eliminated from the page. Since space on the web page is often precious and limited, any opportunity to eliminate data from the web page should be taken. This standard is pretty simple. The datasets contain some fields that are Mandatory or Conditional[185] that must be included in the web design. The datasets also contain fields that are Sender's Option, Business Conditional, and Mutually Agreed that might not be used or supported (depending on the business scenario for that pipeline and the particular dataset). These fields that are not used or supported can be removed from the web page display. The web designer is not required to include a non-mandatory data field on the web page if that field is not used by the pipeline. Many of the data fields in the datasets fall into this category.

All of these standards, together, give the web designer and the pipeline the opportunity to offer a customer experience that reflects the priorities and services of the pipeline. While most of the NAESB web-design-related standards are very directive and are focused on giving the customer a predictable and consistent web experience across all pipelines, this subset of standards gives the pipeline the ability to distinguish itself and present to its personality to the customer.

There are additional web-design-related standards. The NAESB Quadrant Electronic Delivery Mechanisms Related Standards book has standards grouped into functional categories, one category for development of the IPW and one for the development of the CAW. It is important to become familiar with all of these standards and their interrelationship when developing for the web.

In addition to the standards that direct the layout of the web page, there are standards that direct the content of the web page. Each CAW page, unless it is a web page provided as an additional service by a pipeline, is associated with a NAESB WGQ x.4.z dataset; for instance, the Nominations dataset is found in NAESB WGQ 1.4.1[186]. Every web page on a NAESB-compliant website must use NAESB-standard data-element names[187] as the labels for the fields that appear on the web page; NAESB-standard code values and code-value descriptions[188] for those elements that have NAESB-specified code sets as the available values; NAESB common codes to identify the business party[189] for the Shipper (Service Requester), Pipeline (Transportation Service Provider), Upstream Entity (Upstream Shipper), and Downstream Entity (Downstream Shipper).

NAESB WGQ Standard 4.1.13[190] states that the information displayed on the website must be downloadable. That seems simple enough, because the information can be put into a report format or a .pdf (note: Adobe) format. The standard then continues with the statement that the data must be downloaded in a manner that permits the information to be used in applications. This would mean that a shipper could download its nominations from the pipeline's web page and, effectively, load those same nominations into its own gas-transaction management system for tracking of data. The standards permit several different data formats, but the only ones that would accommodate this requirement would be a CSV (Comma Separated Value) format or, possibly, an RTF (Rich Text Format).

A few more important web-design related standards should be considered when presenting information on the CAW. NAESB WGQ Standard 4.1.32[191] requires that the information on a CAW must be either directly contained in one or more associated EDI datasets or must be derivable from the information contained in these datasets. This is an important comparability consideration so that customers who utilize the EDI datasets as a way of communicating and retrieving transactions have the opportunity to have a comparable experience to those customers choosing to use the website for their transaction interaction. An example of information such as this would be if the pipeline provided a view where the nominated quantity, from the Nomination dataset[192], was provided next to the scheduled quantity from the Scheduled Quantity dataset[193] and the allocated quantity from the Allocations dataset[194] and the difference between each of the quantities was displayed.

Standard Nomination View:

Receipt Location	Transportation Contract	Delivery Location	Nominated Quantity
A1492	FK4242	Z1476	1,000 DTH

Standard Scheduled Quantity View:

Receipt Location	Transportation Contract	Delivery Location	Scheduled Quantity
A1492	FK4242	Z1476	1,000 DTH

Standard Imbalance Quantity View:

Receipt Location	Transportation Imbalance Contract	Delivery Location	Allocated Receipt	Allocated Delivery	
A1492	FK4242	Z1476	1,100 DTH	1,000 Dth	+100 DTH

Combined View:

Receipt Location	Transportation Contract	Delivery Location	Nominated Quantity	DIFF	Scheduled Quantity	Allocated Receipt	Allocated Delivery	Imbalance
A1492	FK4242	Z1476	1,000 DTH	100 DTH	1,000 DTH	1,100 DTH	1,000 Dth	+100 DTH

Example B-9.1
An example of the data contained in each of three standard NAESB data views and how the data could be presented in an optional combined view.

Each of the values is available from one of the datasets provided, but the calculated difference between the quantities would be considered to be a derived quantity. If a shipper chose to use only EDI for transactions, then that shipper would be able to retrieve the data through each of the datasets, combine it, and calculate the difference for presentation on that shipper's gas-transaction management system. In contrast, if a pipeline offered the same view and offered a "negotiated settled quantity" alongside the quantities listed above and then a calculated difference between those quantities and the "negotiated settled quantity", then this would be in violation of the standards. First, the "negotiated settled quantity" is not available in any of the EDI datasets and, second, the quantity is not derivable from any of the data contained in any of the datasets.

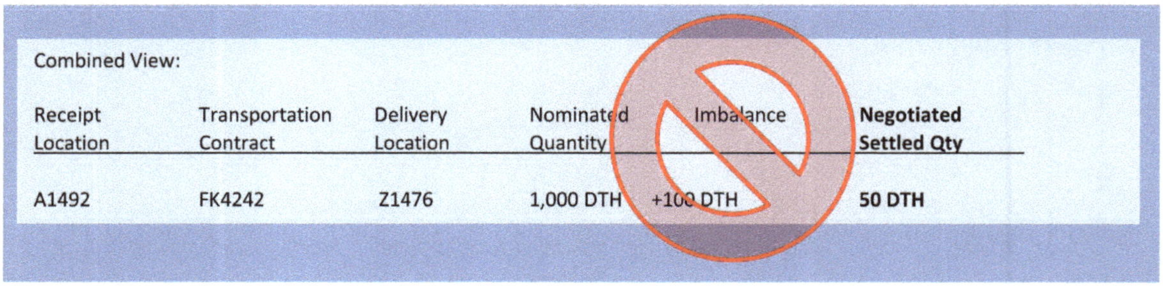

Example B-9.2
An example of an invalid combined view that contains data not available in, or derivable from, any of the standard views.

Because the customer relying on the EDI services as a means of communicating and retrieving transactions does not have access to this same pipeline-provided information through an EDI mechanism, the pipeline is not offering a comparable level of service between EDI and the web and is in violation of the comparability-related standards.

In the same line of pipeline-service offerings, a pipeline may offer views of data in addition to the standard views. These views are referred to as alternate views. NAESB WGQ Standard 4.3.72[195] allows for the use of alternate views as long as they do not replace the required mandatory basic view. Additionally, the alternate views must provide the same business result as the basic view. This last requirement, for the same business result, means that, when a shipper elects to use only the basic views on the pipeline's website to conduct business, then that shipper can achieve all of the same business results as would have been achieved through utilization of the alternate views. The alternate views cannot add a level of service or a transactional capability that is not available in the basic views. This standard, too, points toward comparability of service for customers of the pipeline.

One last requirement for design of CAW pages only applies to the Nominations and Scheduled Quantity related pages. NAESB WGQ Standards 1.3.53 and 1.3.62[196] state that the Nominations and Scheduled Quantity web pages must contain a form and a matrix. NAESB WGQ Standard 4.2.16[197] defines a form as an area that allows for entry, view of a single transaction line item, or both. The form may be a separate single-transaction web page, or it may be contained in the uppermost content area of the web page that also contains the matrix. NAESB WGQ Standard 4.2.17[198] defines a matrix as the lower part of the content area of the web page, and it implies that this information is presented in a grid-type format such as would be presented in an Excel[199] spreadsheet. The matrix may be used for display of information, for entry of data, or for both. The requirement is that both options, the form and the matrix, are provided for both the nominations and scheduled quantity datasets. NAESB WGQ_Standards 1.3.48, 4.3.66, 4.3.76 and 4.3.78[200] also should be considered when developing the required views for the form and the matrix.

Nomination Web Form

Shipper		Contract	
Begin Date		End Date	
Receipt Location		Delivery Location	
Upstream Shipper		Downstream Shipper	
Upstream Contract		Downstream Contract	
Receipt Quantity		Delivery Quantity	
Transaction Type		Package ID	

Nomination Matrix

Shipper	Contract	Begin Date	End Date	Receipt Location	Upstream Party	Upstream Contract	Receipt Quantity	Delivery Location	Downstream Shipper	Downstream Contract	Delivery Quantity	Transaction Type	Package ID

Example B-9.3
An example of a form and marix.

A complete review of all of these standards, in chorus, will provide a comprehensive set of instructions to successfully implement this requirement.

B-10: EDI

The term EDI literally means Electronic Data Interchange. In broad terms, that could mean any exchange of data over any electronic mechanism, such as sending bank information through an app over a smart phone. In NAESB terms and in the terms of most industries who use this term, EDI refers to the ANSI ASC X12 Standards for electronic communication of data through standardized data formats. The ANSI standards apply across many industries. Some of the datasets that NAESB uses for exchange of EDI transactions, in ANSI terms, are generic datasets that may be used for many industry functions. For some of the datasets, NAESB has applied for and been granted datasets that are specific to the transactions that are conducted in the natural gas industry[201].

EDI data is formatted in a hierarchical structure of Heading, Detail, Sub-Detail and, in some cases, Sub-Sub-Detail. The datasets presented in the NAESB manuals have each been designed to utilize this structure and comply with the X12 guidelines for transaction structure. The X12 guidelines are available in documents from DISA (Data Interchange Standards Association). Contact information for DISA is located in Section 5 - Related Standards of each of the NAESB manuals. It is very helpful to have a copy of the complete X12 guidelines when implementing the standards, though the standards datasets do have all of the information required by NAESB. The X12 datasets contain a super-set of capabilities in their design because they have been written to serve the needs of many industries. The NAESB datasets are a subset of those capabilities and use only the portions of the X12 standard that NAESB requires to communicate the transaction information.

The hierarchy of each dataset is generally:

- Heading: who the transaction is from (the sender), who it is being sent to (the recipient), the dates that apply to this transaction set (a single date or a date range), and an overall status of the dataset.
- Detail: this information varies by dataset. In some cases, it identifies the contract number for all of the subsequent information. In other cases, it identifies a specific location, a date range, or both location and date range for the information that will follow.
- Sub-Detail: this information contains the line items of information being transmitted.
- Sub-Sub-Detail: this information contains iterative information about the line item. It may be information by day, by charge, or information broken out for a set of code values, etc.

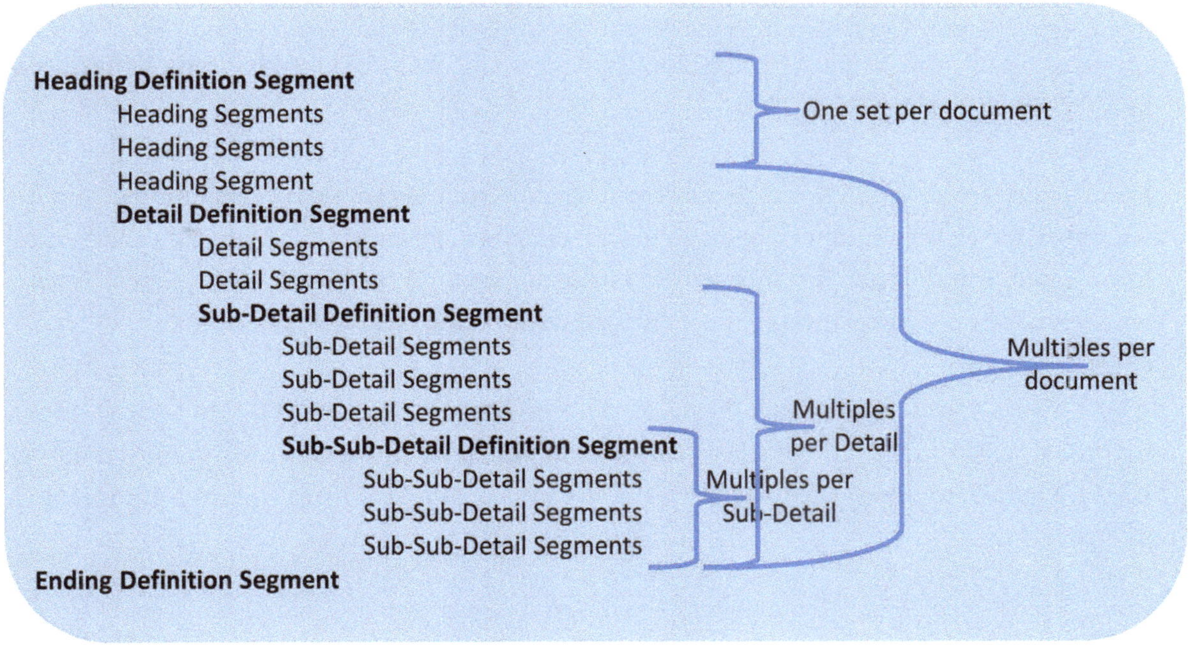

Figure B-10.1
Diagram of the hierarchical levels of an EDI dataset. There may be one header per document, but there may be multiple details per header, multiple sub-details per detail, etc.

Segment Example:

BEG*01*14*20000101**xlk*

BEG	is the segment identifier
*	is the delimiter that has been defined to separate data elements
01	the data value of the first field in the segment
**	two delimiters indicates that there is a null value for the position in the segment

Example B-10.1
An example of how a single segment of an EDI transaction is parsed into data in the translation process.

Each section of the hierarchy discussed above is comprised of segments which, for many people, equates to a line item or section of a record. Each segment is composed of elements. The sum of the segments in a section of the hierarchy goes together to create one unit of information.

Each hierarchical level may appear multiple times within the hierarchical level above. This means that, for one Heading section, there may be many Details; for each Detail section, there may be many Sub-Details, and for each Sub-Detail section, there may be many Sub-Sub Details.

Each segment of an EDI dataset is formatted with a segment identifier followed by the elements for that segment. The information in the segment is separated by a delimiter. In most cases, the default delimiter used is the asterisk (*), but the delimiter to be used can be negotiated between the sending and receiving parties of the dataset.

The EDI instructions for each NAESB dataset, when one is defined, are contained within the x.4.z section of each standards book. For instance, for the Nominations dataset, the EDI instructions are part of the Nominations book and are contained in Standard 1.4.1[202] of that book.

Endnotes

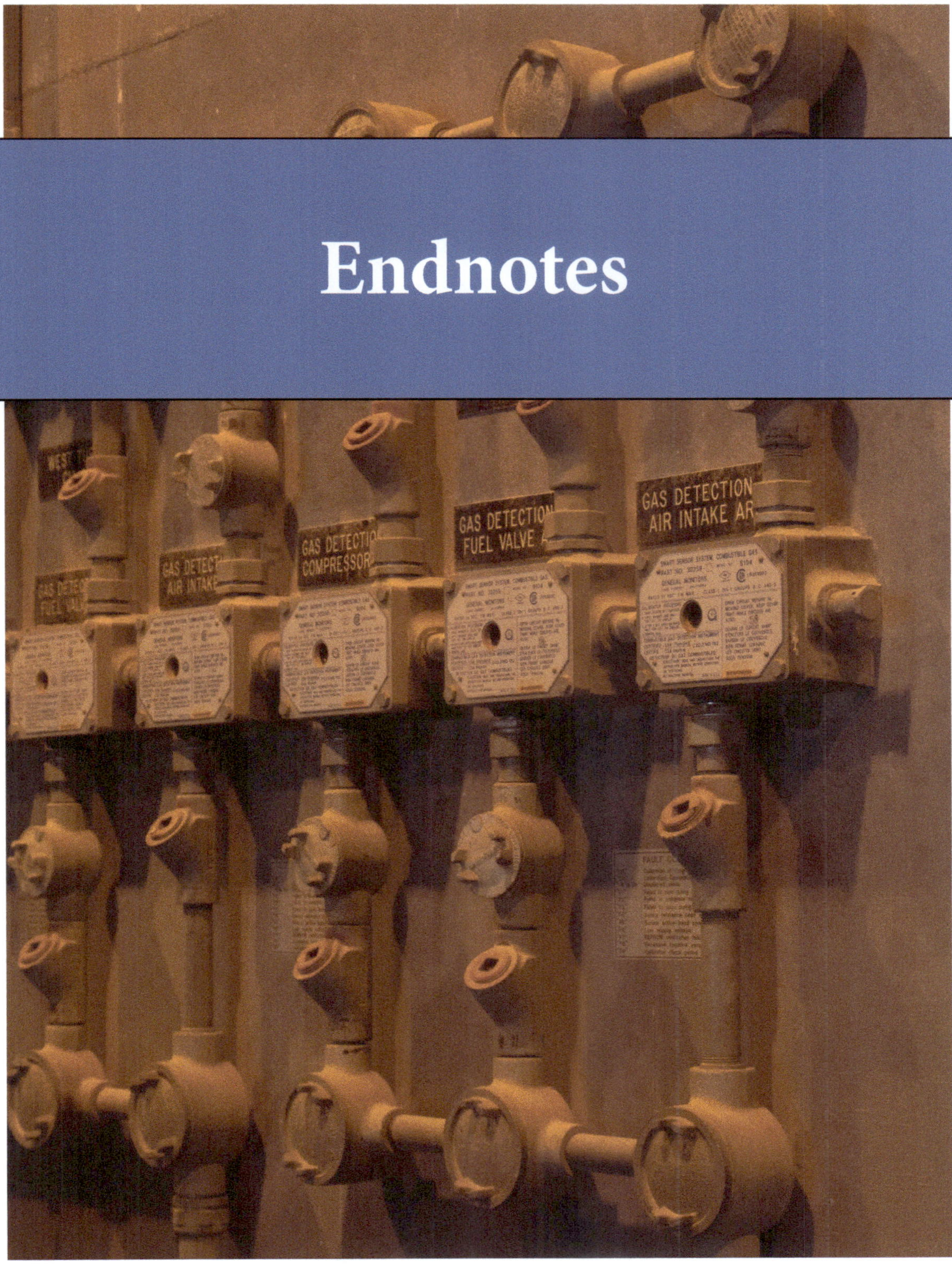
GAS DETECTION
AIR INTAKE AR
GAS DETECTION
FUEL VALVE
GAS DETECTIO
COMPRESSOR
GAS DETECT
AIR INTAKE

Endnotes

1. www.ferc.gov
2. www.naesb.org
3. The best available quantity is a transaction based quantity determined by the best-of the actual allocated quantity, estimated allocated quantity, scheduled quantity, confirmed quantity and nominated quantity.
4. NAESB WGQ Version 3.0 Standards, North American Energy Standards Board, November 14, 2014. https://naesb.org/wgq/imp.asp (This document is password protected). Book 1 – Nominations; Standard 1.4.1 Dictionary
5. See 18 CFR 284.8(h)(3), or FERC Order No 712, June 19, 2008; http://www.ecfr.gov/cgi-bin/text-idx?SID=3538e80d439a8f5930ba738494aa0287&node=se18.1.284_18&rgn=div8
6. aka Retail Access: 18 CFR 284.8(h)(4), or FERC Order No 712, June 19, 2008; http://www.ecfr.gov/cgi-bin/text-idx?SID=3538e80d439a8f5930ba738494aa0287&node=se18.1.284_18&rgn=div8
7. NAESB WGQ Version 3.0 Standards, North American Energy Standards Board, November 14, 2014. https://naesb.org/wgq/imp.asp (This document is password protected). Book 1 – Nominations; Standards related to pooling: 1.2.3, 1.3.17, 1.3.18
8. NAESB WGQ Version 3.0 Standards, North American Energy Standards Board, November 14, 2014. https://naesb.org/wgq/imp.asp (This document is password protected). Book 0 – Additional Standards, Standards related to contract parties: 0.3.1, 0.3.2, 0.3.28; Book 1 - Nominations, Standards related to contract parties: 1.3.75
9. CFR 184.18, FERC Order No 712, June 19, 2008
10. NAESB WGQ Version 3.0 Standards, North American Energy Standards Board, November 14, 2014. https://naesb.org/wgq/imp.asp (This document is password protected). Book 0 – Additional Standards, Standards related to contract locations: 0.3.23, 0.3.24, 0.3.25, 0.3.26, 0.3.27, 0.3.29, 0.4.4
11. Some pipeline tariffs refer to the location-level MDQ as MDRQ for Maximum Daily Receipt Quantity and MDDQ for Maximum Daily Delivery Quantity.
12. Note that a path level MDQ is only relevant if the nomination model type for the contract is wither pathed or pathed non-threaded. A path level MDQ would not apply to a non-pathed model type.
13. NAESB WGQ Version 3.0 Standards, North American Energy Standards Board, November 14, 2014. https://naesb.org/wgq/imp.asp (This document is password protected). Book 1 – Nominations Related Standards, Contracts charges related standards 1.1.16

14. NAESB WGQ Version 3.0 Standards, North American Energy Standards Board, November 14, 2014. https://naesb.org/wgq/imp.asp (This document is password protected). Book 1 – Nominations Related Standards, Contracts charges related standards 1.1.16, Contract fuel standards 1.3.15, 1.3.16, 1.3.28, 1.3.29, 1.3.30, 1.3.31
15. NAESB WGQ Version 3.0 Standards, North American Energy Standards Board, November 14, 2014. https://naesb.org/wgq/imp.asp (This document is password protected). Book 5 – Capacity Release Related Standards 5.4.24
16. The basis price is most often used in energy trading as the price difference between two energy markets or between two locations. For this reference, the basis is between two locations on a physical pipeline system.
17. NAESB WGQ Version 3.0 Standards, North American Energy Standards Board, November 14, 2014. https://naesb.org/wgq/imp.asp (This document is password protected). Book 5 – Capacity Release Related Standards, Bid related standards: 5.3.4, 5.3.26, 5.3.62, 5.3.62a, 5.3.63
18. NAESB WGQ Version 3.0 Standards, North American Energy Standards Board, November 14, 2014. https://naesb.org/wgq/imp.asp (This document is password protected). Book 5 – Capacity Release Related Standards, Standard 5.3.25.
19. NAESB WGQ Version 3.0 Standards, North American Energy Standards Board, November 14, 2014. https://naesb.org/wgq/imp.asp (This document is password protected). Book 5 – Capacity Release Related Standards, Standard 5.3.33
20. NAESB WGQ Version 3.0 Standards, North American Energy Standards Board, November 14, 2014. https://naesb.org/wgq/imp.asp (This document is password protected). Book 5 – Capacity Release Related Standards, Business Process and Practices, page 106 gives comprehensive examples of the calculations of these three bid evaluation methodologies.
21. NAESB WGQ Version 3.0 Standards, North American Energy Standards Board, November 14, 2014. https://naesb.org/wgq/imp.asp (This document is password protected). Book 5 – Capacity Release Related Standards, Business Process and Practices, page 108.
22. © 2014 NAESB, all rights reserved. Reproduction in any form is strictly prohibited without first obtaining permission from NAESB. NAESB WGQ Version 3.0 Standards, North American Energy Standards Board, November 14, 2014. https://naesb.org/wgq/imp.asp (This document is password protected). Book 5 – Capacity Release Related Standards, Business Process and Practices, page 108.
23. NAESB WGQ Version 3.0 Standards, North American Energy Standards Board, November 14, 2014. https://naesb.org/wgq/imp.asp (This document is password protected). Book 5 – Capacity Release Related Standards, Standard 5.4.26.

24. NAESB WGQ Version 3.0 Standards, North American Energy Standards Board, November 14, 2014. https://naesb.org/wgq/imp.asp (This document is password protected). Book 5 – Capacity Release Related Standards, Standard 5.3.20.
25. NAESB WGQ Version 3.0 Standards, North American Energy Standards Board, November 14, 2014. https://naesb.org/wgq/imp.asp (This document is password protected). Book 5 – Capacity Release Related Standards, Standards related to recall/reput: 5.1.2, 5.1.3, 5.2.3
26. NAESB WGQ Version 3.0 Standards, North American Energy Standards Board, November 14, 2014. https://naesb.org/wgq/imp.asp (This document is password protected). Book 5 – Capacity Release Related Standards, Standard 5.1.2.
27. NAESB WGQ Version 3.0 Standards, North American Energy Standards Board, November 14, 2014. https://naesb.org/wgq/imp.asp (This document is password protected). Book 5 – Capacity Release Related Standards, Standard 5.3.45.
28. NAESB WGQ Version 3.0 Standards, North American Energy Standards Board, November 14, 2014. https://naesb.org/wgq/imp.asp (This document is password protected). Book 5 – Capacity Release Related Standards, Standards 5.1.2, 5.1.3, 5.1.4, 5.2.3, 5.3.7, 5.3.8, 5.3.44, 5.3.45, 5.3.46, 5.3.47, 5.3.48, 5.3.49, 5.3.52, 5.3.53, 5.3.54, 5.3.55, 5.3.56, 5.3.57, 5.3.58.
29. NAESB WGQ Version 3.0 Standards, North American Energy Standards Board, November 14, 2014. https://naesb.org/wgq/imp.asp (This document is password protected). Book 5 – Capacity Release Related Standards, Standard 5.3.1.
30. NAESB WGQ Version 3.0 Standards, North American Energy Standards Board, November 14, 2014. https://naesb.org/wgq/imp.asp (This document is password protected). Book 5 – Capacity Release Related Standards, Standard 5.3.2.
31. NAESB WGQ Version 3.0 Standards, North American Energy Standards Board, November 14, 2014. https://naesb.org/wgq/imp.asp (This document is password protected). Book 5 – Capacity Release Related Standards, Standard 5.3.2.
32. NAESB WGQ Version 3.0 Standards, North American Energy Standards Board, November 14, 2014. https://naesb.org/wgq/imp.asp (This document is password protected). Book 5 – Capacity Release Related Standards, Standard 5.3.2.
33. NAESB WGQ Version 3.0 Standards, North American Energy Standards Board, November 14, 2014. https://naesb.org/wgq/imp.asp (This document is password protected). Book 5 – Capacity Release Related Standards, Standard 5.3.2.
34. FERC Order No. 637 at P125.
35. FERC Order No. 637 at P125.
36. FERC Order No. 637 at P125.
37. NAESB WGQ Version 3.0 Standards, North American Energy Standards Board, November 14, 2014. https://naesb.org/wgq/imp.asp (This document is password protected). Book 0 – Additional Standards, Standard 0.3.3, 0.3.4, 0.3.5, 0.3.6,

0.3.7, 0.3.8, 0.3.9, 0.3.10; Book 5 – Capacity Release Related Standards, Standard 5.3.1, 5.3.59 and 5.3.60.

38. NAESB WGQ Version 3.0 Standards, North American Energy Standards Board, November 14, 2014. https://naesb.org/wgq/imp.asp (This document is password protected). Book 1 – Nominations Related Standards, Standard: 1.3.48, 1.3.53, 1.3.55, 1.3.56
39. NAESB WGQ Version 3.0 Standards, North American Energy Standards Board, November 14, 2014. https://naesb.org/wgq/imp.asp (This document is password protected). Book 1 – Nominations Related Standards, Standard 1.3.7.
40. NAESB WGQ Version 3.0 Standards, North American Energy Standards Board, November 14, 2014. https://naesb.org/wgq/imp.asp (This document is password protected). Book 1 – Nominations Related Standards, Standard 1.3.2.
41. NAESB WGQ Version 3.0 Standards, North American Energy Standards Board, November 14, 2014. https://naesb.org/wgq/imp.asp (This document is password protected). Book 1 – Nominations Related Standards, Standard Standard 1.4.1 – Nominations dataset defines this list.
42. NAESB WGQ Version 3.0 Standards, North American Energy Standards Board, November 14, 2014. https://naesb.org/wgq/imp.asp (This document is password protected). Book 1 – Nominations Related Standards, Standard 1.2.2.
43. For example, a data element in a report dataset many be conditional on whether it was provided during the creation of the transaction.
44. © 2014 NAESB, all rights reserved. Reproduction in any form is strictly prohibited without first obtaining permission from NAESB. NAESB WGQ Version 3.0 Standards, North American Energy Standards Board, November 14, 2014. https://naesb.org/wgq/imp.asp (This document is password protected). Book 1 – Nominations Related Standards, Standard 1.2.2
45. NAESB WGQ Version 3.0 Standards, North American Energy Standards Board, November 14, 2014. https://naesb.org/wgq/imp.asp (This document is password protected). Book 1 – Nominations Related Standards, Standard 1.3.27.
46. NAESB WGQ Version 3.0 Standards, North American Energy Standards Board, November 14, 2014. https://naesb.org/wgq/imp.asp (This document is password protected). Book 1 – Nominations Related Standards, Standard 1.4.1
47. NAESB WGQ Version 3.0 Standards, North American Energy Standards Board, November 14, 2014. https://naesb.org/wgq/imp.asp (This document is password protected). Book 1 – Nominations Related Standards, Standards related to nomination elements and validation: 1.1.9, 1.2.5, 1.3.5, 1.3.23, 1.3.24, 1.3.25, 1.3.81
48. NAESB WGQ Version 3.0 Standards, North American Energy Standards Board, November 14, 2014. https://naesb.org/wgq/imp.asp (This document is password

protected). Book 1 – Nominations Related Standards, Standard 1.4.1 Data Dictionary.

49. NAESB WGQ Version 3.0 Standards, North American Energy Standards Board, November 14, 2014. https://naesb.org/wgq/imp.asp (This document is password protected).
50. NAESB WGQ Version 2.1 Standards, North American Energy Standards Board, July 23, 2013. https://naesb.org/wgq/imp.asp (This document is password protected).
51. NAESB WGQ Version 3.0 Standards, North American Energy Standards Board, November 14, 2014. https://naesb.org/wgq/imp.asp (This document is password protected). Book 1 – Nominations Related Standards, Standard 1.4.1.
52. NAESB WGQ Version 3.0 Standards, North American Energy Standards Board, November 14, 2014. https://naesb.org/wgq/imp.asp (This document is password protected). Book 0 – Additional Standards, Related Standards, page 24.
53. NAESB WGQ Version 3.0 Standards, North American Energy Standards Board, November 14, 2014. https://naesb.org/wgq/imp.asp (This document is password protected). Book 1 – Nominations Related Standards, Standard 1.4.1
54. NAESB WGQ Version 3.0 Standards, North American Energy Standards Board, November 14, 2014. https://naesb.org/wgq/imp.asp (This document is password protected). Book 1 – Nominations Related Standards, Standard 1.3.19
55. NAESB WGQ Version 3.0 Standards, North American Energy Standards Board, November 14, 2014. https://naesb.org/wgq/imp.asp (This document is password protected). Book 1 – Nominations Related Standards, Standard 1.3.80
56. NAESB WGQ Version 3.0 Standards, North American Energy Standards Board, November 14, 2014. https://naesb.org/wgq/imp.asp (This document is password protected). Book 1 – Nominations Related Standards, Standard 1.4.1
57. The Minor Correction process in NAESB is used to add and update code values. For more information visit www.NAESB.org.
58. NAESB WGQ Version 3.0 Standards, North American Energy Standards Board, November 14, 2014. https://naesb.org/wgq/imp.asp (This document is password protected). Book 0 – Additional Standards, Standard 0.3.17; Book 1 – Nominations Related Standards, Standards related to nomination timeline: 1.1.4, 1.1.18, 1.2.4, 1.3.2, 1.3.4, 1.3.6, 1.3.8, 1.3.9, 1.3.11, 1.3.13, 1.3.21, 1.3.32, 1.3.33, 1.3.37, 1.3.38, 1.3.42, 1.3.43
59. NAESB WGQ Version 3.0 Standards, North American Energy Standards Board, November 14, 2014. https://naesb.org/wgq/imp.asp (This document is password protected). Book 1 – Nominations Related Standards, Standard 1.2.4, 1.3.13
60. NAESB WGQ Version 3.0 Standards, North American Energy Standards Board, November 14, 2014. https://naesb.org/wgq/imp.asp (This document is password

protected). Book 1 – Nominations Related Standards, Standard 1.2.12

61. NAESB WGQ Version 3.0 Standards, North American Energy Standards Board, November 14, 2014. https://naesb.org/wgq/imp.asp (This document is password protected). Book 1 – Nominations Related Standards, Standard 1.3.2.
62. NAESB WGQ Version 3.0 Standards, North American Energy Standards Board, November 14, 2014. https://naesb.org/wgq/imp.asp (This document is password protected). Book 1 – Nominations Related Standards, Standard 1.4.1, Technical Implementation of Business Process,
63. NAESB WGQ Version 3.0 Standards, North American Energy Standards Board, November 14, 2014. https://naesb.org/wgq/imp.asp (This document is password protected). Book 1 – Nominations Related Standards, Standard 1.3.6
64. NAESB WGQ Version 3.0 Standards, North American Energy Standards Board, November 14, 2014. https://naesb.org/wgq/imp.asp (This document is password protected). Book 1 – Nominations Related Standards, Standard 1.3.2
65. NAESB WGQ Version 3.0 Standards, North American Energy Standards Board, November 14, 2014. https://naesb.org/wgq/imp.asp (This document is password protected). Book 1 – Nominations Related Standards, Standard 1.4.1 – Nomination – see code values dictionary list of additional cycle codes
66. NAESB WGQ Version 3.0 Standards, North American Energy Standards Board, November 14, 2014. https://naesb.org/wgq/imp.asp (This document is password protected). Book 1 – Nominations Related Standards, Title Transfer Tracking Related Standards: 1.1.10, 1.1.11, 1.1.13, 1.1.20, 1.1.21, 1.2.13, 1.2.14, 1.2.15, 1.2.16, 1.2.17, 1.2.18, 1.2.19, 1.3.64, 1.3.65, 1.3.66, 1.3.67, 1.3.68, 1.3.69, 1.3.70, 1.3.71, 1.3.72, 1.3.73, 1.3.74, 1.3.76, 1.3.77
67. NAESB WGQ Version 3.0 Standards, North American Energy Standards Board, November 14, 2014. https://naesb.org/wgq/imp.asp (This document is password protected). Book 1 – Nominations Related Standards, Standard 1.3.64
68. NAESB WGQ Version 3.0 Standards, North American Energy Standards Board, November 14, 2014. https://naesb.org/wgq/imp.asp (This document is password protected). Book 1 – Nominations Related Standards, Standards 1.1.10, 1.1.11, 1.1.13 1.1.20 1.1.21, 1.2.14, 1.2,15, 1.2.16, 1.2.17, 1.2.18, 1.2.19, 1.3.71, 1.3.72, 1.3.73, 1.3.74, 1.3.76, 1.3.78.
69. NAESB WGQ Version 3.0 Standards, North American Energy Standards Board, November 14, 2014. https://naesb.org/wgq/imp.asp (This document is password protected). Book 1 – Nominations Related Standards, Standards related to confirmations: 1.1.22, 1.2.8, 1.2.9, 1.2.10, 1.2.11, 1.3.20, 1.3.22, 1.3.35, 1.3.36, 1.3.40, 1.3.45, 1.3.46
70. NAESB WGQ Version 3.0 Standards, North American Energy Standards Board, November 14, 2014. https://naesb.org/wgq/imp.asp (This document is password

protected). Book 1 – Nominations Related Standards, Standards v1.4.3,1.4.4,1.4.7

71. NAESB WGQ Version 3.0 Standards, North American Energy Standards Board, November 14, 2014. https://naesb.org/wgq/imp.asp (This document is password protected). Book 1 – Nominations Related Standards, Standard 1.4.3
72. NAESB WGQ Version 3.0 Standards, North American Energy Standards Board, November 14, 2014. https://naesb.org/wgq/imp.asp (This document is password protected). Book 1 – Nominations Related Standards, Standard 1.4.4
73. NAESB WGQ Version 3.0 Standards, North American Energy Standards Board, November 14, 2014. https://naesb.org/wgq/imp.asp (This document is password protected). Book 1 – Nominations Related Standards, Standard 1.4.5
74. NAESB WGQ Version 3.0 Standards, North American Energy Standards Board, November 14, 2014. https://naesb.org/wgq/imp.asp (This document is password protected). Book 1 – Nominations Related Standards, Standard 1.3.40
75. NAESB WGQ Version 3.0 Standards, North American Energy Standards Board, November 14, 2014. https://naesb.org/wgq/imp.asp (This document is password protected). Book 1 – Nominations Related Standards, Standard 1.2.1
76. NAESB WGQ Version 3.0 Standards, North American Energy Standards Board, November 14, 2014. https://naesb.org/wgq/imp.asp (This document is password protected). Book 1 – Nominations Related Standards, Standard 1.3.22 contains the terms of this rule.
77. NAESB WGQ Version 3.0 Standards, North American Energy Standards Board, November 14, 2014. https://naesb.org/wgq/imp.asp (This document is password protected). Book 1 – Nominations Related Standards, NAESB standards related to scheduling: 1.3.3, 1.3.39, 1.3.41, 1.3.44, 1.3.51, 1.3.62, 1.3.79
78. NAESB WGQ Version 3.0 Standards, North American Energy Standards Board, November 14, 2014. https://naesb.org/wgq/imp.asp (This document is password protected). Book 1 – Nominations Related Standards, Standards related to scheduling are: 1.1.2, 1.2.12, 1.3.2, 1.3.3, 1.3.21, 1.3.23, 1.3.24, 1.3.59, 1.3.61, 1.3.62, 1.3.65, 1.3.71, 1.3.79, 2.3.51, 2.3.52, 2.3.53, 4.3.54, Order 637 page 205.
79. NAESB WGQ Version 3.0 Standards, North American Energy Standards Board, November 14, 2014. https://naesb.org/wgq/imp.asp (This document is password protected). Book 1 – Nominations Related Standards, Standard 1.3.80
80. This term may also be referred to as a flow day diversion.
81. NAESB WGQ Version 3.0 Standards, North American Energy Standards Board, November 14, 2014. https://naesb.org/wgq/imp.asp (This document is password protected). Book 1 – Nominations Related Standards, Standard 1.4.1 Code Values Dictionary for Transaction Type – code values 56, FDF, FDR, FDT
82. NAESB WGQ Version 3.0 Standards, North American Energy Standards Board, November 14, 2014. https://naesb.org/wgq/imp.asp (This document is password

protected). Book 1 – Nominations Related Standards, Standard 1.4.5 and 1.4.6

83. NAESB WGQ Version 3.0 Standards, North American Energy Standards Board, November 14, 2014. https://naesb.org/wgq/imp.asp (This document is password protected). Book 1 – Nominations Related Standards, Standard 1.4.5 Code Values Dictionary for Reduction Reason Codes.
84. NAESB WGQ Version 3.0 Standards, North American Energy Standards Board, November 14, 2014. https://naesb.org/wgq/imp.asp (This document is password protected). Book 1 – Nominations Related Standards, Standard 1.4.6 Code Values Dictionary for Reduction Reason Codes for Operator.
85. NAESB WGQ Version 3.0 Standards, North American Energy Standards Board, November 14, 2014. https://naesb.org/wgq/imp.asp (This document is password protected). Book 1 – Nominations Related Standards, Standards related to measurement: 2.1.1, 2.1.4, 2.4.5, 2.4.6, 2.4.18
86. NAESB WGQ Version 3.0 Standards, North American Energy Standards Board, November 14, 2014. https://naesb.org/wgq/imp.asp (This document is password protected). Book 1 – Nominations Related Standards, Standard 1.3.14
87. NAESB WGQ Version 3.0 Standards, North American Energy Standards Board, November 14, 2014. https://naesb.org/wgq/imp.asp (This document is password protected). Book 2 – Flowing Gas Related Standards, Standard 2.3.19
88. NAESB WGQ Version 3.0 Standards, North American Energy Standards Board, November 14, 2014. https://naesb.org/wgq/imp.asp (This document is password protected). Book 2 – Flowing Gas Related Standards, Standard 2.4.1
89. NAESB WGQ Version 3.0 Standards, North American Energy Standards Board, November 14, 2014. https://naesb.org/wgq/imp.asp (This document is password protected). Book 2 – Flowing Gas Related Standards, Standard 2.4.1
90. NAESB WGQ Version 3.0 Standards, North American Energy Standards Board, November 14, 2014. https://naesb.org/wgq/imp.asp (This document is password protected). Book 2 – Flowing Gas Related Standards, Standard 2.4.1 PDA Transaction Type Matrix
91. NAESB WGQ Version 3.0 Standards, North American Energy Standards Board, November 14, 2014. https://naesb.org/wgq/imp.asp (This document is password protected). Book 2 – Flowing Gas Related Standards, Standards 2.3.58, 2.3.59
92. NAESB WGQ Version 3.0 Standards, North American Energy Standards Board, November 14, 2014. https://naesb.org/wgq/imp.asp (This document is password protected). Book 2 – Flowing Gas Related Standards, Standard 2.4.3
93. NAESB WGQ Version 3.0 Standards, North American Energy Standards Board, November 14, 2014. https://naesb.org/wgq/imp.asp (This document is password protected). Book 2 – Flowing Gas Related Standards, Standard 2.4.3 Allocation Transaction Type Matrix

94. NAESB WGQ Version 3.0 Standards, North American Energy Standards Board, November 14, 2014. https://naesb.org/wgq/imp.asp (This document is password protected). Book 1 – Nominations Related Standards, Standard 1.3.24, 1.3.71; Book 2 – Flowing Gas Related Standards, Standards 2.1.1, 2.1.2, 2.1.6, 2.2.4, 2.2.5, 2.3.8, 2.3.15, 2.3.16, 2.3.17, 2.3.18, 2.3.19, 2.3.20, 2.3.21, 2.3.22, 2.3.23, 2.3.25, 2.3.27, 2.3.54, 2.3.55, 2.3.57, 2.3.58, 2.3.59, 2.3.60, 2.3.61, 2.3.62, 2.3.63, 2.3.64, 2.4.3, Book 3 - Invoicing Related Standards, Standard 3.3.26; Book 5 - Capacity Release Related Standards, Standard 5.3.69.
95. NAESB WGQ Version 3.0 Standards, North American Energy Standards Board, November 14, 2014. https://naesb.org/wgq/imp.asp (This document is password protected). Book 1 – Nominations Related Standards, Standard 1.3.71
96. NAESB WGQ Version 3.0 Standards, North American Energy Standards Board, November 14, 2014. https://naesb.org/wgq/imp.asp (This document is password protected). Book 2 – Flowing Gas Related Standards, Standard 2.3.21
97. (aka parking-and-lending)
98. NAESB WGQ Version 3.0 Standards, North American Energy Standards Board, November 14, 2014. https://naesb.org/wgq/imp.asp (This document is password protected). Book 2 – Flowing Gas Related Standards, Standard 2.3.27, 2.3.28, 2.3.65, 2.4.4; Book 3 – Invoicing Related Standards, Standard 3.3.14
99. NAESB WGQ Version 3.0 Standards, North American Energy Standards Board, November 14, 2014. https://naesb.org/wgq/imp.asp (This document is password protected). Book 2 – Flowing Gas Related Standards, Standard 2.1.6
100. NAESB WGQ Version 3.0 Standards, North American Energy Standards Board, November 14, 2014. https://naesb.org/wgq/imp.asp (This document is password protected). Book 2 – Flowing Gas Related Standards, Standard 2.2.3
101. Note that some pipelines only use the "make-up" term to resolve imbalances. This is because the make-up is due the pipeline or the make-up is due the shipper. This is a different way of using the same terms and accomplishes the same result.
102. NAESB WGQ Version 3.0 Standards, North American Energy Standards Board, November 14, 2014. https://naesb.org/wgq/imp.asp (This document is password protected). Book 2 – Flowing Gas Related Standards, S Imbalance trading related standards: 2.1.5, 2.2.2, 2.2.3, 2.3.30, 2.3.40, 2.3.41, 2.3.42, 2.3.43, 2.3.44, 2.3.45, 2.3.46, 2.3.47, 2.3.48, 2.3.49, 2.3.50.
103. NAESB WGQ Version 3.0 Standards, North American Energy Standards Board, November 14, 2014. https://naesb.org/wgq/imp.asp (This document is password protected). Book 2 – Flowing Gas Related Standards, Standard 2.3.41
104. NAESB WGQ Version 3.0 Standards, North American Energy Standards Board, November 14, 2014. https://naesb.org/wgq/imp.asp (This document is password protected). Book 2 – Flowing Gas Related Standards, Standard 2.4.9

105. NAESB WGQ Version 3.0 Standards, North American Energy Standards Board, November 14, 2014. https://naesb.org/wgq/imp.asp (This document is password protected). Book 2 – Flowing Gas Related Standards, Standard 2.4.11
106. NAESB WGQ Version 3.0 Standards, North American Energy Standards Board, November 14, 2014. https://naesb.org/wgq/imp.asp (This document is password protected). Book 2 – Flowing Gas Related Standards, Standard 2.4.15
107. Council of Petroleum Accountants Societies. http://www.copas.org/
108. Sarbanes-Oxley Act, July 30, 2002
109. NAESB WGQ Version 3.0 Standards, North American Energy Standards Board, November 14, 2014. https://naesb.org/wgq/imp.asp (This document is password protected). Book 5 – Capacity Release Related Standards, Standard 5.3.22
110. NAESB WGQ Version 3.0 Standards, North American Energy Standards Board, November 14, 2014. https://naesb.org/wgq/imp.asp (This document is password protected). Book 5 – Capacity Release Related Standards, Standard 5.2.4, 5.2.5, 5.3.64, 5.3.65, 5.3.66,5.3.67, 5.3.68, 5.3.69
111. NAESB WGQ Version 3.0 Standards, North American Energy Standards Board, November 14, 2014. https://naesb.org/wgq/imp.asp (This document is password protected). Book 2 – Flowing Gas Related Standards, Standard 2.1.2; Book 3 – Invoicing Related Standards, Standard 3.3.15, 3.3.16
112. NAESB WGQ Version 3.0 Standards, North American Energy Standards Board, November 14, 2014. https://naesb.org/wgq/imp.asp (This document is password protected). Book 2 – Flowing Gas Related Standards, Standard 2.3.7, 2.3.11,, 2.3.40, 2.3.41 ; Book 3 – Invoicing Related Standards, Standard 3.3.15, 3.3.16 3.2.1, 3.3.14
113. NAESB WGQ Version 3.0 Standards, North American Energy Standards Board, November 14, 2014. https://naesb.org/wgq/imp.asp (This document is password protected). Book 3 – Invoicing Related Standards, Standard 3.1.2, 3.2.1, 3.3.3, 3.3.4, 3.3.5, 3.3.6, 3.3.7, 3.3.8, 3.3.9, 3.3.10, 3.3.11, 3.3.12, 3.3.13, 3.3.14, 3.3.23, 3.3.24, 3.3.25, 3.3.26, 3.4.1, 3.4.4
114. NAESB WGQ Version 3.0 Standards, North American Energy Standards Board, November 14, 2014. https://naesb.org/wgq/imp.asp (This document is password protected). Book 3 – Invoicing Related Standards, Standard 3.3.14, 3.3.26
115. NAESB WGQ Version 3.0 Standards, North American Energy Standards Board, November 14, 2014. https://naesb.org/wgq/imp.asp (This document is password protected). Book 3 – Invoicing Related Standards, Standard 3.3.17, 3.3.18, 3.3.19, 3.4.2
116. NAESB WGQ Version 3.0 Standards, North American Energy Standards Board, November 14, 2014. https://naesb.org/wgq/imp.asp (This document is password protected). Book 3 – Invoicing Related Standards, Standard 3.3.21, 3.3.22, 3.4.3

117. Council of Petroleum Accountants Societies. http://www.copas.org/
118. Bylaws for North American Energy Standards Board Approved by GISB Board of Directors; GISB to Go Out of Existence as Separate Organization December 31, 2001, NAESB begins operation January 1, 2002
119. NAESB WGQ Version 3.0 Standards, North American Energy Standards Board, November 14, 2014. https://naesb.org/wgq/imp.asp (This document is password protected).
120. NAESB has developed an excellent tool that is available at NAESB.org. The tool is a matrix of all of the WGQ standards by category and shows all of the standards that apply to a specific topic. It is titled WGQ Business Practice Standards Version n.n Matrix and has a version available to members and non-members at https://naesb.org//wgq/imp.asp.
121. TIBCO Corporation, Foresight software, EDISIM product; http://www.tibco.com/products/automation/application-integration/business-to-business/foresight
122. NAESB WGQ Version 3.0 Standards, North American Energy Standards Board, November 14, 2014. https://naesb.org/wgq/imp.asp (This document is password protected). Book 10 - Internet Electronic Transport Related Standards
123. NAESB WGQ Version 3.0 Standards, North American Energy Standards Board, November 14, 2014. https://naesb.org/wgq/imp.asp (This document is password protected). Book 4 – Quadrant Electronic Delivery Mechanism Related Standards
124. NAESB WGQ Version 3.0 Standards, North American Energy Standards Board, November 14, 2014. https://naesb.org/wgq/imp.asp (This document is password protected). Book 4 – Quadrant Electronic Delivery Mechanism Related Standards; and Book 10 – Internet Electronic Transport Related Standards
125. NAESB WGQ Version 3.0 Standards, North American Energy Standards Board, November 14, 2014. https://naesb.org/wgq/imp.asp (This document is password protected). Book 4 – Quadrant Electronic Delivery Mechanism Related Standards, Standard 4.2.19
126. NAESB WGQ Version 3.0 Standards, North American Energy Standards Board, November 14, 2014. https://naesb.org/wgq/imp.asp (This document is password protected). Book 0 – Additional Standards, Standards related to the Informational Postings Website: 0.3.5, 0.3.26; Book 4 – Quadrant Electronic Delivery Mechanism Related Standards, Standards 4.1.13, 4.1.16, 4.1.17, 4.1.18, 4.1.19, 4.1.20, 4.1.21, 4.1.22, 4.1.23, 4.1.24, 4.1.33, 4.2.1, 4.2.2, 4.2.3, 4.2.4, 4.2.5, 4.2.6, 4.2.7, 4.2.8, 4.2.9, 4.2.14, 4.2.15, 4.3.5, 4.3.16, 4.3.17, 4.3.18,, 4.3.20, 4.3.22, 4.3.23, 4.3.24, 4.3.25, 4.3.26, 4.3.27, 4.3.28, 4.3.30, 4.3.31, 4.3.32, 4.3.33, 4.3.34, 4.3.35, 4.3.36, 4.3.38, 4.3.40, 4.3.41, 4.3.53, 4.3.67, 4.3.80, 4.3.81, 4.3.82, 4.3.86, 4.3.94, 4.3.99, 4.3.101, 4.3.102, 4.3.104; Book 5 – Capacity Release Standards, Standards 5.4.20,

5.4.21, 5.4.22, 5.4.23

127. NAESB WGQ Version 3.0 Standards, North American Energy Standards Board, November 14, 2014. https://naesb.org/wgq/imp.asp (This document is password protected). Book 4 – Quadrant Electronic Delivery Mechanism Related Standards, Standards 4.3.23

128. NAESB WGQ Version 3.0 Standards, North American Energy Standards Board, November 14, 2014. https://naesb.org/wgq/imp.asp (This document is password protected). Book 0 – Additional Standards, Standards, Operationally Available and Unsubscribed Capacity related standards: 0.3.18, 0.3.20, 0.3.21, 0.3.22, 0.4.2, 0.4.3

129. NAESB WGQ Version 3.0 Standards, North American Energy Standards Board, November 14, 2014. https://naesb.org/wgq/imp.asp (This document is password protected). Book 0 – Additional Standards, Standards, Standard 0.4.2

130. NAESB WGQ Version 3.0 Standards, North American Energy Standards Board, November 14, 2014. https://naesb.org/wgq/imp.asp (This document is password protected). Book 0 – Additional Standards, Standard 0.4.3

131. NAESB WGQ Version 3.0 Standards, North American Energy Standards Board, November 14, 2014. https://naesb.org/wgq/imp.asp (This document is password protected). Book 4 – Quadrant Electronic Delivery Mechanism Related Standards, Standards related to posting of gas quality: 4.1.40, 4.3.89, 4.3.90, 4.3.91, 4.3.92, 4.3.93, 4.3.95, 4.3.96, 4.3.97, 4.3.98

132. See 18 CFR 284.13(c); http://www.ecfr.gov/cgi-bin/retrieveECFR?gp=&SID=3538e80d439a8f5930ba738494aa0287&n=pt18.1.284&r=PART&ty=HTML

133. NAESB WGQ Version 3.0 Standards, North American Energy Standards Board, November 14, 2014. https://naesb.org/wgq/imp.asp (This document is password protected). Book 4 – Quadrant Electronic Delivery Mechanism Related Standards, Standards 4.3.z and Book 5 – Capacity Release Related Standards, Standards 5.3.z

134. NAESB WGQ Version 3.0 Standards, North American Energy Standards Board, November 14, 2014. https://naesb.org/wgq/imp.asp (This document is password protected). Book 2 – Flowing Gas Related Standards, Standards 2.3.z

135. NAESB WGQ Version 3.0 Standards, North American Energy Standards Board, November 14, 2014. https://naesb.org/wgq/imp.asp (This document is password protected). Book 4 – Quadrant Electronic Delivery Mechanism Related Standards, Standards 4.3.z

136. NAESB WGQ Version 3.0 Standards, North American Energy Standards Board, November 14, 2014. https://naesb.org/wgq/imp.asp (This document is password protected). Book 11 – eTariff Related Standards

137. NAESB WGQ Version 3.0 Standards, North American Energy Standards Board, November 14, 2014. https://naesb.org/wgq/imp.asp (This document is

password protected). Book 5 - Capacity Release Related Standards, Standards 5.4.2,5.4.,5.4.4
138. NAESB WGQ Version 3.0 Standards, North American Energy Standards Board, November 14, 2014. https://naesb.org/wgq/imp.asp (This document is password protected). Book 4 – Quadrant Electronic Delivery Mechanism Related Standards, Standards 4.3.42, 4.3.43, 4.3.75, 4.3.79, 85
139. NAESB WGQ Version 3.0 Standards, North American Energy Standards Board, November 14, 2014. https://naesb.org/wgq/imp.asp (This document is password protected). Book 4 – Quadrant Electronic Delivery Mechanism Related Standards, Standards 4.1.13, 4.1.19,
140. NAESB WGQ Version 3.0 Standards, North American Energy Standards Board, November 14, 2014. https://naesb.org/wgq/imp.asp (This document is password protected). Book 4 – Quadrant Electronic Delivery Mechanism Related Standards, Standards, Appendix B, Appendix C
141. NAESB WGQ Version 3.0 Standards, North American Energy Standards Board, November 14, 2014. https://naesb.org/wgq/imp.asp (This document is password protected). Book 4 – Quadrant Electronic Delivery Mechanism Related Standards, Standards 4.3.5
142. NAESB WGQ Version 3.0 Standards, North American Energy Standards Board, November 14, 2014. https://naesb.org/wgq/imp.asp (This document is password protected). Book 0 – Additional Standards, Standards 0.3.11, 0.3.12, 0.3.13, 0.3.14, 0.3.15; Book 2 – Flowing Gas Related Standards, Standard, 2.3.63; Book 5 – Capacity Release Related Standards, Standards 5.2.1, 5.2.2, 5.3.70, 5.3.71, 5.4.16
143. NAESB WGQ Version 3.0 Standards, North American Energy Standards Board, November 14, 2014. https://naesb.org/wgq/imp.asp (This document is password protected). Book 5 – Capacity Release Related Standards, Standards 5.4.16
144. NAESB WGQ Version 3.0 Standards, North American Energy Standards Board, November 14, 2014. https://naesb.org/wgq/imp.asp (This document is password protected). Book 4 – Quadrant Electronic Delivery Mechanism Related Standards
145. NAESB WGQ Version 3.0 Standards, North American Energy Standards Board, November 14, 2014. https://naesb.org/wgq/imp.asp (This document is password protected). Book 4 – Quadrant Electronic Delivery Mechanism Related Standards, Standard 4.3.23
146. NAESB WGQ Version 3.0 Standards, North American Energy Standards Board, November 14, 2014. https://naesb.org/wgq/imp.asp (This document is password protected). Book 5 – Capacity Release Related Standards, Standard 5.4.16
147. NAESB WGQ Version 3.0 Standards, North American Energy Standards Board, November 14, 2014. https://naesb.org/wgq/imp.asp (This document is password

protected). Book 4 – Quadrant Electronic Delivery Mechanism Related Standards, Standard 4.3.28

148. NAESB WGQ Version 3.0 Standards, North American Energy Standards Board, November 14, 2014. https://naesb.org/wgq/imp.asp (This document is password protected). Book 4 – Quadrant Electronic Delivery Mechanism Related Standards, Standard 4.3.29
149. NAESB WGQ Version 3.0 Standards, North American Energy Standards Board, November 14, 2014. https://naesb.org/wgq/imp.asp (This document is password protected). Book 5 – Capacity Release Related Standards, Standard 5.4.16
150. NAESB WGQ Version 3.0 Standards, North American Energy Standards Board, November 14, 2014. https://naesb.org/wgq/imp.asp (This document is password protected). Book 0 - Additional Standards, Standard 0.3.7, 0.3.10
151. NAESB WGQ Version 3.0 Standards, North American Energy Standards Board, November 14, 2014. https://naesb.org/wgq/imp.asp (This document is password protected). Book 1 – Nominations Related Standards, Standard 1.3.51 and Book 5 – Capacity Release Related Standards, Standards 5.3.36, 5.3.37, 5.3.38, 5.3.39, and 5.3.40 specify the notification requirements in the case of an intraday bump.
152. NAESB WGQ Version 3.0 Standards, North American Energy Standards Board, November 14, 2014. https://naesb.org/wgq/imp.asp (This document is password protected). Book 0 - Additional Standards, Standard 0.3.14, Book 1 – Nomination Related Standards 1.1.12, 1.1.14, 1.1.15, 1.2.6, 1.3.26, 1.3.34, Book 5 – Capacity Release Related Standards 5.3.36, 5.3.37, 5.3.38, and 5.3.39 provide instructions on the notification requirements in the case of an operational flow order.
153. NAESB WGQ Version 3.0 Standards, North American Energy Standards Board, November 14, 2014. https://naesb.org/wgq/imp.asp (This document is password protected). Book 5 – Capacity Release Related Standards, Standards5.2.1, 5.2.2, 5.3.34, 5.3.35, 5.3.36, 5.3.37, 5.3.38 and 5.3.39 cover email notifications of critical notices
154. NAESB WGQ Version 3.0 Standards, North American Energy Standards Board, November 14, 2014. https://naesb.org/wgq/imp.asp (This document is password protected). Book 5 – Capacity Release Related Standards, Standards5.1.4, 5.3.44, 5.3.45, 5.3.46, 5.3.47, and 5.3.49.
155. NAESB WGQ Version 3.0 Standards, North American Energy Standards Board, November 14, 2014. https://naesb.org/wgq/imp.asp (This document is password protected). Book 5 – Capacity Release Related Standards, Standards 5.3.60 contains the requirements of that email
156. NAESB WGQ Version 3.0 Standards, North American Energy Standards Board, November 14, 2014. https://naesb.org/wgq/imp.asp (This document is password

protected). Book 5 – Capacity Release Related Standards, Standards 5.3.73, and FERC Order to Show Cause, Issued March 20, 2014 – RP14-442-000

157. NAESB WGQ Version 3.0 Standards, North American Energy Standards Board, November 14, 2014. https://naesb.org/wgq/imp.asp (This document is password protected). Standards related to the Customer Activities Website: Book 0 – Additional Standards, Standards 0.3.27, 0.3.28, Book 2 – Nominations Related Standards 1.3.48, 1.3.53, 1.3.55, 1.3.56, 1.3.58, 1.3.62, 1.3.79, Book 2 – Flowing Gas Related Standards2.4.7, 2.4.8, Book 4 – Quadrant Electronic Delivery Mechanism Related Standards 4.1.13, 4.1.15, 4.1.20, 4.1.21, 4.1.22, 4.1.23, 4.1.24, 4.1.26, 4.1.27, 4.1.28, 4.1.29, 4.1.30, 4.1.31, 4.1.32, 4.1.33, 4.2.2, 4.2.3, 4.2.4, 4.2.5, 4.2.7, 4.2.8, 4.2.9 , 4.2.10 , 4.2.13 , 4.2.14 , 4.2.15 , 4.2.16 , 4.2.17 , 4.2.19 , 4.3.5, 4.3.34, 4.3.36 , 4.3.38 , 4.3.39 , 4.3.40 , 4.3.41 , 4.3.42 , 4.3.43, 4.3.44, 4.3.45 , 4.3.46 , 4.3.48 , 4.3.49 , 4.3.50 , 4.3.52 , 4.3.53 , 4.3.54, 4.3.55 , 4.3.57 , 4.3.58 , 4.3.60 , 4.3.61 , 4.3.62 , 4.3.65 , 4.3.66, 4.3.67 , 4.3.68 , 4.3.69 , 4.3.72 , 4.3.75 , 4.3.78 , 4.3.79 , 4.3.80, 4.3.81 , 4.3.82 , 4.3.83 , 4.3.84 , 4.3.85 , 4.3.86 , 4.3.87 , 4.3.100, 4.3.101, 4.3.102, 4.3.103, 4.3.104, Book 5 – Capacity Release Related Standards 5.4.24, 5.4.25, 5.4.26, 5.4.27

158. NAESB WGQ Version 3.0 Standards, North American Energy Standards Board, November 14, 2014. https://naesb.org/wgq/imp.asp (This document is password protected). Book 4 – Quadrant Electronic Delivery Mechanism Related Standards, Standard 4.3.42

159. NAESB WGQ Version 3.0 Standards, North American Energy Standards Board, November 14, 2014. https://naesb.org/wgq/imp.asp (This document is password protected). Book 4 – Quadrant Electronic Delivery Mechanism Related Standards, Standard 4.3.43

160. NAESB WGQ Version 3.0 Standards, North American Energy Standards Board, November 14, 2014. https://naesb.org/wgq/imp.asp (This document is password protected). Book 1 – Nominations Related Standards

161. NAESB WGQ Version 3.0 Standards, North American Energy Standards Board, November 14, 2014. https://naesb.org/wgq/imp.asp (This document is password protected). Book 2 – Flowing Gas Related Standards

162. NAESB WGQ Version 3.0 Standards, North American Energy Standards Board, November 14, 2014. https://naesb.org/wgq/imp.asp (This document is password protected). Book 3 – Invoice Related Standards

163. NAESB WGQ Version 3.0 Standards, North American Energy Standards Board, November 14, 2014. https://naesb.org/wgq/imp.asp (This document is password protected). Book 5 – Capacity Release Related Standards

164. NAESB WGQ Version 3.0 Standards, North American Energy Standards Board, November 14, 2014. https://naesb.org/wgq/imp.asp (This document is password

protected). Book 6 – Contracts Related Standards

165. NAESB WGQ Version 3.0 Standards, North American Energy Standards Board, November 14, 2014. https://naesb.org/wgq/imp.asp (This document is password protected). Book 4 – Quadrant Electronic Delivery Mechanism Related Standards, Standard 4.3.43, 4.3.75, 4.3.79
166. NAESB WGQ Version 3.0 Standards, North American Energy Standards Board, November 14, 2014. https://naesb.org/wgq/imp.asp (This document is password protected). Book 4 – Quadrant Electronic Delivery Mechanism Related Standards, Standard 4.3.29, 4.3.30, 4.3.32, 4.3.34, 4.3.44, 4.3.48, 4.3.50, 4.3.55, 4.3.58, 4.3.68, 4.3.72
167. NAESB WGQ Version 2.1 Standards, North American Energy Standards Board, April 30, 2013. https://naesb.org/wgq/imp.asp (This document is password protected).
168. NAESB WGQ Version 2.1 Standards, North American Energy Standards Board, April 30, 2013. https://naesb.org/wgq/imp.asp (This document is password protected).
169. NAESB WGQ Version 3.0 Standards, North American Energy Standards Board, November 14, 2014. https://naesb.org/wgq/imp.asp (This document is password protected). Book 4 – Quadrant Electronic Delivery Mechanism Related Standards, Standard 4.3.72
170. NAESB WGQ Version 3.0 Standards, North American Energy Standards Board, November 14, 2014. https://naesb.org/wgq/imp.asp (This document is password protected). Book 4 – Quadrant Electronic Delivery Mechanism Related Standards, Standard 4.2.30
171. NAESB WGQ Version 3.0 Standards, North American Energy Standards Board, November 14, 2014. https://naesb.org/wgq/imp.asp (This document is password protected). Book 4 – Quadrant Electronic Delivery Mechanism Related Standards, Standard 4.3.58
172. NAESB WGQ Version 3.0 Standards, North American Energy Standards Board, November 14, 2014. https://naesb.org/wgq/imp.asp (This document is password protected). Book 4 – Quadrant Electronic Delivery Mechanism Related Standards, Standard 4.3.44
173. NAESB WGQ Version 3.0 Standards, North American Energy Standards Board, November 14, 2014. https://naesb.org/wgq/imp.asp (This document is password protected). Book 4 – Quadrant Electronic Delivery Mechanism Related Standards, Standard 4.3.68
174. NAESB WGQ Version 3.0 Standards, North American Energy Standards Board, November 14, 2014. https://naesb.org/wgq/imp.asp (This document is password protected). Book 4 – Quadrant Electronic Delivery Mechanism Related Standards,

Standard 4.3.29

175. NAESB WGQ Version 3.0 Standards, North American Energy Standards Board, November 14, 2014. https://naesb.org/wgq/imp.asp (This document is password protected). Book 4 – Quadrant Electronic Delivery Mechanism Related Standards, Standard 4.3.50
176. NAESB WGQ Version 3.0 Standards, North American Energy Standards Board, November 14, 2014. https://naesb.org/wgq/imp.asp (This document is password protected). Book 4 – Quadrant Electronic Delivery Mechanism Related Standards, Standard 4.3.29
177. NAESB WGQ Version 3.0 Standards, North American Energy Standards Board, November 14, 2014. https://naesb.org/wgq/imp.asp (This document is password protected). Book 4 – Quadrant Electronic Delivery Mechanism Related Standards, Standard 4.3.58
178. NAESB WGQ Version 3.0 Standards, North American Energy Standards Board, November 14, 2014. https://naesb.org/wgq/imp.asp (This document is password protected). Book 4 – Quadrant Electronic Delivery Mechanism Related Standards, Standard 4.3.58
179. NAESB WGQ Version 3.0 Standards, North American Energy Standards Board, November 14, 2014. https://naesb.org/wgq/imp.asp (This document is password protected). Book 4 – Quadrant Electronic Delivery Mechanism Related Standards, Standard 4.3.68
180. NAESB WGQ Version 3.0 Standards, North American Energy Standards Board, November 14, 2014. https://naesb.org/wgq/imp.asp (This document is password protected). Book 4 – Quadrant Electronic Delivery Mechanism Related Standards, Standard 4.3.48
181. NAESB WGQ Version 3.0 Standards, North American Energy Standards Board, November 14, 2014. https://naesb.org/wgq/imp.asp (This document is password protected). Book 4 – Quadrant Electronic Delivery Mechanism Related Standards, Standard 4.3.32
182. NAESB WGQ Version 3.0 Standards, North American Energy Standards Board, November 14, 2014. https://naesb.org/wgq/imp.asp (This document is password protected). Book 4 – Quadrant Electronic Delivery Mechanism Related Standards, Standard 4.3.44
183. NAESB WGQ Version 3.0 Standards, North American Energy Standards Board, November 14, 2014. https://naesb.org/wgq/imp.asp (This document is password protected). Book 4 – Quadrant Electronic Delivery Mechanism Related Standards, Standard 4.3.55
184. NAESB WGQ Version 3.0 Standards, North American Energy Standards Board, November 14, 2014. https://naesb.org/wgq/imp.asp (This document is password

protected). Book 4 – Quadrant Electronic Delivery Mechanism Related Standards, Standard 4.3.34

185. The requirement to use a conditional field is based on whether the condition has been met. Some pipelines will never have a situation where the condition is met for a data element and therefore that data element may be eliminated from the view. For other data elements, however, there may be a situation where the condition is met and therefore the element is required for the view.
186. NAESB WGQ Version 3.0 Standards, North American Energy Standards Board, November 14, 2014. https://naesb.org/wgq/imp.asp (This document is password protected). Book 1 – Nominations Related Standards, Standard 1.4.1
187. NAESB WGQ Version 3.0 Standards, North American Energy Standards Board, November 14, 2014. https://naesb.org/wgq/imp.asp (This document is password protected). Book 4 – Quadrant Electronic Delivery Mechanism Related Standards, Standard 4.3.28
188. NAESB WGQ Version 3.0 Standards, North American Energy Standards Board, November 14, 2014. https://naesb.org/wgq/imp.asp (This document is password protected). Book 4 – Quadrant Electronic Delivery Mechanism Related Standards, Standard 4.3.28
189. NAESB WGQ Version 3.0 Standards, North American Energy Standards Board, November 14, 2014. https://naesb.org/wgq/imp.asp (This document is password protected). Book 0 – Additional Standards, Standard 0.3.x
190. NAESB WGQ Version 3.0 Standards, North American Energy Standards Board, November 14, 2014. https://naesb.org/wgq/imp.asp (This document is password protected). Book 4 – Quadrant Electronic Delivery Mechanism Related Standards, Standard 4.1.3
191. NAESB WGQ Version 3.0 Standards, North American Energy Standards Board, November 14, 2014. https://naesb.org/wgq/imp.asp (This document is password protected). Book 4 – Quadrant Electronic Delivery Mechanism Related Standards, Standard 4.1.32
192. NAESB WGQ Version 3.0 Standards, North American Energy Standards Board, November 14, 2014. https://naesb.org/wgq/imp.asp (This document is password protected). Book 1 – Nominations Related Standards, Standard 1.4.1
193. NAESB WGQ Version 3.0 Standards, North American Energy Standards Board, November 14, 2014. https://naesb.org/wgq/imp.asp (This document is password protected). Book 1 – Nominations Related Standards, Standard 1.4.5
194. NAESB WGQ Version 3.0 Standards, North American Energy Standards Board, November 14, 2014. https://naesb.org/wgq/imp.asp (This document is password protected). Book 2 – Flowing Gas Related Standards, Standard 2.4.3
195. NAESB WGQ Version 3.0 Standards, North American Energy Standards Board,

November 14, 2014. https://naesb.org/wgq/imp.asp (This document is password protected). Book 4 – Quadrant Electronic Delivery Mechanism Related Standards, Standard 4.3.72

196. NAESB WGQ Version 3.0 Standards, North American Energy Standards Board, November 14, 2014. https://naesb.org/wgq/imp.asp (This document is password protected). Book 1 – Nominations Related Standards, Standard 1.3.53 and 1.3.62
197. NAESB WGQ Version 3.0 Standards, North American Energy Standards Board, November 14, 2014. https://naesb.org/wgq/imp.asp (This document is password protected). Book 4 – Quadrant Electronic Delivery Mechanism Related Standards, Standard 4.2.16
198. NAESB WGQ Version 3.0 Standards, North American Energy Standards Board, November 14, 2014. https://naesb.org/wgq/imp.asp (This document is password protected). Book 4 – Quadrant Electronic Delivery Mechanism Related Standards, Standard 4.2.17
199. Excel is a trademark of Microsoft Corporation
200. NAESB WGQ Version 3.0 Standards, North American Energy Standards Board, November 14, 2014. https://naesb.org/wgq/imp.asp (This document is password protected). Book 1 – Nominations Related Standards, Standard 1.3.48, Book 4 – Quadrant Electronic Delivery Mechanism Related Standards, Standard 4.3.66, 4.3.76 and 4.3.78
201. NAESB WGQ Version 3.0 Standards, North American Energy Standards Board, November 14, 2014. https://naesb.org/wgq/imp.asp (This document is password protected). Book 4 – Quadrant Electronic Delivery Mechanism Related Standards, Standard 4.1.6, 4.1.7, 4.1.10, 4.1.12, 4.1.33, 4.1.34, 4.1.35, 4.1.36, 4.1.37, 4.1.38, 4.1.39, 4.2.11, 4.2.12, 4.2.18, 4.2.20, 4.3.1, 4.3.2, 4.3.3, 4.3.47, 4.3.80, 4.3.81, 4.3.82, 4.3.86
202. NAESB WGQ Version 3.0 Standards, North American Energy Standards Board, November 14, 2014. https://naesb.org/wgq/imp.asp (This document is password protected). Book 1 –Nominations Related Standards, Standard 1.4.1 – EDI Subtab

Glossary

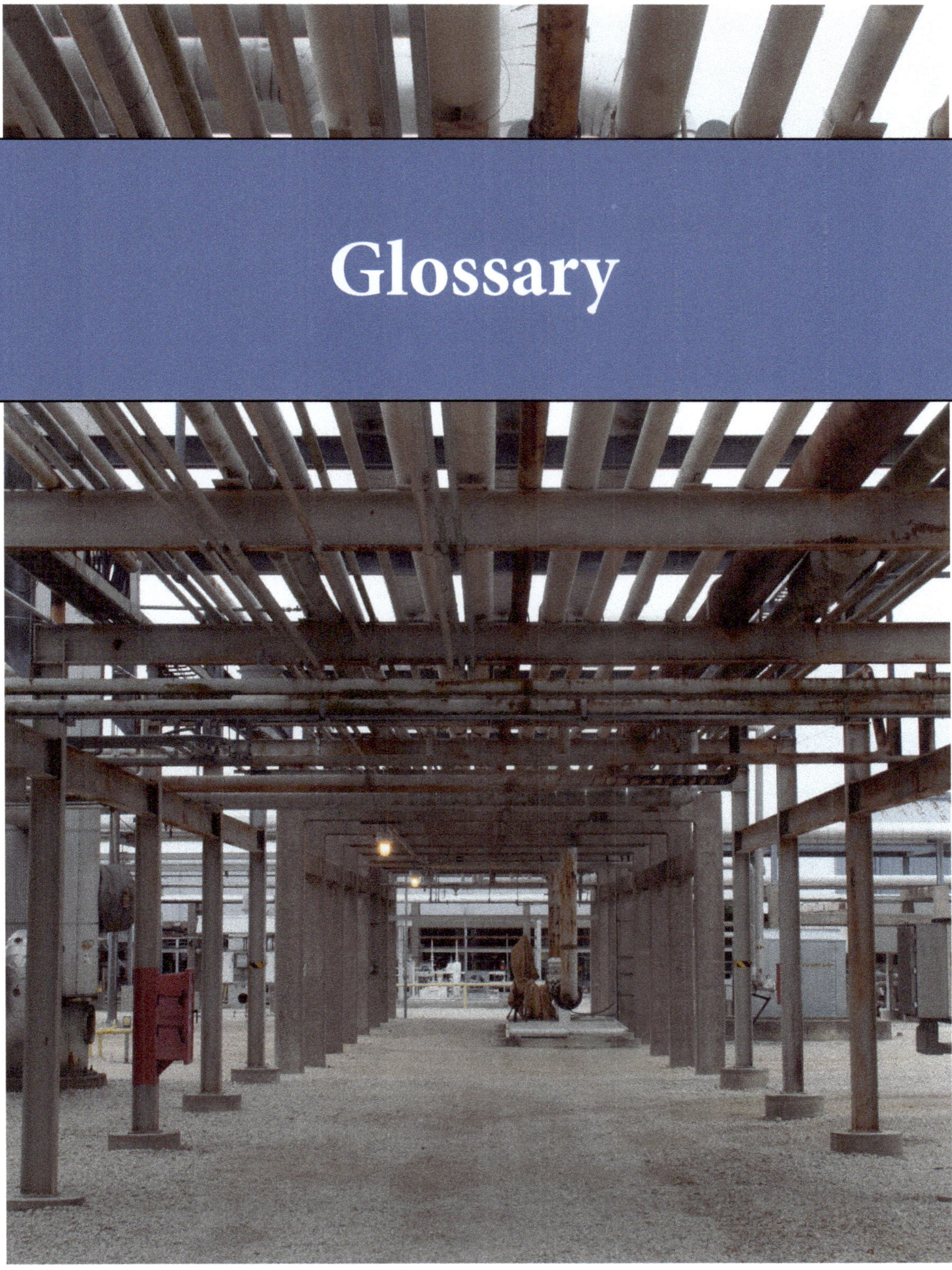

Glossary

311 pipeline: Instrastate pipeline subject to section 311(a)(1) of the Natural Gas Policy Act that requires it to file rates and charges and a tariff or Statement of Operating Conditions with FERC. Includes all intrastate pipelines that transport gas on behalf of other intrastate or local distribution pipelines served by an interstate pipeline.

ACA: Acronym for "Annual Cost Adjustment." For definition, see "Annual Cost Adjustment."

Accounting party: Receives invoices and accompanying reports for transportation contract. May be shipper, agent, or other party designated in contract.

Additional Standards: One of a series of nine NAESB Wholesale Gas Quadrant books in which NAESB standards are codified; contains standards that apply generally to other books of NAESB standards and contains standards that do not fit into other categories.

Agent: Through a contractual relationship with pipeline and shipper or operator, acts as a representative to conduct business on behalf of shipper or operator.

Aggregate: When shippers combine various packages of gas into one larger amount.

Allocations: Process whereby the pipeline reconciles the gas that was scheduled to flow with the actual flow of gas on the pipeline and allots to its customers the portion of the gas for which they contracted.

Annual Cost Adjustment: Fee charge by interstate pipeline. Also known by acronym "ACA."

Asset manager: Entity in special relationship between shipper and agent with enhanced rights to transport its own or its customer's gas without violating the "Shipper must have title rule."

Associated contract: Designates a contract other than shipper's transportation contract that is important to a transaction, such as a storage contract.

Auto-confirmation: Agreement between two interconnected parties in which any nomination entered for a location is automatically assumed to be confirmed to enable the pipeline to proceed with scheduling process.

Balancing service: Method used to keep shipper in balance at all times between the amount it delivers onto the pipeline and the amount it receives off the pipeline. Pipelines may have specific contracts or may use storage contracts for this purpose.

Beginning date: Date on which service requester wishes gas flow on a pipeline nomination to start.

Beginning time: Time at which service requester wishes gas flow to start on pipeline on beginning date. May either be start of gas day or one of a set of beginning times pipeline permits shippers to request.

Best available quantity: A quantity determined by a hierarchy of priorities of the quantities on a transaction. The best available quantity is most often the latest quantity but may be the quantity with the highest priority. On a nomination transaction, the best available quantity is the actual allocated quantity, estimate allocated quantity, scheduled quantity, confirmed quantity or nominated quantity in descending order.

Biddable: Term pertaining to capacity release indicating that the capacity release offer terms are such that the offer is eligible for bids.

Bid transportation rate: Used by pipelines to offer shippers the ability to indicate the rate they wish to pay for transportation on a particular nomination.

Bid-up indicator: Used to tell pipeline that shipper is willing to have its rates raised incrementally higher than negotiated rate until the rate is high enough to secure scheduled quantity of transportation.

British Thermal Units: Unit to measure the heating value of natural gas. The amount of energy necessary to raise the temperature of one pound of water by one degree Fahrenheit. Usually abbreviated "BTUs."

BTUs: Abbreviation for "British Thermal Units." See "British Thermal Units" for a definition.

Capacity release: When shipper holding firm service on pipeline decides not to use all or portion of service for a period of time and to make it available for bid to highest bidder. First transaction FERC allowed pipelines to conduct electronically in Order 636.

Capacity Release: One of a series of nine NAESB Wholesale Gas Quadrant books in which NAESB standards are codified; details transactions and contains supporting datasets related to posting and trading of contractual capacity.

Capacity Release Offer dataset: Used to post available capacity being offered from firm service agreements.

Capacity type indicator: Tells pipeline locations on a nomination are using specific capacity rights.

Cash-out: Mechanism used by a pipeline to resolve imbalances in a shipper's account in which, at the end of an imbalance period, the shipper pays monetary amount to pipeline for gas the shipper received over the amount specified in its nomination in case of "imbalance due pipeline" or the pipeline pays shipper a monetary amount for deficit in amount of gas a shipper did not receive in amount owed under its nomination agreement in case of "imbalance due shipper."

CAW: Abbreviation for "Customer Activities Website." See "Customer Activities Website" for definition.

Charges: Amount assessed to the shipper, calculated by the quantity of gas for which a shipper contracted and received off the pipeline and the rate and charge types agreed on by the shipper and pipeline, adjusted by any imbalances that may have occurred during gas transportation.

Charge type: One of any number of fees that a pipeline may assess a shipper for service on the pipeline contract. One contract may have multiple charge types.

Commodity fee: Fee pipeline assesses to all shippers for transportation based on volume or quantity of gas transported.

Compression: Process used to bring gas from a low-pressure pipeline to a high-pressure pipeline and to keep gas at a level of pressure needed to push the gas down the pipeline.

Confirmation: Interchange between pipeline and operator to communicate and confirm transactions expected to flow and associated volumes of gas to be received onto the pipeline and delivered off of the pipeline.

Confirmation quick response: EDI transaction that provides validation error and warning codes and messages to tell the sender of the information that one or more pieces of data contained in the transmission were unable to be processed.

Constraint-focused: Pipeline on which constraints are addressed first in scheduling process.

Contract: Foundation of the relationship between the shipper and the pipeline which outlines the agreement under which the pipeline will transport or store natural gas for the shipper and defines the time period, type, and location of service, the rate for service, and any exceptions to the pipeline's pro-forma agreement.

Contracts: One of a series of nine NAESB Wholesale Gas Quadrant books in which NAESB standards are codified; details model and standard contracts for use in natural gas industry.

Contract inventory: Monitoring by pipeline of a shipper's pipeline inventory to ensure levels on the contract and at various points are not exceeded during nomination process.

COPAS: Acronym for Council of Petroleum Accountants Society. For definition, see "Council of Petroleum Accountants Society."

Council of Petroleum Accountants Society: Professional organization that establishes accounting principles for specific accounting practices to ensure compliance with regulations in the Natural gas and other petroleum-based industries. Also known by the acronym "COPAS."

Credit: Process that determines services for which a shipper is able to contract transportation on pipeline whereby pipelines can assess and reduce financial risk.

Cubic feet: Unit of measurement for natural gas volume. Usually abbreviated MCF for "thousand cubic feet" or MMCF for "million cubic feet."

Customer Activities Website: Section on pipeline's website reserved for customers secured by login that contains data available only to that specific customer's log-in, and the site online where transactions occur to initiate and manage the flow of gas. Also known by its acronym "CAW."

Cycle: Nomination deadlines that identify the times in a gas day when a shipper may submit nominations on the pipeline and may expect to receive nomination processing results from the pipeline.

Cycle indicator: Gives shipper ability to elect in nomination the cycle in which it wishes to begin flow of gas.

Deal type: Used to specify pre-negotiated arrangements between the shipper and the pipeline.

Dekatherm: Measurement of quantity for purified natural gas equal to one MMCF with a heating value of one. Unit of measurement usually used in natural gas transportation contracts in the United States. May also be spelled "Decatherm." Abbreviated "DTH."

Delivered quantity: Used by pipeline in EDI transactions to allow shipper to provide amount of gas delivered in nomination transaction.

Delivery location: End point for a transaction at which shippers receive natural gas off of a pipeline. Also known as "delivery point."

Delivery point: See definition "Delivery location."

Delivery quantity: In non-EDI transactions, this quantity tells the pipeline the quantity of gas the shipper intends to deliver at the delivery location. May be reduced by any in-kind fuel the pipeline retains.

Delivery rank: Applied by shipper to downstream unthreaded portion of pathed non-threaded nomination to indicate how shipper wants nomination ranked in case of delivery cut.

Demand charge: Fee pipeline charges firm-contract holders to reserve capacity on pipeline regardless of whether or not contract holder utilizes the capacity for transportation of gas. Also known as "reservation fee."

Disaggregate: When shippers divide a large amount into various packages for delivery onto a market.

Displacement capacity: Quantity of gas that reduces the flow at a receipt meter by the quantity being delivered at the receipt meter through a reversal of flow direction. Likewise, a quantity of gas that reduces the flow at a delivery meter by the quantity being received at the delivery meter.

Distribution pipeline: Pipeline that moves gas from the high-pressure pipeline to the local distribution company. Usually an intrastate pipeline that is governed by regulatory entities within its state of operation.

Downstream: In gas transportation, the disposition of gas after it is received off of a pipeline. Ultimate delivery to a business or residential consumer lies on this side of gas transportation.

Downstream contract identifier: Used to designate service-requester contract to which shipper is delivering a particular package of gas.

Downstream identifier: Party receiving gas from the service requester in the nomination. Also known as downstream shipper.

Downstream package ID: Tells pipeline which unique package of gas can be matched to nomination for confirmation purposes for delivery on pipeline at downstream location.

Dry gas: Pure-methane gas that has been processed to remove impurities.

DTH: Abbreviation for Dekatherm. For definition, see "Dekatherm."

EDI: Abbreviation for "Electronic Data Interchange." For definition, see "Electronic Data Interchange."

EDM: Abbreviation of "Electronic Delivery Mechanisms."

Elapsed-prorated-scheduled quantity: Quantity presumed to have flowed on pro-rata basis during hours of gas day that elapsed prior to change in flow. Also known by acronym "EPSQ."

Electronic Data Interchange: Any exchange of data over any electronic mechanism using ANSI ASC X12 Standards for electronic communication of data through standardized data formats. Also known by acronym "EDI."

Electronic Delivery Mechanisms: Two of a series of nine NAESB Wholesale Gas Quadrant books in which NAESB standards are codified; contains instructions for electronic exchange of data in NAESB process and for public view of interstate pipeline tariff via Informational Postings. NAESB has divided the EDM books into the QEDM – or quadrant-specific EDM manual and IET – or internet electronic transport manuals. Also known by acronym "EDM."

Ending date: Date on which service requester wishes gas flow on pipeline to end.

Ending time: Time at which service requester wishes gas flow to cease on pipeline on ending date. Optional for shipper to send and pipeline to support. Usually the end of gas day.

EPSQ: Abbreviation for "elapsed prorated scheduled quantity." See definition under "Elapsed-prorated-scheduled quantity."

eTariff: One of a series of nine NAESB Wholesale Gas Quadrant books in which NAESB standards are codified; contains instructions for interstate pipeline to file its periodic tariff updates with FERC in electronic mechanism.

Ethane: Lower carbon gas with formula of C2H6, sometimes an impurity in natural gas. Natural gas must be processed in order to remove ethane and other secondary components before the gas can be transported.

Export declaration: Used for transportation crossing border from Canada into United States.

Facility: Usually refers to a functional area on a pipeline, including those used for storage and processing.

Federal Energy Regulatory Commission: Regulatory agency of the federal government that sets rules and governance relating to interstate gas transportation and influences all areas of gas transportation in which interstate transportation is involved. Also known by the acronym of "FERC."

FERC: Acronym for "Federal Energy Regulatory Commission." For definition, see "Federal Energy Regulatory Commission."

Firm service: Type of service offered by a pipeline whereby shipper has designated space for transportation on pipeline for contracted period of time. Because pipeline reserves space for shipper, shipper pays either reservation charge or demand charge for number of DTH specified in its contract regardless of whether or not it uses transportation. Pipelines give firm service higher scheduling and allocation priority.

Flow-day redirect: When shipper changes an existing nomination, through a point of constraint, in subsequent cycle to move current receipt point to new receipt point or to move current delivery point to new delivery point.

Flowing Gas: One of a series of nine NAESB Wholesale Gas Quadrant books in which NAESB standards are codified; concerns transactions related to gas flow and distribution of gas after flow.

Fuel: Energy used to compress gas on pipeline. Also, a contractual retainage of gas quantity used to operate a pipeline.

Gas control: After quantities scheduled, creates a plan to set valves for meters so scheduled flow can be received and delivered.

Gas flow: Physical movement of gas onto, through, and off of a pipeline, including monitoring by gas control and use of meters to measure the gas.

Gas Industry Standards Board: Working group first formed by FERC to address areas in industry needing major change. Later became the North American Energy Standards Board. Also known by the acronym "GISB."

Gatherer: Entity, pool, or pipeline that receives gas from numerous wellheads before delivering to a high-pressure pipeline for transportation.

Gathering pipeline: Pipeline that collects gas from numerous wellheads and moves it onto a high-pressure pipeline for transportation. Usually intrastate pipeline that is governed by regulatory entities within its state of operation.

Gigajoules: Measurement of quantity for purified natural gas used in Canada.

GISB: Acronym for the "Gas Industry Standards Board." For definition, see "Gas Industry Standards Board."

Hinshaw pipeline: A pipeline with transactions that are received, delivered, and consumed within one state and governed by that state's public utility commission. Hinshaw pipelines are not subject to FERC jurisdiction.

Hub service: Service where physical location on pipeline intereconnects with many pipelines. Similar to pooling service.

Imbalance: Difference between the amount of gas scheduled to flow on a pipeline and the amount of gas that actually flowed. Pipelines use various methods to rectify imbalances in gas flow.

Imbalance-due-pipeline position: Caused when shipper takes more gas off of pipeline than it receives.

Imbalance-due-shipper position: Caused when shipper receives less gas off of pipeline than it delivers onto the pipeline.

Imbalance trading: Mechanism used by a pipeline to resolve imbalances in a shipper's account.

Index-based: Rate option for transportation contract based on price indices.

Informational Posting Website: Website in public domain of pipeline's system available for anyone to view. Also known by abbreviation "IPW."

Injection season: Time of year when shippers typically inject gas into storage facility.

Interactive flat files: Format of files that may be exchanged between pipelines and service requesters in electronic formats via the CAW.

Internet Electronic Transport: One of a series of nine NAESB Wholesale Gas Quadrant books in which NAESB standards are codified; contains standards for data exchange and communication through EDI or flat files.

Interstate pipeline: Pipeline that operates between states or one that crosses one or more state lines. Such pipelines are governed by regulations set down by the Federal Energy Regulatory Commission.

Interruptible: Type of service offered by a pipeline in which shippers engage the pipeline for transportation of gas on an as-needed basis, and paid for via a commodity charge. Offers more risk to shipper because of the lack of guaranteed space on the pipeline. Usually given a lower scheduling and allocation priority by a pipeline.

Intraday-1: Cycle with nomination deadline of 10 a.m. for flow that begins on same gas day at 2 p.m. during gas day.

Intraday-2: Cycle with nomination deadline of 230 p.m. for flow that begins on same gas day at 6 p.m. during gas day.

Intraday-3: Cycle with nomination deadline of 7 p.m. for flow that begins on same gas day at 10 p.m. during gas day.

Intraday-noms: Nominations that occur during the course of the gas day, after the timely nomination deadline.

Intrastate pipeline: Pipeline that operates within one state. Could be a gathering pipeline that moves gas from a wellhead to a high-pressure pipeline or a distribution pipeline that moves gas from the high-pressure pipeline to the local distribution company. Governed by regulatory entities within their state of operation.

Inventory: Supplies of gas maintained by pipeline and managed by operational balancing agreements to maintain balances in shippers" accounts. Types of inventory include contractual, storage, park, and imbalance.

Invoicing: Process whereby the pipeline assembles charges assessed to a shipper into a comprehensive bill that is accompanied by back-up statements that support charges listed on the invoice. Invoices are issued according to regulatory timeline after charge calculations are complete and verification of charges accomplished.

Invoicing: One of a series of nine NAESB Wholesale Gas Quadrant books in which NAESB standards are codified.

IPW: Abbreviation for "Informational Postings Website."

Lesser-of-rule: Outlines decision pipeline and operator make when quantities in confirmation process do not match after confirmation process is complete, whereby lesser quantity becomes confirmation quantity.

Local distribution company: Entity on the downstream side of the gas business responsible for delivering gas to local users. May be the utility that delivers gas to business or residential consumers or the LDC may deliver to one or more utility companies that, in turn, deliver to consumers. In many states, may also be the open-access transporter that offers transportation services to other entities or may purchase and sell gas for delivery to consumers. Also known by the acronym "LDC."

Location: Term used by NAESB to identify receipts and deliveries on a pipeline. May be physical location such as meter station or logical location such as accounting for exchange of gas ownership. Also known as "point."

Make-up: Mechanism in which shipper brings gas onto pipeline in case of "imbalance due-pipeline" because shipper received more gas off of pipeline than it delivered onto pipeline.

Mandatory: Described information sender must provide for data element as part of transaction and which receiver must use and process if data element is something receiver can use.

Market-focused: Pipeline scheduling scenario to maximize the deliveries flowing out of the pipeline to the market area.

Maximize-Throughput: Pipeline scheduling scenario focused on keeping most available volume flowing through pipeline.

Maximum Daily Delivery Quantity: Used in pipeline tariffs to refer to the greatest amount of gas a shipper may receive on a daily basis at a specific location on pipeline. Also known by the abbreviation "MDDQ."

Maximum Daily Quantity: Total maximum quantity that can be used across all locations and paths on a given day for a contract. Used to assess reservation/demand charge on a firm contract. Also known by abbreviation "MDQ."

Maximum Daily Receipt Quantity: Used in pipeline tariffs to refer to the greatest amount of gas a shipper may deliver onto a pipeline at a specific location on a daily basis. Also known by the abbreviation "MDRQ."

Maximum rate indicator: Used by shippers to indicate to pipeline it is willing to pay the maximum rate permitted under the pipeline's tariff, rather than its negotiated rate, in order to get its transportation to flow.

MCF: Abbreviation for "thousand cubic feet," unit of volume measurement for natural gas.

MDDQ: Abbreviation for "Maximum Daily Delivery Quantity." For definition, see "Maximum Daily Delivery Quantity."

MDQ: Abbreviation for "Maximum Daily Quantity." For definition, see "Maximum Daily Quantity."

MDRQ: Abbreviation for "Maximum Daily Receipt Quantity." For definition, see "Maximum Daily Receipt Quantity."

Measurement: Recording active flow of gas on pipeline at given time or interval using data from electronic-flow devices, manual entry, gas-quality lab results, and weather data.

Meter: Physical device to measure gas at a location and at a rate. Affected by temperature, pressure, and other factors.

Methane: Single-carbon gas with scientific formula of CH4 and a BTU factor of 1.0 that comprises natural gas.

Mileage-based: Rate option for transportation contract based on distance with per-mile charges.

Minimum delivery quantity: Used by shipper to indicate to pipeline the minimum quantity that it will accept as scheduled quantity less than the nominated quantity if pipeline is unable to delivered requested quantity.

Minimum receipt quantity: Used by shipper to indicate to pipeline the minimum quantity that it will accept as scheduled quantity less than the nominated quantity if pipeline is unable to delivered requested quantity.

MMBTU: Caloric quantity that ensures all participants in flow of gas on pipeline are treated equally from heating-value perspective. Measurement calculated by multiplying MMCF by BTU.

MMCF: The abbreviation for "million cubic feet," a unit of volume measurement for natural gas.

NAESB: The acronym for the North American Energy Standards Board. For a definition, see "North American Energy Standards Board." NAESB is pronounced [nays-bee].

NAESB standards: Codified standards agreed to by the participants working on the North American Energy Standards Board that govern the way business is conducted in the natural gas industry. Standards are published in a nine-volume set of books known as the NAESB Wholesale Gas Quadrant Standards (WGQ).

Natural gas: A common term for mix of methane gas and secondary components such as water, sulfur, or other carbon gases. Single-carbon methane gas with scientific formula of CH4 and BTU factor of 1.0 that that has been processed for industrial or residential use.

Natural gas liquids: Heavier carbon gasses, often an impurity in natural gas that must be removed through processing before natural gas can be transported. Sought-after commodity because products are highly marketable. Also known by acronym "NGLs."

NGLs: Acronym for "Natural Gas Liquids." For definition, see "Natural Gas Liquids."

Nomination: Order submitted by the shipper to the pipeline to initiate the flow of gas, which includes the terms under which the shipper requires the gas to flow throughout the pipeline, including gas make-up requirements, length of service requested, and rate. NAESB nomination cycles govern nominations on interstate pipelines.

Nomination dataset: Contains 64 data elements used to comprise nominations.

Nomination key: Group of data elements in a nomination that causes a new nomination to be created when a value in one or more elements is different.

Nominations: One of a series of nine NAESB Wholesale Gas Quadrant books in which NAESB standards are codified; contains all the datasets related to transactions that occur before gas flows, such as nomination transactions, confirmation transactions, and reporting of scheduled quantities.

Nominator's tracking ID: Used by shipper on EDI dataset transmission to distinguish each nomination line item.

Non-biddable: Term pertaining to capacity release indicating a capacity release offer that is not subject to public bidding.

Non-pathed model type: Nomination model type identified by NAESB in which shipper submits upstream data and downstream data in separate transactions that can be used to route portions of shipper's gas in diverse paths. Non-pathed models only require that the receipt and deliveries be in balance before submitting the nomination. Abbreviated "NPT."

NOPR: Acronym for "Notice of Proposed Rulemaking." For definition, see "Notice of Proposed Rulemaking."

North American Energy Standards Board: Industry-formed and represented organization that develops standards for the energy industry, including wholesale gas, on a voluntary, consensus-building basis. Also known by the acronym "NAESB."

Notice of Proposed Rulemaking: Issuance by FERC staff notifying interested parties of an concern observed in market/industry about which FERC staff perceives a change needs to be made. Also known by acronym "NOPR."

NPT: Abbreviation for "non-pathed model type."

OBA: Acronym for "operational balancing agreement." For definition, see "Operational balancing agreement."

Operational balancing agreement: Standing contract between pipeline and operator used to maintain balances with operators at interconnects to maintain balance between quantity of gas shipper delivers to pipeline and quantity shipper receives off pipeline. Also known by acronym "OBA."

Operational impact area: A physical area on a pipeline designated as the boundary within which imbalances may be traded. May span multiple zones and segments.

Operator-provided value: Allocation method which gives operator ability to assign fixed values to one or more transactions at a location.

Package ID: Used by shipper that allows it to distinguish one nomination transaction from another nomination that would otherwise be the same.

PAL: Acronym for "parking and loaning" or "parking and lending." For definition, see "Parking and loaning."

Parking and loaning: Service provided by pipeline that permits shipper to park gas for short time on pipeline before delivering gas off, or to borrow gas from pipeline for short time when shipper receives more gas off pipeline that it delivered to pipeline. Considered low-level interruptible service. Also known as "parking and lending." Also known by acronym "PAL."

Pathed model type: Nomination model type identified by NAESB and used most often on North-American pipelines in which a specific receipt location on a pipeline is tied to a specific delivery location. Abbreviated "PTH."

Pathed non-threaded model type: Nomination model type identified by NAESB in which a specific receipt location on a pipeline is tied to a specific delivery location but in which upstream-supply and downstream-market transactions are not directly associated with the contract. Instead, the shipper assigns ranks to the upstream suppliers and the downstream market, which allows the shipper to control which supplies of gas get cut in the event of reductions. Abbreviated "PNT."

Payback: Mechanism in which pipeline gives gas to shipper to make up deficit in case of "imbalance due shipper" in which shipper received less gas off of pipeline than it delivered onto pipeline.

Payment remittance: Mechanism provided via EDI or the pipeline website on which the shipper can inform the pipeline of any invoices not being paid, of any partial payments, and of any reasons for differences between invoiced amount and amount paid.

PDA: Abbreviation for "pre-determined allocation." For definition, see "Pre-Determined Allocation."

Penalty range: The level of percentage of imbalance in a shipper's account at which pipelines begin imposing penalties.

Pentane: Carbon gas, C5H12, often an impurity in natural gas in a low quantity. The natural gas must be processed in order to remove pentane and other secondary components before the gas can be transported.

Percentage: Allocation method in which gas at a location is distributed based on percentage rights operators assign to nomination transactions rather than on quantity originally scheduled.

Pipeline: System used to gather, process, store, transport, and distribute gas from one location to another, whether a state-level pipeline, intrastate pipeline, interstate pipeline, a network of pipelines. This term may encompass the physical transportation pipeline, gathering facilities, gas-processing plants, storage facilities, and distribution companies.

Plant operator: Party in control of the physical operation and maintenance of a gas processing plant.

PNT: Abbreviation for "pathed non-threaded model type." For a definition see "pathed non-threaded model type."

Point: Also known as "location." Used by some business entities to identify receipts and deliveries on a pipeline.

Point of constraint: Location on pipeline where compression, junction of pipes, or other physical limitations cause reduced gas flow.

Point operator: Also known as operator of a location. Pipeline delivering gas at a location or receiving gas at a location. May be third party contracted to measure and to allocate gas at location.

Pooling: Service that permits shipper to collect gas supply transactions into one larger unit and disaggregate the gas into markets. Service must be offered by interstate pipelines.

PPA: Abbreviation for "prior-period adjustment." See definition at "Prior-period adjustment."

Pre-Determined Allocation: Dataset that enables service requester to provide allocation instructions to pipeline, depending upon the operational configuration and business practices of the pipeline. Also known by abbreviation "PDA."

Primary location: Locations listed on firm service contract as those with primary scheduling rights on the contract.

Prior-period adjustments: Issued by pipeline to correct volumes from estimate value to actual value when the final actual measured volume and actual allocated quantity are not available for measurement at calendar cut-off date. Also known by abbreviation "PPA."

Processing rights indicator: Used by shippers to provide notice that it has elected to use its processing rights to transportation service providers that offers processing services.

Processing service: Used to extract non-methane components out of natural gas to make it suitable for long-distance transportation.

Producer: A collective term for entities involved on the production side of the natural gas industry, responsible for overseeing the progression of natural gas from its removal from the ground, through processing, and into mainline transportation. Producer is a collective term for a group that includes, among others, the well operator, gatherer, plant operator, and transporter.

Propane: Lower carbon gas, C3H8, sometimes an impurity in natural gas. The natural gas must be processed in order to remove propane and other secondary components before the gas can be transported.

Pro-rata: Allocation method where portion measured to each party is determined by its percentage of the original overall scheduled quantity for a location.

PTH: Abbreviation for "pathed model type." For a definition see "pathed model type."

Quantity: Used on nomination transactions that require only one quantity to be provided.

Quantity-based: Rate option for transportation contract versus a flat rate.

Quantity-type indicator: Tells pipeline whether quantity provided is for receipt or delivery or both.

Rank: Method of allocation wherein transactions are assigned numeric priorities to determine which receives first distribution of measured gas.

Reduction-reason code: Required by NAESB for explanation to shipper when scheduled quantity on pipeline is reduced from original nominated quantity.

Recall: Term offered as part of offer and bid in capacity-release process in which releasing shipper may ask for capacity to be returned for part or all of the remainder of the term of release.

Receipt location: Beginning point at which shippers deliver natural gas onto a pipeline for transportation. Also known as receipt point.

Receipt point: See definition "Receipt location."

Receipt quantity: Quantity of gas the shipper intends to receive at the receipt location.

Receipt rank: Applied by shipper to upstream unthreaded portion of pathed non-threaded nomination to indicate how shipper wants nomination ranked in case of receipt cut.

Reput: Term offered as part of offer and bid in capacity-release process in which releasing shipper releases capacity at end of recall period either to original acquiring shipper or to another shipper.

Request for confirmation: Dataset used to initiate confirmation process from one party at interconnected point. Contains data elements related to receipt side and delivery side of nomination depending on the point of view of the location.

Reservation fee: Fee pipeline charges firm-contract holders to reserve capacity on pipeline regardless of whether or not contract holder utilizes the capacity for transportation of gas. Also known as "demand fee."

Reticulated pipeline: System on which gas has option of flowing more than one direction to get to same delivery location on same system.

Revenue-based: Pipeline where scheduling priorities are based on projected revenue of transportation transactions.

Scheduled quantity: Culmination of confirmation and scheduling processes that will be used to configure the pipeline for gas flow.

Scheduling: Process whereby pipeline accumulates all quantities nominated and determines how much gas can flow through each location and through each segment of pipe for a given cycle.

Secondary locations: In some contracts, all locations on pipeline other than primary locations are regarded as secondary locations. In other contracts, the secondary locations may be explicitly listed.

Segment: Division for a pipeline that identifies specific sections that operate in the same manner. May be separated by operational constraints, points of connection, locations where pipe sizes change, or where compression causes operational capacity to vary.

Segmentation: Provides an opportunity for firm-contract holder to fully utilize its transportation capacity by dividing capacity into multiple segments.

Service requester: Entity requesting transportation service on a pipeline. May be a shipper, agent, or asset manager.

Service requester contract: NAESB designation for contract used to transport one or more packages of gas.

Shipper: Owns transportation contract for capacity on pipeline or at service facility.

"Shipper must have title" rule: The federal regulation that requires an entity holds title to any gas it transports on an interstate pipeline.

SOC: Acronym for "Statement of Operating Conditions." See definition under "Tariff."

SOX compliance: Acronym for "Sarbanes-Oxley Act."

Standing confirmation: Agreement between operator and pipeline where gas flow is expected to be relatively constant with contracted parties taking gas on long-term basis.

Statement of Account: Issued by pipeline to inform shipper of invoices issues, payments that have been received, and outstanding balances due to pipeline. May accompany invoice or be issued separately from invoice.

Statement of Operating Conditions: Another name for a pipeline's tariff. Also known by the acronym "SOC." For a definition, see "Tariff."

Stepped rate: Rate option for transportation contract where one rate is applied to entire block of gas when volume falls within a range of volumes with rate based on range of volume.

Storage inventory: The quantity of gas in a shipper's contracted storage account, the balance of which is the sum of all the shipper's injections and withdrawals on the storage facility.

Storage ratcheting: Spacing out times and amounts shipper may inject into or withdraw from storage facility to prevent all injections or withdrawals occurring during peak periods.

Storage service: Service offered by a pipeline to hold gas for a shipper for a period of time. Gives shipper option of buying gas during non-peak season and delivering gas to market during peak season. Storage facility may be underground salt dome, underground gas facility that has been exhausted, or above-ground facility built by pipeline.

Sulfur: Sometimes an impurity in natural gas that decreases the heating component of the gas. The natural gas must be processed in order to remove sulfur and other secondary components before the gas can be transported. The sulfur removed from natural gas is usually sold on a secondary market.

Supply-focused: Pipeline scheduled to maximize the receipts flowing onto pipeline.

Swing: Allocation method in which one or more designated transactions absorb the excess quantity when measured quantity is greater than, or receives a lesser quantity when the measured quantity is smaller than, total scheduled quantity.

Tariff: Also known as a "statement of operating conditions," this is the governing document for a pipeline, which explains the pipeline's service offerings, the rules for the service offerings, the rates and charges, and the business rules the pipeline uses to govern transactions. An interstate pipeline must file its tariff with the Federal Energy Regulatory Commission.

Tiered rate: Rate option for transportation contract where one rate is applied to first block of flow volumes, second rate applied to second set of flow volumes, and third rate applied to third set of flow volumes.

Timely cycle: The first cycle in the gas day where nominations are submitted the day before the gas is requested to flow. Also a time to synchronize transportation requests across pipeline grid.

Timely nomination: Deadline before which all nominations are considered timely for a particular cycle.

Timestamp: System-generated verification of time when pipeline receives a nomination from a shipper.

Title Transfer Tracking: Process where TSP tracks exchange of ownership of gas when bought, sold, or exchanged between two or more parties at a location. Required service on FERC-regulated pipelines. Also known by abbreviation "TTT."

Trade window: Period of time after accounting period for active operational period has closed in which imbalances may be traded to resolve "imbalance due pipeline" or "imbalance due shipper" positions.

Transactional reporting section: Section on pipeline's informational postings website.

Transportation service: The movement of gas on a gas pipeline from a receipt location to a delivery location.

Transportation Service Provider: An all-encompassing proper name coined by NAESB to describe any entity that provides services to transport gas for other parties, which may include the physical transportation pipeline, gathering facilities, gas-processing plants, storage facilities, and distribution companies. In the industry, these entities are also commonly referred to as "pipelines." Also known by the abbreviation "TSP."

Transporter: A pipeline or other entity responsible for moving natural gas from one location to another.

TSP: The abbreviation for "Transportation Service Provider." For a definition, see "Transportation Service Provider."

TTT: abbreviation for "Title Transfer Tracking." For a definition, see "Title Transfer Tracking."

Upstream: In gas transportation, the disposition of gas before it is delivered onto a pipeline.

Upstream contract identifier: Used to designate service-requester contract under which a particular package of gas was serviced prior to title being held by the service requester.

Upstream identifier: Party delivering gas to service requester in a nomination. Also known as upstream shipper.

Upstream package ID: Tells pipeline which packages of gas can be matched to nomination on upstream pipeline for confirmation purposes.

Utility company: Usually the ultimate sales entity that buys natural gas and distributes it to local business and residential consumers.

Validation: Occurs when pipeline has received the nomination, finds it to be correct, and accepts it, or informs shipper through series of pre-approved error codes that the pipeline found errors or warnings in nomination line item. This term may also apply to the receipt process of confirmations, pre-determined allocations, capacity release offers and bids.

Volumetric-based: Rate option for transportation contract.

Water: Sometimes an impurity in natural gas that decreases the heating component of the gas. The natural gas must be processed in order to remove water and other secondary components before the gas can be transported.

Well operator: An entity on the production side of the natural gas business. The individual or company that controls the location and the wellhead mechanism where natural gas is removed from the ground.

Wellhead: The mechanism in the ground to remove natural gas for sale.

Wet gas: Natural gas that is not pure methane and contains secondary components that affect the quality and heating value of the gas.

WGQ: Acronym for NAESB Wholesale Gas Quadrant.

Withdrawal season: Time of year when shippers typically withdraw gas from storage facility during peak seasons.

Zone: Division for a pipeline. Used to identify boundaries of a specific area for transportation on a pipeline.

Index

INDEX

www.ingramcontent.com/pod-product-compliance
Lightning Source LLC
LaVergne TN
LVHW070831220926
848486LV00030B/268